Citizens by Degree

Studies in Postwar American Political Development

Citizens by Degree

Higher Education Policy and the Changing Gender Dynamics of American Citizenship

DEONDRA ROSE

OXFORD
UNIVERSITY PRESS

OXFORD
UNIVERSITY PRESS

Oxford University Press is a department of the University of Oxford. It furthers
the University's objective of excellence in research, scholarship, and education
by publishing worldwide. Oxford is a registered trade mark of Oxford University
Press in the UK and certain other countries.

Published in the United States of America by Oxford University Press
198 Madison Avenue, New York, NY 10016, United States of America.

© Oxford University Press 2018

Catalogue record is available from the Library of Congress.
ISBN 978–0–19–065095–7 (pbk.)
ISBN 978–0–19–065094–0 (hbk.)

3 5 7 9 8 6 4 2

Paperback printed by Webcom, Inc., Canada
Hardback printed by Bridgeport National Bindery, Inc., United States of America

For my mother, Donna Elaine Rose.

"Remember the ladies."

—*Abigail Adams, 1776*

CONTENTS

ACKNOWLEDGMENTS

Writing this book has been one of my life's most thrilling endeavors, and I would like to express sincere thanks to the many people whose support helped me bring the project to completion. I am most grateful to the policymakers, activists, former legislative staff members, and other experts who shared their knowledge about the National Defense Act, the Higher Education Act, and Title IX with me. My sincere thanks go to the Honorable Senator Birch Bayh, Dr. Bernice Sandler, Dr. Mary Allen Jolley, Ms. Margaret Dunkle, Mr. Richard Green, Dr. Donna Nelson, Ms. Marilyn Stapleton, Ms. Val Bonnette, and Dr. Wendy Mink. I am especially grateful to Dr. Mary Allen Jolley for sharing Rep. Carl Elliott's archived papers with me. Thanks also go to Mrs. Helen Nycz, Mr. David Drennen, Dr. Elizabeth Sanders, Mrs. Millie Rowe-Sanders, and Mrs. Shirley Williams Lynch for the inspiring biographical narratives that help to bring the history to life. The US Department of Education allowed me to use restricted-access data from the National Postsecondary Student Aid Study, the US Library of Congress provided access to archived congressional papers, and the Oregon Historical Society provided me with access to Rep. Edith Green's archived papers.

My journey as a political scientist, political historian, and policy feedback scholar has been profoundly shaped by Suzanne Mettler's extraordinary mentorship. In addition to being a world-class intellectual and a trailblazer among political scientists, Suzanne offers a model of excellence in scholarship that I strive to emulate. I am eternally grateful to Suzanne for her generous feedback on this project at every stage of its development and for permitting me to use the Social and Governmental Issues and Participation (SGIP) dataset for this research. I am grateful to Theodore J. Lowi for unwavering faith in this project and for serving as an unrivaled inspiration. His recent passing was a tremendous loss, and I'm sad that I won't be able to show him the final product. But his characteristic enthusiasm, insightful feedback, and rousing pep talks were integral to its existence. I am also extremely grateful to Michael Jones-Correa for brilliant insights and generous feedback that have greatly benefited this book. Michael's wisdom, generosity, and unstinted support have played a central role in my development as a scholar, and I will forever appreciate his mentorship. Christopher J. Anderson offered valuable questions, insights, and advice that have made a tremendous difference to my work, and this project in particular. This book also benefited from Peter Enns's generous feedback and thoughtful suggestions. Finally, I am grateful to Elizabeth Sanders, whose wisdom, infinite kindness, vast intellect, and friendship have made valuable contributions to my development as a scholar and to this project.

Cornell University's Government Department, the University of Notre Dame's Political Science Department, and the Sanford School of Public Policy at Duke University provided vibrant intellectual communities that sustained and inspired me as I wrote. Many thanks go to the Cornell Institute for Social and Economic Research (CISER) and to Dr. Warren Brown, Pam Baxter, Kim Burlingame, and Lynn Martin for all of their help in securing and housing my restricted-access data. I also offer sincere thanks to Aurora D'Amico at the National Center for Education Statistics (NCES), Tracy and Dan at NCES, Francoise Vermeylen and Shamil Sadigov at the Cornell Statistical Consulting Unit (CSCU), Tyler Ransom at the Duke Social Science Research Institute, and the incredible reference librarians at Cornell's Olin Library—especially Lynn Thitchener, Maureen Morris, and Peter Campbell. I am very grateful to my excellent team of undergraduate research assistants at Duke University— Kathryn Eckhart, Blaine Elias, Hilary Greenberg, Sophie Haet, Sophia Mamilli, Lexi Mendes, and Martina Tiku—and for generous funding from the Eads Fellowship, which made it possible to engage them.

At Cornell, I benefited from a tremendous community of people. In addition to the scholars mentioned previously, I am grateful to Richard Bensel, Ronald Herring, and Tina Slater. I offer a high salute to the dear friends who have gone the distance with me: Phillip Ayoub, Chris Zepeda-Millán, Jaimie Bleck, Idrissa Sidibe, Maria Sperandei, Sreedevi Muppirisetty, Leila Ibrahim, Igor Logvinenko, Don Leonard, Sophia Jordan Wallace, Julie Ajinkya, Benjamin Brake, Pablo Yanguas, Berk Esen, Janice Gallagher, Tariq Thachil, Simon Gilhooley, Pinar Kemerli, Noelle Brigden, Lucia Seybert, Simon Cotton, and Desmond Jagmohan. And I don't know what I would have done without the support of Marin Clarkberg, Kris Corda, Kat Empson, J. Ellen Gainor, Cindy Grey, Christine Holmes, Barb Knuth, Sheri Notaro, Laurel Southard, and Brenda Wickes.

The two years that I spent as a Moreau Postdoctoral Fellow at the University of Notre Dame were crucial to the continued development of this project. I am especially grateful to Dianne Pinderhughes and Christina Wolbrecht for their generous mentorship during my time there. I am also grateful to Ruth Abbey, Peri Arnold, Jaimie Bleck, Eileen Hunt Botting, David Campbell, Darren Davis, Michael Desch, Amitava Dutt, Karen Graubert, Alexandra Guisinger, Victoria Tin-bor Hui, Joshua Kaplan, Geoffrey Layman, David Nickerson, Paul Ocobok, Richard Pierce, Emilia Powell, Benjamin Radcliff, Ricardo Ramirez, Naunihal Singh, Ernesto Verdaja, and Dana Villa for valued friendship and colleagueship.

The Sanford School of Public Policy has provided an extraordinary place for bringing the book to completion. It is a privilege to work at an institution that prioritizes service in the leadership of society and that values the role that government programs can play in fostering equal opportunity. Words fall short of conveying my deep gratitude to the brilliant Kristin Goss, who read the entire manuscript and offered insightful feedback that significantly strengthened it. Many thanks also go to Elizabeth Ananat, Charles Clotfelter, and Robert Garlick whose generous feedback helped me tremendously. Furthermore, I offer heartfelt thanks to Catherine Admay, Susan Alexander, David Arrington, Carolyn Barnes, Sarah Bermeo, Tony Brown, Kelly Brownell, Nick Carnes, Kerri Carnes, Phil Cook, Sandy Darity, Lynette Edgerton, Christina Gibson-Davis, Elise Goldwasser, Heather Griswold, Kerry Haynie, Carol Jackson, Ashley Jardina, Bruce Jentleson, Belinda Keith, Judith Kelley, Karen Kemp, Bob Korstad, Anirudh Krishna, Helen "Sunny" Ladd, Pam Ladd, Cassie Lewis, Mary Lindsley, Joel Luther, Linda Lytvinenko, Frederick "Fritz" Mayer, Paula McClain, Manoj Mohanan, Candice Odgers, Jackie Ogburn, Jenni Owen, Stan Paskoff, Jay Pearson, Gunther Peck, Dirk Philipsen, Billy Pizer, Marcos Rangel, Ken Rogerson, Seth Sanders, Steve Schewel, Steve Sexton, Quinton ("Q") Smith, Jessi Streib, Don Taylor, Peter Ubel, Kate Walker, Anna White, Kate Whetten, and Sarah Zoubek. I also want to say a big thank you to Lisa Garcia-Bedolla for her valuable mentorship, which has served as a guiding light as I have brought this project to completion.

And my acknowledgments would be incomplete without my most sincere thanks to Michelle Ballif, Larry Nackerud, Jim Coverdill, Alex Kaufman, Audrey Haynes, Judi Rogers, Nancy Ward, and David Seago for early inspiration that helped to make this book possible.

I am especially grateful to the incomparable Steven M. Teles for his enthusiasm about this project and for the opportunity to contribute to Oxford's Series on Postwar American Political Development. It has also been a privilege to work with editor David McBride, Claire Sibley, Helen Nicholson, Kathleen Weaver, and everyone at Oxford University Press. Moreover, I would also like to offer my deepest thanks to the anonymous reviewers, whose thoughtful, generous, and spot-on feedback helped me to do greater justice to this topic. I am grateful to *Studies in American Political Development* and the *Journal of Policy History* for allowing me to reprint material from articles published there.

Thanks always to my dear family for their endless support, infectious enthusiasm, good humor, and love. I thank my grandmother, Shirley Williams Lynch, for encouraging me to reach for the stars and for exuding a spirit of excellence that I strive to emulate. I am grateful to my aunt, Dionne, for her kindness, generosity, and enthusiasm. Without her love and support, I could never have completed this book. Additionally, I owe a debt of gratitude to my uncle, Don, for his valued encouragement and considerable wisdom; and to my cousins Mario Walker and Tanisha Walker-Wilson for being kindred spirits. My sisters—Mercedes and Brandy—are two of my very best and most valued friends. I'm extremely grateful to them for constant support, encouragement, and years of witty repartee. I'm also grateful to my little nephew, Aiden, a wise lad of ten years whose animated support and good cheer make it all worthwhile. I want to convey deep gratitude to Willie Lynch, Kym Rose, Destiny Fae Rose, Jonathan Rose, Rose Snell, Mekia Snell (and little King and baby Mason), Walter "J. R." Snell, Brandon Bulger, James Johnson, David, Leslie, and Desiree Wilson, Johnny and Karen Williams, Darren Walton, SaBrina McIntire, Jozelia Grace, Jakiya McIntyre, India Walton, and the memory of my father, David L. Walton. Finally, I offer sincere thanks to my dear friends Loren Aguillard-Carcassole, Jerry Anthony, Marian Arnold, Jacqueline Bress, Alicia Calvin, Bernette Finley-Drawe, Anna Goehner, Mario Gurrero, Alisha Harland, Susan Hoerger, Aubrey Johnson-Duke, Stephanie Johnson, Joey Nelson, Helen Nycz, Brecht Putman, Alex Rahn, Ruth Solom, Diva Thomas, Michele Thomas-Johnson, Liz Wayne, and Kara Zetzman—you light up my life.

This book is dedicated to my mother, Donna Elaine Rose, whose love, unwavering support, and unflinching confidence have enabled me to go the distance with any endeavor, not least of all—this book. Ignoring the warnings of doctors who said that my premature birth would hinder my intellectual development, my mother worked tirelessly to prove them wrong. Even as a young woman, she was a visionary who saw potential where others did not. I am grateful for all of the love and confidence that she poured into me, and if I have been able to contribute even a little to our understanding of higher education, public policy, and American political development, as the saying goes—I got it from my mama.

Deondra Rose
Durham, North Carolina
December 2016

Citizens by Degree

Higher Education Policy
and Women's Citizenship

Legislation is vitally needed if women are to be accorded the fair treat-
ment that is the birthright of their brothers.
—Dr. Bernice Sandler, *chair of the Action Committee for*
Federal Contract Compliance in Education, Women's
Equity Action League (WEAL), 1970[1]

Like many young women in American colleges and universities, Michelle—a psychology major at the University of Missouri–Kansas City—could be described
as a "go-getter."[2] Focused squarely on a career in family therapy, Michelle works
hard to maintain an excellent grade point average and to make the most of her
educational opportunities. When she is not exploring internship possibilities
or thinking about graduate school applications, she can be found participating
in extracurricular activities or seeking career counseling. Michelle unapologeti-
cally describes her serious attitude about higher education and her intense focus
on long-term career plans as the result of "perfectionist" tendencies. Without
question, she views higher education as the key to long-term success. She is in
good company. Since the mid-twentieth century, the proportion of American
women earning college degrees has increased dramatically. While men earned
more degrees than women for more than three hundred years after the establishment of higher educational institutions in America, women have earned more
college degrees than men since 1981. By the 2016–2017 academic year, women
made up a full 57.6 percent of American college students.

For many young Americans, the increasing higher educational attainment
of American women has inspired a reimagining of traditional gender roles.
Consider, for example, Michelle's fiancé, who has sampled a smorgasbord of
undergraduate majors, devoting himself to a career in dentistry one week and
environmental science the next. While Michelle is preparing for graduate study,
her fiancé has no plans to pursue advanced training—in fact, due to his fluctuat-
ing interests, Michelle and her friends question whether he will even complete

his undergraduate degree. Michelle expects that she and her fiancé will settle into a family life that challenges traditional gender norms, with Michelle assuming the traditionally masculine role of "breadwinner," while her fiancé devotes his attention to the private sphere, taking on the role of stay-at-home dad—and, by extension, the customarily feminine duties of childcare, cooking, and housework.

The wealth of possibilities that young women like Michelle enjoy demonstrate the progress that American women have made since the mid-twentieth century. Over the last fifty years, women have made strides that underscore a firm movement toward first-class citizenship in terms of full inclusion in American economic, social, and political life. They made up 47 percent of paid workers in the United States in 2015—up from 35.3 percent in 1969.[3] Moreover, women have increasingly participated as equal—if not principal—players in the socioeconomic well-being of their families. In 2012, for example, 63.3 percent of American mothers were either the sole or cobreadwinner for their families, and a significant proportion of these were families headed by single mothers.[4] For the millions of American families that rely on the income generated by female householders, women's access to valuable employment opportunities tend to be especially important.

Women have also made noteworthy strides in terms of participation in the exercise of political power. Throughout much of the nation's history, American women occupied the margins of American political life. Women did not gain the right to vote until the Nineteenth Amendment to the Constitution was ratified on August 18, 1920, and their participation in mass- and elite-level politics trailed that of men.[5] Yet, over the next sixty years, the resilient gender gap in political involvement began to narrow. Consider, for example, the gender dynamics of voter turnout in US presidential elections (Figure 1.1). Data from the US Census Bureau illustrate that during the 1980 presidential election, American women voted at higher rates than men, and they have continued to do so in every presidential election since. Although the nation has seen declines in overall voter participation since the mid-twentieth century, it is important to note that this decline has occurred more steeply for men than for women.

What explains the progress that women have made since the mid-twentieth century? The conventional wisdom suggests that the 1970s—with the emergence of a strong women's rights movement, fervent activism on the part of feminist organizations like the National Organization for Women (NOW), and a renewed push for the Equal Rights Amendment—marked the crucial turning point for gender equality in the United States.[6] This book, however, ventures beyond the received wisdom to provide a new explanation for the progress that American women have made. While scholars have established the importance of education to the various elements of citizenship, we have yet to consider the role

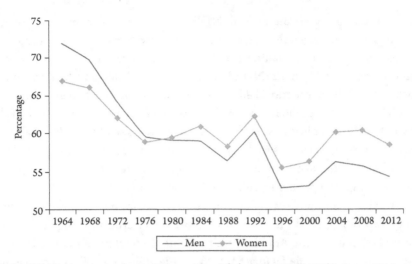

Figure 1.1 Voter turnout during US presidential elections, 1964–2012. *Source*: US
Census Bureau. Table A-1. Reported Voting and Registration by Race, Hispanic Origin, Sex and Age
Groups: November 1964 to 2014.

of federal higher education policies in shaping the gender dynamics of US citizenship since the mid-twentieth century. This book takes a step in that direction by examining the relationship between federal higher education policies and the gender dynamics of US higher educational attainment, attitudes toward the government, and mass political involvement.

I argue that landmark US higher education policies enacted during the mid-twentieth century have played an important role in the promotion of women to first-class citizenship. Passed prior to and apart from the feminist movement, the National Defense Education Act of 1958 (NDEA), the Higher Education Act of 1965 (HEA), and Title IX of the 1972 Education Amendments made it possible for women to gain knowledge and skills that not only are valued in the labor market but also facilitate political engagement and enhance the probability of being tapped to participate in political activities.[7] In what could be described as a one-two punch sequence in an assault against gender inequality in higher educational access, the NDEA and the HEA provided financial aid that helped to make college affordable for women, and Title IX outlawed sex discrimination in college admissions. Through this combination of redistributive and regulatory policy, US lawmakers promoted equal opportunity for women and significantly expanded their access to college degrees and the socioeconomic and political benefits that they yield. Thus, these policies have played an important role in women's promotion to first-class citizenship.

Taken together, the NDEA and HEA constitute the core of government provisions for student financial aid and remain the pillars of US higher education policy. The unlikely creation of the NDEA represented a dramatic departure from higher education policy precedents and, more broadly, US social policies because it provided substantial benefits in a broad-reaching, gender-neutral fashion. The neutrality of the NDEA is a case of what I call "accidental egalitarianism." Rather than intentional efforts to expand educational access for women, the NDEA's gender egalitarianism resulted from lawmakers' efforts to carefully negotiate delicate political issues—in this case, the issue of racial inequality. In working carefully to avoid stumbling into the contentious realm of race politics and political battles over school desegregation, lawmakers inadvertently opened the door for greater gender equality in educational opportunity.

Given the significance of higher education policy for providing equal opportunity for women, I make the case that it represents a crucial, though frequently overlooked, pillar of the American welfare state. Federal higher education programs provided valuable financial aid that made attending college a possibility for many young women who might not have considered higher education absent federal support, while also establishing institutional regulation that leveled the playing field of college admissions. My examination of the relationship between US higher education policy and women's opportunity demonstrates the significance of the US welfare state for promoting equality and full citizenship for marginalized groups. The significant expansion of women's access to higher education—and the socioeconomic and political benefits associated with it— worked against the medley of social, economic, and political inequality that had historically relegated American women to second-class citizenship in the United States. Thus, federal aid for higher education represents a significant, though frequently overlooked, component of the American welfare state.[8]

To consider the influence that landmark higher education policies have had on the extent to which women are incorporated as full citizens in the United States, I begin by examining the political development of these path-breaking programs, paying particular attention to how they were fashioned and probing how—in contrast to other landmark social welfare program precedents—they included women on equal terms with men. Then, I draw on empirical analysis to examine how federal higher education policies have shaped the gender dynamics of social and political citizenship in the United States. These questions warrant careful examination because their answers shed light on the effectiveness of social policy for promoting equality and full citizenship for marginalized populations.

The historical analysis of women's higher education and US higher education policy presented in chapter 2 reveals that a combination of private and public forces have shaped the gender dynamics of US higher educational attainment since the seventeenth century. Through much of the nation's history, the federal government exercised restraint when it came to intervening in higher education.

Early activities were limited to the provision of land grants to support the establishment of state colleges, and during the Great Depression, the federal government offered the first direct aid to college students by way of modest work-study benefits. After World War II, the government offered the first substantial direct financial aid for college students under the Serviceman's Readjustment Act ("the GI Bill") of 1944. While this landmark program helped to expand college access for an entire generation of American men, it exacerbated the long-standing gender gap in higher educational attainment because its benefits were targeted toward returning war veterans, who were overwhelmingly male. In tandem with lawmakers' creation of higher education programs that significantly expanded women's access to college degrees during the mid-twentieth century, the rate at which women earn college degrees began to increase and has continued, unstinted, in subsequent decades. To fully appreciate the significance of federal higher education programs for women's citizenship, we must understand the historical and political contexts in which they were developed.

The creation of the National Defense Education Act of 1958 and the Higher Education Act of 1965, which I examine in chapters 3 and 4, marks the birth of modern higher education policy in the United States, as well as women's invitation into a new relationship with the state. Examining the politics surrounding their creation sheds light on the role that intentionality has played in higher education policy development. Given the unprecedented level of educational support that the NDEA and HEA extended to women, the question of whether lawmakers genuinely hoped to achieve this end represents one of the most interesting features of their development. As we will see, the particular value of the NDEA and the HEA for women was a matter of inadvertent outcomes, rather than deliberate efforts to provide them with benefits.

Moreover, unlike lawmakers' numerous failed attempts to pass a federal financial aid program for college students, those championing the NDEA were successful in harnessing formidable political factors—namely, the *Sputnik* crisis, the domestic struggle over civil rights, and the politics of the Cold War—that provided a favorable context for the establishment of student loans. I find that a political context shaped by unified government and strong presidential leadership enabled the reinforcement of the NDEA's commitment to expanding access to higher education for young Americans through the passage of the Higher Education Act. Under these favorable political conditions, lawmakers took the liberty of expanding existing student loan provisions while adding the first federal grant program, which was the earliest iteration of today's Pell Grant program.

Analysis of the political development of the National Defense Education Act and the Higher Education Act also enhances our understanding of the history of US welfare state development and prompts a revision of our traditional understanding of the role that Southern Democrats played in its development during the mid-twentieth century. Scholars have recognized that Southern Democrats played a central role in obstructing the passage of federal social welfare proposals on the grounds that federal intervention through social policy could enable the federal government to wield greater influence in southern states, which were vigilant about maintaining states' rights in the face of calls for desegregation and other progressive policy objectives. Contrary to this trend, however, the NDEA and the HEA were championed by Southern Democrats. Thus, these case studies offer valuable insights that enhance our understanding of US social policy and American political development.

While many narrowly associate higher education policy with student financial aid programs, federal regulation represents an integral component in government efforts to expand access to college. As such, chapter 5 turns to the development of Title IX, which invoked the regulatory powers of the state to ensure that women and men enjoyed equal access to higher education. Given the redistributive nature of higher education policy precedents, lawmakers' decision to use regulatory policy to expand women's access to college in the 1970s is noteworthy because it represents the birth of gender-conscious higher education policy. I find that a growing appreciation for sex discrimination in American institutions promoted a change in how lawmakers thought about inequality in college access and prompted a shift from focusing on affordability to addressing discriminatory admissions policies. Taking a regulatory approach was integral to lawmakers' ability to remove institutional barriers that represented the last major obstacle limiting women's access to college degrees. Moreover, it demonstrated a full-throated commitment to women's treatment as first-class citizens. To analyze the political development of the NDEA, the HEA, and Title IX, I draw upon a wide range of primary and secondary materials including elite and expert interviews, transcripts of congressional committee and subcommittee hearings, presidential commission reports, archived congressional papers, oral history interviews, newspaper articles, and historical poll data. In doing so, I gain insight into the political and historical context within which each of these policies unfolded.

In chapter 6, I examine the feedback effects that federal student aid policies have had for the gender dynamics of social citizenship in the United States using empirical analysis of data from three national surveys—the Social and Governmental Issues and Participation Study (SGIP), the National Postsecondary Student Aid Study (NPSAS), and the Cooperative Institutional Research Program (CIRP) Freshman Survey. I find that federal student aid programs have contributed to the significant increase in women's educational attainment that we have seen since the mid-twentieth century. Moreover, they have also promoted women's inclusion as full citizens in the United States by promoting greater gender parity in socioeconomic status.

What about the feedback effects of federal higher education policies for women's engagement in politics? I use a difference-in-differences approach to consider whether higher education programs have promoted greater political interest, efficacy, and participation in women. I find that federal student aid programs have contributed to increasing gender parity in political engagement by providing access to higher education—a resource that yields knowledge and skills that are valuable for political engagement. By promoting greater educational attainment among American women, these policies have helped to narrow the gap in US political engagement and have thus promoted greater gender parity in terms of political citizenship. Although political scientists have long recognized education to be a significant determinant of political involvement, this book provides the first empirical investigation of the effects of federal higher education policies on gender parity in political engagement.

In chapter 8, I conclude the analysis by considering the significance of the two-pronged approach that lawmakers employed to promote women's equality in and via higher education, as well as the importance of these programs for how we conceptualize the American welfare state. My analysis suggests that the NDEA, the HEA, and Title IX hold powerful lessons for those interested in the politics of public policy, gender, higher education, and inequality. The combination of redistributive policy and regulatory policy that lawmakers used to expand women's access to college degrees institutionalized women's treatment as first-class citizens under US social policy while simultaneously strengthening gender equality in terms of social and political citizenship. In addition to highlighting the importance of political context to the viability and effectiveness of policies intended to enhance equality, I demonstrate the power of a mixed-policy approach for ameliorating inequality that is rooted in both individual-level and institutional challenges.

In addition to well-recognized social, demographic, and economic shifts that have facilitated the progress that American women have made since the 1960s, this book provides evidence that federal higher education policies have played a central role in promoting gender equality in the United States. In doing so, it highlights government education programs as an indispensable component of the American welfare state. Perhaps more than any other federal social programs, landmark higher education policies have played a crucial role in American women's advancement from second-class to first-class citizenship.

Gender Equality and Degrees of Citizenship

In the most general sense, citizenship characterizes the relationship between individuals and the state. In her powerful analysis of citizenship, Judith Shklar characterizes it as one's status, or "standing," in the polity, which provides individuals with "a sense of one's place in a hierarchical society."[9] In the United States, a tradition of unequal standing among groups has made this aspect of citizenship a particularly interesting one for students of politics. While the nation's political creed centers upon the principles of equality, democracy, and liberty, history abounds with instances in which the full and equal standing that are part and parcel of "first class" citizenship were narrowly restricted to groups like white male landowners. Women, racial and ethnic minorities, and low-income citizens, on the other hand, were relegated to a status of "second class" citizenship whereby they experienced systematic discrimination by the state, unequal protection under the law, and exclusion from full participation in the nation's social, economic, and political life. "It is because slavery, racism, nativism, and sexism, often institutionalized in exclusionary and discriminatory laws and practices, have been and still are arrayed against the officially accepted claims of equal citizenship," says Shklar, "that there is a real pattern to be discerned in the tortuous development of American ideas of citizenship."[10]

Historically, gender has marked a powerful determinant of whether Americans enjoy first- or second-class citizenship. The Fourteenth Amendment of the US Constitution, for example—which was ratified in 1868—explicitly provides that all American citizens are entitled to fair treatment and equal protection under the law. Nevertheless, for nearly a century, the government continued to employ different standards when dealing with women and men, and gender inequality in citizenship represented an egregious affront to the nation's purported core values. Women's second-class citizenship in America reaches back to the colonial era in which the status of married white women was rooted in English common law. Under this legal system, the principle of "coverture" shaped their citizenship status. Coverture was the idea that married women held no legal identity as individuals but were considered charges of their husbands. The exclusion of women—as well as racial minorities and some white men—from the privileges of full citizenship in the United States served to signal their subordinate status in the polity, while indicating that full citizenship was a valued commodity.[11]

From the beginning, women's exclusion from the right to vote cast them as second-class citizens in the United States. Despite their status as legal citizens, women's exclusion from the right to exercise political power rendered them subjugated members of the polity. Even after women gained the right to vote in 1920, US social policies routinely differentiated between women and men in ways that made clear men's status as first-class citizens and women's status as second-class citizens.[12] Prior to the 1930s, veterans' pensions and support for widows and their dependent children made up the bulk of social provision in the United States. As beneficiaries of the nation's nascent welfare state, women's inclusion was generally predicated on their roles as wives and mothers.[13] With the New Deal came social programs that stratified women and men by incorporating white men under the auspices of national social programming and by subjecting women and black men to the variability of state government standards for relief.[14] As a result, New Deal programs yielded two distinct, gender-stratified standards of citizenship for Americans. As a result of such gender stratification in the ways in which the state interacted with men and women, American men enjoyed a status as first-class citizens, while women were relegated to second-class citizenship.

Political philosopher T. H. Marshall focuses on the specific requirements of first-class standing, defining citizenship as "a status bestowed on those who are full members of a community."[15] He asserts that "all those who possess [citizenship] are equal with respect to the rights and duties with which the status is endowed."[16] By this definition, the criterion of equality is central to the achievement of full citizenship, and one's status as a first-class citizen requires that she or he possess certain rights. Marshall identifies three types of rights—civil, social, and political—which, taken together, are part and parcel of full citizenship.[17] The civil element of citizenship, which corresponds most closely to what we think of as legal citizenship, includes individual rights and freedoms, as well as the responsibilities associated with membership in a society. This includes a number of personal freedoms, such as freedom of speech and religion, as well as the right to property ownership and equal protection under the law.

The social element of citizenship refers to the right of socioeconomic security and the ability to enjoy a standard of living that reflects the standards of contemporaneous society. Moreover, it includes the right of individuals to participate as full members of social society. The social element of citizenship includes access to social and economic security and the right to full participation in society, which is due to any of its members by virtue of association.[18] Social policy is seen as a viable mechanism for improving social citizenship, as it has the potential to enhance a central factor associated with full citizenship: independence.[19] Historically, women's status as dependents has severely limited their control over their own lives. Their ability to participate in social life has been largely shaped by the socioeconomic status of their husbands, fathers, brothers, or other male relatives. Marshall highlights the education system and social programs as the primary institutions shaping social citizenship.

Marshall characterizes the political element of citizenship as the right to take part in wielding political power, either directly or indirectly, by participating in the selection of representatives.[20] The nation's democratic system of government is predicated upon the notion of popular sovereignty and the presumption that the expressed will of the governed reflects the preferences of the nation's *entire* citizenry. In the United States, full citizenship includes the ability to participate in activities that are intended to shape the election of government officials and their subsequent actions. Such activities include voting, contributing to political campaigns, volunteering on campaigns, and contacting elected officials.[21]

Data from the American National Election Studies (ANES) reveal that over the last half century, the United States has seen important shifts in the gender dynamics of political engagement. In addition to the fact that women have voted at higher rates than men in every presidential election since 1980, women's engagement in a number of political activities has increased since 1960, while rates of men's participation has decreased. For example, as Figure 1.2 shows, the proportion of men reporting that they care "a good deal" about who wins the presidential election declined from 68 percent in 1960 to 63 percent in 2008. We saw the reverse for women, with 78 percent of women expressing strong interest in the results of the presidential election in 1960, compared to 82 percent

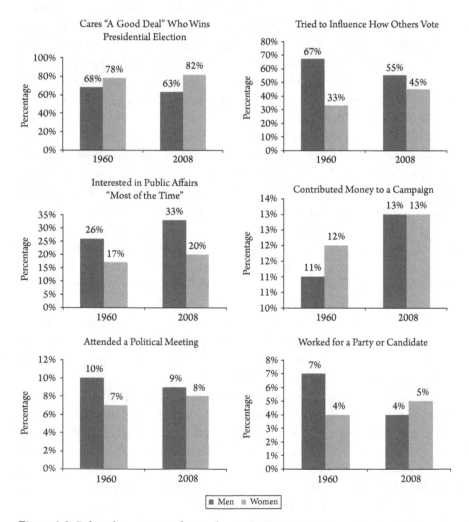

Figure 1.2 Political engagement by gender: 1960 versus 2008. *Source*: The American National Election Studies. The ANES Guide to Public Opinion and Electoral Behavior.

of women offering the same response in 2008. Similarly, the rate at which men report trying to influence how others vote declined from 1960 to 2008 (67 percent to 55 percent), while the rate at which women worked to persuade others increased from 33 percent in 1960 to 45 percent in 2008. Both women and men have become more likely to report higher levels of interest in public affairs, though 33 percent of men say that they are interested in public affairs "most of the time," compared to 20 percent of women. Data also show that women and men contribute to political campaigns, attend political meetings, and work for political parties or candidates at virtually equal rates. Although the rates at which men attend political meetings and work for parties and candidates have declined since 1960, they have increased slightly for women.

Although persisting challenges like unequal pay for women and men, the United States' lack of parental leave policies, and unequal political representation signal that there is still progress to be made in women's movement toward achieving true first-class citizenship, the strides that women have made since the mid-twentieth century have helped to marshal them toward full and equal participation in the nation's economic, social, and political life. Government social programs have played an important role in women's movement toward first-class citizenship, and I suspect that federal higher education programs were particularly important to this movement. It is possible that—absent government support in the form of education, income support, health care, and other social programs—the progress that women have made since the mid-twentieth century might have been more modest.

Women and the March Toward First-Class Citizenship

A history of social, economic, and political inequality had cast American women as second-class citizens well into the twentieth century. Prior to the passage of landmark higher education programs, women's status as second-class citizens was evident in their treatment by government social programs, like the aforementioned New Deal programs that stratified benefits on the basis of gender. The gendered treatment of Americans via social programming continued with the creation of the GI Bill, which privileged an entire generation of American men by providing World War II veterans with generous government financial aid to pursue college education and technical training. Because the veterans who were eligible to take advantage of GI Bill benefits were overwhelmingly male, the federal government essentially paved the way for millions of American men who would otherwise not have obtained college degrees to do so, while doing little to expand higher educational access for women.

By setting a new standard for how federal social policies treat women and men, the landmark higher education programs that were enacted after the mid-1950s yielded a significant change in the gender dynamics of American citizenship. The National Defense Education Act of 1958 engendered a new relationship between the federal government and American women by incorporating women as equal beneficiaries of the student aid that was created by the path-breaking program. Rather than tying higher education benefits to gendered requirements like military service or requirements that student aid beneficiaries pursue training in traditionally male fields like engineering, these programs granted valuable financial support to students on the nongendered basis of financial need. The Higher Education Act of 1965 continued in this vein, allocating federal support broadly to both men and women. Seven years later, when lawmakers passed Title IX of the 1972 Education Amendments, the federal government made clear women's full and equal standing in society and in the polity by prohibiting sex discrimination in federally supported education programs. The development of the NDEA and the HEA initiated a watershed change in women's status as citizens in the United States, and the passage of Title IX signaled the government's commitment to asserting women's right to equal standing and full social citizenship. While conventional wisdom suggests that such momentous advances would occur as a result of organized activity on the part of women's rights activists, in fact these important advances occurred prior to the development of the contemporary feminist movement.[22]

By expanding women's access to higher education through a combination of redistributive and regulatory higher education programming, the federal government has also enhanced women's social citizenship. The financial assistance provided by the National Defense Education Act and the Higher Education Act and Title IX's prohibition on sex discrimination in college admissions significantly expanded women's access to college. This promoted significant increases in women's socioeconomic status by providing them with greater access to college degrees. As a result, by helping women gain the qualifications necessary to work in well-paying jobs that require higher education, these programs have been crucial to helping American women achieve greater socioeconomic status and greater independence. With greater access to college degrees and the socioeconomic benefits that tend to come with them, women have become increasingly able to support themselves and their families.

In addition to strengthening women's citizenship by treating women as first-class citizens and strengthening their social citizenship, the nation has witnessed a transformation in women's incorporation in the polity. Political scientists have long recognized that higher educational attainment represents one of the most consistent predictors of political engagement. Americans who have more education are more likely to express interest in politics, to possess high levels of political efficacy, and to participate in a range of political activities. As American women and men have increasingly participated in American life as equals, women have advanced beyond their long-standing second-class citizenship to achieve first-class standing. By employing higher education policy in a way that has transformed the gender dynamics of American citizenship, the federal government has played an important role in this process.

Previous accounts of the progress that women have made since the 1960s have emphasized the social, cultural, and economic shifts that have helped to usher women toward first-class citizenship. The decline of "domesticity"—the notion that the private sphere represents the most appropriate arena for American womanhood—and the influence of the US civil and women's rights movements helped to catalyze women's increasing engagement in mass politics. At the dawn of the twentieth century, changes in American industry began to loosen women's ties to the private sphere. With the emergence of innovative information technologies, employers found themselves in need of additional office and clerical staff and found women to be suitable candidates for these positions.[23]

Women's movement into the labor force continued steadily throughout the twentieth century. Since the early 1970s, declining employment rates and wage stagnation for men have challenged the traditional male breadwinner model for many families. Moreover, as Elizabeth Warren and Amelia Tyagi note in *The Two-Income Trap*, the high cost of housing in high-quality school districts has placed considerable strain on families and has driven many women into the labor force since the 1970s.[24] As a result of increasing participation in paid labor, women were less reliant on the traditional structure of domesticity for economic survival. Women's large-scale movement into the labor force rendered significant shifts in the nature of their citizenship.[25] Moreover, experience with work-related activities such as supervising others, organizing meetings, and public speaking often translates into "human capital" that facilitates civic and political engagement.[26] Women and men who participate in the workforce are also more likely to be tapped by political parties and interest groups to take part in political activities.[27]

As women gained financial independence and devoted more energy to engaging in careers outside of the home, important demographic changes followed. Not only did women get married later and have fewer children, but also the nation's divorce rates increased precipitously.[28] The emergence of oral contraception—known popularly as "the pill"—in the 1960s and the legalization of abortion in 1973 provided women with increased control over family planning, thus facilitating greater labor force participation among women.[29] Thanks to more extensive and sustained labor force participation, American women now compose a significant proportion of the once male-dominated labor force and more fully engage their role as citizens.

In addition to women's increasing economic independence, social movements represent what is perhaps the dominant explanation for women's enhanced citizenship since the mid-twentieth century. Some consider the civil rights movement of the 1960s to be the turning point of women's political engagement because it provided lessons in how to effectively demand equal treatment as citizens.[30] Others argue that the women's liberation movement of the 1970s marks the turning point for women's civic and political engagement.[31] Many of the women who became politically involved to support—or to oppose—the Equal Rights Amendment gained the important experience of working through government institutions to pursue political, social, and economic interests.[32] Indeed, by providing women with tools needed to engage fully as US citizens and by altering their expectations regarding citizenship, social movements made women increasingly aware of the importance and effectiveness of civic and political engagement to their status in the polity.

Have women truly achieved first-class citizenship? It is safe to say that, while women have moved toward first-class citizenship, the quest for perfect equality continues. This is particularly true when it comes to achieving amplification of political voice and securing equal representation in governing institutions.[33] Nevertheless, absent programs like the NDEA, the HEA, and Title IX, the strides that women have made in the last fifty years would likely have been much more modest. As women have moved from second-class citizenship toward first-class citizenship proper, US higher education policies have played a pivotal role in the progress women have made.

The Education of American Women: Trends over Time

Political scientists have identified education as a central component shaping socioeconomic status and a weighty factor in the calculus of political engagement. Thus, the notion that increased higher educational attainment has been central to the progress that women have made since the mid-twentieth century seems intuitive. Americans who have higher levels of education tend to enjoy higher incomes and work in more prestigious occupations, and they are significantly more likely to be politically engaged than those who have less education.[34] Furthermore, one's educational attainment shapes the extent to which she or he will engage in political activities.[35] Education not only provides information and skills that facilitate political learning and participation but also, as scholars have argued, increases the normative impetus to engage in politics, as educational institutions may bestow upon students a heightened sense of civic duty.[36] In terms of recruitment and mobilization, citizens with higher levels of education are most likely to be tapped for participation by political parties, interest groups, candidates, and other political activists.[37] By providing access to knowledge and skills that correspond to socioeconomic opportunity

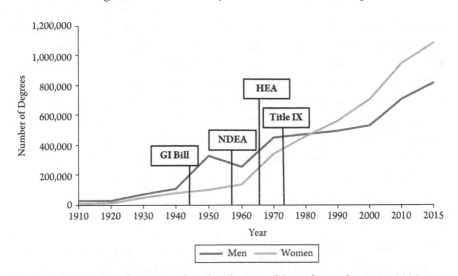

Figure 1.3 Bachelor's degrees conferred in the United States by gender, 1910–2015.
Source: US Department of Education, National Center for Education Statistics (NCES).

and high levels of political engagement, higher education offers a powerful pathway to full citizenship.

Historically, men outpaced women as the recipients of college degrees from the establishment of higher education in the Colonies in 1636 through the 1970s. As Figure 1.3 shows, prior to the 1940s, relatively few Americans earned college degrees; among those who did, men consistently earned more degrees than women. In 1910, for example, men earned more than three times as many bachelor's degrees than women. In 1940, although women were more likely than men to earn high school diplomas, they were less likely than men to complete four years of college.[38]

Throughout the remainder of that decade, a significant increase in the number of degrees earned by men—which was fueled by the passage of the GI Bill in 1944—precipitated the emergence of a considerable gender gap in the number of bachelor's degrees earned by Americans. Moreover, women's presence in higher education was suppressed by active discrimination in college admissions. While some schools simply refused to admit women, others limited women's presence by invoking strict gender quotas or by only permitting women to matriculate into particular degree programs. In 1960, there were 1.6 male undergraduates for every female undergraduate in American colleges and universities.[39]

Through the 1960s and 1970s, there was a significant increase in women's college degree attainment, and by the beginning of the next decade, the gender gap in college degree attainment had virtually disappeared. In 1981, in an astounding reversal of the historical trend whereby men obtained higher education at higher rates than women, women began to earn bachelor's degrees at higher rates than men.[40] Since then, a new gender gap has emerged, with women steadily earning more degrees than their male counterparts. By 2003, there were 1.3 female college students for every male student.[41] Women's advances in higher educational attainment were not limited to undergraduate degrees. In recent years, American women have earned an increasing proportion of advanced degrees. In 2008, women surpassed men as the recipients of doctoral degrees for the first time, and by 2010, they earned a full 60 percent of the master's degrees awarded in the United States.[42] Not only has increased educational attainment enhanced women's opportunities in the labor force, but also it has yielded a combination of social and political advancements that have contributed to an increase in women's status in the United States while altering the gender dynamics of American citizenship.

Given the strides that women have made in obtaining higher education and the socioeconomic and political benefits that it has promoted, it is easy to forget the extent to which women were marginalized in US higher education throughout much of the nation's history. For many families, limited resources often meant choosing between funding higher education for a son or a daughter. Parents were rarely willing to spend as much on their daughters' education as their sons' education.[43] In addition to the challenges women faced in securing financial support from family members, women had difficulty securing college funding from other sources, as scholarships for women were scarce, and women faced limited opportunities to work their way through school.[44]

Prior to the 1970s, women's access to college degrees was further limited by institutional barriers. Most American colleges and universities used gender quotas and exclusionary admissions policies to suppress the number of women permitted to study on their campuses. In addition to discriminatory admissions policies, institutions and private organizations that offered merit- and need-based scholarships to undergraduates rarely offered financial support for young women, and when they did, scholarships offered rarely approached the level of funding offered to young men. In the decades since, American women have come to not only meet but also exceed the rates at which men complete college degrees.

Higher Education Policy: A Novel Approach to Equal Opportunity

Higher education policy represents an innovative approach to expanding equal opportunity. Financial aid programs helped to make attending college affordable for those who lacked the means to pay for postsecondary education. Access to financial aid has become especially important as the cost of college has increased precipitously since the mid-twentieth century. According to the National Center for Education Statistics, the average cost of tuition and fees for undergraduates enrolled full time in degree programs grew nearly 200 percent from 1963 to 2015. The cost of attending a full-time undergraduate program during the 1963–1964 academic year was $3,900, compared to $11,487 during the 2014–2015 academic year.[45] In offering financial aid to students, lawmakers have helped to combat the need for low-income students to engage in full- or part-time employment while enrolled in college courses. The ability to devote full attention to academics helps to increase the probability that students will successfully complete their degrees. In addition to offsetting the cost of undergraduate study, the ability to use government support for pursuing an undergraduate degree could make it more likely that students will be able to direct additional financial resources toward the pursuit of graduate or professional degrees.

While few studies have focused on the relationship between public policies, citizens' educational attainment, and their engagement in politics, scholars have begun to shed light on this relationship by examining the impact of the GI Bill for educational attainment and civic and political engagement among veterans.[46] Evidence has shown that the GI Bill promoted high levels of educational attainment for an entire generation of American men.[47] In providing resources that helped to make college affordable, the GI Bill made completing a college degree a feasible goal for many veterans who would not have otherwise undertaken postsecondary training.[48]

GI Bill usage also promoted higher levels of political efficacy among participants.[49] Thus, in addition to the resources offered by the GI Bill program, use of its benefits for college education and vocational training provided veterans with an experience that influenced their perception of and feelings about the state. GI Bill usage often yielded shifts in recipients' attitudes toward the government, making them increasingly aware that the government is committed to serving people like them.[50] This supports the notion that federal higher education policies have the capacity to increase citizens' levels of political efficacy and to shape their conceptualizations of themselves as citizens.

The benefits provided by the gender-neutral federal financial aid programs enacted since 1958 represent an important departure from US social policy precedents. In the context of US social policy development, the broad-reaching, gender-neutral design of the National Defense Education Act and the Higher Education Act has deviated from the gendered, more narrowly targeted program design that has characterized other social welfare programs. Previously enacted welfare state policies like Old Age Insurance, Aid to Dependent Children, and Unemployment Insurance treated women and men differently in ways that reinforced inequality.[51] Although GI Bill benefits were not explicitly restricted to men but to military veterans during an era of military conscription, the program proved more in line with gendered social policy precedents than not. Of the 2.2 million World War II veterans who attended college using the GI Bill, only 64,728—fewer than 3 percent—were women.[52] Not only were women largely excluded from the financial aid that the GI Bill provided for an entire generation of American men, but also they were excluded from the enhanced socioeconomic mobility and heightened civic engagement that program usage facilitated. Unlike their male counterparts, American women did not broadly receive federal education funds to support higher educational training that would usher millions of citizens into the middle class. Furthermore, they were virtually excluded from the experiences of GI Bill participation, which transmitted the message that, as first-class citizens, beneficiaries have a claim to political inclusion. In their exclusion, women did not gain this opportunity to develop a sense of gratitude for the state's generosity or the related desire to engage in civic activism as a way of showing appreciation for benefits received.

The political dynamics shaping federal higher education programs have differed in ways that have made this approach to social policy a powerful one. The need-based and non-need-based federal student loan and grant programs that were created under the National Defense Education Act in 1958 and the Higher Education Act in 1965 were distinctive because they treated women and men equally, expanding higher educational access through the provision of financial aid. For the first time, a significant proportion of American women had the opportunity to attend college with the support of government financial resources. Title IX further expanded women's access to college degrees. Although the regulation was created to prohibit colleges and universities from discriminating against women, it banned sex discrimination in higher education programs, giving both women and men a legal claim against gender discrimination. The universal approach that lawmakers used to craft the NDEA, the HEA, and Title IX have played a central role in their political resilience. As Theda Skocpol notes, although social policies that target benefits narrowly to the neediest citizens tend to represent the most efficient use of public resources, such policies often fall short of the broad-reaching political support necessary to sustain them over time.[53] While broad-reaching, universal policies may extend benefits in a less efficient manner, they tend to elicit higher levels of political support by virtue of their extended reach.

Reconceptualizing the American Welfare State

Compared to other prominent welfare state programs like Temporary Assistance to Needy Families (TANF), Medicaid, and food stamps, federal higher education programs are generally viewed positively and have proved relatively resilient in the face of political opposition. This can be credited, at least partially, to the universal approach to policy design that lawmakers took to craft them and the resulting fact that a broad swath of the population shares a stake in their continuation. It also reflects the fact that higher education policies are not fraught with the same negative connotations that surround programs that we typically associate with the term "welfare." Federal student aid programs do, indeed, resemble welfare policies in that they provide public assistance with the goal of promoting socioeconomic stability and well-being among the population. Nevertheless, when we think of welfare policies in the United States, Pell Grants, Perkins Loans, and Stafford Loans rarely come to mind. This is likely related to the fact that support for higher educational pursuits is more closely associated with "earned" benefits like Social Security and Unemployment Insurance that resonate with American political values like individualism, equality of opportunity, and social mobility in a way that social policies like income supports and food stamps do not. This has important implications for the extent to which social policies can expand opportunity to marginalized Americans. By providing millions of women with funds to attend college and by ensuring equal access to higher educational institutions, federal higher education policies have represented a crucial—if frequently overlooked—component of the American welfare state.

Public Policy Feedback and Gender Equality in US Citizenship

My hypothesis that federal higher education programs enacted after the mid-twentieth century expanded women's access to higher education and contributed to the narrowing gender gap in US political engagement is rooted in what public policy scholars call the theory of policy feedback effects. Policy feedback theory centers on the idea that public policies have the capacity to act as both outputs of and inputs into the political process. As such, policies can alter citizens and the political environment by reshaping not only the social and economic orientations of citizens but also their rates of involvement in politics and what they come to expect from government.[54]

Scholars have recognized two primary mechanisms through which policy feedback effects are transmitted. The first is through resource effects. Resource effects occur in the form of incentives—such as monetary payments, goods, and services—that have implications for citizens' material well-being and their life opportunities. These effects typically reshape the costs and benefits of engaging in politics. Providing an example of the resource effects of public policy utilization, Andrea Campbell has shown that the Social Security program provides valuable benefits that make its most dependent beneficiaries more likely to maintain a high level of interest in politics and to engage in political activity if they suspect that their benefits are in danger.[55] Sidney Verba, Kay Lehman Schlozman, and Henry Brady have demonstrated that possessing resources, such as higher levels of education, income, and political efficacy, makes citizens more likely to participate in politics.[56] I hypothesize that federal higher education policies have altered the calculus of political participation by providing citizens with a resource—educational attainment—that significantly increases the probability that they will engage in politics.

In addition to resource effects, policy feedback may also be transmitted through a second mechanism—interpretive effects. Interpretive effects are the ways in which policy usage, in and of itself, serves as a source of information and meaning that shapes citizens' inclination to participate in politics. Scholars note that policies send messages to program participants that indicate their value as citizens, while also teaching the appropriate roles of citizens and the government.[57] Public policies send messages reflecting the social construction—or "cultural characterizations or popular images"—of the individuals they affect.[58] These messages, in turn, shape citizens' orientations toward government. This type of effect arises from features of policy design, the form that benefits take, and the scope of eligibility. Public policies also have the capacity to shape what citizens believe, their aspirations, and how they think about themselves.[59] Joe Soss, for example, has shown that welfare beneficiaries learn to expect subpar treatment from the government by way of their experiences with government agencies.[60] This yields a decreased sense of external efficacy and makes welfare beneficiaries less likely to participate in politics. Staffan Kumlin and Bo Rothstein have found that universal social programs help to increase social trust among beneficiaries because they transmit the lesson that equal treatment shapes the "rules of the game" that organize society. Means-tested programs, on the other hand, tend to undermine social trust.[61] In another example of interpretive effects, Suzanne Mettler has demonstrated that the GI Bill sent messages that veterans were first-class citizens. In doing so, it promoted strong feelings of civic duty and heightened political efficacy among beneficiaries, thereby contributing to high levels of political engagement among them.[62] I hypothesize that the higher education policies enacted since the late 1950s exerted similar interpretive effects by providing women with a positive interaction with the government (i.e., government-facilitated access to higher education) and by signaling women's status as first-class citizens.

In examining the claim that federal student aid usage influences the gender dynamics of educational attainment, attitudes toward government, and political participation in the United States, I do not undervalue the importance of previously identified demographic and socioeconomic background characteristics.

Instead, this analysis provides a serious consideration of the influence of public policy on US gender politics vis-à-vis these established explanations.

Education Policy and Women's Equality

This analysis demonstrates that—in a show of surprising gender egalitarianism—lawmakers dramatically altered the gender dynamics of US higher educational attainment when they passed the NDEA and the HEA, essentially paving the way for women to surpass men as the recipients of college degrees. These programs promoted not only greater gender parity in socioeconomic status by significantly expanding women's access to college but also gender parity in political engagement. While the student aid provided under the NDEA and HEA mounted an assault on gender inequality in US higher education by providing women with financial support for pursuing college degrees, the Title IX regulation dealt a powerful blow to gender inequality in higher education by prohibiting gender discrimination in college admissions.

In what follows, I argue that federal student loans, Pell Grants, and Title IX reshaped the gender dynamics of American citizenship by facilitating greater higher educational attainment among women and contributing to a narrowing of the gender gap in political engagement. Federal higher education programs enacted since 1958 have not only augmented women's status within the polity by altering the standard by which the government interacts with women but also facilitated women's advancement from second-class to first-class citizenship. By considering the importance of federal higher education policy to the gender dynamics of citizenship in the United States, this book aims to enhance our understanding of gender equality, recognizing that the federal government began to promote gender equality apart from—and, indeed, prior to—the feminist movement. In what follows, we will see that federal higher education policy has played a significant, though overlooked, role in the gender dynamics of American citizenship. In addition to significant societal changes that have promoted gender equality in the last fifty years, the federal government has contributed to the increasing gender equality in the United States.

The Gendered Roots of American Higher Education

Why should girls be learne'd and wise?
Books only serve to spoil their eyes.
The studious eye but faintly twinkles
And reading paves the way to wrinkles.
                    —John Trumbull, *The Progress of Dulness*, 1773

Growing up on a farm in Alabama's Limestone County, Mildred "Millie" Rowe distinguished herself as an excellent student with a bright future. After graduating from high school at the age of sixteen, the daughter of two schoolteachers set her sights on a college education. When she began her studies at Athens College in the fall of 1936, there were no federal student loans or grants available to help fund her education. For Millie and her family, private funds represented the only available resources for meeting the cost of attending college. Because Millie's parents could not afford to fund their daughter's education, she worked her way through school as a staffer in the college dining hall. Millie's parents were, however, able to supplement their daughter's earnings by donating produce from the Rowe family farm to her school, and Athens College credited these donations toward her tuition costs. In 1939, after three rigorous years of coursework and on-campus employment, Millie completed her bachelor's degree and embarked upon a career as an educator.[1] Her accomplishment is especially noteworthy when we consider that, in 1940, only 3.8 percent of American women over the age of twenty-four had completed at least four years of college, compared to 22.7 percent of men.[2]

Millie Rowe's reliance on private means to fund her higher education contrasts greatly with the experience of her younger brother, George. As a military veteran who had served in the armed forces during World War II, George Rowe was eligible to receive education benefits under the GI Bill. Through this program, the US government provided George and millions of veterans—a group that was overwhelmingly male—with grants that covered college tuition and fees and even provided a generous stipend to support them and their families as they worked toward their degrees. Considering the dearth of resources available to help women pay for college and women's low educational attainment prior to the 1960s, Millie Rowe's completion of a baccalaureate degree was remarkable.

Through much of American history, higher education was reserved for the most privileged citizens. From the founding of the nation's first college in 1636 to the post–World War II era, the beneficiaries of higher education were over-whelmingly white, male, and well-to-do. Women, racial minorities, and low-income Americans remained at the margins of postsecondary training until the mid-twentieth century when dramatic social, economic, and political changes effectively democratized higher education in the United States.[3] As a result of crucial changes that emerged during and after the late 1950s, groups that were long denied equitable access to higher education and excluded from full par-ticipation in postsecondary programs now maintain a strong presence in the nation's colleges and universities.

American women represent the most prominent example of this phenom-enon. Prior to the twentieth century, women found limited access to higher education via land-grant colleges and state universities, particularly those in the Midwest and the West.[4] Land-grant institutions were generally more amena-ble to the idea of educating women than their private counterparts, a fact that reflected their central mission of educating the broader public and providing cit-izens with a wide range of skills. In the twentieth century—particularly after the 1960s—women moved rapidly into higher education. This trend represents per-haps the most striking change that has occurred since the early days of American higher education.[5]

Given the complex history of women's higher education in the United States, the rapid increase in women's bachelor's degree attainment since the 1960s is particularly striking. The movement of women into higher education has occurred in tandem with a dramatic increase in federal support for higher education. Although the federal government long resisted taking an active role in higher education, in the last seventy years it has come to provide extensive support for college students and their families. Contrary to political rhetoric suggesting otherwise, the federal government has used higher education to pro-mote national interests like producing an educated labor force and promoting national security objectives by expanding access to high-quality training in sci-ence and technology fields.[6] To answer this book's central question of whether federal higher education policies have helped to promote gender equality in higher educational attainment and political engagement in the United States, we must begin by analyzing the history of women's participation in American higher education and the federal government's historical role in shaping who has access to it.

The Birth of American Higher Education in the Colonial Era (1636–1776)

The founding of Harvard College in 1636 marked the birth of American higher education. In its early years, Harvard demonstrated a firm commitment to Calvinism, training young men typically bound for careers in the clergy.[7] In 1693, the British monarchy chartered the College of William and Mary, and in 1701 a third college was added to the nation's roster of higher educational institutions with the founding of the Collegiate School, which later became Yale University. The original colonial colleges set the tone for higher education in the young nation. They heralded the creation of institutions that had small faculties and student bodies, that maintained strong ties to the church, and whose students were typically destined to assume leadership positions therein. During this period, colleges were responsible for producing gentlemen and for providing what was termed "Republican Education"—a curriculum that cultivated virtues like selflessness, patriotism, and leadership.[8] With the founding of the College of New Jersey in 1746, which was established via an unprecedented compromise between the Presbyterian Church and the New Jersey colony, the church's firm grasp on America's nascent higher educational institutions began to weaken.[9] College enrollments grew steadily during the mid-eighteenth century, and in the years immediately preceding the Revolutionary War, approximately 750 students were enrolled in colonial colleges. Seventy-five percent of those students attended the four oldest colleges.[10]

Given that higher education in the colonial era was a strictly male arena built around the objective of training the nation's future religious, political, economic, and military leaders, it comes as little surprise that none of the existing higher educational institutions offered college training for women.[11] Women's absolute exclusion from higher education during the colonial period was rooted in the widely held notion that they—as the weaker sex—were incapable of advanced learning.[12] This view centered on two premises: first, that women were mentally inferior to men, and second, that they possessed a physical and emotional frailty that was unsuited to the rigors of higher education.[13] Not only did such views exemplify the formidable social barriers that women faced when it came to the pursuit of college study, but also they proved resilient, shaping Americans' attitudes about which citizens were the natural or rightful participants in higher education and their expectations regarding college access. As a result, these attitudes have had a significant influence on the long-term trajectory of women's higher education in the United States. They have also fostered the long-standing assumption that men's and women's education must—by virtue of each sex's fundamentally dissimilar natures—be different.[14] As such, the very prospect of educating women was deemed questionable, and women's ability to pursue higher education typically required that they carefully avoid attracting male resentment.[15]

The Growth of Higher Education in a New Nation
(1777–1879)

As the nation's founders deliberated at the Constitutional Convention in 1787, they considered and rejected proposals that would have institutionalized federal support for higher education. As a result of the framers' firm commitment to localism, the US Constitution makes no formal provisions for higher education.[16] This set an important precedent that would, for centuries, shape lawmakers' decisions regarding postsecondary training. In the years hence, American lawmakers would continue to question the propriety of federal intervention in the area of higher education, many arguing that attending to the postsecondary educational needs of society is best left to the states.

In the early years of American independence, the number of higher educational institutions operating in the new nation continued to grow, and it was during this era that higher education became regarded as the nation's "cottage industry."[17] Throughout the several states, citizens worked to establish institutions of higher learning. Between 1782 and 1791, Maryland, Georgia, South Carolina, North Carolina, and Vermont passed policies to support college education in their states.[18] With the creation of the state-chartered University of Georgia in 1785 and University of North Carolina in 1789, this period marked the beginning of significant—albeit limited—federal intervention in higher education.[19] For sixty-five years after 1796, the federal government supported college building in the states through the provision of seventeen congressional land grants.[20] This institution-centered approach to supporting higher education established a lasting precedent that would shape lawmakers' efforts in that area for more than 130 years.

In the nineteenth century many Americans viewed higher education as a mechanism for utilitarian ends—particularly, the development of discipline in young people.[21] As the nation's system of higher education grew during this era, it served a variety of purposes and provided new opportunities for various groups of citizens. In the South, the College of South Carolina and the University of Virginia exemplified higher education in the region, catering to the sons of politically and socially prominent planters.[22] New institutions were established to provide women, African Americans, and Catholics—groups that the nation's colleges and universities had typically discriminated against—access to higher education.[23] The 1820s and 1830s saw a continued expansion of higher education in the United States, and in the 1850s, free African Americans gained access to higher education via Pennsylvania's Ashmun Institute (later called Lincoln University) and Ohio's Wilberforce University.[24] By 1860, the number of colleges had grown from the original 9 colonial colleges to approximately 250 institutions.[25] From the first, American higher education was imagined without women in mind. With its separate institutions catering to specific segments of the population, the developing system of American colleges and universities institutionalized the belief that women and other marginalized groups could be justifiably segregated into institutions offering education at varying degrees of quality. Moreover, it reflected the lack of seriousness with which many considered higher education for women and racial minorities. This foundational posture toward women made no question of their second-class status in American life. It also fueled resilient disparity in how institutions treated women, and in Americans' attitudes regarding the propriety of women's education.

Debating Higher Education for Women

With the expansion of colleges in the late eighteenth and early nineteenth centuries, Americans began to debate the propriety of extending advanced education to women. Mary Wollstonecraft's 1792 *Vindication of the Rights of Women* stirred this debate, boldly advocating for women's education and making the case that it would ultimately strengthen society. Those sharing the British feminist's view that women ought to have equal access to education faced staunch opposition from those who believed that women were inherently unsuited for higher learning. One line of reasoning held that women's innate intellectual shortcomings precluded their ability to benefit from advanced education.[26] For example, although Thomas Jefferson was a vocal supporter of broad-reaching education who found great amusement in educating his own daughters at home, he viewed this undertaking as a mere hobby—one that could, at best, serve his daughters in their roles as mothers.[27]

Others argued that the frail constitution of the female sex made women wholly unsuited for college learning, fearing that higher education would precipitate nervous breakdown or moral corruption among the nation's young ladies. Reverend John Todd articulated this view in the early 1870s: "Must we crowd education on our daughters, and for the sake of having them 'intellectual,' make them puny, nervous, and their whole earthly existence a struggle between life and death?"[28] Women's supposed frailty meant that higher education could prove hazardous. Dr. Edward Clarke's 1873 book *Sex in Education; or a Fair Chance for Girls* provided a most compelling account of this frailty.[29] Based on case studies of seven Vassar College students, Dr. Clarke asserted that the mental exertion involved in pursuing the same advanced education as men rendered women susceptible to "neuralgia, uterine disease, hysteria, and other dangerments of the nervous system."[30] In addition to fearing the potential health hazards of women's education, others feared that extensive education would make women reluctant or unable to undertake their "feminine duties" of marriage and childrearing.[31] One Vanderbilt student captured this attitude well, saying, "No man wants to come home at night and find his wife testing some new process for manufacturing oleomargarine, or in the observatory sweeping the heavens for a comet."[32] The prospect of women's higher education represented a potential threat to the traditional family structure that many Americans had come to revere. Yet a final source of opposition to women's higher education revolved around the possibility that women would not only meet the challenges of advanced education but also exceed them. In this regard, women were viewed as a potential threat to the gendered order of society whereby men reigned supreme.[33]

While opponents of women's higher education emphasized the irrationality of educating women and the deleterious outcomes that such an ill-advised course could yield, supporters recognized the pragmatism of educating women. Some argued, for example, that cultivating women's intelligence would enable them to better perform their roles as wives and mothers. College-educated women, according to this line of reasoning, could provide intelligent wives for the clergy. Moreover, they would be especially suited for the vital role of "Republican Motherhood," which cast women as the cultivators of patriotism, duty, and morality in the citizens of the next generation.[34] In this regard, motherhood was characterized as a vital component in American life, offering a natural form of social control.[35]

In addition to strengthening their ability to serve the nation as wives and mothers, supporters of women's higher education believed that the presence of women could have a good influence on the men studying on college campuses. Highlighting the potential institutional effects of educating women, some college faculty members supported the idea of coeducation on the grounds that women's presence would tame male student populations that were prone to fighting and that exhibited ever-increasing apathy toward academics.[36] The presence of women could also prove useful for providing future members of the clergy with practice dealing with women, a valuable skill for leading congregations or taking on wives.[37]

Finally, the need for teachers provided a particularly noteworthy impetus for including women in advanced education. In addition to allowing women to work in an area that was viewed as compatible with their supposed predisposition to nurturing, those who supported training women as teachers noted that female teachers could be compensated at lower rates than male teachers and that the professionalization of women teachers would strengthen education in the nation's common schools.[38] This emphasis on the utility of women's higher education provided some of the most compelling arguments in its favor. Arguments advocating for women's education for the sole or primary purpose of their enrichment were not nearly as persuasive as calls to develop the intellectual capacities of women to promote social purposes like teaching schoolchildren or providing resourceful wives for clergymen. As more Americans recognized the value of extending college education to women, the inevitability of their inclusion in advanced education became increasingly apparent.

A New Frontier: Women's Movement into Higher Education

Institutional Changes

Women's welcome into higher education was an uneven one. Beginning in the early nineteenth century, women gained access to seminaries (also known as academies), which provided gender-specific training for women, and normal schools that provided teacher training.[39] Troy Female Seminary became the first institution to train women for the teaching profession when it opened in 1821; and, in the late nineteenth century, the nation saw the rapid creation of women's colleges, beginning with the Georgia Female College (now known as Wesleyan College) in 1836.[40] Women's colleges offered some of the earliest opportunities for women to pursue advanced education.

Before the high-profile establishment of Vassar in 1861, approximately forty women's colleges offered degrees to women.[41] However, there was broad-reaching concern over whether women's institutions would provide an education comparable to that which was provided in men's colleges.[42] By many accounts, early higher educational institutions that catered to women were little more than high schools or "finishing schools" that aimed to produce suitable wives.[43] Between 1861 and 1875, Matthew Vassar, Henry Wells, Sophia Smith, and Henry Durant established women's colleges that were intended to provide the same standard of higher education that characterized the nation's most elite male colleges, which staunchly refused to admit women.[44] In the decades that followed, Wellesley College (1875), Smith College (1875), Spelman College (1881), Bryn Mawr (1885), and Barnard College (1889) were founded with the purpose of providing high-quality educational opportunities for women.[45] Women's colleges were noteworthy because they offered educational spaces that catered specifically to women and that incorporated them as full and equal participants in campus life.

After being excluded from the colleges that had taught their brothers since Harvard's 1636 founding, women finally gained the opportunity for coeducation in 1833, when Oberlin College became the first higher educational institution in the United States to admit both men and women.[46] The land-grant colleges and state universities of the Midwest took the lead in pioneering coeducation.[47] In 1855, the University of Iowa became the first public or state college to admit both women and men. The University of Wisconsin followed suit in 1863, as did the University of Kansas, Indiana University, and the University of Minnesota in 1869.[48] While many of these schools were reluctant to admit women, they were compelled to do so by women taxpayers who took issue with the use of public funds—generated from both male and female taxpayers—to support higher educational institutions that refused to serve both women and men.[49]

Throughout the nineteenth century, women's campaigns for admission played an important role in their newfound inclusion on college campuses. Women's organizations and parent–teacher associations demanded that state legislatures and institutional boards of regents offer the daughters of taxpaying citizens access to vocational training.[50] A number of older women applied pressure on colleges, insisting that they admit women; and some of the wealthiest sympathizers, as economist Mable Newcomer puts it, "bought women's way in."[51] At the University of Michigan and at the Johns Hopkins Medical School, for example, women gained admission only after female activists raised $100,000 for each school and declared that the gifts' bestowal was contingent upon each institution agreeing to admit women.[52] Although many prestigious men's schools continued to deny women access, some college founders, like Ezra Cornell and John Purdue, had worked to ensure that women would enjoy equal opportunities at land-grant colleges.[53] By 1869, 41 percent of postsecondary academic institutions were coeducational, and women made up approximately 21 percent of the nation's college students.[54]

While many American women gained greater access to higher education during the late nineteenth century, black, Jewish, and Catholic women did not.[55] In 1860, the US population included 4.5 million blacks; a full 4 million of them were slaves who were subjected to laws that prevented their learning to even read or write.[56] For blacks residing in non-slave-holding states, advanced education was reserved for men. Historians estimate that before 1840, bachelor's degrees were awarded to fifteen black men and to no black women.[57] With the founding of Spelman College in 1881, higher educational opportunity for black women increased substantially.

Catholic and Jewish women also faced discrimination in higher education. During the late nineteenth century, they were admitted to women's colleges in small numbers, or as Lynn Peril put it, "'by ones and twos' . . . as long as they didn't rock the boat."[58] For many colleges and universities, limiting the presence of women was deemed critical to maintaining institutional quality. Considering the prevalence of such discrimination, these women eventually benefited from the creation of institutions that were established with them in mind. The 1896 founding of Maryland's College of Notre Dame, for example, provided greater access to higher education for Catholic women.[59] As these examples illustrate, although American women saw progress in higher educational attainment throughout the nineteenth century, this progress did not occur at the same rate for everyone. In spite of noteworthy steps toward greater inclusion for women, institutional barriers would continue to limit women's access to higher education well into the twentieth century.

Double Standards on Campus

By the 1840s, women were increasingly permitted to learn beside their male counterparts. They were, nonetheless, subjected to glaring double standards on campus. Oberlin College, the institution that pioneered coeducation in the United States, provides an excellent example. In terms of curriculum, men and women were typically segregated into "sex-traditional" fields.[60] From women's earliest inclusion at Oberlin, they were automatically enrolled in the "Ladies' Course," which provided a curriculum deemed appropriate to women's preordained roles as wives and mothers. Beginning in 1841, women were given the option of enrolling in the men's course of study; however, they were not permitted to engage in public speaking. Furthermore, the school invoked a strict, gendered division of labor whereby women were required to cook, to sew, and to do male classmates' laundry, and male students handled heavier chores.[61]

On campus, women were often greeted with hostility and found themselves treated as second-tier students. Upon entering classrooms during the late nineteenth century, for example, women students at the University of Wisconsin were expected to remain standing until their male classmates were seated.[62] While some male and female students forged friendships, some social organizations maintained an "anti-coed" policy that discouraged the men from fraternizing with the women.[63] Male students' feelings of hostility toward coeducation and their female classmates were often palpable.[64] Many men at newly coeducational eastern colleges felt that women's presence signified their lower status vis-à-vis all-male schools like Harvard and Yale.[65]

Women's academic excellence was not met with the same esteem as excellent achievement among male students, and women were often denied honors like Phi Beta Kappa keys on the grounds that granting such awards to women would come at the unnecessary expense of men.[66] As one woman was told, "when it came to finding a job, men needed [academic] honor[s] more than women did."[67] Although women students were required to pay student activity fees, they were denied the opportunity to participate in most student organizations.[68] Women's second-class status on coeducational campuses was also evident in their limited access to college facilities. Before 1900, women in coeducational

institutions rarely enjoyed access to on-campus amenities that were comparable
to the comfortable dorm accommodations and well-appointed athletic facilities
that their male counterparts took for granted.[69] All things considered, women's
second-class status served as a palpable reminder that they were somehow less
deserving of college education than their male counterparts.

Early Higher Education Policies

The Civil War represents a critical juncture in the gendered history of American
higher education. This historical moment rendered a substantial number of
young women without male familial support, compelling many to turn to the
labor force—and higher education—in hopes of better supporting themselves.[70]
By the end of the war, women represented the majority of the nation's teachers,
and over time, teacher education programs catered primarily to women.[71]

In addition to marking the beginning of an era in which higher education
took on a measure of exigency for many American women, the Civil War also
represents a pivotal political moment that enabled lawmakers to successfully
pass legislation that had previously languished in Congress.[72] Among the most
prominent of these policies was the Morrill Land-Grant program, which had
been vetoed by President James Buchanan in 1859.[73] Three years later, President
Abraham Lincoln signed the Morrill Land-Grant Act of 1862, which provided
government land to each state for establishing and supporting at least one college, thus marking the beginning of federal intervention in higher education.
This policy allocated government support for the establishment of some of the
nation's earliest and most important state universities.[74] Further, the policy held
that the resources generated from federal lands would be used to support education in "agriculture and the mechanic arts in such a matter as the legislatures of
the States may respectively prescribe, in order to promote the liberal and practical education of the industrial classes in the several pursuits and professions in
life."[75]

The Morrill Act supported the establishment of land-grant institutions that
welcomed both men and women and, in doing so, promoted women's inclusion
in higher education.[76] These institutions would also serve the national objective
of providing practical education that would prove useful for common citizens.
In this vein, providing women with training for crucial occupations like teaching
served important national goals. Although the Morrill Land-Grant Act did not
specifically mention gender, it promoted coeducation by supporting the establishment of higher educational institutions in the sparsely populated western
states, where the admission of women and men proved an economically advan-
tageous policy. Lincoln's signing of the first Morrill Land-Grant Act resonated

with his expressed commitment to providing all Americans with "an unfettered start, and a fair chance in the race of life"; and, in passing the landmark program, lawmakers distinguished the United States as "the first nation in the world, whether in peace or war, to systematically commit its resources for the support of higher education."[77] Of the more than one hundred land-grant colleges that were supported by the Morrill Land-Grant Act of 1862, many became leading academic institutions in the United States.[78]

After a show of lobbying support from the presidents of land-grant colleges who were interested in securing direct government funding on an annual basis, a second Morrill Land Grant was passed in 1890.[79] This policy reinforced the federal commitment to higher education by institutionalizing annual appropriations to benefit state colleges, including land-grant colleges in the South that catered to women and African American students.[80] Taken together, the Morrill Land-Grant Acts helped to significantly expand higher educational opportunity in the United States by providing unprecedented federal resources to support postsecondary institutions.

American Higher Education During the Progressive Era (1880–1920)

The Progressive Era provided the backdrop for sweeping changes in American higher education. By the end of the nineteenth century, the primary purpose of higher education had shifted from imparting broad learning and intellectual discipline to producing an educated labor force that would meet the needs of the nation's rapidly growing economy.[81] The period saw continued growth in the number of colleges operating in the United States and a continuous movement of women into higher educational institutions. Although the total proportion of the American population pursuing advanced education remained low—a mere 3 percent of Americans between eighteen and twenty-one years old were enrolled in college in the 1890s—and although colleges continued to represent the domain of the elite, attaining higher education became a celebrated ideal for white males.[82] Furthermore, college education became increasingly associated with socioeconomic mobility. Not only did higher education pave the way to increased earnings, but also it offered social respectability for "nouveau riche" families.[83] In terms of growth in higher education during the Progressive Era, coeducation stood out as an area experiencing significant expansion.[84] As a result, the "college woman" emerged as a cultural figure during this period.[85] For men and women, higher education began to represent an increasingly beneficial undertaking.

Reaching a High Point
in Women's Postsecondary Education

The Progressive Era saw important changes in women's higher education. First, women were becoming increasingly prepared for pursuing postsecondary degrees. In 1890, when few Americans had more than a fifth-grade education, girls outnumbered boys as high school graduates.[86] Still, at that point in time, the majority of women students were enrolled in women's colleges, which were typically less rigorous than men's.[87] The University of Chicago's 1892 founding was noteworthy because of college president William R. Harper's strong commitment to equitable coeducation. During the institution's earliest years, Harper recruited women undergraduates, graduate students, and faculty members. By the 1890s, Cornell University, Syracuse University, Boston University, Stanford University, the University of Michigan, the University of Wisconsin, and other schools had already transitioned into coeducation, and they shared in the commitment to providing more rigorous training for women students.[88]

While a number of colleges in the northeastern and southern United States continued to resist coeducation, institutions in the nation's midwestern and western regions—which were more vulnerable to financial pressure from its supporters—proved more amenable to coeducation.[89] In the South, state colleges in Texas, Arkansas, and Mississippi were the first to adopt coeducation, as were the region's historically black colleges. Schools in the Old South—the southern states of the original thirteen colonies—were among the last to permit women and men to pursue advanced education side by side.[90] Nationwide in the year 1900, fewer than thirty thousand Americans—a mere 0.04 percent of the population—had earned bachelor's degrees, and of those who had, approximately 81 percent were men, and only 19 percent were women.[91] In terms of the entire population of young Americans between the ages of eighteen and twenty-one years old, only 2.8 percent of women earned bachelor's degrees that year.[92]

Women college students in the late nineteenth century tended to hail from middle-class families in which the fathers worked in the professions, in business, or in agriculture.[93] Although women enjoyed greater access to advanced education during the Progressive Era, they faced many challenges. On one hand, institutions still discriminated against them. Schools like Harvard, Yale, Princeton, and Columbia resisted calls to admit women. Instead of inviting women students into their institutions, they established coordinate colleges—essentially, "sister schools"—to accommodate women.[94] The increasing number of women on many of the nation's college campuses evoked considerable backlash from coast to coast. Fearing that their schools would be taken less seriously or that they would be mistaken for "women's schools," a number of institutions, such as the University of Michigan and Stanford University, adopted gender quotas that restricted the number of women who would be granted admission.[95] Consider Stanford University in 1899. Stating a commitment to ensuring that Stanford did not become a female seminary, the founder's widow unilaterally institutionalized a gender quota that permanently capped female enrollment at the university—which had reached 40 percent of the student body in the late nineteenth century—at five hundred students.[96] The University of Rochester, Tufts University, and Western Reserve University established separate schools for women, while the University of Chicago placed women and men in sex-segregated classes during their first two years of study.[97] Boston University mounted a "More Men Movement" to recruit more men, and Wesleyan University simply stopped admitting women between 1902 and 1915.[98]

For men and women during the early twentieth century, financing college education was challenging for those who did not come from well-heeled families. As historian Barbara Miller Solomon notes, "No college women (or men) could count on scholarships or loans . . .. Education between 1870 and 1920 was a privilege for the fortunate or a reward to be earned through one's own efforts."[99] While men of modest means could often work their way through college or take advantage of the rare scholarship, women with limited resources struggled when it came to financing their own higher educational pursuits. Although some women worked as teachers to earn money for college, they generally had great difficulty finding positions that would enable them to work their way through school, and they enjoyed ever less access to scholarship funds than men.[100] While a small number of schools like Boston University and the University of Chicago provided gender-egalitarian scholarship aid during the late nineteenth century, most scholarship aid was available to men but not women. In 1906, Tulane University provided two hundred scholarships for men, while reserving only nine for women.[101]

In the early twentieth century colleges saw a growth in the number of self-supporting college women.[102] By 1917, college deans had begun to recognize and publicize the need for greater financial support for students.[103] On some campuses, young women organized funds to help support their self-supporting classmates. Other financial assistance came from external sources. *Ladies' Home Journal*, for example, hosted a contest that offered funding for a four-year education at Vassar, Wellesley, or Smith College to the young woman who sold the most magazine subscriptions.[104] As the publication noted, many parents understand the "thousand and one advantages which college education means for a girl" and desire higher education for their daughters, but, too often, "the desire is there, but not the means."[105] Such instances illustrate an increasing awareness of the returns that higher education could provide for women and the creative approaches that many women took in hopes of securing that education.

World War I and Its Effects on American Higher Education

During World War I, American colleges and universities saw declining enroll-ments as male students were drafted into combat. At Harvard and Yale, for exam-ple, enrollments declined by approximately 40 percent in one year due to the war.[106] This precipitated a shift in the gender dynamics of US higher educational institutions, as women's presence on college campuses grew during the war.

   With the end of World War I, budget constraints and increasing application pools led elite colleges to become more selective in admitting students. With this new emphasis on selectiveness, schools became particularly concerned about the social backgrounds of their students and whether these backgrounds rein-forced or undermined their elite images. As a result, American colleges during the post–World War I era became more likely to discriminate against applicants on the basis of demographic factors like gender, race, and religion. Columbia University, for instance, developed an admissions system that limited the num-ber of Jewish students accepted each year. Soon thereafter, Princeton, Yale, and Harvard adopted similar guidelines to restrict the number of Jewish students attending their institutions.[107] Thus, elite institutions worked in opposition to the increasing accessibility of higher education that had begun to transform col-leges and universities during the preceding decades.[108] This regression toward discrimination threatened to undermine the progress that women and minori-ties had achieved, while contributing to the power of institutional barriers that limited their access to college degrees.

Depression-Era Higher Educational Attainment and Access (1921–1943)

During the interwar period, the nation saw modest growth in women's pres-ence in higher education, as well as the rise of junior, or community, colleges in the United States. By 1920, the number of Americans with four-year degrees rose to more than 48,000—0.05 percent of the population. During the same time frame, normal schools, which continued to supply the nation with a steady stream of trained teachers, provided postsecondary education to an increas-ing number of students, many of whom were women.[109] Teachers' colleges also maintained a strong presence throughout the country, educating a growing num-ber of students, as did two-year colleges, which enrolled approximately 10,000 students.[110] Over the following decade, the number of Americans earning bach-elor's degrees increased dramatically, and the nation's colleges and universities saw doubled enrollments. In 1930, more than 120,000 Americans reported having earned at least a bachelor's degree, and the gender gap in educational attainment continued to narrow, as 60 percent of Americans with bachelor's degrees were men, compared to approximately 40 percent who were women.[111]

The National Youth Administration's Work-Study Program

On June 26, 1935, President Franklin Delano Roosevelt issued Executive Order No. 7086. As part of the New Deal initiative to rehabilitate the nation from the economic woes of the Great Depression, Roosevelt invoked the executive power delegated to him by the Federal Emergency Relief Appropriation Act (FERA) of 1935 to establish the National Youth Administration (NYA). According to Roosevelt's executive order, the NYA would

> initiate and administer a program of approved projects which shall pro-
> vide relief, work relief, and employment for persons between the ages
> of sixteen and twenty-five years who are no longer in regular attendance
> at a school requiring full time, and who are not regularly engaged in
> remunerative employment.[112]

Two months later, in August 1935, Roosevelt expanded the NYA's charge to include administering a college work-study program that would provide federal aid for college students facing financial difficulties that endangered their ability to continue their education.[113] The NYA represented an important program under the FERA, and Roosevelt charged the Works Progress Administration (WPA) with administrating it. The program would be monitored by a system of national, state, and local advisory committees that included civic and professional leaders, as well as representatives from colleges, state agencies, and private organizations.[114]

Although the modest allocation of $50 million—out of the FERA's $5 billion budget—to operate the work-study program limited its ability to provide extensive support to college students and precluded the program from becoming a mechanism for expanding access to higher education, its emergence revolutionized US higher education policy.[115] Historically, federal efforts had centered on providing federal support for infrastructure or resources for particular programs, like vocational education. NYA work-study benefits provided the first federal aid targeted directly to college students. Admittedly, the program's short-term effects were modest.[116] Nevertheless, the modesty of the program's short-term effectiveness pales in comparison to the significance of its long-term effects.

In addition to shifting the federal government's higher education efforts from institutional support and program provisions to direct student aid, it also set an enduring precedent for gender-egalitarian higher education policy by providing benefits to both male and female students, without regard to sex. In doing so, the

NYA work-study program helped to set the stage for the development of subsequent student aid programs that would allocate benefits on a gender-egalitarian basis. In addition to its gender egalitarianism, the NYA was noteworthy in its racial egalitarianism, initiating the nation's first federal affirmative action program, as well as allocating aid for African American students pursuing graduate degrees.[117]

World War II and the Postwar Era (1944–1960)

During World War II, women maintained a substantial presence in American colleges and universities, occupying seats that were vacated by men who were serving in the armed forces.[118] As scholars have noted, American higher educational institutions founded with the purpose of educating men have become increasingly amenable to the prospect of admitting women when male enrollments are in decline or when financial pressures compel them to admit a larger number of students.[119] World War II signaled the beginning of a dramatic, worldwide expansion of higher education. In the immediate postwar era, approximately 30 percent of Americans between the ages of eighteen and twenty-two were enrolled in college.[120] However, women's presence as a proportion of college students declined significantly during the postwar era.[121] In hopes of creating space for returning veterans, some schools implemented quotas for women and nonveterans.[122] Schools that would have welcomed women during the war now routinely rejected them. This postwar attempt to free up space in colleges and universities by relegating the women—who had sustained these institutions during the war—to the sidelines is reminiscent of early debates over the propriety of educating women. Echoing the utilitarian rationale that was popular in the nineteenth century, many felt that society and higher educational institutions should invest in women's education insofar as such investment would yield returns to society. In other words, they felt that educating men took priority over educating women at a time when the nation's economy grappled with the challenge of accommodating returning war veterans. Although a considerable amount of time had elapsed, attitudes regarding women's higher education remained strikingly unchanged in this regard.

During the early twentieth century, American women and men obtained college degrees at steadily increasing rates. Although men had consistently earned degrees at higher rates than women, they began to outpace women by a significant margin around 1930.[123] This growing disparity was fueled, at least in part, by the gender dynamics of the Depression-era labor market. As many Americans struggled with unemployment, higher education represented a possible path to labor force participation. Yet during the 1930s, regulations barring women from certain professions made higher education less valuable for them and contributed to an expansion of the gender gap in college degree attainment.[124] After World War II, the gender gap in US higher educational attainment increased dramatically, and much of this trend was directly related to federal intervention into higher education during the postwar era. With the creation of the Serviceman's Readjustment Act (the "GI Bill") of 1944, the federal government significantly expanded access to higher education for military veterans—98 percent of whom were men.[125] When lawmakers enacted the program at the end of World War II, they fundamentally changed the gender dynamics of American higher education while setting an important precedent for federal higher education policy.

The GI Bill of 1944

On June 22, 1944, lawmakers signed the GI Bill into law, providing a variety of benefits to veterans returning home from World War II.[126] Those who served in active duty for more than ninety days and who had been honorably discharged were eligible to take advantage of the bill's generous grants for higher education. To reward veterans for their service and to temper the effect of their return to the labor force by steering a significant portion of them into colleges and universities, the federal government provided grants to cover tuition and fees. In addition to generous tuition grants, GI Bill benefits also included a monthly stipend of $75 for single veterans, $105 for veterans with one dependent, and $120 for those with two or more dependents.[127]

The GI Bill was undeniably successful at expanding veterans' access to higher education in the postwar era. More than 2 million citizens took advantage of the program's benefits, costing the federal government more than $5.5 billion.[128] Historical data indicate that the GI Bill was a resounding success in promoting increased access to higher education for veterans, and this success is closely associated with the program's effectiveness in expanding access to higher education.[129] Immediately after World War II, approximately 70 percent of male students enrolled in America's postsecondary institutions were veterans.[130] Compared with 1.5 million total students before World War II, an astounding 1.1 million World War II veterans were enrolled in postsecondary programs in 1947.[131] For all its success, however, the GI Bill failed to reflect the gender-egalitarian precedent set by the NYA work-study program. Instead, these federal resources were awarded overwhelmingly to American men, and American women were virtually excluded from the government's unprecedented support for college students.

As Millie Rowe's story illustrated at the beginning of this chapter, women had a markedly different experience with the GI Bill. During World War II, American women actively contributed to the war effort, fighting on the home

front by stepping into positions that were previously held by men. As nonveterans, however, they were not eligible for the rewards of the GI Bill. At the end of
the war they were encouraged to act as "responsible citizens" by returning to the
home so that male veterans could have full access to jobs in the labor force.[132]
The resulting exodus of women from the workforce coincided with an emphasis
on the notion that men had the greatest claims to higher education because they
had an economic imperative to participate in the labor force. They were, according to dominant gender norms, the rightful beneficiaries of the knowledge and
skills that higher education would provide.

Although women were largely ineligible for GI Bill benefits by virtue of their
nonveteran status, a small number of women—making up 2 percent of soldiers
serving in active military duty during World War II—were eligible veterans.[133]
Considering this small proportion, it comes as little surprise that fewer than
3 percent of World War II veterans who used the GI Bill to attend college—that
is, 64,728 of more than 2.2 million veterans—were women.[134] Of the female
GIs who were eligible to take advantage of the program's benefits, many did not
use them because they were not aware of their eligibility, because their family
responsibilities made it impossible to pursue a college degree, or because they
did not feel entitled to the same benefits as their male counterparts.[135] Given that
female World War II veterans generally hailed from more privileged socioeconomic backgrounds and were typically encouraged to pursue higher education
as children, their surprisingly low rate of program uptake signals the potency of
postwar gender norms.[136]

The small group of women who did take advantage of GI Bill benefits often
received benefits that paled in comparison to those enjoyed by their male counterparts. They also faced open hostility from the organizations charged with
administering veterans' benefits—the same organizations that enthusiastically
helped male veterans to claim their GI benefits.[137] Thus, gender inequality in the
administration of GI Bill benefits advantaged men while placing women at a significant disadvantage. As Suzanne Mettler notes, "Had the female veterans been
different in only one regard—sex—they would have used the G.I. Bill at higher
average rates than male veterans did. Gender was the sole factor that stood in the
way of their G.I. Bill usage."[138]

Indeed, the administration of the GI Bill program was fraught with discrimination against women.[139] Banks and postsecondary institutions, in particular,
were notoriously less than helpful—if not downright hostile—to women claim-
ing benefits. Moreover, during the postwar era, the focus on providing opportunity for male veterans coupled with social norms to precipitate a decline in
higher educational attainment among women. Women who shared Millie
Rowe's interest in obtaining postsecondary training—like Millie's elder sisters,
who had briefly attended nursing school—were urged to devote themselves to

raising families and to leave work and educational opportunities for men who needed to resume their roles as breadwinners.[140] The overwhelmingly female group of Americans who were ineligible for GI Bill benefits often had difficulty securing funds for college.[141] While women had composed almost half of all students during the war, they represented only 28.8 percent of students in 1948.[142] Although the GI Bill provided access to higher education for a significant portion of Americans who otherwise would not have obtained advanced training, women were largely excluded from these benefits.

Higher Education Since the Mid-Twentieth Century (1960–Present)

The history of higher education in the United States yields important lessons for thinking about the effect that government programs have had on the gender dynamics of American citizenship since the mid-twentieth century. As we have seen, higher educational institutions in the United States were established with men in mind, and for approximately three hundred years after the establishment of the nation's first college, women were still working toward achieving equal access to postsecondary institutions. Fortunately, during the early twentieth century, the federal government established landmark precedents that set the stage for increasing government intervention in higher education and helped to expand college access for erstwhile marginalized groups like low-income veterans. Having considered the complex history of gender and opportunity in American higher education, let us turn to three landmark federal policies—the National Defense Education Act of 1958, the Higher Education Act of 1965, and Title IX of the 1972 Education Amendments—that have helped to reshape the gender dynamics of US higher education since the mid-twentieth century.

Scaring Up Money for College

How the Politics of Crisis Set the Stage for Gender-Egalitarian Student Aid

If the United States is to maintain a position of leadership and if we are to further enhance the quality of our society, we must see to it that today's people are prepared to contribute the maximum to our future progress and strength and that we achieve the highest possible excellence in our education.

—President Dwight D. Eisenhower, *1958*[1]

Because of your commitment to education, I received an NDEA loan to go to teacher's college. I graduated in 1963 and taught high school English for twenty-four years . . . . To repay my country for the difference education made in my life, I decided to sell everything I own, cash in my life savings and spend it all getting a doctorate in education at Harvard . . . . When I finish . . . I aim to dedicate my second career to helping school reform recover from the damage done over the last six years of the Republican administration.

—*NDEA beneficiary Jan Eagle, February 1989, in letter to Carl Elliott*

Given the lengthy history of women's marginalization in higher education and limited public support for female college students, which were discussed in chapter 2, the creation of a federal financial aid program that significantly expanded women's access to college in 1958 was unlikely. By the late 1950s, the time-honored tradition of state and local predominance in the area of kindergarten through twelfth-grade education and state dominance in higher education made the prospect of expanding the federal role in educating citizens a dim one.[2] As the Eighty-Fifth Congress got underway in January of 1957, there was little reason to expect that lawmakers would pass a program for federal aid for higher education. For years, Sen. Lister Hill (D-AL) and Rep. Carl Elliott (D-AL) had proposed legislation that would channel federal funds toward education, but political challenges repeatedly foiled their attempts. Federal support for higher education faced formidable opposition from a range of political actors, including

President Dwight Eisenhower and conservative Republicans who were suspicious of federal intervention in the area of education. Southern Democrats also opposed federal student aid, fearing that federal education policies would enable the government to force integration in slowly desegregating school systems throughout the South.[3]

Women's marginalization in elite- and mass-level politics during the 1950s also contributed to the improbability of passing a student aid program that would significantly expand educational opportunity for women. Of the 435 members of the US House of Representatives serving in the Eighty-Fifth Congress, only 14 were women; and Margaret Chase Smith (R-ME) was the lone woman serving in the 100-member Senate. In terms of mass politics, women voted and participated in other political activities at lower rates than men, and they expressed lower levels of political efficacy.[4] It was unlikely that women would constitute a vocal, well-organized interest group demanding support to pursue college degrees.

Nevertheless, on September 2, 1958, the US Congress passed and President Eisenhower signed the National Defense Education Act (NDEA). The creation of this program marked a watershed moment in the development of US higher education policy because it created the first need-based federal student loans. What's more, the passage of the NDEA marked a significant moment for gender equality because it provided American women with the first broadly accessible public support for pursuing college degrees and paved the way for future programs that would employ federal intervention to promote equal access to higher education for American women and men. Given the formidable political barriers that made it unlikely that lawmakers would enact such a program in the 1950s, the successful passage of the National Defense Education Act in 1958 presents a puzzle for students of public policy. In this chapter, I seek to understand how lawmakers successfully passed such a path-breaking student aid program at that historical moment and how it has contributed to women's educational attainment in subsequent decades. Using historical analysis, I examine the NDEA's surprising and highly significant departure from US social policy precedents, paying particular attention to how the program was fashioned and what its passage meant for women's status as citizens.

The creation of the NDEA and its impact for women marked a dramatic departure from existing higher education policy precedents. Unlike the 1862 and 1890 Morrill Land Grant Acts and the 1917 Smith-Hughes Act, which provided government funds to build college infrastructure and to support vocational programing, the NDEA provided aid directly to students. The National Youth Administration's 1935 work-study program was gender egalitarian in that it provided support to both men and women, but the fact that benefits reached only a narrow segment of students who were already enrolled in college during the

Great Depression meant that its benefits did little to help expand women's access to college degrees. The 1944 GI Bill pioneered the use of large-scale student financial aid as a tool to expand higher educational opportunity, but its military service–based eligibility requirements meant that women were overwhelmingly excluded from its benefits. By providing substantial financial support for college students on the basis of financial need, the National Defense Education Act blazed a trail for gender parity in public support for college students.

In addition to the extent to which it deviated from higher education policy precedents, the NDEA was also distinctive in its departure from US social policy precedents, more broadly. Early social welfare programs like veterans' pensions, support for widows, and safety net programs established under the New Deal exemplified an institutionalized standard of differential treatment for men and women.[5] Women's participation in these programs was typically predicated on their roles as wives and mothers.[6] By allocating benefits on the basis of financial need, the NDEA treated women and men equally and signaled a shift in how women were treated under US social policy. Additionally, in providing the first occasion on which a broad spectrum of American women could qualify for federal student aid, the passage of the National Defense Education Act marked a crucial moment in the expansion of women's higher educational opportunity— an accomplishment that would have reverberating effects for women's status as full and equal citizens in the American polity.

Historical analysis suggests that women's incorporation as full citizens under US social policy is rooted in the political development of the NDEA, which was shaped by Cold War politics on the international stage and contention over civil rights on the domestic front. The concerted influence of these factors was central to lawmakers' success in passing a student assistance program that institutionalized gender-egalitarian support for college students and contributed to a narrowing of the gender gap in higher educational attainment that had been exacerbated by the GI Bill. These factors were also integral to the NDEA's radical departure from the gendered style of previous social policies and its ability to actualize a significant shift in the gender dynamics of US citizenship.

This case study of the political development of the NDEA provides valuable lessons for our understanding of agenda setting and policy design. In terms of agenda setting, it reveals the powerful force that the politics of crisis and the emergence of a political window of opportunity can have on upsetting the status quo, offering scholars of public policy and political development valuable lessons for achieving sweeping policy change in the midst of political contexts that are fraught with contention. Recognizing the significance of the politics of crisis for their ability to pass a higher education program, Lister Hill and Carl Elliott strategically designed their proposal to place the issue of national security front and center. Doing so was crucial to their capacity to generate enough political support to achieve its passage. Additionally, the creation of the NDEA offers a powerful example of accidental egalitarianism resulting from vague policy design. Rather than reflecting a deliberate attempt to target government support to women who had been excluded from public support for pursuing college degrees, women's inclusion as full and equal beneficiaries of the NDEA was a matter of lawmakers' attempts to make the NDEA proposal so vague that it would invite little opposition from lawmakers concerned about which groups would be included or excluded from the program. This technique was a direct attempt to deflect attention from issues related to race and religion, which had proved insurmountable for previous education policy proposals. It had the inadvertent effect of substantially reshaping college affordability for American women.

Moreover, this case offers insight into how lawmakers can use strategic policy design to generate crucial political support for social programs. Concern regarding the impact that federal financial aid could have on the racial order of schools in the South and the possibility that federal support could be directed toward Catholic institutions were central issues shaping consideration of the NDEA, and lawmakers grappled with how—or whether—to signal that the NDEA's benefits would be distributed without discrimination. To secure the political support of liberals and conservatives in Congress, Lister Hill and Carl Elliott strategically designed their proposal to successfully negotiate these issues, which had doomed previous education proposals.

The creation of the National Defense Education Act provides a powerful example of how a combination of political forces can collide to foster nonincremental policy change. It also enhances our understanding of American political development by greater illuminating the role that Southern Democrats played in the development of US social policy. Contrary to the well-known role that they played in inhibiting the creation of federal social programs during the mid-twentieth century, the creation of the NDEA reveals that Southern Democrats led the way in creating the financial aid programs that constitute the pillars of US higher education policy.

A Fortuitous Alignment of Political Factors and the Departure from Precedent

Based on the precedent established by the GI Bill, we might have expected policymakers in 1958 to enact a student aid program that approximated its national security–centered approach by targeting federal education funds to students who would embark upon careers in the crucial—and male dominated—fields of engineering and science, the military, or other areas deemed directly related to national security. Instead, the NDEA provided federal loans to undergraduates, absent requirements that students pursue any particular area of study.[7] Moreover, the bill omitted any reference to race, religion, and sex when identifying program beneficiaries. By using broad, highly generalized criteria for benefit eligibility, Sen. Lister Hill (D-AL) and Rep. Carl Elliott (D-AL) were able to convince their liberal colleagues that the program was inherently antidiscriminatory, while simultaneously assuring Southern Democrats that the bill would have no substantial bearing on the racial order of southern institutions of higher education. This chapter provides strong evidence that a timely alignment of political factors enabled lawmakers to pass the NDEA in 1958 and, as a result, to incorporate women as full citizens under US social policy.

The first factor facilitating passage of the NDEA was the Soviet Union's launch of the *Sputnik* satellites. This event provided what John W. Kingdon calls a "window of opportunity" that enabled lawmakers to move existing goals and proposals for federal higher educational aid through Congress.[8] Throughout the 1940s and early 1950s, Hill and Elliott had attempted to pass legislation that would provide federal funding to Americans pursuing college education, but these proposals succumbed to contention over issues like the expansion of federal power and what funding Catholic schools would mean for the separation between church and state.[9] Hill and Elliott recognized the opportunity that the *Sputnik* crisis presented and took great pains to develop a proposal that would successfully clear the House and the Senate. Political entrepreneurs capitalized on the United States' disappointing showing in the space race by using the occasion to emphasize the need for federal student financial aid programs that they had been previously unable to pass.

The second force that contributed to the passage of gender-egalitarian federal student aid was the domestic struggle over civil rights. Southern lawmakers had a keen interest in securing federal resources to support education in southern states, which were taxed by the strain of maintaining segregated, and thus dual, school systems.[10] Throughout the 1940s and early 1950s, efforts to obtain federal funds for higher education were thwarted by opponents who feared that such aid would increase federal control over southern states, empowering the federal government to force school integration in the South by threatening to withhold education funding. Because Southern Democrats and Republicans (from all regions) typically opposed federal student aid proposals, NDEA proponents intentionally crafted their student assistance proposal to be as vague and ostensibly innocuous as possible, leaving matters such as the administration of proposed funds and their effects on the racial order of southern colleges and universities to institutional administrators. As Rep. Carl Elliott would later note, his efforts to expand higher educational access were meant to extend support to a diverse range of beneficiaries and to ensure that "the sons and daughters of the working men and women of this nation would have the opportunity to achieve the highest level of education commensurate with their ability, unfettered by economic, racial or other artificial barriers."[11]

As a result, the gender inclusiveness of the National Defense Education Act was more a matter of political exigency than a strong commitment to expanding women's access to college degrees. Lawmakers' preoccupation with race during the late 1950s made it unlikely that they would forcefully advocate for student aid policies that boldly addressed gender inequality. Rep. Adam Clayton Powell (D-NY) and the National Association for the Advancement of Colored People (NAACP), however, were notable exceptions. During deliberations over education policy proposals, Representative Powell forcefully advocated for an NAACP-crafted nondiscrimination amendment that would require benefits to be allocated without regard to race, color, religion, sex, or national origin.

Cold War politics represents the third force that promoted women's full and equal inclusion as beneficiaries of the NDEA's student aid provisions. While scholars have recognized Cold War politics as valuable to the efforts of civil rights activists, they have stopped short of recognizing its significant—if understated—influence on the issue of women's rights.[12] When the Soviet Union launched the *Sputnik* satellites, Lister Hill and Carl Elliott strategically harnessed the conservative rhetoric of anticommunism and public anxiety over Soviet technological advances to advocate for government student aid.[13] The authors of the NDEA refrained from incorporating sex-based restrictions into their legislative proposals to drive home the Cold War argument that the nation's security depended on its ability to harness *all* available intellectual resources, or "manpower," in competition with an increasingly sophisticated Soviet Union.[14] Thus, the gender egalitarianism of the National Defense Education Act reflects a political imperative specific to Cold War politics. Taken together, the window of opportunity presented by the *Sputnik* crisis, controversy related to civil rights, and the politics of the Cold War made it possible for enterprising lawmakers to create an educational reform that would provide unprecedented public support for women pursuing college degrees.

Against All Odds: The Improbability of Passing Women-Empowering Federal Student Aid in the Postwar United States

During the postwar era, contention over a variety of issues undermined the probability that the federal government would extend support for college students beyond GI Bill provisions. The topic of public support for college students evoked spirited debate among the president, members of Congress, and a variety of interest groups. For President Eisenhower—who embraced a "God helps those who help themselves" philosophy on social policy—support for education was best left to state and local governments. Although the administration expressed tepid support for modest education proposals like federal aid for school construction and tax credits for families paying college expenses, it refrained from taking initiative in the area of education. In terms of expanding higher educational opportunity for women in particular, while Eisenhower expressed concern about gender inequality in employment in his 1956 State of the Union address, he made no comment on the sizeable gender gap that characterized college degree attainment.[15]

In August of 1957, the President's Committee on Education Beyond High School encouraged the president to push for increased federal support for higher education in familiar forms—land grants, GI Bill benefits, and funding for the recently established National Science Foundation. The committee also suggested that the federal government implement a system of tax deductions to assist low-income students and their families in financing college education. With the exception of tax deductions, which represented a novel proposal for student aid, these recommendations reflected a strong inclination to build upon programs that were already in place. Of the financial aid policies proposed—GI Bill benefits and tax deductions—the latter could have promoted gender parity in higher educational attainment because the tax credits would have been granted on the gender-neutral basis of need, as opposed to the masculine criterion of military service. However, lawmakers would not seriously consider higher education tax credits until the late twentieth century.

In Congress, existing proposals represented a much greater span of alternatives than the school construction and tax deduction possibilities being considered by the Eisenhower administration. In the late 1940s and early 1950s, educational reformers prioritized curriculum improvement in the areas of science and mathematics.[16] In the mid-1950s, members of Congress had proposed scholarships for needy students, federal student loans and loan assistance, financial aid for students studying to become teachers, and the establishment of a United States Science Academy. They also presented more Eisenhower-friendly proposals for school construction and grants to the National Science Foundation. In the national legislature, policymakers presented financial aid proposals that had the capacity to increase women's access to college; yet without fail, these proposals became casualties of political battles over racial discrimination. When federal aid proposals were considered, liberal reformers like Rep. Adam Clayton Powell (D-NY)—an African American representative from Harlem, New York, who was a vocal proponent of civil rights—insisted that the legislation explicitly denounce racial discrimination. As a result, the programs in question typically suffered defeat at the hands of Southern Democrats.

As members of Congress considered early proposals for federal student aid, interest groups were quick to weigh in on the issue.[17] Supporters of federal student aid included the National Education Association (NEA), the American Federation of Labor and Congress of Industrial Organizations (AFL-CIO), and the military-defense industry.[18] The AFL-CIO established the Conference on Federal Aid to Education, which included numerous interest groups such as the American Federation of Teachers, the NAACP, the National Veterans' Committee, the American Association of University Women, and the National Council of Jewish Women. Supporters of federal aid for education disagreed as to whether the government should provide general aid, which would provide schools with unrestricted financial support, or categorical aid, which would grant federal funds to the states and to local school systems for specific, pre-defined purposes or for select groups of students. Professional educators were stalwart supporters of general aid, while other federal aid supporters rejected the idea on the grounds that the government could not be trusted to effectively allocate federal funding.[19]

The US Chamber of Commerce, the National Association of Manufacturers, the American Legion, and various businessmen's and taxpayers' associations were vocal opponents of federal student aid measures.[20] These groups were particularly suspicious of categorical aid proposals, which they saw as a "Trojan horse for federal control."[21] Historically, the threat of federal control represented perhaps the most "rhetorically and politically potent" argument inhibiting lawmakers' efforts to enact programs that would provide federal support for higher education.[22] The possibility that student aid policies could provide the federal government with an additional mechanism by which to control the states provoked the ire of Southern Democrats, who would mount the most vocal opposition to proposals for federal student aid. The objections of Southern Democrats posed a serious obstacle to passing any federal financial assistance program, let alone aid that overtly expanded college access for groups that were underrepresented in higher education, like women and racial and ethnic minorities. Regardless of the public's support for federal aid to education in the early 1950s and despite increasingly egalitarian views toward women, Congress repeatedly rejected proposals for general aid to students on the grounds that such support would increase the federal government's control over education.

Institutionalizing Equal Opportunity Through the Policymaking Process

A dominant approach to explaining the public policymaking process emphasizes the incremental nature of program development. From this perspective, the policies that lawmakers produce tend to differ marginally from existing programs.[23] "Policy does not move in leaps and bounds," asserts Charles Lindblom.[24]

Instead, he claims, public administrators in Western democracies choose to enact policies that differ incrementally from existing programs, which permits them to both simplify the range of proposals under consideration and ensure that these proposals are relevant.[25] Historical institutionalists have emphasized the tendency of policymakers to build upon previously enacted programs when developing new policies.[26] Paul Pierson argues that, by increasing momentum down a particular policy avenue, the feedback effects of already established policies "render previously viable alternatives implausible."[27]

Based on this framework emphasizing the "lock-in" effects that emanate from previously enacted public policies, we would expect lawmakers crafting a federal education program in 1958 to have designed a policy that closely resembled existing federal education programs—namely, the Morrill Land Grant Acts, the Smith-Hughes Act, or the GI Bill—or previously enacted social policies. Had they adhered to an incremental approach to policymaking in 1958, the National Defense Act would have reflected the style of the Morrill Land Grant Acts by allocating federal funds for classroom construction or the approach taken by the Smith-Hughes Act by providing assistance for the sole purpose of enhancing the quality of instruction in a particular academic area. Similarly, it might have resembled the GI Bill by providing federal grants to military veterans or to students who were enrolled in programs specifically related to national security.

If policymakers had built primarily upon existing social programs, the education program that emerged in 1958 would have treated men and women differently—most likely targeting student aid to men, whose use of education benefits would presumably enhance their capacity to act as breadwinners for their families. Instead, lawmakers produced the National Defense Education Act—a gender-neutral, federal aid program that provided National Defense Student Loans directly to individual college students, irrespective of their fields of study.[28] Because it provided federal funds directly to students on the nongendered basis of need, the NDEA represents a dramatic departure from the GI Bill and other programs that had provided federal funds to support college infrastructure and academic programming.

While the incremental approach fails to capture the emergence of the National Defense Education Act in 1958, the theories of agenda setting and policy design offered by John W. Kingdon and Frank R. Baumgartner and Bryan D. Jones provide insight into the dramatic change that lawmakers successfully institutionalized in passing the NDEA.[29] Policy windows, Kingdon argues, offer occasional opportunities for policy action; however, they appear infrequently and are short in duration.[30] The *Sputnik* crisis provided such a window. In line with popular perceptions of the significance of the NDEA, Rep. Alan Wheat (D-MO) described the policy as "a furious and eloquent reaction against the Russians' launch of Sputnik."[31] But viewed in the context of long-range ramifications, the

NDEA was even more consequential because, through it, political entrepreneurs capitalized on the opportunity presented by the loss of the space race to institutionalize broad-reaching federal support for higher education.

Baumgartner and Jones provide further theoretical support for understanding the dramatic change precipitated by the passage of the National Defense Education Act. They argue that "policymaking in the United States is punctuated by bursts of activity that modify issue understandings and lead to nonincremental policy change."[32] Central to fully understanding agenda setting and policy change is fully appreciating the generation and maintenance of policy issues.[33] Lawmakers who supported federal student aid drew upon the *Sputnik* crisis as a focusing event that enabled them to dramatically alter the national discourse regarding appropriate government support for education. Prior to the fall of 1957, lawmakers focused primarily on the problems presented by a national classroom shortage, and proposals for federal education support generally revolved around aid for school construction. The *Sputnik* launches facilitated a significant shift in Americans' understanding of the educational demands facing the nation, and this shift shaped federal higher education policy for years to come.

This analysis will illustrate the process by which lawmakers—whose primary objective was to strategically avoid obstacles that would prevent them from providing federal funds to higher education—inadvertently revolutionized the gender dynamics of American higher education. By passing the National Defense Education Act of 1958, these political actors promoted gender egalitarianism in college affordability, while paving the way for future government programming that would provide additional support for women and men as they pursued postsecondary degrees.

The Politics of Crisis: How *Sputnik*, Civil Rights, and the Cold War Facilitated the Creation of Gender-Egalitarian Student Aid

Scaring Up Money for College

Although the Eisenhower administration, members of Congress, and various interest groups held defined positions on the propriety of federal involvement in education, the issue failed to gain traction until October 4, 1957. On that day, the Soviet Union won the race to space in spades. By successfully launching *Sputnik I*, the first satellite to orbit Earth, Soviet scientists debunked Americans' belief that the United States was the most technologically advanced nation in the world. In the midst of Cold War tensions, this surprising demonstration of scientific prowess was broadly interpreted as signifying the United States' weakness in science and technology and facilitated the ascent of education to the top of the nation's political agenda. Senate staff member Stewart McClure recalls that the public panicked: "people were fretting in the streets about, 'oh, my God, we're behind.' "[34] Now that the Soviet Union had successfully placed a satellite in space, Americans feared that the Soviets would soon be able to gather intelligence of US military capabilities via satellite or even launch nuclear missiles from space.[35] These fears were intensified on November 2, when the Soviet Union launched *Sputnik II*. This time, the satellite launched by Soviet scientists carried a dog, which gave the Soviet Union the additional distinction of being the first country to successfully send a living organism into outer space. These triumphs were viewed as a clear demonstration of Soviet prowess in science and technology and a decided victory for communism.

In the wake of the Soviet Union's triumphant launches, a growing sense of crisis swept the nation, and Americans sought to identify the root of the nation's failure to keep pace with the Soviets. Although many pointed to the perceived failures of the nation's scientists, disaccord at the Pentagon, and suboptimal prioritizing of Cold War concerns by President Eisenhower, a disproportionate amount of criticism fell on the nation's educational system.[36] Critics pointed to shortages in school infrastructure, a chronic lack of science equipment in many high school classrooms, American students' underachievement in mathematics, perilous secondary school dropout rates, and underwhelming levels of college attendance as reasons for the nation's disappointing showing on the space science and engineering front, as well as indicators of vulnerability in the area of national security. Popular publications like *Life* magazine and *The Nation* printed articles highlighting glaring deficiencies in American education.[37] These lackluster characterizations of American schools contrasted sharply with the accounts of US officials, like US Commissioner of Education Lawrence Derthick, who returned from visits to the Soviet Union singing the praises of its rigorous, efficient, and broad-reaching educational system.[38]

The panic that resulted from the *Sputnik* launches and the emergent concern for education in the United States sparked a national outcry.[39] Educational shortcomings were characterized as directly related to the nation's ability to survive in an increasingly competitive international arena, and citizens expected the federal government to secure the nation's safety by providing support for education. [40] Six days after the launch of *Sputnik I*, the American Council on Education (ACE), which advocated on behalf of higher educational institutions, considered the relationship between the nation's failure to win the space race and the lack of federal support for higher education during a meeting held in Washington, DC.[41] While Americans' heightened interest in the quality of the nation's educational system was piqued by perceived shortcomings in science and mathematics, they expressed concern for the system in its entirety—across academic fields and educational levels. Citizens had come to regard education as directly related to the nation's ability to survive in an increasingly competitive international arena, and they made clear their expectation that the federal government could secure the nation's safety by providing support for education.

The *Sputnik* crisis reflected the zeitgeist of the Cold War, growing from an "all-inclusive ideology" characterized by "a grim rhetoric of survival."[42] Capitalizing on Americans' surprise following the Soviet triumph and the disappointment with which they viewed the United States' comparative capabilities, political entrepreneurs who favored federal aid for education instigated public fears regarding the nation's security in the face of Soviet scientific—and presumably militaristic—advantage. This method of securing support for federal education policy drew upon Cold War politics to achieve the arguably unrelated goal of steering federal funds toward higher education. Lawmakers emphasized the necessity of shoring up US "manpower" and preventing the waste of talent to ensure the nation's ability to survive in the face of increasingly sophisticated communist nations. By successfully juxtaposing Cold War politics with the shortcomings of American education, lawmakers and the media took advantage of the window of opportunity that the *Sputnik* crisis provided for expanding access to higher education.

While struggling to reassure the nation of its safety, President Eisenhower took seriously citizens' concerns with the country's educational well-being.[43] In a special address delivered in Oklahoma City, Oklahoma, on November 13, 1957, a little more than one month after the launch of the first *Sputnik* satellite, Eisenhower formally acknowledged the significance of education to national security, specifically addressing the relationship between higher education and the nation's safety.[44]

> Young people now in college must be equipped to live in the age of intercontinental ballistic missiles. However, what will then be needed is not just engineers and scientists but a people who will keep their heads and, in every field, leaders who can meet intricate human problems with wisdom and courage. In short, we will need not only Einsteins and Steinmetzes, but Washingtons and Emersons.[45]

He also emphasized the strides that the Soviet Union had made in education in the recent forty years.[46] One week prior to delivering this message, Eisenhower had met with top administrators in the Department of Health, Education, and Welfare (HEW), charging them with the task of constructing an education program on behalf of the administration that reflected "the public mood."[47] As such, the president expected his administration to produce a temporary policy proposal that directly responded to concerns related to the *Sputnik* crisis. Eisenhower planned to propose this program at the beginning of the congressional session in January of 1958.

Southern Democrats as the Unlikely Champions of Gender Egalitarian Student Aid

Given their Alabama roots, Sen. Lister Hill and Rep. Carl Elliott were unlikely champions of federal student aid. Typically, when lawmakers considered proposals that would extend federal financial support to students, Southern Democrats (along with conservative Republicans from all regions) voted against them. Why, when Southern Democrats typically opposed higher education policy, did Hill and Elliott spearhead proposals for broad-reaching—and, thus, gender-egalitarian—federal support for college students? For most Southern Democrats, federal student aid was viewed as a potential mechanism for federal intrusion into the affairs of individual states. Many of these lawmakers represented constituencies that would have been angered by the possibility that a student aid program could force integration upon southern colleges and universities by withholding funds from institutions that were not in compliance with the Supreme Court's 1954 *Brown v. Board of Education* decision. Hill and Elliott recognized what the *New York Times* described as "prickly" political problems related to religious, racial, economic, and educational issues in their home state.[48]

Although Hill and Elliott hailed from the South, they were nonetheless national politicians who recognized the value of federal higher education aid for their region. They also hailed from northern Alabama, a region known for its populist politics. In fact, Hill and Elliott were not the only lawmakers from their region who recognized the benefits that federal support could yield for their state. According to Elliott's former legislative aide, Mary Allen Jolley, "In looking at the Alabama delegation in those years, it was a very sophisticated, progressive group of people. Both of the US senators and then four of the nine congressmen made up a really progressive group, and they did a lot of good things for the state of Alabama."[49] Stewart McClure, the chief clerk of the Senate's Committee on Labor, Education, and Public Welfare under Lister Hill, echoed this sentiment, noting the surprisingly liberal delegation of lawmakers hailing from Alabama, which included Carl Elliott, John Sparkman, Bob Jones, and Albert Rains. Thinking about their liberalism, he said, "I don't understand it, really, except that the time they were elected, the issues in the South were economic, pulling themselves up, needing federal help, public works, and other things. These men knew how to get it and could work up there effectively."[50] Thus, for Hill and Elliott, the benefits that could be derived from steering federal funds to their impoverished

region outweighed the potential political costs of championing this type of legislation. Commenting on his support for federal social programming during
the contentious postwar political era, Elliott once commented to a friend, "The
people of Alabama need this, and I'm going to sponsor it. It will probably ruin
my career."[51] Nevertheless, Hill and Elliott were committed to passing a broad-
reaching student aid program that would provide a large number of young citizens with human capital that could yield economic gains for the South.

For Hill, a strong interest in education had emerged from his earliest days of
campaigning in northern Alabama, a region that was historically characterized
by populist political views.[52] By the 1950s, Hill had become known in the Senate
as a strong proponent for public health programs. His interest in student aid
represented an extension of his commitment to using social welfare programs
to support citizens. For Elliott, his personal experience as a struggling college
student shaped his commitment to expanding higher educational access for
young Americans. After setting off to college at the University of Alabama with
only $2.38 in his pocket, Elliott spent his college years hustling between a full
load of courses and the numerous jobs that he held to pay for tuition and living expenses. He knew firsthand the challenges that low-income students faced
in financing higher education, and passing a federal student aid program represented one of the central legislative goals of his career.[53]

While the NDEA and its gender-egalitarian style of expanding access to college degrees were championed by male Southern Democrats—a group not
typically associated with support for growth of the US welfare state—women's
groups, the presumptive champions of women's access to public support for college degrees, were surprisingly reticent. While women participated in many of
the interest groups that advocated on behalf of federal student aid, the interests
of women's groups lay elsewhere. In the mid-1950s, these organizations did not
consider higher education to be a central "women's issue." When, for example, the
League of Women Voters and the General Federation of Women's Clubs—two
of the nation's largest women's organizations—produced policy statements alert-
ing Congress of their primary political concerns in the spring of 1956, neither
higher education nor education at the primary and secondary level were listed
among their principal policy concerns.[54] Granted, the National Women's Party
had brought the issue of women's rights before Congress on numerous occasions
in supporting the Equal Rights Amendment, but the goal of increasing gender
equality in higher educational opportunities failed to generate organized support
from women's groups.[55] Not surprisingly, women's issues did not represent a central part of Democrats' or Republicans' legislative agendas in the 1950s. This may
have reflected the fact that women's political activism in the 1950s did not resemble the women's suffrage movement that had immediately followed World War
I or the women's liberation movement that would occur in the late 1960s and

1970s.[56] After World War II, the influence of women's organizations was particularly limited in the social welfare domain of national policy, as their bureaucratic
allies—particularly the Children's and Women's Bureaus—had experienced a
substantial decline in political power.[57] Additionally, women's organizations faced
the confines of Cold War politics, whereby vocal advocates for liberal policies
intended to combat inequality could be labeled communist sympathizers. While
a few women participated in congressional hearings on the NDEA, they testified
on behalf of educational organizations or to share the perspective of interested
undergraduate students. Women's groups did not take the opportunity to weigh
in on the proposed program or to highlight women's stake in it.

While the muted nature of women's groups' political activism in the postwar era did little to promote the passage of a federal college aid program that
would help both women and men, the prospect of Congress's producing such a
policy was augmented by the emergence of increasingly egalitarian public opinion. Two postwar surveys revealed Americans' progressive views regarding the
higher education of women. In an April 1945 survey, 73 percent of Americans
said that if they had a daughter graduating from high school, they would prefer
for her to attend college.[58] Five years later, in July of 1950, a Roper Commercial
Survey reported that 68 percent of Americans thought that women and men
should be taught the same curriculum in college.[59] These trends indicate that
Americans increasingly viewed higher education as a worthwhile pursuit for
both men and women. Thus—in the event that lawmakers decided to enact a
federal student aid program—the decision to provide aid to both genders would
have resonated with public opinion.

The Cold War's Unheralded Influence on Women's Rights

Unlike progressive-era social policies that benefited women at the behest of
women's groups, the gender-egalitarian effects of the NDEA were rooted in lawmakers' strategic subversion of Cold War politics coupled with extreme caution
regarding civil rights and a commitment to taking advantage of the window of
opportunity presented by the *Sputnik* crisis. These factors enabled proponents
of federal student aid to significantly expand the nation's commitment to supporting citizens' higher educational pursuits.[60] The arguably accidental establishment of gender egalitarianism in US higher education was a byproduct of
this noteworthy feat.

Scholars have shown that civil rights activists effectively drew upon the politics
of the Cold War to effectively highlight the hypocrisy of US advocacy for democracy and fairness abroad, despite the fact that a significant portion of the nation's

own citizens were subjected to race-based discrimination.[61] At the same time, scholars have portrayed the Cold War era as yielding little in the way of promoting equal opportunity for American women. In his insightful analysis of the relationship between national security and efforts to secure equal rights in the United States, John Skrentny asserts that the Cold War did little to promote gender equality.[62] Admittedly, the issue of women's rights occupied a subjugated position on the roster of US priorities during the 1950s. In the area of employment, for example, lawmakers were repeatedly unsuccessful in proposing equal pay legislation. Yet, I find that, although public policies expanding rights for racial and ethnic minorities were front and center during this era, the passage of the NDEA represents a crucial moment for women's progress. In his book *See Government Grow*, Gareth Davies asserts that President Lyndon Johnson's Great Society initiative marks the emergence of education policies as increasingly potent mechanisms of progressive change. He describes the 1960s as "a brief liberal moment" that had reverberating effects.[63] However, historical evidence suggests that federal student aid programming has been a significant tool for progressive politics since the Cold War era, when lawmakers passed the NDEA. By successfully providing broad-reaching federal support directly to young women in the form of need-based federal student loans, the NDEA offered an important precedent that informed the subsequent passage of additional financial aid programs and likely contributed to the durability of education policy as a mechanism for the progressive change that Davies describes.

In the Cold War context, the political currency of emphasizing American women's civic engagement and asserting their full integration into democratic society enhanced the likelihood that US lawmakers would pass a gender-neutral federal student aid program.[64] They had an incentive to emphasize women's active participation in electoral politics and to promote the nation's full utilization of women's skills and talents. Compared to the Soviet Union, however, the United States failed to fully utilize the talents of its women. While many Soviet women obtained advanced education, worked in crucial science and engineering fields, and directly contributed to the nation's prowess in science and technology, American women obtained higher education at much lower rates than men and were rarely employed in fields related to science and technology. Lawmakers argued that, to compete with the Soviet Union and to protect American democracy, it was imperative that the United States take advantage of all available "manpower." Just as "showcasing American women's political involvement became a particularly common way to deprecate Soviet life," educating women and drawing upon their talents in the name of democracy resonated with Cold War politics.[65] In this context, the political currency of emphasizing American women's full integration into American higher education increased the probability that lawmakers would advocate for a higher education program that would significantly expand educational access for both women and men.

The Politics of Enactment: Design, Deliberation, and Passage of the National Defense Education Act

Designing Federal Student Aid: Two Proposals

Having already convened subcommittee hearings on the topic of education in 1957, Rep. Carl Elliott (D-AL) recognized the political currency of the *Sputnik* launches and made plans to strategically argue that providing federal support for education in general—and higher education in particular—was crucial to ensuring the nation's security.[66] The idea to take advantage of the unique window of opportunity that *Sputnik* provided came from Stewart McClure, who noted that unlike previous education proposals, the NDEA "was wrapped in the flag and safe."[67] McClure later described the role that he played in devising the strategy, saying:

> It was my idea . . . to do something and to grab this opportunity which would never come again, when the public was all upset and people were fretting in the streets about "oh, my God, we're behind," and all that stuff. So it was, as the Latins used to say, *carpe diem*, "seize the day," and we did, and we did.[68]

Over the December 1957 holiday season, Hill and Elliott assembled their teams in Birmingham to design a federal student aid proposal that they could present to their respective legislative chambers when Congress reconvened in January of 1958. Carl Elliott's former legislative assistant, Mary Allen Jolley, recalls an atmosphere filled with the recognition that the *Sputnik* situation had provided a valuable window of opportunity:

> So when they came together in Birmingham—I was there for those meetings—the conversation was "What is it that we can get passed?" You know, "Now we've got a chance . . . let's load it up with everything that we ever tried to do or ever wanted to do." And, so they got some things in it that had never been tried—[funds for] guidance counseling . . . for language and area studies, for audiovisual equipment.[69]

Hill and Elliott also focused on carefully tying their previous proposals for educational aid to national security in a way that would preclude both rejection by their conservative colleagues and the presidential veto. This cautious approach to policy design illustrates Douglas Arnold's thesis that lawmakers are mindful of the existing and potential preferences and reactions of the public, their opponents, and the media when crafting public policy.[70]

For Hill and Elliott, that meant designing a student aid proposal that was powerful enough to offer substantial support to needy college students while withstanding three controversial issues that had long precluded the passage of federal education proposals—expanding federal control over education, maintaining the separation of church and state, and dealing with segregated schools.[71] The Hill-Elliott measure, which was developed in close consultation with HEW Associate Secretary Elliot Richardson, was strategically named the "National Defense Education Act" and authorized $1.6 billion over the course of five years to provide forty thousand merit-based scholarships to undergraduate students, federal student loans, a work-study program, and money for vocational education.[72] Stewart McClure later recalled:

> I invented that God-awful title: the National Defense Education Act. If there are any words less compatible, really, intellectually, in terms of what is the purpose of education—it's not to defend the country; it's to defend the mind and develop the human spirit, not to build cannons and battleships. It was a horrible title, but it worked. It worked. How could you attack it?[73]

Although Carl Elliott was particularly interested in passing a scholarship program, the decision to expand the menu of financial aid offered under the NDEA reflected lawmakers' interest in exploring a range of possible options. Mary Allen Jolley recalls the point during NDEA hearings at which lawmakers became interested in the prospect of providing loans to students:

> They hinged that loan program on the testimony of a man named Ralph Birdie. I never will forget him. He was out in Chicago, and he said that the University of Minnesota had a student loan program that they administered, and I guess they had raised funds sometime . . . . [T]he college administered it and he said, "We have a better loan repayment rate than the commercial banks in Minneapolis," because he had checked it out. Now, that really caught their attention, so everybody said, "Well, by gosh, if the students are going to pay it back, let's give them a loan." And, so that's where the program came from.[74]

In addition to providing scholarships and loans to talented students pursuing higher education, the NDEA proposal also included funding for teacher training centers and instructional equipment to enhance learning at all levels of education.[75]

Hill and Elliott recognized the potential value of the *Sputnik* crisis for giving higher education proposals a fighting chance and the possibility that it held for "coupling solutions to problems." Aware that the policy window presented by the *Sputnik* crisis would be "of short duration," Elliott worked to quickly and effectively tie his aid proposal to the contemporaneous Cold War crisis.[76] The lawmakers understood that the strongest student aid proposals would emphasize a broad allocation of benefits and an expressed intent of strengthening national security. Although Elliott and Hill packaged their proposal as a temporary response to this particular crisis that would increase America's talent resources in areas like technology and science, they had no intention of scaling back federal aid to education once it had been enacted or of limiting the scope of beneficiaries by academic field. As Elliott later wrote:

> Although training scientists and engineers was a primary focus, we were looking far past the immediate crisis. We were looking at opening the doors of education across the board, in the humanities as well as the "hard" sciences. The crisis gave us a focal point to get our bill made into law—that's how we came up with the title the National *Defense* Education Act. But we realized this bill's effects would extend beyond the current climate of that time. It was education in general, from physics to philosophy, that we wanted to make available to the best young minds of this country.[77]

Elliott's assertion makes clear his intent in crafting the NDEA. Hill and Elliott knowingly and purposefully took advantage of the window of opportunity provided by the *Sputnik* launches to promote substantial and long-lasting federal support for college students.

To create a broad-reaching federal student aid program, it was imperative that Hill and Elliott frame their education bill in a way that would be agreeable to Southern Democrats. Central to this objective was preventing Rep. Adam Clayton Powell (D-NY) from insisting that the federal student aid legislation include an antidiscrimination clause. The "Powell amendments," as these riders were known, proposed that the policies to which they were attached—typically school construction aid and military programs—prohibit benefit allocation on the basis of race, color, religion, nationality, or sex. These amendments proved especially controversial because, in addition to gaining the support of "big-city Democrats" who agreed with their central premise, they garnered the votes of Republicans and Southern Democrats who wished to kill the legislation.[78] These lawmakers would vote in support of the antidiscrimination amendment and then vote *against* the entire bill on the grounds that the antidiscrimination amendment made the proposal disagreeable to their constituents.

To save the National Defense Education Act from such a fate, Hill and Elliott carefully designed the program so that it was vague enough to be interpreted by liberals as inherently nondiscriminatory and by Southern Democrats as innocuous. This was done by omitting Powell's antidiscrimination amendment and offering a means test and enrollment at a US institution of higher education as the only formal criteria for financial aid eligibility. Providing federal aid directly to individuals, rather than to schools, enabled Hill and Elliott to successfully avert the segregation issue. As Barbara Barksdale Clowse recognizes, by awarding scholarships, states "could still practice segregation as long as their commissions made these [federal financial aid] awards without discrimination."[79] In other words, any low-income student could feasibly receive a federal grant, but the student would still have to gain admission to an institution of higher education to utilize the award. The fact that the bill would provide federal aid to any student who met these criteria satisfied the liberals in Congress, while Southern Democrats were reassured by the enrollment criteria. While this framing did little to expand African Americans' access to southern colleges and universities in the mid-twentieth century or women's access to male-only colleges and universities, it did institutionalize racial and gender equality in college affordability.[80]

Aware that Lister Hill and Carl Elliott were crafting a federal student aid proposal in the wake of the *Sputnik* crisis, President Eisenhower charged HEW Associate Secretary Elliot Richardson with producing a proposal on behalf of the administration. The result of his efforts, the Educational Development Act of 1958, was "much more bare-bones" than the Democrats' NDEA proposal.[81] It proposed awarding ten thousand need-based scholarships to students with exceptional academic records. Although it did not require that recipients pursue higher education in any particular fields, it did target scholarships to students with solid backgrounds in science and mathematics. The administration's proposal was presented to Congress by Sen. H. Alexander Smith (R-NJ) and Rep. Carroll D. Kearns (R-PA). The Smith-Kearns bill proposed a $1 billion program that centered upon modest scholarships for students and grants to the National Science Foundation. It also allocated money for the improvement of education-related statistical services and foreign language programs. Per Eisenhower's insistence, the Republican proposal emphasized the temporary, emergency-related nature of the proposed legislation.

Hill and Elliott's central objective in proposing the National Defense Education Act was raising the intellectual level of all Americans.[82] As such, the Democrats took issue with Eisenhower's insistence that aid should be awarded on the basis of merit. Under such a system, the federal government would provide assistance to a smaller group of especially talented students instead of granting aid broadly, on the more inclusive bases of citizenship and need. Hill and Elliott adamantly objected to Eisenhower's proposal, which flew in the face of their overall goal of democratizing access to college.

Passing Federal Student Aid During the Era
of Strong Committees

It was clear, from the start, that the battle over federal student aid would be an intense one. On January 20, 1958, Rep. Thomas Pelly (R-WA) urged his colleagues not to allow unease over national defense to compel them to rush into federal student aid:

> Meeting and outmatching Soviet technological progress is a matter requiring careful study and it may well be that shortages in engineering and scientific personnel could be overcome by making these ultimate careers more attractive. In other words, rather than by a hysterical crash program and trying by scholars to mass produce our youth into physicists and other scientific calling, that we consider other means of correcting any deficiencies.[83]

Indeed, the battle over federal student aid was a bipartisan struggle that pitted conservative Republicans and Southern Democrats against liberal Democrats.[84] In the late 1950s, the House of Representatives was the more conservative of the national legislature's two chambers, as Southern Democrats in the House tended to be more conservative than liberal Republicans in the Senate. This meant that the successful passage of the NDEA depended on Carl Elliott's ability to win the support of moderate Republicans in the House, a feat that would enable him to compensate for a lack of support from Southern Democrats.[85] The House of Representatives represented a crucial hurdle for federal education aid proposals, and the success or failure of the National Defense Education Act would depend largely on that chamber's deliberations.

Because congressional committee chairs were particularly powerful during this period, committees represented decisive battlefields for social policy proposals—points at which many met their demise. When lawmakers began what would be an eight-month process of considering educational proposals on January 27, 1958, Lister Hill and Carl Elliott in Congress and Elliott Richardson at HEW knew that getting a viable bill through the necessary committees would require a great deal of work. In the House, Education and Labor Committee Chair Graham Barden (D-NC)—whom one Senate staff member described as a "tough, thick-necked, immutable, immoveable, rock-ribbed chairman"—proved a formidable opponent of federal aid for education, and his opposition generally meant that such proposals never survived committee deliberations.[86]

More important, the *Sputnik* crisis gave these proposals a fighting chance. It was fortuitous that lawmakers had been working to produce federal education legislation when *Sputnik I* launched. Their readiness to take advantage of this opportunity significantly increased the probability that an education proposal would gain passage during the Eighty-Fifth Congress.[87] Under other circumstances, complicated political and ideological issues would likely have made it impossible that either the Hill-Elliott or Smith-Kearns bills would enjoy a fate that was any different from the host of unsuccessful federal aid proposals that had been presented to Congress in the postwar era. However, members of a new guard of liberal lawmakers had joined the Education and Labor Committee—Representatives Carl Elliott (D-AL), Edith Green (D-OR), Frank Thompson (D-NJ), and Stewart Udall (D-AZ)—forming a coalition that championed the cause of federal support for education.[88]

Within the House Education and Labor Committee, Chairman Barden's decision to reject the dominant practice of adhering to seniority when selecting subcommittee chairs in 1957 may have also enhanced the probability that an education bill would successfully emerge from the committee.[89] In filling the last of five subcommittee chairs, Barden made the unconventional decision to skip over Rep. Adam Clayton Powell (D-NY) to appoint a fellow southerner, the more-junior Carl Elliott. While Elliott acknowledged that Chairman Barden's decision may have been based on racism, he maintained that "for me and the rest of the committee members eager to finally get an education bill in motion" the decision was fortunate because "any subcommittee headed by Adam Clayton Powell was dead in the water from the beginning."[90] This view was rooted in the political controversy created by Powell's insistence that federal education programs be nondiscriminatory, which invoked the ire of Southern Democrats, who represented locales that would presumably use federal funds to support segregated school systems. Elliott and other members of the Education and Labor Committee believed that the representative from Alabama could produce higher education proposals that dealt with school segregation in a fashion that would be less inflammatory than any method that Powell was sure to adopt.

Accidental Egalitarianism: Gender Equality as a Political Imperative

As the newly appointed chairman of the House Special Education Subcommittee, Carl Elliott approached the task of designing a viable student aid proposal with the utmost care. He immediately consulted with national education lobbyists, including the American Council on Education, the Association of American Colleges, and the National Education Association, as he and his staff began to craft an education bill. He also charged his legislative aides with studying existing higher education statutes.[91] Beginning in August of 1957, Elliott chaired cross-country hearings before a Special Education Subcommittee, traveling from Washington, DC, to cities in Wisconsin, South Dakota, Utah, and Oregon. After the launch of *Sputnik I* and after Hill and Elliott devised the strategy to connect their education proposals to the Cold War crisis, subcommittee members began to emphasize the necessity of providing federal educational support so that the nation could redeem itself from its disappointing loss in the race to space.

The significance that a federal higher education program could have for American women did not emerge as a topic of discussion during hearings and subsequent deliberations. Looking back on the topics that shaped lawmakers' discussions regarding the proposed NDEA and the question of whether gender figured into these discussions, Mary Allen Jolley says, "I don't think it came up at all, or I don't remember it in our hearings or anywhere. It just wasn't talked about very much." While women's stake in the NDEA was not at the forefront of discussions about the proposed legislation, women did play a role in supporting Lister Hill and Carl Elliott as they worked to steer it through the legislative process. In addition to Mary Jolley's role as an important member of Elliott's staff who helped to marshal the program from drafting to legislative hearings through passage, Hill and Elliott also benefited from the support of another influential woman. To aid his early efforts to persuade his congressional colleagues of the necessity of federal support for education and the importance of moving the NDEA through the Rules Committee, Carl Elliott turned to a wealthy woman from New York named Mary Lasker, who had been a solid supporter of Lister Hill's efforts to improve health care in the United States. The widow of businessman Albert Lasker, Hill's benefactress was one of the richest women in the world. After her husband's death, she used her estimated $8 million inheritance to support a variety of progressive causes.[92] Lasker took particular interest in the Hill-Elliott proposal for education aid and underwrote early efforts to disseminate informational materials to members of Congress and the media in hopes of rallying support for the measure.[93]

Lister Hill and Carl Elliott used NDEA committee hearings to construct a solid case for federal student aid. They engaged a broad range of witnesses who offered testimony that pointed toward education as the solution to the nation's defense troubles. Elliott later characterized these witnesses as "heavy artillery"— "some of the most recognizable and influential minds of the time" and "voices neither Howard Smith nor anyone else involved with this bill could ignore."[94] Leading the roster of witnesses were administration officials, including John A. Perkins, HEW undersecretary; Dr. Lawrence G. Derthick, US education commissioner; Marion B. Folsom, HEW secretary; and Ralph C. M. Flynt, director of the Higher Education Programs Branch of the HEW Division of Higher Education. Additional witnesses included university officials, male and female undergraduates, and representatives from the National Education Association, the US Chamber of Commerce, the national Academy of Sciences, the National Research Council, the NAACP, the American Chemical Society, the National

Science Foundation, the American Association of Land-Grant Colleges and State Universities, and the State Universities Association.[95] Describing their strategy in engaging such an illustrious roster of witnesses, Stewart McClure recalled:

> We got the cream of the brains of this country, so that when we went to the floor we could say, "Well, now, does the senator mean that he challenges the distinguished leader of the National Council on Science, Detlev Bronk, who says . . . ." We hammered them into the ground. And, of course, if anybody brought up socialism or something like that, the dreadful spectre of socialism, we had Edward Teller and the Hydrogen Bomb to clobber them with! Well, hearings, as you well know, really can shape the form of anything. You get the right witnesses and ask the right questions and they give the right answers, your opposition is slaughtered before they can open their trap. That's one of the tactical secrets of functioning on this Hill.[96]

Members of Congress brought their most compelling arguments to the debate over federal student aid. For decades, the specter of federal control had effectively thwarted lawmakers' attempts to enact federal aid for higher education.[97] Opponents of federal student assistance objected to national government intervention on the grounds that such support would inappropriately involve the federal government in education—a policy area traditionally and best reserved for state and local governments.[98] Champions of federal student aid countered this argument with assurances that any federal program would be modest and temporary and allow the state and local governments to remain the principal arbiter on matters related to education. Opponents countered, however, that large federal programs are rarely temporary and that they tend to grow rather than decline, becoming increasingly unwieldy over the course of their existence. In the Senate, Strom Thurmond (D-SC) and Barry Goldwater (R-AZ) took particular issue with the Hill-Elliot proposal and raised loud objections to it. Thurmond questioned the relevance of the NDEA for promoting national security, citing the absence of a requirement that students pursue postsecondary training in disciplines directly related to defense as a glaring omission. Goldwater objected on the grounds that the federal aid proposal represented what would surely become a nonretractable, ever-expanding demand on the federal government.[99]

Contention also revolved around the effect that federal involvement in education would have on the issues of race and religion in the United States. Some feared that federal support for education would blur the separation of church and state by permitting the federal government to provide funds to Catholic schools.[100] Others took issue with the possibility that the national government could use education funding to influence the nature of (de)segregation in southern schools.[101] In the wake of the Supreme Court's landmark 1954 decision in *Brown v. Board of Education,* which ruled school segregation to be a direct violation of the Fourteenth Amendment of the US Constitution, congressional representatives from the South saw federal education aid as a potential tool that would allow the federal government to punish segregated schools by withholding federal funds, effectively forcing desegregation upon schools that had been integrating with "all deliberate speed."[102]

Throughout the congressional hearings for the NDEA, the topic of gender was far less contentious than that of race or religion; nevertheless, women's full and equal inclusion as beneficiaries of direct federal student aid was not a foregone conclusion. Rep. Donald W. Nicholson (R-MA) raised the question of whether educating women could be deemed a waste, pointing out that, even if girls and women were to go to college, they would probably get married and "miss out on all the things [they] could do" with that education.[103] Rep. Edith Green (D-OR) took issue with that logic, saying that if educating women is wasteful, "it seems to me there is a tremendous amount of waste in educating young men who go to war and are shot. That is completely wasted, is it not?"[104] HEW Secretary John A. Perkins expressed his opinion that education is never wasted and made clear the administration's position that federal aid should be targeted to both women and men, asserting:

> Women usually do not attend college in the numbers which their abilities indicate they should. If a family is perhaps pressed financially and they have sons and daughters, they are apt to educate the sons before they will extend themselves to educate the daughters. Then, too, it is more difficult for ladies to work themselves through college than it is for a young man to do so.[105]

He continued by addressing Nicholson's assertion that marriage frequently precludes women's ability to gain the full value on the returns of higher education, saying, "There is an interesting quip, 'You educate a man and you have educated one person; but you educate a mother and you have educated a family.' There is some great truth to that."[106] Hill and Elliott framed their education proposal as a general provision that would support the higher educational pursuits of both men and women. They worked to establish a tone of gender egalitarianism during committee sessions, as is evinced by Carl Elliott's opening statement before the Special Education Subcommittee. Framing men's and women's education as a national imperative, Elliott asserted that "America is rich in native intelligence . . . . We need only to shape our talents, to educate with discernment to develop to the utmost the latent endowments everywhere among us, to train each boy and girl to the highest attainable degree, consistent with his or her ambition."[107] These deliberations demonstrate an emphasis on the propriety of including women as the beneficiaries of federal student aid and the value that doing so would have for the nation.

After addressing the problems that stem from wasting intellectual talent, the discussion turned to the form that federal support should take. When lawmakers asked the HEW representatives to discuss the basis on which benefits should be allocated to students, Perkins and his colleague, Ralph C. M. Flynt, advocated for need-based scholarships. Flynt, HEW's director of higher education programs, told the committee that 50 percent of young women and 46 percent of young men identified financial need as the most important barrier to obtaining higher education. Providing need-based federal aid directly to students would effectively remove this barrier for young women and men.[108] To drive home this point, lawmakers invited male and female undergraduates to testify before the committees. These testimonies revealed the daunting challenges faced by many young women and men who face the task of funding their own postsecondary education. Some committee members were skeptical regarding the value of student loans, particularly for women who might find it difficult to repay them. Charles Brooks, executive staff assistant to Sen. Wayne Morse (D-OR), predicted that student loans would be "useless" because of the low probability that women would "avail themselves of a program that leaves them with a debt of $4,000 to $5,000 or more upon graduation."[109] US Education Commissioner Lawrence G. Derthick added that a young woman would likely avoid accepting student loans because of "looking forward to marriage; she does not want to bring her husband-to-be a great debt."[110] During hearings on the student loan proposal, the witnesses invited to testify included Sharon Swanson, a seventeen-year-old high school senior from Hixton, Wisconsin. Carl Elliott used the following exchange with Swanson in an effort to rebut arguments doubting women's inclination to borrow money to attend college or their capacity to repay student loans:

MISS SWANSON: I want to do something useful with my life, which lies ahead of me—something which will not just benefit me but other people as well. I believe that going to college will best help me to accomplish this goal.

MR. ELLIOTT: Sharon, you are a senior in high school this year. The problem we are talking about is immediate with you, is it not?

MISS SWANSON: Yes, it is.

MR. ELLIOTT: It is something you have to look right away and try to find the solution for. I would like to say, first, of course, that I hope the problem can be solved because I have been impressed with the fact that you are a very intelligent young lady, and I hope that you are able to find a scholarship, or a

loan, or a work arrangement that will enable you to finish your college education . . .. Your situation would be much simpler if you were assured now that
loans were available that would pay a substantial portion of your education,
would it not, Sharon?

MISS SWANSON: Yes, it would.

MR. ELLIOTT: Do you believe enough in the future of America and the future of
Sharon Swanson to be willing to borrow some money and pay it back at a rea-
sonable rate of interest, if that opportunity were available to you?

MISS SWANSON: Yes, I would be willing to borrow the money.

MR. ELLIOTT: I think that is the spirit that America is made of.[111]

As lawmakers debated the necessity of federal student aid and the appropriate
forms that it should take, several participants in the House and the Senate committee hearings emphasized the importance of expanding higher educational
opportunities for women in light of the Soviet Union's extensive use of women
in science and engineering, which contrasted with American women's meager
presence in these areas.[112] Henry H. Hartly, superintendent of schools in North
Bend, Oregon, addressed this contrast in a letter to the House Subcommittee on
Education and Labor. He wrote:

> I am sure you are aware that Russia considers its women in a different
> light than do we and that the numerical superiority of Russian scientists
> is achieved, in part at least, by utilizing the brains of its women. In this
> country, when a family has to make a choice between a college educa-
> tion for a son or a daughter, the son is generally favored.[113]

Bearing in mind this contrast with the Soviet Union, lawmakers emphasized the
necessity of educating American women to fully utilize the nation's available
brainpower. Driving home this theme, Sen. Wayne L. Morse (D-OR) insisted
that "we need to watch out that we do not waste brainpower in our country.
I do not think we have any right to deny to a boy and girl a college education if
he or she has the mental potential to do satisfactory college work."[114] From this
perspective, national security depended on its ability to fully and effectively utilize the nation's "manpower." The first line of defense in the post-*Sputnik* battle
against communism, then, was to cultivate the skills and talents of every capable
man, woman, and child through education.

Although their support for women's equality in higher education did not
come in the form of intensive, organized lobbying by female constituents or
women's groups, women were, nonetheless, important participants in the congressional hearing phase of the NDEA's consideration.[115] The aforementioned
financial backing of Mary Lasker, for example, was central to Carl Elliott's early

efforts to generate support for the NDEA by increasing awareness among his colleagues and the media.[116] Moreover, a number of female witnesses who testified during congressional hearings on federal education aid provided important information that enabled the successful passage of the program.[117]

While differing dramatically from the participation of women's groups during the fight for women's suffrage during the interwar period or the subsequent battle for women's rights in the late 1960s and 1970s, women's involvement in the design and enactment of the NDEA could be described as a "quiet storm." In the context of the Cold War, where those who vocally demanded equality or political change were often labeled communist sympathizers, women expressed their interest in equality and equal opportunity via membership in mainstream groups that weighed in on policy proposals being considered by lawmakers, but rarely attempted to set a feminist agenda.[118] Thus, women generally focused on the political issues that emerged from male-dominated political institutions and drew upon the political techniques that were generally rewarded therein. When federal student aid came under consideration, for example, social activist Agnes E. Meyer adopted Cold War rhetoric in advocating for federal student aid, urging Americans to "wake up and realize that the cold war has shifted from a competition in arms to a competition in brains."[119] All things considered, Cold War politics played an important role in shaping individual women's interest in and activity related to the National Defense Education Act in 1958. For women's groups, however, federal support for education was not embraced as a women's issue and, thus, was not a focus of their political activism.[120]

While women's groups had not been actively involved in lobbying for the NDEA, they supported the bill as it made its way through the final stages of the political process. Once the bill emerged from committee deliberations, it remained captive in the House Rules Committee for a considerable amount of time. On July 28, 1958, a number of groups—including the American Association of University Women, the American Federation of Teachers, Delta Kappa Gamma (honor society of women legislators), the National Association of Colored Women's Clubs, the National Council of Jewish Women, the National Council of Negro Women, the YWCA, and the United Church Women—submitted a letter to House Speaker Sam Rayburn insisting that Congress remain in session until it had successfully acted on the federal education aid bill.[121] As the legislative session moved rapidly toward adjournment, Carl Elliott and other federal student aid supporters grew anxious. An August 11, 1958, *Time* editorial noted that as "the *Sputnik*-inspired sense of urgency" subsided, "the fair weather for the school bills [had] turned into dead calm." As panic over the *Sputnik* launches cooled, and as the United States successfully launched its own satellites, Elliott recognized the necessity of acting on the NDEA before the window of opportunity provided by the Soviet triumph closed.

Going the Distance: Debating Federal Student Aid
on the Floor

The momentum generated by committee hearings and the media propelled the NDEA forward, as it emerged from the Rules Committee during the first week of August and headed to the floor of the House for consideration by the Committee of the Whole.[122] During this phase of deliberation, members of the House devoted a considerable amount of time to discussing proposed amendments. Carl Elliott's legislative assistant, Mary Allen Jolley, recalled the nature of debate over the NDEA on the floor of the House and the bipartisan efforts that ensured the retention of the proposal's original substantive content:

> When the NDEA was on the floor, Republicans offered an amendment to strike everything after the enacting clause and substitute a Republican bill. Carl was managing the debate, and he didn't say one word against the amendment. Instead, the Republicans on Carl's committee got up and defended the original bill. They said, "Mr. Elliott has listened to our views, we've made an impact on this bill, he's accepted some of our ideas." Short version, "Don't mess with this bill," you know? And, we got the bill through, without him having to say a word about it. That's the kind of skillful legislator he was.[123]

Additional concern revolved around the prospect that Rep. Adam Clayton Powell would propose a "Powell amendment" to the bill. During floor deliberations, the New York congressman successfully submitted the antidiscrimination amendment that would ensure the award of financial aid "without discrimination based on race, color, religion, national origin, or sex."[124] When Carl Elliott convened discussion of the NDEA bill in the House of Representatives on August 8, 1958, Powell rose to voice his "complete support" for the proposal and confirmed his plan to propose the attachment of the Powell amendment. After describing the significance of this rider for ensuring nondiscrimination on the basis of race, color, religion, and national origin, Powell offered a discussion of the importance of women's equal access to higher education support that proved particularly forward thinking at a time when gender equality was on few minds when it came to the NDEA. Commenting on "Sex"—the fifth identity indicated in Powell's amendment—he said, "Because here there seems to be a blind spot. I noticed in the debate that scientists and engineers are referred to as 'young men' as if the field of science and engineering was for men only. Women have as much right as men to participate in this program."[125]

In what proved a stunning blow to Carl Elliott's and Lister Hill's original intentions in designing the National Defense Education bill, House members voted to remove its scholarship provision during the final stages of consideration. Because the scholarship provision represented one of the most controversial items in the bill, one that faced solid opposition from conservative members of the House, Rep. Walter Judd (R-MN) managed to successfully submit an amendment striking scholarships from the bill and moving the proposed authorizations to a title providing student loans.[126] Toward the end of the NDEA's consideration in the House, Rep. H. Alexander Smith (R-NJ) created further controversy by appending a loyalty oath to the bill, exemplifying what Barbara Barksdale Clowse describes as the "leitmotif" of the Cold War: "an obsession with national survival."[127] Nevertheless, on August 9, 1958, the House of Representatives voted to pass its version of the NDEA by a roll-call vote of 265 to 108, thus sending it to the Senate.[128]

Once the bill was presented on the floor of the Senate, its consideration was relatively smooth. Unlike the House of Representatives, the Senate retained the scholarship measure that was included in the original Hill-Elliott proposal. Shortly before midnight on August 13, the Senate passed its version of the National Defense Education Act by a sixty-two to twenty-six roll-call vote.[129] While thirty-five Democrats and twenty-seven Republicans supported the bill, ten Democrats and sixteen Republicans voted against it. The Democrats who opposed the bill hailed primarily from the Deep South, while the Republican objectors tended to represent districts in the Midwest and West.[130]

In the version of the NDEA that emerged from the House and Senate conference committee, the scholarship provision and Adam Clayton Powell's antidiscrimination amendment were high-profile casualties of the political process. Conference committee members attempted to allay the concerns of liberal Democrats by arguing that the bill was inherently nondiscriminatory. The deliberate scrapping of the antidiscrimination amendment was part of a political strategy employed by congressional proponents of federal aid who intentionally left parts of the legislation vague to preclude prohibitive actions on the part of conservatives—particularly Southern Democrats—who would likely reject the bill if they feared extensive federal control.[131] To reassure liberals in the House who had reservations about approving the conference bill absent the "Powell amendment," Elliott presented a letter written by HEW Associate Secretary Elliot Richardson that declared the NDEA to be "inherently antidiscriminatory."[132]

The conference committee's bill gained bipartisan support—and bipartisan opposition—in the House and the Senate. While Republicans tended to hold more conservative views, members of the Democratic Party—who represented "a conflicting mix of white Southerners, Catholics, urban blue-collar workers, and ethnic and minority groups"—were divided ideologically.[133] As consideration of the NDEA neared an end on August 23, 1958, Rep. Harry Haskell (R-DE) offered an urgent reminder to his colleagues:

> The Soviet Union today has one of the most dangerous weapons in the whole world—the atheistic, scientific trained mind—and it has them in plentiful supply . . . . The Soviet colleges and universities graduated twice as many engineers and scientists as we did in 1956. They have more than double the number of science students in their higher educational institutions this year than we have. Tuition in colleges is free— they pay students salaries—(stipends they have named them)—there are bonuses in addition for those with high scholastic marks, particularly in science.[134]

In the final legislative action on the National Defense Education Act, the House of Representatives passed the bill on August 23, 1958—the penultimate day of the Eighty-Fifth Congress—by a roll-call vote of 212 to 85. President Eisenhower signed the NDEA, PL 85-864, into law on September 2, 1958.[135] While partisanship was not an important source of division on this legislation, ideology was, as liberals and conservatives in both chambers failed to see eye to eye on this bill.[136] In addition to ideological considerations, as Barbara Barksdale Clowse notes, the looming elections may have served to garner additional support for this federal student aid legislation.[137]

The enactment of the National Defense Education Act represents a critical juncture in the politics of federal support for higher education and for gender egalitarianism in college access. It paved the way for future higher education programs that would continue to expand access to higher education for Americans who were traditionally underrepresented in postsecondary institutions. Following the successful passage of the NDEA, US Education Commissioner Lawrence Derthick celebrated the program's creation, calling it an act that would "open up many opportunities for increasing our vital reservoir of trained manpower, a reservoir we need to provide leaders in all fields from science to statesmanship."[138] Beneficiaries of the program would express their thanks for decades to come. After Carl Elliot became the inaugural recipient of the Kennedy Center's Profiles in Courage Award in 1989, profiles recounting his work in creating the NDEA and his legacy of expanding access to college for young Americans engendered an outpouring of gratitude from NDEA beneficiaries. Soon letters poured in from NDEA program participants expressing their gratitude to the retired statesman. Bill Rover of Boston offered Elliott his sincere thanks, saying, "Your National Defense Loan bill for disadvantaged college students propelled many youngsters at that time to college, including myself . . . . Because of you, I was able to attend college and receive a Bachelor's

Degree and then go on to become a dentist." Women's correspondence with
Elliott reveal the program's special significance for expanding women's access to
college degrees. Hubertien Scott recalled the significance of the NDEA to her
educational trajectory, noting:

> My husband was the beneficiary of the GI Bill. I am the beneficiary of
> the NDEA. I had no intention of acquiring a Ph.D. when I went back
> to college in 1959 as a freshman at age 32, mother of three children,
> and a fourth two years later. However, when I got my BA in 1962, I was
> encouraged to apply for an NDEA scholarship for graduate study, and
> was awarded a three-year scholarship which paid me to go to graduate
> school all the way to a Ph.D.[139]

In February of 1989, Margaret Voland of Bridgewater, Massachusetts, wrote Carl
Elliot saying that she and her husband "could not have gone to college except
for National Defense Student Loans" and other financial aid. In March of 1989,
Sally Grimes of Rockport, Massachusetts, wrote that

> without the National Defense Loan Program I would not have been able
> to pursue college. It was a lifesaver. I studied Special Ed at [the] Univ.
> of Ill. & later rec'd a masters Degree in Education from Harvard. I have
> tested, taught, counseled people (mostly young ones!) for twenty years.
> I served on our School Board & am a real advocate of the underpriv-
> ileged. Without my education my words and actions would not have
> been as effective as I hope they've been . . .. Thank you.[140]

In addition to making college affordable for thousands of American women
and men, the NDEA dramatically altered the federal government's posture toward
education. Writing four years after the program's passage, Homer D. Babbidge
Jr. and Robert Rosenzweig recognized that the distinctiveness of the National
Defense Education Act lay in the fact that "the Congress of the United States had
never before declared that it was a goal of *national* policy that 'no student of ability
will be denied an opportunity for higher education because of financial need.' "[141]
Stewart McClure also noted that the passage of the NDEA marked "the end of
opposition to federal aid to education, by both the Democrats and Republicans.
Thereafter, as [the Labor, Education, and Public Welfare] committee history
shows, we passed anything you could think of."[142] The NDEA dramatically altered
Americans' conceptualization of appropriate government support for education,
heralding a shift in the dominant form of federal education aid from support for
expanding school infrastructure and improving academic programming to assistance provided directly to students in the form of financial aid.

The creation of the NDEA set an important precedent that framed education aid as a security issue and facilitated the emergence of new interest groups.[143] Women, in particular, represent one such group. In the years following its passage, the NDEA successfully expanded access to higher education for tens of thousands of American women.[144] In implementing the NDEA, lawmakers emphasized federal control over the program and required that the substantial resources flowing into it be distributed in a nondiscriminatory fashion. This form of policy implementation departed from the decentralized administration of federal student aid under the National Youth Administration (NYA) work-study program and the GI Bill. The level of local and institutional discretion that characterized these landmark policy precedents was conducive to discriminatory benefit allocation that often disadvantaged women. Under the NDEA, the federal government determined student eligibility using a standard formula to gauge financial need. It also established aid amounts and ensured that any needy student—male or female—who had gained acceptance into an accredited college or university would be eligible to receive benefits. This high level of federal control over program administration ensured that NDEA benefits would be allocated in a patently egalitarian manner. Although men tended to borrow slightly more money from the NDEA's National Defense Student Loans than women, many were surprised by the willingness of American women to borrow funds for higher education.[145] In 1959, National Defense Loans were awarded to 7,199 women and 14,958 men. By 1960, the numbers increased dramatically, with 38,886 women and 67,487 men receiving these benefits.[146] The loan forgiveness provision for students planning to teach in primary and secondary schools made the NDEA particularly attractive for students pursuing degrees in education—most of whom were women.[147] By 1961, women made up approximately 33 percent of American college students and the same proportion of student loan beneficiaries.[148]

Conclusion

The creation of the National Defense Education Act—and the birth of need-based federal student loans—represents a watershed moment in the history of American social policy. By institutionalizing gender equality in college affordability, this program expanded equal opportunity in the United States and marked a significant moment in women's movement toward first-class citizenship. Granted, in passing the NDEA, lawmakers' central focus was to create a federal financial aid program that would increase college access for low-income young people, rather than a particular interest in enhancing women's educational opportunity. Although the NDEA's gender-egalitarian nature was more a matter of necessity than a matter of conscious effort on the part of lawmakers, the program provided women with unprecedented public support for pursuing college degrees and the citizenship-enhancing benefits that tend to accompany them.

As we have seen, the NDEA's broad-reaching policy design offers a valuable example of universally targeted social programs that successfully avert many of the political shortcomings that challenge more targeted ones. Moreover, the NDEA's gender-neutral benefit allocation also reflects the combination of international and domestic political forces that shaped the historical moment at which it was created. The 1957 *Sputnik* launches—and the politics of crisis that accompanied it—provided a window of opportunity that enabled lawmakers to successfully pass student financial aid programs. In the context of the Cold War, lawmakers who supported the NDEA emphasized the necessity of strengthening American higher education to ensure that the nation could effectively compete with the Soviet Union. Because the Soviets efficiently utilized all available national resources by fully integrating women and men into the fields of science and engineering, the failure of the United States to do the same would place democracy at risk.

Moreover, domestic politics—particularly contention regarding racial discrimination—was a critical factor shaping the design of the NDEA. To appease liberals, who wished to include language condemning racial discrimination in the provision of federal aid, and Southern Democrats, who would object to such framing, lawmakers intentionally left the NDEA's allocation criteria vague, awarding aid irrespective of students' race, religion, area of study, or gender. They were able to assure liberals that the bill was inherently antidiscriminatory while also assuring Southern Democrats that the program would have little bearing on the racial order in southern higher educational institutions. Thus, lawmakers allocated federal student aid in a gender-egalitarian fashion not because they were particularly interested in gender equality, but because they wanted to avoid potentially harmful controversy on the issue of race. The sense of crisis generated by the Soviet Union's *Sputnik* launch, combined with the politics surrounding the domestic struggle for civil rights and the politics of the Cold War on the international stage, provided a window of opportunity that facilitated the passage of an unprecedented commitment to providing higher educational support for the nation's young men and women.

Although women's organizations did not vocally participate in the politics surrounding the creation of the National Defense Education Act, women's interests were incorporated in the design of the program as a result of proponents' subversion of Cold War ideology and rhetoric for the purpose of passing long-standing student aid objectives. Political entrepreneurs working to tie their federal student aid proposals to the panic that resulted from the *Sputnik* launches emphasized the necessity of fully developing and utilizing American brainpower in the interest of national survival. All things considered, the *Sputnik* crisis provided a window of opportunity that permitted lawmakers to commit the federal government to providing higher educational aid to the nation's young people while also paving the way for future programs that would expand this relationship. Contrary to considerable received wisdom suggesting that major policy shifts typically emerge as a result of pluralist politics and widely held notions that US welfare state development was driven primarily by the efforts of liberal politicians and inhibited by nonliberals, especially Southern Democrats, the creation of the NDEA proves otherwise. This chapter has shown that the NDEA originated not with intensely mobilized women's organizations but with an unlikely group of political entrepreneurs—many of whom were political moderates hailing from southern states.

By clearing the crucial hurdle of successfully passing the NDEA with its unprecedented government support for college students, lawmakers established a public commitment to removing financial barriers that had long restricted women's access to college degrees. While the GI Bill significantly expanded college access for a substantial portion of American men during the postwar era and dramatically increased the gender gap in US higher educational attainment, the NDEA counteracted this effect by providing federal funds to both women and men as they pursued college degrees. By enabling a broad spectrum of American women to qualify for federal student aid, the NDEA significantly expanded women's higher educational opportunity. It also broke with the tradition of previously enacted federal higher education policies that either provided financial support for school infrastructure and programming or granted financial aid on the gendered basis of military service. In so doing, the National Defense Education Act critically altered the gender dynamics of college affordability.

4

Sustaining Gender Parity in College Aid

The Higher Education Act of 1965

The problem of educating young people is not confined to low-income families. Middle-income families, faced with the prospect of educating more than one member of the family, are often hard pressed either to find the funds or to select which child should be educated. The case is often presented where the oldest member is enrolled in school but when his younger brothers and sisters reach college age they are unable to attend due to expenses already incurred.
—Rep. Harrison "Pete" A. Williams Jr. (D-NJ),
June 1, 1965 (Remarks from statement made during the
"Higher Education Act of 1965 [HR 3220]"
Subcommittee Hearings)

In the next school year alone, 140,000 young men and women will be enrolled in college who, but for the provisions of this bill, would have never gone past high school. We will reap the rewards of their wiser citizenship and their greater productivity for decades to come.
—President Lyndon B. Johnson, *November 8, 1965*
(Remarks made in Higher Education Act signing statement)

In the early months of 1960, Vice President and Republican presidential nominee Richard Nixon and his Democratic rival, Sen. John F. Kennedy of Massachusetts, faced off in a battle to succeed Dwight Eisenhower as president of the United States. Not long into the course of the election, the topic of securing economic prosperity for the American people quickly became a focal point. For Nixon, investing in higher education represented a valuable tool for promoting economic growth. Capitalizing on the popularity of the National Defense Education Act (NDEA), he advocated for more federal student loans and also recommended the creation of a federal scholarship program.[1] Kennedy also recognized the value of higher education for strengthening the nation's economic prospects, and he advocated for increased federal support for college students.[2]

Nixon's and Kennedy's support for expanding federal aid to college students reflected Americans' growing appreciation of the relationship between higher educational opportunity and socioeconomic well-being. In one of the closest electoral victories in modern history, Kennedy would defeat Nixon to become the nation's thirty-fifth president. Unfortunately, his assassination three years later left fulfillment of his commitment to higher education to his successor.

As we saw in chapter 3, modern student aid and a public commitment to using redistributive policy to ensure college affordability for women resulted from the efforts of political entrepreneurs who seized the window of opportunity presented by the politics of crisis in 1958. For President Kennedy's successor, Lyndon B. Johnson, higher education represented a central component in his "War on Poverty," and the Higher Education Act (HEA) of 1965 made his commitment to the nation's college students clear. While the National Defense Education Act initiated a new relationship between the federal government and the nation's women by making federal student aid available to them for the first time, the HEA took this relationship to a new level. In the seven years between the creation of the National Defense Education Act and the passage of the Higher Education Act, Americans increasingly regarded higher education as a solid mechanism for improving socioeconomic status. In this chapter, I consider how lawmakers drew upon auspicious political circumstances to further entrench higher education programming in the fabric of US social policy and to amplify individual-level aid for college students with the Higher Education Act of 1965.

This case study offers important lessons that enhance our understanding of the significance of policy design for sustaining and even reinforcing social policy reform. Two aspects of the Higher Education Act's design played a particularly important role in its capacity to effectively expand women's access to college. First, the HEA provides a valuable example of how "targeting within universalism" can help to generate broad political support for a social policy.[3] This approach to policy design is characterized by devising a program that will provide support to the neediest citizens and then broadening the scope of benefit allocation as much as possible, typically incorporating groups not typically associated with the receipt of social policy, such as middle-class or high-income Americans. This way, the program provides valuable support for those with the greatest need. Moreover, a diverse set of beneficiaries have a stake in the program, which increases the probability that efforts to disrupt the program would be met with substantial opposition.

Second, the creation of the Higher Education Act provides a powerful example of the role that path dependency has played in the development of higher education policy. The HEA amplified and extended the government support that was first provided under the NDEA, despite lawmakers' original portrayal of the NDEA as a temporary emergency measure that would presumably be scaled back once the nation recovered from the *Sputnik* crisis. Seven years after passing the NDEA, rather than scaling back federal support for college students, lawmakers built upon the landmark program, providing additional need-based student loans, the first federal scholarships for needy students, funds for school infrastructure, support for developing institutions, and urban extension programs. The "Title IV Programs" contained in the HEA's eponymous core title extended the NDEA's National Defense Student Loan program, created the new Guaranteed Student Loan (GSL) program, and offered need-based Basic Educational Opportunity Grants.[4]

Rather than moving away from the financial aid–centered approach that characterized the National Defense Education Act, lawmakers continued on that pathway, reinforcing it by creating additional need-based loans for college students and by creating the first need-based grants. This was due, at least in part, to the fact that the National Defense Education Act generated lessons for policymakers—especially regarding the political value of extending broad-reaching federal support to college students. In the years following the passage of the National Defense Education Act, Americans became accustomed to receiving federal funds for higher education, and government support for college students became an increasingly salient issue on the political stage.[5] Between 1955 and 1965, college enrollments increased considerably, as the number of students attending American postsecondary institutions grew from 2.4 million to 4.8 million.[6] In this context, higher education maintained a position of unprecedented prominence on the political agenda. Lawmakers' sustained support for a financial aid–centered approach to expanding access to college degrees also reflects an appreciation for the support that the NDEA generated among beneficiaries and a recognition that moving away from financial aid programs could prove costly for lawmakers. In fact, lawmakers sought to expand the scope of student aid beneficiaries by expanding the reach of student aid to include middle-class constituents under the non-means-tested Guaranteed Student Loan Program.

In addition to illustrating the significance of policy design to the political viability of social policy reforms, this case study highlights the pivotal role that executive leadership has played in the development of US higher education policy. Unlike the uphill battle that characterized the NDEA's passage, historical analysis reveals that the politics surrounding the creation of the Higher Education Act were relatively smooth, owing largely to the success of the NDEA, the existence of a political context that advantaged liberal lawmakers who favored federal education assistance, and the formidable political acumen of another southern politician: President Lyndon B. Johnson. President Johnson and members of the executive branch of government played active roles in crafting the Higher Education Act, and the president's leadership was central to the program's successful movement through the political process. Akin to the accidental egalitarianism that characterized the NDEA's creation, President Johnson's support for the inclusion of women under the HEA was more a matter of his commitment to achieving comprehensive equal educational opportunity for young Americans, rather than an explicit focus on expanding higher educational opportunity for women in particular.

The Higher Education Act's passage was greatly influenced by the decided victories that Democrats won in the 1964 elections, whereby many of the lawmakers who had opposed the provision of direct aid to college students during the late 1950s lost their congressional bids.[7] Moreover, deliberations over the HEA reflected President Johnson's emphasis on the role that student aid could play in combating poverty, thereby facilitating the inclusion of women as presumed beneficiaries of proposed programs. Lawmakers focused primarily on the amount of federal resources to direct to student aid programs and the style that the benefits should take. The soundness of investing federal financial aid in women college students, a question that had been a focal point of NDEA deliberations, seemed to represent a basic assumption for lawmakers considering the Higher Education Act as an antipoverty measure. Taken together, this set of political forces was central to lawmakers' ability to use the Higher Education Act to reinforce and build upon the gender-egalitarian higher education policy that had emerged during the late 1950s.

From the Kennedy Administration to the War on Poverty

Shortly after taking office in 1961, President Kennedy appointed Purdue University's president, Frederick L. Hovde, as chairman of a task force on education. The Hovde Commission provided the president with recommendations that included the allocation of approximately $9.4 billion for grants and loans to students between 1961 and 1965.[8] As Hugh Davis Graham notes, "The Hovde report envisioned a massive and *permanent* [government] role in education."[9] In addition to the Hovde Commission, Kennedy established the President's Commission on the Status of Women, which emphasized the importance of higher education for women's socioeconomic status. In its final report to the president, the committee noted that "men and women are equally in need of continuing education, but at present women's opportunities are more limited than men's."[10] In explaining the cause of women's limited opportunities, the report pointed to the fact that women were typically excluded from "the substantial arrangements for advanced training provided by businesses for their executives," as well as "the educational and training of the armed forces."[11] The

President's Commission on the Status of Women emphasized the importance of higher education to women's well-being and recommended that the federal government increase its efforts to promote women's college attendance.

In 1961, the Kennedy administration produced a higher education bill that proposed the provision of need- and merit-based federal scholarships for undergraduate students and institutional loans to tackle the ongoing problem of classroom shortages. Kennedy emphasized the fact that the administration's proposal dodged the perennially contentious issue of maintaining the separation of church and state while providing much-needed federal assistance for education, saying that

> We are aiding the student in the same way the GI bill of rights aided the student. The scholarships are given to the students who have particular talents and they can go to the college they want. In that case it is aid to the student, not to the school or college, and, therefore, not to a particular religious group.[12]

The president's proposal, however, was ultimately unsuccessful; old disagreements concerning the effects of federal student aid on the scope of government power proved insurmountable.

The following year, Kennedy's college aid proposal met a similar fate. Because Republican lawmakers objected to the bill's scholarship provisions and because many non-Catholics objected to providing grants to religious higher educational institutions, Kennedy's 1962 proposal for expanded federal support for higher education failed.[13] By 1963, the Kennedy administration had jettisoned the student scholarship component of its higher education bill, limiting its new proposal to federal funds for school construction. In February of that year, *New York Times* columnist Fred Hechinger noted that the administration's proposal was distinctive because it was the first postwar education proposal that did not directly address Cold War objectives.[14] On December 16, 1963, in the wake of President John F. Kennedy's assassination, Congress passed, and recently inaugurated President Lyndon B. Johnson signed, the Higher Education Facilities Act (PL 88-204; also known as the Morse-Green bill), which provided federal funds to support campus infrastructure.[15]

The 1964 elections brought major victories for the Democratic Party. Johnson's defeat of Barry Goldwater in the presidential election and large Democratic majorities in Congress heralded the emergence of a political climate that would prove amenable to educational reform. Moving forward, the Johnson administration sought to take unprecedented action in expanding educational opportunity. Reflecting this objective, as James Hearn noted, the mid-1960s "brought the seeds of extraordinary change to federal policy in education," with lawmakers undertaking "a wide-ranging initiative in education, passing more than two-dozen acts aimed directly at American schools and colleges."[16] Johnson intended to use this era of unified Democratic government to tackle inequality head on, emphasizing the value of higher education as a mechanism for promoting equal opportunity and combating poverty.[17]

In 1964, Johnson clearly outlined his goals for education in a series of speeches and public statements. For higher education, he expressed a commitment to expanding and improving colleges and to making greater access to college a central priority for his administration.[18] During this same year, Johnson appointed John W. Gardner, the president of the Carnegie Corporation, as chair of a task force charged with identifying the greatest challenges facing education in the United States and recommending specific policy proposals that could be incorporated into an education bill.[19] Members of the Gardner Task Force included US Commissioner of Education Francis Keppel; William B. Cannon, chief of the US Bureau of the Budget's Division of Education, Manpower, and Sciences; Hedley W. Donovan, editor of *Time* magazine; White House liaison Richard Goodwin; and numerous university presidents, professors, and business leaders. The resulting report—which the task force submitted to President Johnson—emphasized the necessity of expanding the federal government's efforts in higher education, particularly those intended to promote greater college access for less privileged Americans.[20] One mechanism by which the task force proposed to do this was via a program of guaranteed student loans that are backed by the government.[21] Under such a program, the federal government would step in to repay the debt if a student failed to repay the loan amount.

The Politics of Presidential Leadership: Enacting the Higher Education Act

President Lyndon Johnson's forceful leadership represents perhaps the biggest factor contributing to the successful passage of the Higher Education Act and its capacity to expand gender egalitarianism in US higher educational attainment. As a policy issue, increasing educational opportunity represented a central priority for the president. In a speech during the White House Conference on Education during July of 1965, Johnson said: "I think most of you know the enveloping role which education has played in my own life. It really was the instrument which took a boy from the countryside of Texas and opened to him the boundless dreams and the opportunities of American life."[22] As Sally Davenport notes, the HEA reflected social policy themes that, in 1965, had recently emerged. For Johnson, college education represented a powerful antipoverty measure that offered "a means of mainstreaming the poor, not just providing minimum levels of 'welfare.' "[23] From this perspective, federal higher education programs could potentially raise the educational attainment—and standard of living—of a significant segment of the US population. The president's use of higher education policy to promote equal opportunity was heavily influenced by the precedent set by the National Defense Education Act.[24] It was also shaped by Johnson's appreciation for the effect that the GI Bill had on equal opportunity. Former Michigan congressman William D. Ford noted in 1985 that in advocating for the Higher Education Act, "essentially President Johnson was proposing that the benefits of the GI Bill be made available to all our citizens. Opening the doors of opportunity and investing in the human resources of our nation remain the principal goals of the Higher Education Act as they were the principal benefits of the GI Bill."[25]

The political context of the mid-1960s proved an asset to Johnson's pursuit of federal legislation that would significantly expand college access. Taking advantage of sweeping Democratic victories in 1964, the president prioritized pushing a comprehensive student aid proposal through the legislature that would further the NDEA's efforts to expand college access for the nation's young men and women.[26] Johnson also benefited from the fact that, by the time the Higher Education Act came under consideration, political issues that had long dogged proposals for federal student aid had become less contentious. The 1964 Civil Rights Act had prohibited the transfer of federal dollars to segregated schools, thus setting a standard for subsequent programs. The NDEA's provision of financial aid directly to students rather than to institutions settled arguments that federal student aid would jeopardize the separation of church and state. The successful passage of the National Defense Education Act in 1958 and the Civil Rights Act in 1964 provided a winning strategy for successfully passing the HEA. Furthermore, the recent passage of the Elementary and Secondary Education Act (PL 89-10) on April 11, 1965, placed education on the minds of legislators and their constituents.

Designing the Higher Education Act: A Unilateral Process

Fueled by Johnson's vocal commitment to passing an extensive program of support for higher education, the policy design phase of the Higher Education Act centered upon the White House and its liaisons in the Office of Education, the Bureau of the Budget, and the Treasury. With the goal of successfully passing legislation that would significantly expand access to higher education, the president and his administration spent much of 1964 constructing its proposal so that it could "hit Congress with a full package of legislative proposals, rush the bills through committee, and then force a floor vote before [Johnson] lost his election momentum."[27] Throughout the process of constructing the administration's student aid proposal, President Johnson wielded "tight executive control" over the policy's design.[28] As Michael Parsons notes, "Congress would have input, but it would come after the administration had formed the policy, thus forcing Congress to respond on Johnson's terms.[29]

In adopting this hands-on approach, Johnson worked closely with his staff to construct a bill that would succeed in providing federal scholarships, a goal that had eluded Democratic lawmakers since the 1940s. Douglas Cater, a special assistant to the president, was known as the "education man" in the White House. Cater acted as a chief liaison for matters related to education. During the formulation of the Higher Education Act, Cater—in communication with President Johnson—was responsible for crafting the proposal that would be submitted to Congress.[30] Working closely with Education Commissioner Francis Keppel and US Office of Education officials Peter Muirhead and Samuel Halperin, Cater actively sought the input of representatives from the higher education establishment, who were closely aligned with the Office of Education. Doing so ensured their political support once the proposal came under congressional consideration.[31] Cater also consulted with the US Bureau of the Budget, which "determined the feasibility of the [HEA] in terms of cost and funding levels," and the Department of the Treasury, which offered a second opinion on the feasibility of the administration's proposal and actually constructed the Guaranteed Student Loan Program.[32]

Taking into account the interests of actively engaged groups like the American Council on Education (ACE), the American Library Association, and the Association of Research Lobbies who actively lobbied the US Office of Education, the administration produced a proposal that provided support to numerous areas related to higher education. The proposed Higher Education Act included $25 million in federal support for an urban land-grant extension program that would provide financial support to urban universities (Title I); $65 million in funding for college libraries (Title II); and $30 million in aid to struggling postsecondary institutions, such as historically black colleges and universities (Title III).[33] The core of the HEA, however, was found in Title IV, which provided student financial assistance in the form of need-based scholarships, guaranteed student loans for middle-class students, extended the need-based loans established by the NDEA, and updated the work-study program by shifting its jurisdiction from the Office of Equal Opportunity (OEO) to the Office of Education (OE).[34]

On January 12, 1965, Johnson delivered a special message to Congress wherein he stressed the importance of providing equal educational opportunity for all Americans and offered a preview of the administration's higher education aid proposal, asserting that "higher education is no longer a luxury, but a necessity."[35] During his address, Johnson emphasized the necessity of providing

$130 million of federal assistance to support needy men and women who wished to attend college, asserting that "loans authorized by the National Defense Education Act currently assist nearly 300,000 college students," but nonetheless, "an estimated 100,000 young people of demonstrated ability fail to go on to college because of lack of money."[36] In addition to requesting that Congress authorize additional support for student financial aid, Johnson proposed expanding the work-study program to include middle-class students.[37] On January 19, 1965, seven days after the president delivered this special education message, the Johnson administration submitted its higher education proposal to Congress along with a letter from the president emphasizing the proposal's utmost importance to the administration.

Enacting the Higher Education Act During an Era of Democratic Control

The political context within which the Higher Education Act made its way through Congress differed greatly from that which had surrounded the National Defense Education Act only seven years earlier. Unlike the NDEA, which was largely propelled by congressional initiative, the president provided the driving force behind the HEA. In Congress, a Democratic majority facilitated the bill's relatively smooth journey from subcommittee deliberations to floor consideration and, ultimately, to successful passage. The replacement of Rep. Graham Barden (D-NC)—a stalwart opponent of federal education aid—with Rep. Adam Clayton Powell (D-NY) as the chair of the Education and Labor Committee in the House of Representatives also contributed to a political climate that favored the HEA.

Women's presence in the labor force rose steadily during the mid-twentieth century. At the same time, Americans increasingly viewed education as a useful antipoverty tool. According to the US Census Bureau's Current Population Survey, 45.2 percent of women between ages twenty-five and fifty-four participated in the labor force in 1965. For the increasing number of women making their way into the paid labor market, higher education represented a valuable credential that could open doors to occupational opportunity and higher income. Agnes Meyer, chairwoman of the National Committee for Support of the Public Schools, submitted a report during the House Subcommittee on Education's hearings on the HEA proposal that advocated on behalf of additional support for higher education to promote women's labor force prospects:

> There should be much more careful planning of women's education
> to take account of the thousands who enter upon lifelong careers and
> the rising proportion of women who enter gainful employment before

marriage and again after their children are in school or are post school age. To permit more and more women to enter the labor market without adequate training would be disadvantageous to them and to the economy.[38]

Lawmakers recognized the value of education for combating poverty. As Rep. Everett Burkhalter (D-CA) noted on the House floor, "No matter what authority on poverty you approach you will find that education is generally accepted as one of the most powerful forces that we have at our command in the fight to give all the disadvantaged some opportunity to obtain adequate food, housing, medicine, jobs, and opportunity to escape the ranks of the poor."[39] The probability of successfully passing the HEA was further enhanced by substantial public recognition of and concern regarding the challenges of funding higher educational opportunity. According to a poll conducted by Louis Harris and Associates in March of 1965, 48 percent of Americans identified financial worries as the most challenging problem facing their children in their attempts to obtain higher education. On May 14, Sen. Harrison Williams (D-NJ) alluded to the challenges that many talented students face in funding higher education during his remarks on the Senate floor: "In June 1961, 400,000 high school seniors who graduated in the upper half of their classes failed to continue their education. The determining factor for one-third to one-half of these young men and women was lack of financial resources."[40]

On May 30, 1965, the Johnson administration's higher education proposal was presented to Congress with Rep. Edith Green (D-OR) acting as chief sponsor. The bill proposed both federal student loans and grants, which resembled the scholarships that, seven years prior, were jettisoned from the National Defense Education Act; a work-study program for undergraduates; and assistance for developing institutions, among other provisions. Soon after the bill's introduction, the Education and Labor Committee's Special Subcommittee on Education, which was chaired by Representative Green, commenced hearings on the proposal, as did the Senate's Labor and Public Welfare Committee's Subcommittee on Education, which was chaired by Sen. Wayne Morse (D-OR). In both chambers, professional organizations, academics, and student aid officers were particularly engaged in the process of providing lawmakers with information to help them determine what measures would ultimately be included in the bill that the Johnson administration had so enthusiastically endorsed. As Chávez notes, the HEA subcommittee hearings offered higher education officials and others interested in student aid "perhaps their last opportunity for participating in the policy-making process for the HEA."[41] Not surprisingly, the Johnson administration closely monitored congressional action at this phase of the legislative process, drawing upon active lines of communication between President

Johnson and Douglas Cater at the White House and Representative Green and Senator Morse at the Capitol.[42]

Between February 1 and May 1, 1965, the Special Education Subcommittee of the House held hearings on the HEA proposal. A broad array of lawmakers, Johnson administration officials, professional educators, university administrators, and other interest group representatives provided information and recommendations to the members of the subcommittee. On the first day of the hearings, an exchange between Anthony J. Celebrezze, secretary of the Department of Health, Education, and Welfare, and Rep. John Brademas (D-IN) exemplified the gender-inclusive tone that would characterize the debate over government efforts to promote equal opportunity in higher education:

SECRETARY CELEBREZZE: At this point in our history I think we are trying to pinpoint [higher education] to the lower economic group, to the elimination of poverty. I am hopeful that as this program takes root and as these young men get out into the professional world, into the academic world—

MR. BRADEMAS: And women, Mr. Secretary.

SECRETARY CELEBREZZE: And women, as they get out, they, themselves, will start lifting the rest of the family up.[43]

As this exchange illustrates, lawmakers were attuned to the relevance of the Higher Education Act for both women and men and intended to consider the proposed legislation in a way that fully incorporated women.[44]

In addition to this women-inclusive goal of expanding access to higher education, the HEA subcommittee hearings reflected an emphasis on expanding college access for low-income students. During his testimony, Secretary Celebrezze presented data from the Office of Education that highlighted the fact that women were less likely than men of similar scholastic aptitude to enter college within one year of completing high school. As his data illustrated, this was particularly true for students whose annual family income was less than $3,000 (see Table 4.1). Among especially talented students who fell in the 90th percentile (top 10 percent) for aptitude, 10.2 percent of male students did not enter college immediately after completing high school, whereas a full 33.1 percent of women failed to do so. For students of similar aptitude whose family income was at least $12,000 per year, the difference is not nearly as stark: 2.9 percent of highly talented male students did not move directly from high school to college, compared to 4.4 percent of similarly talented female students. Among students from low-income families who were ranked in the top 50th percentile in terms of academic aptitude, the data presented by Secretary Celebrezze showed that women were considerably less likely than men to attend college directly after high school. For students falling in the top 25 percent of their peers in terms of

Table 4.1 **Percentage of High School Graduates Who Did
Not Enter College Within One Year of Completing
Twelfth Grade**

| | Family Income | | | |
| | Less Than $3,000 | | $12,000 and Up | |
Aptitude Level	Males	Females	Males	Females
Top 10%	10.2	33.1	2.9	4.4
Top 25%	18.4	36.9	6.3	7.4
Top 50%	37.9	57.9	10.5	15.6
Below 50%	80.4	82.6	50.3	52.4

Source: "Higher Education Act of 1965 (HR 3220)" Subcommittee
Hearings 1965, pp. 32–39; Department of Health, Education, and Welfare;
Office of Education.

aptitude, twice as many women as men (36.9 compared to 18.4 percent) failed to enter college within one year of completing the twelfth grade. For students in the top 50 percent, 57.9 percent of women failed to enter college immediately after high school, compared to 37.9 percent of men. Echoing Celebrezze's emphasis on the difficulty of attaining higher education for low-income students, American Federation of Labor and Congress of Industrial Organizations (AFL-CIO) representative Lawrence Rogin called the federal aid proposal a "badly needed and long-overdue mechanism that can be used by many of our youth to help overcome the otherwise prohibitively high cost of higher education."[45]

Like the debate in the House subcommittee, many witnesses who came before the Senate's Subcommittee on Education between March and June of 1965 expressed fervent support for the legislation and its significance for Johnson's Great Society initiative. Prominent voices from the administration emphasized what Office of Economic Opportunity Director R. Sargent Shriver called the "birthright of opportunity." According to Shriver, "The war on poverty is an integral part of the establishment of the Great Society. And the pursuit of excellence in education follows direction from this Nation's commitment to secure" the promise of equal opportunity. The HEA, asserted Shriver, offered a powerful step toward reclaiming this entitlement for women and men in the United States.[46]

Other witnesses focused on the role of financial hardship as the central challenge to broad higher educational opportunity in the United States. US Education Commissioner Francis Keppel emphasized financial disparity and the ways in which it inhibits equal access to postsecondary education. "The evidence is very strong," he declared, "that young men and young women without family means to help them out are not going into college in numbers—and it is into the one hundred thousands—because they know they don't have the financial support."[47] In memorable testimony before the committee, Ms. Carolyn Steele, a high school counselor, recounted the story of a student named Judy, who came from a single-parent family in Minneapolis, Minnesota:

> Judy . . . is [an African American] girl who graduated last year in the top tenth of her class, was active in school organizations, and had good college capabilities. Her stepfather deserted Judy and her mother when she was nine, and they have existed to a large extent on Aid to Dependent Children funds, which of course ceased for Judy by the time of her graduation. Judy's aim is psychology or pre-law; but because of finances, she took a full-time job, and began this year with only one course in night school . . .. Funds from S.2490 [the proposed HEA] might make Judy a full time college student and make another job open for someone else.[48]

In sharing this example, Ms. Steel emphasized the difference that federal student aid would mean for low-income young women like Judy, while suggesting an additional value to the nation's economy.

For these witnesses, the federal financial aid proposed by the HEA would provide crucial assistance that would greatly expand higher educational opportunity for American men and women. Speaking before the National Conference of Governor's Commission on the Status of Women, Vice President Hubert Humphrey reiterated his party's attitude that higher education represents an important mechanism for opportunity—particularly for women, whose talent too often goes to waste. He asserted that women's employment opportunities were frequently limited by a lack of education. Although women made up 51 percent of Americans graduating from high school in 1964, "when it comes to college the girls, their parents and even their teachers and counselors have some second thoughts."[49]

For the Higher Education Act—as was the case with the National Defense Education Act—federal support for education failed to incite intense mobilization on the part of women's organizations.[50] How policy issues are defined significantly influences which groups and individuals become involved in their politics.[51] As Kristin Goss and Theda Skocpol note, during the 1960s women's groups were "reluctant or unable to use their presumptively 'different voice'" to advocate for social policy issues—such as federal support for higher education—that were important to them.[52] While women have historically been highly interested in the provision of student loans, women's organizations did not focus intensely on the Higher Education Act of 1965 and its potential benefits for women.[53] Expanding access to higher education, especially for needy citizens, was viewed as an issue of general concern—rather than a "women's issue." Not surprisingly, only a small handful of women's groups like the American Association of University Women (AAUW) expressed vocal support for the Higher Education Act in 1965. During committee deliberations, the AAUW submitted a statement in support of the legislation. According to the association's general director, Dr. Pauline Tompkins, the AAUW was "impressed" by the proposed HEA and expressed enthusiastic support for its passage.[54]

Although women's groups were not particularly engaged in lobbying for the Higher Education Act, historical analysis reveals that many of the men and women testifying during HEA subcommittee hearings recognized the importance of expanding higher educational access for American women. In arguing for increased federal financial support for students from low-income families, witnesses who testified in favor of the bill noted the interaction between gender and financial hardship for young people struggling to afford college. George O. McClary, president of the American School Counselor Association, noted that in large, female-headed families, "there is no money for savings which might be used for financing college. There is usually financial brinksmanship. The financial struggle is communicated to the girl in the form of 'get yourself a husband' and to the boy in the form of 'be a man on your own and find yourself a job to help out.'"[55] As such, McClary expressed strong support for the scholarship provisions included in the HEA.[56]

Women's access to educational resources has grown in tandem with changing social perceptions of women's roles.[57] Like President Johnson, US Commissioner of Education Francis Keppel recognized the significance of federal financial aid programs for providing women with access to the kind of public support for college that men had enjoyed under the GI Bill. In describing his recommendations for the proposed Higher Education Act during Senate hearings in March of 1965, he asserted:

> It will be necessary to expand student aid legislation to something approaching the universality of the G.I. Bills. This legislation was, to be sure, suited to the special problems of postwar adjustment to peace. It was also limited, in that it failed to make due provision for the education of women, whose great potentials we cannot afford to neglect.[58]

On March 6, Sen. Harrison Williams (D-NJ) highlighted the importance of gender inclusiveness in opportunity in the United States, observing that "in our efforts to meet the serious problems confronting our youth, we invariably concentrate our attention on the American male . . . . In view of the exceedingly important role of women in our society, this is unfortunate." He went on to encourage his colleagues to "make every effort to ensure that the rising generations of young women from low-income families are properly equipped and able to meet the complex demands of our expanding industrial society."[59]

Echoing the argument that HEW Secretary John Perkins offered in favor of women's full inclusion under the NDEA seven years before, Rep. Donald M. Fraser (D-MN) emphasized the benefits that educating women would yield for American families.[60] He goes on to characterize the fact that many young women did not go to college as "a national waste."[61] Others highlighted the ways in which the HEA could provide capable workers for businesses—including women, who represented an often untapped economic resource—thus providing valuable support for the US economy. Dorothy McBride-Stetson notes that 1960 marked the beginning of an era in which higher education became linked with the economic status of women and their employment opportunities.[62] This notion is apparent in a statement submitted to the House subcommittee by the National Association of State Universities and Land-Grant Colleges, noting that the community extension portion of the proposed Higher Education Act would provide needed support for "groups that have not had adequate opportunities," like women. The HEA would provide women who have left the labor market with training to re-enter "useful professions" such as nursing.[63]

In one particularly interesting exchange, supporters who recognized the significance of the HEA proposal's financial aid provisions for women's access to college disagreed on whether women should be afforded flexible loan repayment options in cases where they exit the labor force upon raising a family. Rep. Neal Edward Smith (D-IA) proposed an amendment to offer an interest-free, easy-payment plan where loan recipients would repay the money they borrowed when they have steady income. Smith advocated for this amendment on the floor of the House on August 26, 1965, saying:

> There are a lot of girls who really do not want to obligate themselves for future years. They do not know what years they will not be able to work. Under my amendment, when they are not able to work they do not repay. Some would be glad to repay after they have raised a family and are earning money . . . .. This makes the National Defense Educational Act discriminatory against women. I think that the committee and subcommittee handling of this bill are responsible for tens of thousands of girls not going to college who would have gone to college because they insist upon keeping a rigid repayment plan on loans instead of having an easy repayment plan.

Smith's colleague, Representative Green (D-IA), rose in opposition to the amendment, saying:

> I am sure I do not qualify to speak as one of these "girl college stu-
> dents," but the gentleman from Iowa has made reference to the fact that
> there would be girls who might borrow and who would find it difficult
> to repay. I am sorry, but I refuse to accept that kind of discrimination.
> I believe that any woman who is attending college and who wants to
> earn a degree and who has borrowed money to go to college is just as
> interested in meeting her obligation to repay a loan as any man is.[64]

Unlike these enthusiastic supporters of the Higher Education Act, some witnesses voiced staunch opposition to the bill. Bankers' associations were particularly averse to the provisions of the HEA. Speaking on behalf of the American
Bankers Association, Keith G. Cone complained that the administration's subsidized loan program posed "a very real danger" because it created "an incentive
for parents to disregard their fundamental obligations to make at least a partial
contribution to the education of their children."[65] A representative testifying on
behalf of an interest group known as Liberty Lobby asserted that the HEA "promotes, glorifies, and finances the ideology of socialism, through its support of
the 'social worker' approach to social and economic problems." "As a 'pork bar-
rel' bill," he continued, "it should be rejected."[66] The Liberty Lobby spokesman
went on to suggest that the federal government should instead adopt a program
that emphasized income tax credits for parents, students, and school taxpayers.

It is interesting to note that while opposition to the Higher Education Act
mirrored NDEA opponents' qualms with the prospect of expanding federal control in the area of education, the note of skepticism over women's inclusion as
student aid beneficiaries that colored the NDEA debate was absent from HEA
deliberation. For the Higher Education Act, opponents were skeptical of the
propriety of using federal funds to provide scholarships and additional loans
to students. Led by Senators Abraham Ribicoff (D-CT) and Winston Prouty
(R-VT), conservative members of Congress—particularly Republicans, though
some Democrats shared this view—argued that proposals for tuition tax credits, which would permit students coming from middle-class backgrounds to
take advantage of federal assistance for higher education, represented the only
responsible mechanism for expanding access to college.

Moreover, they argued, the idea of providing federal tax credits for higher
education enjoyed considerable public support. According to a Gallup poll conducted in January of 1958, when asked "Should parents with children in college
be able to deduct from their income tax the amount of money spent for tuition, board and room at college?," 81 percent of Americans agreed that families

should be able to make such deductions, compared to only 13 percent who said they should not. Democratic leaders managed to fend off attempts to make tuition tax credits a central mechanism by which the federal government provided aid for higher education by emphasizing the potential burden that such credits could place upon the government.[67] Additionally, the fact that the Higher Education Act—unlike the NDEA— made federal student loans available to students from middle-class backgrounds garnered the support of lawmakers who may have otherwise pushed for higher education tax credits.[68] Although tax credit proposals failed to gain approval by Congress in 1964, they became a staple in future debates over federal aid for higher education.

Over the course of subcommittee deliberations, lawmakers accepted a number of amendments that largely enhanced the requests made by the Johnson administration. The House subcommittee did away with library research grants but increased the funding authorizations for community extension programming and provided increased funds for extending the Higher Education Facilities Act. It also enhanced the program's capacity to promote greater higher educational access for American women and men by expanding eligibility for Title IV scholarships to include all students in need of financial support, and not simply those from families in the lowest-income brackets. The House subcommittee's revised bill did, however, depart from the administration's proposal in one major respect: it abandoned the Student Guaranteed Loan Program (SGLP), which provided loans to students from middle-class families.[69] Some members of the subcommittee viewed this alteration as an unresolved issue, even after they approved the HEA on May 18, thus sending it to Chairman Powell's Education and Labor Committee for consideration. The Senate's Education Subcommittee also added amendments to the proposed HEA during the hearings phase, including the addition of provisions for creating a National Advisory Council for Extension and Continuing Education; additional funds for junior colleges and developing institutions; loan forgiveness for student borrowers who enter the field of teaching; and additional scholarship funding for students from low-income families who exhibit exceptional academic achievement.[70]

On August 26, 1965, the House of Representatives debated the merits of the Higher Education Act. During this debate, some lawmakers took issue with the bill's proposed scholarships. In the past, the Senate had approved scholarship provisions in proposed education legislation, only to have such measures stripped from the House version of the bill. In a dramatic break with political precedent, House members rejected an amendment to jettison the scholarship proposal in the HEA by a 58 to 88 standing vote.[71] The House of Representatives approved the HEA by a 367 to 22 roll-call vote that same day.[72] The successful passage of the Higher Education Act by the House of Representatives was particularly significant because it marked the first time that the House had approved a proposal for federal scholarships for college students. Six days later, on September 1, 1965, the Senate Labor and Public Welfare Committee reported its version of the bill to the Senate; and on September 2, that chamber approved the legislation with a 79 to 3 roll-call vote.[73] In the Senate, John C. Stennis (D-MS), A. Willis Robertson (D-VA), and James O. Eastland (D-MS) opposed the HEA's passage.

Once the HEA was approved by both chambers of Congress, their respective proposals were streamlined in a conference committee. Conference debate centered on two items: the HEA's scholarship provision for needy students and the Teacher Corps program. Some lawmakers, such as Representative Green, objected to the entitlement format of Basic Education Opportunity Grants, preferring instead merit-based aid for needy students. Lawmakers also disagreed about the propriety of the Teacher Corps program, which involved providing federal funds to select, train, and pay teachers who would volunteer to teach at schools in impoverished areas of the country.[74] Conservative members of the conference committee argued that such a program would require an inappropriate level of federal control over personnel in participating schools. Ultimately, although Congress authorized funding for the Teacher Corps program, it failed to appropriate funds for the program.

On October 19, 1965, a conference committee of House and Senate members filed a compromise version of the Higher Education Act that closely resembled the Senate's version of the bill including the annual student aid appropriations set forth in the Senate bill and its provisions for amending the National Defense Student Loan Program.[75] Commenting on the conference bill as it returned to each chamber for final approval, Rep. Adam Clayton Powell (D-NY), the chairman of the Education and Labor Committee, proclaimed that "both chambers and both sides of the aisle sought compromise with one goal in mind—the enactment this year of legislation that will revitalize the tired blood of our anemic colleges and universities and pump needy students into the all too upper class main stream of academic life."[76] On October 20, both the House and the Senate approved the conference report with a vote of 313 to 63 in the House and a unanimous voice vote in the Senate.[77] The HEA emerged from Congress replete with eight titles that met the requests made by President Johnson in his January 12 education message. The legislation authorized more than $800 million for higher education in fiscal year 1966, approximately $42 million for interest subsidies for student loans, and financial aid to developing institutions.[78]

On November 8, 1965, Lyndon Johnson signed the Higher Education Act into law at his alma mater, Southwest Texas State College. In his remarks commemorating the occasion, Johnson proclaimed that

> to thousands of young men and women, this act means the path to knowledge is open to all that have the determination to walk it . . .. It

means that a high school senior anywhere in this great land of ours can apply to any college or any university in any of the 50 States and not be turned away because his family is poor.[79]

In his signing statement, he asserted that the nation would "reap the rewards of their wiser citizenship and their greater productivity for decades to come."[80] The Higher Education Act was immensely popular among Americans. When a December 1965 Harris Survey asked respondents whether they approved or disapproved of specific legislation passed by Congress that year, a full 89 percent indicated that they approved of the college scholarships that were created by the HEA, while only 11 percent expressed disapproval.

Building upon the National Defense Education Act, the Higher Education Act of 1965 further expanded access to postsecondary education for millions of American men and women. While Cold War politics and the domestic struggle over civil rights catalyzed the passage of the NDEA, Lyndon Johnson's War on Poverty and the emphasis that his administration placed on economic opportunity fueled the creation of the HEA. In the years immediately following the passage of the Higher Education Act, the number of college degrees earned by women continued to increase precipitously. Sixteen years after its passage, women surpassed men as the recipients of four-year degrees.

After passing the Higher Education Act in 1965, lawmakers adopted the same centralized method of program administration that characterized NDEA implementation. In the years following the policy's enactment, HEA grants, loans, and work-study support supported millions of students as they pursued college degrees. In 1972, lawmakers overhauled the Higher Education Act's Basic Educational Opportunity Grant (BEOG) program as part of the 1972 Education Amendments, an omnibus reauthorization bill extending and amending the programs established by the NDEA and the HEA. In 1982, BEOGs were renamed in honor of Sen. Claiborne Pell (D-RI), a chief proponent of the legislation. By and large, the redistributive student aid programs established under the Higher Education Act have helped to make college affordable for millions of college students, while successfully reinforcing the NDEA's gender-egalitarian approach to ensuring college access for traditionally underrepresented students.

Conclusion

Like the National Defense Education Act, the 1965 Higher Education Act furthered lawmakers' objective of expanding access to college degrees. In addition to promoting equal opportunity for women in higher education, the HEA helped to reinforce a new dynamic of women's treatment under US higher education policy and social policy, more generally. By incorporating women as full and equal beneficiaries, the HEA confirmed women's first-class status in the polity and signaled the achievement of a substantial change in how the federal government treats women relative to men.

The Higher Education Act significantly expanded the federal government's role in facilitating access to higher education for American men and women. For President Lyndon Johnson, higher education represented a powerful anti-poverty tool, and he was committed to constructing a higher education program that would surpass the efforts of the NDEA. Strong presidential leadership and a fortuitous political context enabled Democratic lawmakers to successfully pass the HEA, thereby fortifying the government's commitment to expanding access to higher education with a combination of federal grants and student loans that provided a broad segment of men and women with financial support to help them attain college degrees.

Like the NDEA, the HEA was constructed as a gender-egalitarian policy that provided benefits equally to women and men. By expanding women's access to higher education, the National Defense Education Act of 1958 and the Higher Education Act of 1965 not only narrowed the gender gap in higher educational attainment that emerged after the GI Bill's enactment during the postwar era and paved the way for women to eventually surpass men as the recipients of college degrees, but also altered the gender dynamics of American citizenship in terms of status by institutionalizing a standard of full incorporation of women under US social programs. Taken together, the National Defense Education Act and the Higher Education Act set a new standard for federal involvement in higher education and for the incorporation of female citizens as the full and equal beneficiaries of federal social policies. In so doing, these programs not only dramatically reshaped the gender dynamics of higher educational attainment in the United States but also revolutionized the gender dynamics of American citizenship in terms of status by treating women as first-class citizens.

5

Opening Doors for Women

Title IX and the Death of "Women Need Not Apply"

> One of the basic concepts upon which our democracy was founded was the idea that people can only be free and equal where there is equality of opportunity. If women are unreasonably denied access to public places and public educational institutions (which they support with taxes), then women cannot be considered full and equal citizens. Women should be fully integrated into the educational institutions of our Nation as students (and teachers), and accepted as mature individuals with potential and worth.
>
> —Ms. Virginia A. Allen, *chair of the President's Task Force on Women's Rights and Responsibilities*[1]

> A strong and comprehensive measure is needed to provide women with solid legal protection from the persistent, pernicious discrimination which is serving to perpetuate second-class citizenship for American women.
>
> —Sen. Birch Bayh (D-IN), *1972*

When Marvella Belle Hern completed high school in the early 1950s, she had little doubt that higher education was in her future. Over the past four years, the wheat farmer's daughter gained a reputation as an academic and extracurricular power house: she was a straight-"A" student, she presided over the Girls Nation program, and she was a former governor of the Oklahoma Girls State program. When it came time to apply for college, Marvella set her sights on her dream school, the University of Virginia (UVA). Despite her solid academic and leadership credentials, her application to UVA was returned with a note that simply said: "Women need not apply."[2] As we saw in chapters 3 and 4, in passing the National Defense Education Act (NDEA) and the Higher Education Act (HEA), US lawmakers used redistributive policy to mount a powerful assault on financial barriers limiting women's access to college degrees. Nonetheless, by the early 1970s, women continued to grapple with formidable institutional barriers that suppressed the number of women earning college degrees. Sex

discrimination in college admissions, faculty hiring, and program offerings represented the significant remaining barrier to women's full and equal access to
higher education in the United States. Thus, although women enjoyed access to
federal funds to help meet the cost of earning a postsecondary degree, discriminatory admissions policies limited the number of women who would have the
opportunity to utilize such financial aid in the first place.

It was not uncommon for women to be denied college admission on the basis
of their sex.[3] While most schools invoked gender quotas restricting the number
of women allowed in a particular class, others simply refused to admit female students.[4] Harvard, Princeton, and the University of North Carolina, for example,
set strict gender quotas that limited the number of women permitted to study
in their institutions, while Dartmouth excluded women entirely.[5] To win one of
the coveted "women's seats" in a college, female applicants generally had to have
better grades and higher test scores than their male counterparts. Other higher
educational programs discriminated against women who were married, pregnant, or parenting. For example, in 1966, when Luci Baines Johnson—daughter
of President Lyndon Johnson—attempted to return to nursing school after her
marriage, she was refused readmission because Georgetown University's school
of nursing prohibited married women from enrolling as students.[6]

Title IX changed all of this. Adopted as part of the 1972 Education
Amendments, an omnibus bill that revised and reauthorized the programs that
originated under the Higher Education Act, Title IX prohibited sex discrimination in federally funded education programs. A brief paragraph in an otherwise
rambling bill, the pithy statute established that

> "No person in the United States shall, on the basis of sex, be excluded
> from participation in, be denied the benefits of, or be subjected to dis-
> crimination under any education program or activity receiving federal
> financial assistance" (PL 92-318).

In addition to significantly increasing women's access to college, vocational
training, and graduate school, Title IX successfully fostered gender equality
in faculty hiring and compensation, promoted fair treatment for pregnant and
parenting students, and prohibited sexual harassment in schools. This chapter offers a final case study of landmark higher education policy development,
exploring how the political context of the early 1970s and the efforts of a handful
of political elites revolutionized the federal government's approach to expanding access to college degrees. It offers important lessons for our understanding
of just how important policy design has been for the capacity of federal higher
education policy to expand equal opportunity for women. By departing from
the redistributive policy design of the NDEA and the HEA and employing a

regulatory approach to expand access to higher educational institutions, law-makers ventured beyond offering direct support to students to reform institu-tional practices. This technique of leveraging multiple policy tools to expand access to college degrees signaled an important shift in higher education pol-icy and proved crucial to lawmakers' ability to promote equal opportunity for women. This case study also reveals an interesting shift in the intentionality of lawmakers when it came to expanding women's access to college degrees. While the substantial benefits that women received from the NDEA and the HEA were byproducts of broader political forces that supported their inclusion as inciden-tal and even accidental beneficiaries, Title IX was crafted with the explicit pur-pose of expanding women's access to higher educational institutions.

In both popular and scholarly conceptualizations, Americans have come to associate Title IX with gender equality in sports.[7] Given the regulation's sweep-ing effects for expanding athletic opportunities for women and girls, this rec-ognition is warranted. During the academic year immediately preceding the passage of Title IX, more than 170,000 men participated in collegiate athlet-ics, while fewer than 30,000 women did so. By the 2004–2005 academic year, the gender gap in collegiate athletic participation had narrowed dramatically, with approximately 295,000 men and 209,000 women participating in college sports.[8] However, our narrow association of Title IX with gender equality in athletics obscures the broader significance of the groundbreaking public policy. Not only did the regulation—itself a novel departure from the redistributive for-mat of erstwhile higher education policy precedents—contribute to important changes in the gender dynamics of US higher educational institutions, but also it marked the birth of gender-conscious higher education policy in the United States. For the first time, federal lawmakers fashioned a higher education pro-gram in a way that explicitly addressed gender disparity.

This novel approach to US higher education policy was a timely, though highly unlikely, innovation. Historically, federal higher education policy had tra-ditionally taken the form of redistributive, gender-neutral institutional support and student financial aid. Title IX represents a bold departure from this trend—one that contributed to a change in the gender dynamics of American higher educational institutions and marked a dramatic shift in US higher education pol-icy. It also provided a bold reinforcement of the government's commitment to ensuring women's treatment as first-class citizens. Unlike postwar financial aid programs that stopped short of attempting to correct for gender disparities in college accessibility, Title IX voiced a full-throated call for gender equality in access to the nation's colleges and universities. Rather than incremental change at the margins of existing programs, this movement from gender-neutral finan-cial aid to gender-conscious institutional regulation illustrates dramatic policy change at a critical juncture.[9]

The creation of such a bold regulation ensuring women's access to higher educational institutions seems particularly unlikely when we consider the political factors that shaped the policymaking process in the early 1970s. Although women represented a majority of the US population and more than half of registered voters in 1972, they held fewer than 3 percent of seats in the House of Representatives (11 of 435 seats), and Margaret Chase Smith (R-ME) was the sole woman serving among the 100 US senators. In terms of mass political engagement, women voted at lower rates than men, and they were less likely to engage in activities like contributing money to political campaigns and contacting elected officials. Moreover, women—who represented one-third of the labor force—were paid, on average, 60 cents for every dollar earned by their male counterparts.[10]

To fully appreciate the remarkable development of Title IX—particularly the historical moment at which the regulation was passed and the novelty of invoking federal regulation in higher education policy—we must take seriously the politics surrounding its creation and implementation. Thus far, by focusing primarily on the impact that Title IX has had for gender equality in athletics, analyses of the program have largely overlooked the politics surrounding its passage and its central objective, which was to end gender discrimination in college admissions.[11] What political factors facilitated the passage of Title IX in 1972 and, as a result, the dramatic shift to gender-conscious higher education policy? How, given women's marginalized status in American politics and the absence of a highly organized women's movement advocating on behalf of educational opportunity for women, did Title IX successfully emerge from the political process? I find that, in the wake of passing landmark civil rights policies that used federal regulation to address institutional discrimination against racial and ethnic minorities, Americans and their lawmakers in Congress grew increasingly aware of the obstacle that institutional discrimination posed to women's access to colleges and universities. As such, this context facilitated a shift in how policymakers characterized barriers to equal opportunity in higher education, shifting their focus from affordability to institutional access. Moreover, this shift was made possible by the strategic maneuverings of policy advocates who recognized sex discrimination in college admissions as an affront to equal opportunity in the United States.

"Women Need Not Apply": Sex Discrimination and a New Course for Higher Education Policy

Among the numerous factors that made it unlikely that lawmakers would turn their efforts to expand access to college from financial aid for students to regulatory policies that compelled colleges and universities to use gender-egalitarian admissions criteria was the fact that, well into the mid-twentieth century, sex discrimination was largely conceptualized as a matter of individual misfortune, rather than a systematic barrier that widely limited equal opportunity for women. As Title IX activist Dr. Bernice Sandler notes, "The word 'sex discrimination' was relatively new" in the 1960s and 1970s. While there was concern for the unfair treatment of women, sex discrimination was not perceived as a formal concept, and women tended to attribute discriminatory treatment to the idiosyncrasies of a particular person or individual department.[12] According to Sandler, "You [didn't] think about it as a pattern. It's just an individual instance here and there."[13] For many women, individual instances of unfair treatment by higher educational institutions were all too common, and some were beginning to notice a trend.

Sandler's personal experience being passed over for a faculty position because she "came on too strong for a woman" piqued her interest in gender discrimination in higher education. Working with Vincent Macaluso, the assistant director of the US Department of Labor's Office of Federal Contract Compliance, Sandler attempted to challenge sex discrimination in faculty hiring. She based her claim against discriminatory university hiring on Executive Order 11246. Issued in 1965, this order prohibited federal contractors from discriminating on the basis of sex, race, religion, or national origin when making hiring and other employment decisions. Sandler inundated the Office of Civil Rights (OCR) at the US Department of Health, Education, and Welfare (HEW) with hundreds of charges against American colleges and universities that were not in compliance with the order. As the OCR investigated these complaints, the government withheld federal grants from a number of institutions until they produced plans for improving the treatment of women faculty, graduate students, and staff.[14] Meanwhile, Bernice Sandler found an ally in Rep. Edith Green (D-OR), whose interest was piqued upon receiving a copy of Sandler's complaint.[15]

Representative Green, who would eventually author Title IX, had first-hand experience with the discrimination that women and girls faced in education.[16] After winning election to Congress in 1955, Green distinguished herself as a capable proponent for educational opportunity and emerged as a champion of gender equality. In the late 1970s, she recalled her dismay during a subcommittee hearing a decade prior during which school superintendents advocating for programs to prevent at-risk boys from dropping out of school were unabashedly unconcerned with the attrition of at-risk girls. The educators and Green's male colleagues on the committee took for granted that the academic well-being of boys was more important than that of girls because, as Green recalled, "[boys] were going to be the breadwinners."[17] In the Senate, Birch Bayh (D-IN) would emerge as the principal proponent of Title IX. Senator Bayh's interest in gender equality in higher education was rooted in the discrimination experienced by his first wife, Marvella Hern Bayh, whose story opened this chapter.

It is important to note that the emergence of political efforts to end sex discrimination in college admissions emanated not from a large and organized women's movement but from a small cadre of elites who had first-hand experiences with sex discrimination. The women's rights movement had not yet become an organized force that could support the fight against sex discrimination in higher education. Social policy expert and early Title IX advocate Margaret Dunkle recalls that contemporary women's organizations were just beginning to form at the time that Title IX was considered by Congress.[18] A 1972 *Congressional Quarterly Weekly Report* described the nascent women's movement as a "disorganized, heterogeneous, and fragmented" movement that struggles with "disagreements on the proper tactics" to employ to achieve equal rights.[19] The established women's groups, such as the American Association of University Women, which boasted more than one hundred thousand members; the Business and Professional Women's Foundation; and the League of Women Voters, had limited knowledge regarding equity issues and remained at the sidelines during the early stages of Title IX's development.[20] Rather than emerging from strong and broad-reaching activism, the development of Title IX, as Margaret Dunkle describes it, "was really [by] a few people who made a huge change."[21]

The growing consciousness among political elites that sex discrimination represented an important challenge to educational opportunity in the United States occurred in a political context that was increasingly aware of discrimination and amenable to the use of federal regulation to combat it. The previous decade marked a defining period in American politics during which US policymakers invoked the power of the state to challenge discrimination. Congress took steps to alleviate sex discrimination in employment wages with the Equal Pay Act of 1963. The following year, lawmakers passed the Civil Rights Act of 1964, which made it illegal to discriminate against students and employees on the basis of race, color, or nationality.[22] In Title VI of the Civil Rights Act, lawmakers banned such discrimination in any program receiving federal financial aid. Title VII of the act prohibited sex discrimination, but only in the area of employment. Although these landmark civil rights programs promoted race and gender equality in employment and race equality in education, lawmakers had yet to address the significant barrier that discriminatory admissions policies posed to gender equality in higher education.[23] In a 1971 report, the Ford Foundation noted, "Discrimination against women, in contrast to that against minorities, is still overt and socially acceptable within the academic community."[24] The successes of the civil rights movement cast an even brighter light on the gender inequality that remained in the late 1960s and early 1970s.

In the wake of the civil rights movement, Representative Green, Senator Bayh, and Bernice Sandler began to think seriously about how the government could address discrimination against women in college admissions. Although lawmakers had drawn upon federal regulation as a powerful tool to promote equal treatment in American institutions during the 1960s, the use of federal regulation represented a promethean approach to expanding access to higher education. It was only after lawmakers began to reimagine equal access to college as a matter of institutional change rather than one of personal finance that this approach to higher education policy became a legitimate option. To successfully adopt this unorthodox approach to expanding access to college education, lawmakers would have to make a solid case that sex discrimination by higher educational institutions represented a barrier requiring federal intervention. It would also require that lawmakers adopt a strategic approach for moving their antidiscrimination proposal through the political process, drawing upon growing consciousness regarding gender discrimination.

Representative Green and her allies looked to civil rights legislation as a template for achieving institutional change. The value of using the regulatory power of the state to compel institutional compliance with nondiscrimination laws influenced Edith Green's decision to pursue a regulatory approach to addressing sex discrimination in college admissions. As Margaret Dunkle notes, "There is a long-established tradition at the federal level of coupling a stick—[such as] a prohibition against discrimination or a requirement to do something—with a carrot, [like] student aid."[25] In the 1960s, a similar pairing generated a significant expansion of higher educational opportunities to African Americans. While the National Defense Education Act and the Higher Education Act had extended need-based student aid to low-income African Americans, the Civil Rights Act prevented racial discrimination in higher educational institutions from severely restricting black students' usage of that aid. In the case of the Title IX regulation, lawmakers were "basically playing catch up" by challenging sex-based discrimination that hindered women from broadly using the financial aid benefits that were provided under the NDEA and the HEA.[26]

Shedding Light on Sex Discrimination in College Admissions

The politics of the early 1970s paved the way for lawmakers to take decisive steps to reduce sex discrimination in higher education. In Congress, liberal lawmakers began to highlight issues related to sex discrimination. In June of 1970, Rep. Martha Griffiths (D-MI) and Sen. Birch Bayh began lining up support for the

Equal Rights Amendment, which proposed amending the US Constitution to guarantee women and men equal rights.[27] That same month, as chair of the House Committee on Education and Labor's Special Subcommittee on Education, Representative Green held hearings on discrimination against women in education and employment.

Representative Green's subcommittee hearings on sex discrimination represent a critical juncture in the process by which discriminatory admissions policies became the focus of federal efforts to expand access to higher education.[28] They yielded valuable testimony confirming the need for legislation that would protect women and girls from sex discrimination in education, and they marked the genesis of Title IX. Witnesses providing testimony during these crucial hearings included women's rights activists; college professors; a number of Green's female congressional colleagues; and representatives from colleges, professional organizations, and advocacy groups like the American Association of University Women and Bernice Sandler's Women's Equity Action League (WEAL).

Beyond these groups, interest in Representative Green's investigation into sex discrimination in education and employment was sparse. Catherine Stimpson recalls the lack of seriousness with which the Education Subcommittee's fifteen male members treated the hearings, noting that "no more than four of them ever appeared at one time to listen to the testimony, a comment either on the nature of congressional subcommittee hearings or on the prevailing attitude of men in government towards the issue of women's rights."[29] Also conspicuously absent from the hearings on sex discrimination were the major education organizations like the National Education Association (NEA), the American Council on Education, and the American Federation of Teachers (AFT). These groups paid little attention to the proceedings because they did not regard sex discrimination in education as a particularly pressing issue.[30]

The statements presented at the subcommittee hearings suggested otherwise. While witnesses highlighted the many forms of discrimination that challenged American women in a range of areas, chronic gender disparity in higher education soon became a focal point of the hearings. Among the discriminatory practices that witnesses discussed, their remarks regarding sex discrimination in university admissions were particularly striking. Although men had always pursued postsecondary education at higher rates than women, the gender gap in enrollment was expanding in the late 1960s and early 1970s.[31] A major source of this trend was the fact that many colleges and universities maintained quota systems that restricted the number of women admitted each year.[32] For example, a few years before the hearings, 21,000 women applied for college admission in the state of Virginia and were rejected, while not a single man who applied for admission was rejected.[33] Many schools made it clear that, to gain admission, women needed to be "especially well qualified."[34] Men, however, were not held to such lofty standards. It was not unusual for incoming freshman classes to be characterized by substantial gender imbalances. In 1970, the University of North Carolina's freshman class consisted of 1,900 men and only 426 women.[35]

Such inequality characterized the gender dynamics of American higher education more broadly. While men had traditionally earned more college degrees than women, the expanding gender gap in bachelor's degree completion indicated that the nation was moving backward when it came to equal educational opportunity. In 1940, 4.5 percent of women over the age of twenty-five had completed at least four years of college, compared to 5.4 percent of men. In 1967, the gap had expanded significantly, with 7.6 percent of women and 12.8 percent of men over twenty-five holding bachelor's degrees.[36] Representative Green's subcommittee hearings demonstrated the magnitude of gender inequality in American higher education. When the hearings came to a close, she placed a special order with the federal printing office to produce a whopping six thousand copies of the hearing transcripts, which she promptly mailed to the presidents of major colleges and universities, as well as members of committees and organizations that dealt with education.[37]

The statements presented during these hearings provided Edith Green and her allies with valuable evidence to support their argument that sex discrimination represented an egregious barrier to equal higher educational opportunity. They drew upon this information to make the case that institutional regulation represented a natural shift for US higher education policy—one that was not only necessary but also a simple matter of fairness. As such, Green's subcommittee hearings were crucial to redefining the problem of educational access as one of institutional discrimination rather than financial need.

Although the Education Subcommittee's sex discrimination hearings revealed gender inequality to be a significant national problem, it became apparent when the hearings concluded in July of 1970 that Edith Green's original plan of appending an amendment prohibiting sex discrimination in education to the Civil Rights Act might not be the most effective approach. Requesting that she tread carefully around the fragile progress that the 1964 Civil Rights Act had achieved, Assistant Attorney General Jerris Leonard and African American leaders suggested that Green and her allies present their proposal as separate legislation.[38] Rather than amending the Civil Rights Act, Leonard suggested that Green should use it as a blueprint for a unique proposal.[39] Representative Green decided to present Title IX as an amendment to the omnibus education bill that Senator Claiborne Pell (D-RI) introduced to reauthorize the student aid provisions of the National Defense Education Act and the Higher Education Act, which were scheduled to expire on June 30, 1971. In a special message to Congress on March 19, 1970, President Richard Nixon emphasized the administration's commitment to enhancing federal support for higher education in the form of student loans, grants, and aid to community colleges.[40] This placed the topic of higher education in a prominent position on the political agenda. The following month, the President's Taskforce on Women's Rights and Responsibilities issued a report entitled "A Matter of Simple Justice," highlighting the problem of sex discrimination in the United States.[41] This focus on higher education and a growing awareness of problems related to sex discrimination provided an amenable political context for the introduction of Title IX.

Two Chambers, One Goal: Pushing Title IX Through the Political Process

With the beginning of the Ninety-Second Congress in January of 1971, the Republican president and the Democrat-controlled House and Senate prioritized the task of reauthorizing the landmark federal student aid programs that were created under the National Defense Education Act of 1958 and the Higher Education Act of 1965. In a message to Congress on February 22, 1971, President Nixon proclaimed that it would be "a year of national debate on the goals and potentials of our system of higher education." The year could also provide "a time of opportunity to discover new concepts of mission and purpose, which are responsive to the diverse needs of our country."[42] Nixon revealed the administration's proposal for continuing federal aid for higher education, which was drafted by Associate Secretary Elliot Richardson and the staff at HEW. Known as HR 5191, "The Higher Education Opportunity Act of 1971," Nixon's proposal expressed a commitment to continued financial aid for needy students but revealed a new interest in providing assistance for higher-income students as well.[43] While Nixon expressed a strong commitment to providing funds to colleges and universities that traditionally serve black Americans—calling these institutions "an indispensable national resource"—he placed no such emphasis on the importance of providing aid to women's colleges.[44]

"Low Key" Politics in the House of Representatives

Rep. Edith Green decided to attach her sex discrimination proposal to HR 7248, the congressional version of the omnibus reauthorization bill, which was known simply as "the Education Amendments." As Sen. Birch Bayh notes, Edith Green was a stalwart proponent of gender equality in higher education and, in the politics surrounding the anti–sex discrimination regulation, "the real trooper in the House."[45] Recognizing the value of the landmark 1964 legislation for providing a blueprint for addressing discrimination, Green drew upon the exact language used in the Civil Rights Act, which had banned discrimination on the basis of race, color, and nationality in all federally funded programs, when drafting Title IX.[46] Bernice Sandler remembers Representative Green's approach to drafting the statute, saying, "She changed it, took the wording from Title VI—put 'sex' instead of race, color, national origin in it and limited it to education."

Occupying a brief paragraph in the lengthy reauthorization bill, Green's proposal prohibited sex discrimination in federally funded education programs.[47] The purpose of Title IX was to outlaw the use of federal funds to support education programs that engaged in sex discrimination. Title IX addressed a broad range of issues related to gender equality in education, providing legal recourse for gender discrimination in admissions and employment, sexual harassment, and discrimination against pregnant and parenting students and faculty members.[48] Along with congressional representatives Shirley Chisholm (D-NY) and Patsy Mink (D-HI) and Senators Birch Bayh (D-IN) and George McGovern (D-SD), Representative Green and her allies in Congress began working to secure support for the regulation in both legislative chambers.

A crucial component in the successful passage of Title IX was Representative Green's strategy for maneuvering the regulation through Congress. To avoid provoking intense objection to Title IX, Green asked allies to forgo lobbying on behalf of the proposal.[49] Margaret Dunkle describes Edith Green's strategy as keeping Title IX "under the radar," submitting it nonchalantly—as something that simply followed the pattern of Title VI of the Civil Rights Act.[50] As WEAL activist Bernice Sandler recalls, "Edith Green was a superb politician." She continues:

> I remember this meeting, there were maybe, I don't know, seven, eight of us, in '72, and we came and we said, "We're ready to lobby. You just tell us what you want us to do, and we'll do it." She said, "I don't want you to lobby at all." And we thought, "What?" And she said, "If you lobby, people are going to ask what's in this bill, and if they find out what's in it, they're not going to vote for it." She said, "They're going to vote for it, it's going to pass." And she was absolutely right. We were horrified—we thought she was wrong. We didn't know as much as she did.[51]

This low-key approach to steering Title IX through Congress can be credited with averting demands for exemptions that would significantly weaken its ability to promote women's access to college.[52] If Title IX had attracted too much attention, says Dunkle, "[it] would have had so many exclusions that it would have looked like Swiss cheese."[53] The strategy that Edith Green and her allies used to maneuver Title IX through Congress has been described as "stealth politics."[54] According to Jean C. Robinson, Pamela Barnhouse Walters, and Julia Lamber,

proponents of Title IX consciously downplayed the extent to which the regulation would reshape higher education and minimized discussion of the initiative
to avoid opposition.[55] Yet, although historical analysis confirms that Edith Green
intentionally avoided attracting unnecessary attention to Title IX as it made its
way through the House of Representatives, the historical record also suggests
that—ultimately—Title IX's movement through the political process fell short
of perfect stealth. While the amendment failed to garner extensive attention during committee deliberations on the education reauthorization bill, on a number
of occasions lawmakers engaged in discussion about gender discrimination in
higher education and the importance of equal access for women. At one point,
when the issue of sex discrimination in faculty hiring came up during committee
hearings, Representative Green and her colleague Rep. John Brademas (D-IN)
engaged in the following good-humored exchange:[56]

MRS. GREEN: Congressman Brademas.
MR. BRADEMAS: Thank you, Madam Chairman. Let me say we have a very effec-
    tive "women's lib" leader here [referring to Representative Green]. She is rap-
    idly converting me. I noticed that at the University of California at Berkeley,
    Madam Chairman, in 1923, 2.6 percent of the professors were women, and in
    1960 and 1970, it is 2.3 percent.
MRS. GREEN: Would my colleague yield?
MR. BRADEMAS: Of course.
MRS. GREEN: The rapid conversion reminds me of the 1954 decision: "with all
    deliberate speed."
MR. BRADEMAS: Madam Chairman—
SECRETARY RICHARDSON: I think the Congressman deserves credit for con-
    version, since he is an overseer of Harvard University and Harvard has
    signed . . . an agreement with the Office of Civil Rights.
MRS. GREEN: I do know, but I do want you to know it was not instantaneous.
MR. BRADEMAS: Madam Chairman, it is never too late to be saved.

When the education reauthorization bill made its way out of committee
deliberations and onto the House floor, the bulk of discussion revolved around
the financial aid provisions that it reauthorized and its provisions for busing to
facilitate school desegregation. Although debate over Title IX represented a
small fraction of congressional deliberation over the omnibus bill, a number of
Representative Green's female colleagues in the House voiced strong support for
the measure. Rep. Patsy Mink (D-HI), for example, emphasized the impropriety
of providing federal tax dollars—which are drawn from male and female citizens
alike—to institutions that subject women to unfair treatment. Addressing her
colleagues from the House floor, she offered a clarification of Title IX's reach,

framing it as a simple matter of fairness that resonated with the awareness that gender discrimination is unfair. "Any college or university which has an undergraduate admission policy which discriminates against women applicants," she said, "is free to do so under our bill, but such institutions should not be asking the taxpayers of this country to pay for this kind of discrimination . . . . [J]ust as we insist that schools be color-blind, we must insist also that they be sex-blind as well."[57] Throughout deliberations, Green and her colleagues framed the inclusion of Title IX as resonating with the contemporaneous appeals to equal opportunity.

On a small number of occasions, members of Congress acknowledged the problem of sex discrimination in higher education and even alluded to evidence presented during Representative Green's earlier subcommittee hearings on sex discrimination.[58] Supporters of Title IX voiced objection to the allocation of federal funds to support institutions engaging in discriminatory admissions policies. As such, they appealed to the right of all women who contributed into the federal treasury to withhold their tax dollars from supporting institutions engaging in sex discrimination.[59]

Although Edith Green's strategy of minimizing fanfare around Title IX in hopes of avoiding intense opposition afforded the regulation a relatively smooth journey through the political process, and although the passage of the Equal Rights Amendment had recently signaled lawmakers' interest in promoting gender equality, Title IX was not without opposition. Many of Title IX's opponents took issue with the idea of the federal government regulating college admissions. Speaking on behalf of Harvard, Princeton, Yale, Notre Dame, and other elite private institutions, Rep. John Erlenborn (R-IL) disagreed that the federal government should force colleges to admit women and men equally. Such a policy, he argued, would place undue burden on those institutions.[60] In a letter to Edith Green, John Honey, vice president of governmental affairs and research at Syracuse University, urged the exclusion of Title IX from the reauthorization bill, saying that the proposal failed to represent "an appropriate subject for congressional action."[61] Some universities objected on the grounds that gender-egalitarian admissions policies could prove detrimental to the financial well-being of their institutions. Harvard, Yale, Princeton, and other elite institutions claimed that male alumni donated more money to their schools than female alumni and that admitting a greater proportion of women would significantly reduce financial support.[62]

While some opponents took overt exception to the notion of admitting women and men to higher educational institutions on an equal basis, others framed their objections as rooted in concerns regarding an overreaching of government power, rather than opposition to equal opportunities for women. In the House, Representative Erlenborn emerged as a strong opponent of Title

IX. The federal government, he argued, had no place dictating whether institutions of higher education should admit women and, if they do, how many they should agree to accommodate. According to Erlenborn: "Passage of Title IX would establish a dangerous precedent . . . . [I]f Congress permits the Federal Government to take away from colleges their right to determine the composition of their own student bodies, it will plant the seed of destruction for our system of higher education as we know it."[63] To support his argument, he produced a number of letters from elite higher educational institutions decrying the prospect of having to admit women and men at equal rates. He responded to these objections by proposing an amendment that would exempt all undergraduate institutions from the Title IX regulation.[64] Citing support from Father Theodore Hesburgh, Civil Rights Commission chair, and Harris Wofford, a former member of the US Commission on Civil Rights, Representative Erlenborn assured his colleagues that they need not worry that supporting an amendment exempting undergraduate programs from Title IX would signal a lack of support for civil or human rights:

> So Members do not feel a vote for this amendment means a vote against civil rights or human rights, I would like to point out that I have received a telephone call from Father Hesburgh, president of Notre Dame University, currently Chairman of the Civil Rights Commission, in support of this amendment. He understands the impact of the language on the individual undergraduate schools, particularly those such as his, that would be thinking in terms of moving away from the single sex concept and moving toward having both sexes in their institution.[65]

Providing for gender equality in graduate and professional degree programs, he argued, would provide a great deal of opportunity to women without burdening higher educational institutions. Among those who objected to the idea of exempting undergraduate programs from the Title IX regulation, Rep. Edith Green raised strong objection, saying, "I say to the Members that any amendment to [Title IX] that says we are going to end discrimination and then excepts 95 percent of the institutions in this country, is pure fraud." She went on to address Erlenborn's reference to his call from Father Ted Hesburgh, saying:

> I want to say that I admired and had great respect for Father Hesburgh over a period of years, but I apologize for him for his stand on this. How a person as Chairman of the Civil Rights Commission of the United States can make eloquent statements about having to end discrimination in this country and then say it is perfectly all right to continue the

discrimination against over 50 percent of the people in this country
I do not know.[66]

Rep. Patsy Mink (D-HI) also rose in opposition to the Erlenborn amendment
to Title IX, saying, "It is utter nonsense to argue that the Federal Government
has the responsibility to protect the civil rights of its citizens, and to exclude
women from this protection! That is the essence of the Erlenborn amendment."
She added: "I would remind my colleagues that this vote will be seen by women
all across the United States as a true test of our commitment to this cause."[67]
Despite such vocal objection, Erlenborn's amendment prevailed. Approved by
a close vote of 194 to 189, the Erlenborn amendment significantly weakened
Title IX in the House version of the Education Amendments by exempting all
undergraduate programs from the prohibition against sex discrimination.[68] On
November 4, 1971, the House of Representatives passed its version of the omnibus reauthorization bill—which included a weakened Title IX—by a vote of
332 to 38, sending the proposal to the Senate.

Less-Than-Stealthy Politics in the Senate

By adroitly drawing upon burgeoning gender consciousness in the political
environment to frame gender equality in college access as a natural extension of
US higher education policy, Representative Green facilitated Title IX's successful movement through the House of Representatives. While the amendment's
movement through the House could be described as surprisingly "low key," considering the magnitude of change it proposed, its movement through the Senate
could be described as anything but stealthy. On August 5, 1971, Sen. Birch Bayh
(D-IN) introduced the Title IX prohibition against sex discrimination in education on the floor of the Senate, asserting that the proposed amendment would
"guarantee that women, too, enjoy the educational opportunity every American
deserves."[69] Pointing to the recommendations offered by President Nixon's Task
Force on Women's Rights and Responsibilities and the 1964 Civil Rights Act's
failure to include sex discrimination, Bayh asserted that passing Title IX would
yield "a forward step, both in higher education and in protecting equal rights for
all Americans."[70] A number of his colleagues, however, failed to see Title IX as
such a clear-cut remedy for protecting citizens' rights. Although most accounts
of the passage of Title IX suggest that it moved through Congress with relatively
little fanfare, analysis of Senate proceedings reveals that the proposal generated
contentious debate.

As the Senate deliberated over the education reauthorization bill in early
1972, it was clear that, in the wake of civil rights policies that challenged race
discrimination in the United States, Americans were becoming increasingly

concerned about the problem of sex discrimination.[71] One women's rights advocate poignantly characterized sex discrimination as "the last socially acceptable prejudice."[72] During his State of the Union address on January 20, 1972, President Nixon expressed support for extending the authority of the Civil Rights Commission to include sex discrimination, and in Congress, lawmakers continued to strategize on how best to guide Title IX through the political process.[73] While some lawmakers objected to the notion of federal regulation over access to college admissions, this increasing gender consciousness made it difficult to advocate for continued sex discrimination in admissions.[74]

In probing the effects that Title IX would have on universities, Sen. Peter Dominick (R-CO) made a point of questioning how it would affect a number of areas far removed from college admissions. It was through this probing that opponents focused on the potential redistributive effects of Title IX, and it was along these lines that the question of how the regulation would affect athletics was raised. Senator Dominick asked whether the ban on sex discrimination would require women and men to play on the same football teams and to share athletic equipment and facilities.[75] As a slippery slope of seemingly preposterous outcomes that could result from Title IX offered a politically expedient way to defeat the proposal, discussion shifted away from Title IX's intended objective of ensuring equal college access for women. In addition to requiring men and women to play on the same sports teams, to use the same locker rooms, and to share athletic equipment, opponents argued, Title IX would fly in the face of appropriate gender norms. Sen. Strom Thurmond (R-SC) expressed outrage at the possibility that Title IX could require gender integration in military academies like the Citadel, which was located in his home state.[76] Despite Senator Bayh's feeble attempts to emphasize that gender equity in college admissions was the primary aim of the law, this line of questioning provided opponents with a mechanism for casting doubt on the propriety of the amendment. By emphasizing the amendment's impact on activities outside of admissions, opponents successfully emphasized Title IX's redistributive effects in a way that piqued the attention of organized interests—namely, sports groups—that would come to dominate Title IX politics.

Once the topic of athletics entered the political discourse, Birch Bayh had a difficult time keeping the Senate focused on the amendment's central objective of ensuring gender equality in higher education by providing women and men with equal access to college admissions. Contesting the germaneness of Title IX to the education reauthorization bill, Strom Thurmond prompted the Senate chair to abruptly end its consideration.[77] This sequence of events marks the point at which sports became a dominant issue in the politics of Title IX. Opponents like Peter Dominick and Strom Thurmond recognized the benefits of emphasizing the potential redistributive effects of Title IX—that it could require schools to reallocate resources for women wishing to play sports and that military schools could be forced to accommodate women and, thus, turn away male applicants. Such arguments resembled earlier objections to the Equal Rights Amendment that invoked a slippery slope of implications, from unisex public restrooms to women in military combat.

The sports issue was a particularly potent point of disagreement because it cast doubt on the amendment while not taking the politically risky approach of directly opposing women's right to equal access to higher education. Once sports became a topic of interest, athletic directors at top programs became concerned. Senator Bayh notes that the athletic directors of Notre Dame and the University of Alabama were among the earliest opponents of Title IX. Expressing fears that the regulation would "destroy" their football programs, they asked the senator to reconsider his support for the bill.[78] As former Office of Civil Rights staff member Valerie Bonnette recalled, "When it became clear that athletics was going to be covered by Title IX in the early 1970s, many people thought it would be the end of college sports as we knew them."[79] Bernice Sandler remembers typical lamentations about the burden that Title IX would place on athletic programs. As a typical argument went, "We have football; we don't have money for an extra program for girls. It's going to cost money, and where are we going to get the money?"[80]

As such, controversy over the sports issue provided opponents with an opportunity to galvanize well-organized interest groups that could mount formidable opposition to Title IX's potential redistributive effects. As more people began to recognize the possible redistributive effects of Title IX and to understand the weight of the reform under consideration, additional resistance surfaced. After the Senate's initial debate and the introduction of the sports issue, the *Washington Post* and the *New York Times* produced multiple editorials in opposition to Title IX.[81] Senator Bayh was unable to raise the issue of sex discrimination in education again in the Senate until February of 1972, when the chamber revisited the omnibus education reauthorization bill.

Taking into account the controversy evoked by the inclusion of military academies under Title IX, Bayh submitted a revised amendment that exempted these institutions from the ban on sex discrimination. In presenting Title IX, Bayh focused on the importance of rectifying one of the last "socially acceptable" forms of discrimination in the United States: "The rationale for denying women an equal education is vague, but its destructive presence is all too clear." He continued:

> We are all familiar with the stereotype of women as pretty things who go to college to find a husband, go on to graduate school because they want a more interesting husband, and finally marry, have children, and

never work again. The desire of many schools not to waste a "man's place" on a woman stems from such stereotyped notions. But the facts absolutely contradict these myths about the "weaker sex" and it is time to change our operating assumptions.[82]

In hopes of preventing his colleagues from scrapping the proposal entirely and to allay concerns that the reach of Title IX would extend beyond the call of ensuring gender equality in college admissions, Senator Bayh accepted a number of exemptions that would shield certain institutions and programs from Title IX regulation. While private undergraduate programs, traditionally sex-segregated institutions like military academies, and single-sex programs like beauty pageants were excluded from Title IX, the regulation would prohibit sex discrimination at all public colleges and universities—which traditionally serviced the vast majority of American undergraduates and enrolled a full 78 percent of college students in 1972—as well as all graduate degree programs.[83] The revisions satisfied his colleagues, and the Senate voted to approve Title IX by a voice vote on February 28, 1972. That same day, the Senate passed its version of the omnibus education reauthorization bill, Title IX and all.

　　Three months later, the House and Senate conference committee worked to reconcile their respective versions of the education reauthorization bill. In the wake of Congress's passage of the Equal Rights Amendment on March 22, 1972, conference committee members devoted careful attention to how their higher education proposals dealt with the issue of sex discrimination. The chief difference between the House version of Title IX and the Senate version of Title IX was that the House version had severely weakened the amendment's power to challenge sex discrimination in higher education by exempting all undergraduate institutions from the regulation. The Senate version, on the other hand, exempted private undergraduate programs but subjected all public undergraduate programs to the regulation. Members of the conference committee managed to strengthen Title IX by adopting the Senate language, thereby subjecting all public undergraduate institutions to the Title IX regulation.[84] Conferees submitted the compromise bill—officially entitled "The Education Amendments of 1972"—to the House and the Senate on May 22 and 23. On May 24, the Senate approved the education reauthorization bill by a vote of 63 to 15, and the House passed it by a vote of 218 to 210.[85]

Regulating Opportunity with Gender-Conscious Higher Education Policy

On June 23, 1972, President Richard Nixon signed the 1972 Education Amendments (PL 92-318) into law. The successful passage of Title IX marked a pivotal moment for US higher education policy: the birth of one of the most significant antidiscrimination policies of the twentieth century and a dramatic shift in US higher education policy. As political scientist Eileen McDonagh and journalist Laura Pappano note, Title IX was intended "to gain for women the educational access that the G.I. Bill paid for and secured for economically disadvantaged men and that Title IV of the Civil Rights Act of 1964 guaranteed successfully to African American men."[86] This brief, unprepossessing paragraph effectively banned sex discrimination in public undergraduate programs and all vocational, graduate, and professional programs receiving federal funding. The only programs not subject to the regulation were private undergraduate programs, schools whose single-sex nature was based on long-standing religious tenets, military schools, social fraternities and sororities, youth programs like Girls and Boys Nation/State, father–son/mother–daughter activities, and beauty pageants.[87]

Departing from the financial aid approach to expanding access to higher education that had long characterized federal higher education policies, Title IX mirrored civil rights legislation, invoking the regulatory powers of the state to reform postsecondary access. In providing women with a legal claim against sex discrimination in higher education, Title IX forever reshaped the nation's colleges and universities and paved the way for a dramatic increase in women's educational attainment after the 1970s. As a result of its passage, overt sex discrimination in college admissions has declined precipitously, and lawmakers institutionalized awareness of women's issues on college campuses across America.[88]

By prohibiting gender quotas and the exclusion of women from public colleges and universities, Title IX significantly increased women's access to higher education. In 1971, the year immediately preceding its adoption, men outnumbered women as students at degree-granting institutions by more than 1.4 million people. By 1977, only five years after the passage of Title IX, the gender gap in college enrollment had narrowed considerably, with male college students outnumbering their female counterparts by fewer than 300,000 people. Six years later, in 1983, women students outnumbered men by more than 400,000 people.

As a result of its role in reforming college admissions, Title IX helped to narrow the gender gap in US higher educational attainment. While only 18 percent of young women and 26 percent of young men had completed at least a bachelor's degree in 1971, that number had increased to 27 percent for both women and men by 1994.[89] Before Title IX's passage in 1972, women received only 9 percent of medical degrees, 7 percent of law degrees, and 1 percent of dental degrees. By 1997, women earned 38 percent of medical degrees, 43 percent of law degrees, and 38 percent of dental degrees.[90]

Noting women's rapidly increasing presence in higher education after the landmark regulation's passage, Title IX expert and former US Department of Education Office of Civil Rights (OCR) staff member Valerie Bonnette recognized the importance of Title IX for achieving rapid progress: "I don't think that the number of women in higher education would be anywhere near what we see today were it not for Title IX." She continued, "I think we would have made progress very, very gradually."[91] Title IX also promoted greater gender equality in faculty hiring and compensation, required fair treatment for pregnant and parenting students, and prohibited sexual harassment in schools. Using the regulatory powers of the state, US lawmakers compelled higher educational institutions to subject women and men to equal treatment.

A New Day: Unbridled Access to Higher Education for Women

In June of 1997, US lawmakers paused to commemorate the twenty-fifth anniversary of Title IX. A quarter century after passing the landmark regulation, lawmakers—and Americans, more broadly—had a great deal to celebrate. The Title IX regulation changed how higher educational institutions treat women. In passing the landmark program, US lawmakers effectively utilized the regulatory power of the state to not only institutionalize gender equality in college admissions but also demonstrate an unprecedented gender consciousness in higher education policy. Unlike the GI Bill, the National Defense Education Act, and the Higher Education Act, which expanded access to college via gender-neutral federal financial aid, Title IX broke with higher education policy precedent by invoking gender-conscious federal regulation to increase women's access to college. In doing so, this landmark policy contributed to an enormous shift in the gender dynamics of US higher educational institutions. Lawmakers affirmed women's status as first-class citizens, demonstrated a commitment to their incorporation as full and equal beneficiaries of the nation's colleges and universities, and set the stage for women to outpace men as the recipients of bachelor's degrees. After Title IX's passage in 1972, the proportion of women attending American colleges and universities increased precipitously, and by 1981, women had surpassed men as the recipients of bachelor's degrees. Speaking on the floor of the House, Rep. Patsy Mink (D-HI) lauded the program that had "opened the doors of educational opportunity to millions of girls and women" by challenging discriminatory admissions policies and by prohibiting discrimination against pregnant and parenting students and girls and women interested in participating in athletics programs.[92]

Title IX marked a dramatic shift in US higher education policy. In the first two decades after World War II, the federal government had focused its higher education efforts on the task of expanding access to college degrees by providing financial aid to students. In the early 1970s, a burgeoning gender consciousness in the political environment and a growing awareness of institutionalized sex discrimination in American colleges and universities fueled a shift in how lawmakers conceptualized barriers to equal opportunity and higher educational access. Shifting their focus from financial need to barriers limiting institutional access, lawmakers reimagined how best to approach the objective of expanding access to higher education. This transformation illustrates Baumgartner and Jones's assertion that US policymaking "is punctuated by bursts of activity that modify issue understandings and lead to non-incremental policy change."[93] No longer was affordability the challenge that prevented equal access to the nation's postsecondary institutions. Rather, discriminatory admissions policies that unfairly limited the number of seats made available to women emerged as the new barrier that required federal attention.

We have seen that the successful passage of civil rights legislation in the years immediately preceding lawmakers' consideration of Title IX yielded a political context in which lawmakers took seriously the problem of discrimination and the value of regulatory policy for addressing institutionally driven inequality. Within this context, policymakers recognized sex discrimination in college admissions as an institutional barrier to equality that constituted an affront to women's status as first-class citizens, as well as the most significant remaining barrier to gender equality in higher education. The success of civil rights policies also provided Rep. Edith Green with a powerful template to use when drafting the ban on sex discrimination. Drawing directly upon the language used in Title VI of the Civil Rights Act of 1964, Green crafted Title IX as an unprepossessing amendment to a large omnibus education reauthorization bill.

Representative Green and her small cadre of political allies developed a political strategy to avert intense opposition against the proposed regulation. Although elite higher educational institutions and their allies in Congress successfully championed exemptions that relieved private undergraduate programs and traditionally single-sexed programs from regulation under Title IX, the amendment successfully compelled women's equal admission to public undergraduate programs—which serve the greatest number of American college students—and all vocational, professional, and graduate programs. As a result, this landmark higher education policy significantly increased women's access to college, paved the way for dramatic increases in women's higher educational attainment, and demonstrated the government's commitment to ensuring full citizenship for women.

Fortunate Sons and Daughters

Financial Aid and the Gender Dynamics of Social Citizenship

> I know in my generation there was just simply no state or federal help
> for women to go [to college]. Families, I think, made the decision that
> if there were limited resources, that money would be spent on the boys
> of the family. I can remember the shock when a brother-in-law of mine,
> as late as the mid-sixties, said, "We've got to save enough money to put
> the two boys through college." I said, "What about Kathy?" He said,
> "Well, she'll get married soon." . . . I think that while education bills can-
> not be labeled as women's issues, they probably had as much or more to
> do with the progress that women have made than anything else.
>   —Rep. Edith Green (D-OR), *1978*[1]

> Learn, baby, learn so you can earn, baby, earn!
>   —Rep. Adam Clayton Powell (D-NY)

For as long as she could remember, Shirley Williams had dreamed of going to
college and becoming a lawyer. Her dreams were dashed in February of 1965
when—only four months shy of graduating from high school—she was forced
to quit school to find work. One of six children growing up in a low-income
Cleveland family, and the eldest daughter living at home, Shirley had fought hard
to juggle schoolwork and the responsibility of helping to care for her younger sib-
lings. When her mother decided that she could no longer afford to support her
teenage daughter, Shirley had no choice but to quit school and find a job. Soon
after, she got married and started a family of her own. By the early 1970s, Shirley
was a divorced mother of three. Struggling to support her family as a single parent, she worked two—sometimes three—jobs that eventually led to a painful
back injury and even hospitalization for exhaustion. More than ever, she wanted
to pursue a college degree. Like many women of her generation who postponed
college degrees until their children were grown, Shirley began to think seriously
about returning to school in 1989, when her youngest child was finishing high
school. Inspired by a longtime friend who had escaped poverty by becoming

a registered nurse in her forties, Shirley set her sights on nursing school. As a low-income student, the availability of government support in the form of Pell Grants and federal Perkins Loans was critical to her ability to pursue a degree. Once enrolled, Shirley focused intensely on her academic work, distinguishing herself as an "A" student, and after two years of hard work, she graduated with an associate's degree in nursing, achieving greater educational attainment, income, and occupational prestige than she or anyone in her immediate family had ever known. Years later, she reminisced about the federal student aid that supported her pursuit of a college degree, saying, "To me, it was my ticket out of poverty."[2]

By treating women and men as the full and equal beneficiaries of US social policy and by helping to remove affordability and institutional discrimination as barriers to higher educational access, the federal student aid programs enacted since the late 1950s signaled a significant change in the tenor of US higher education policy and demonstrated the federal government's commitment to ensuring equal opportunity for women. Upon their passage, the landmark student aid programs established under the National Defense Education Act, the Higher Education Act, and the 1972 Education Amendments were poised to become crucial components of the American welfare state—ones that had the capacity to help usher women into the status of first-class citizenship. Thus far, we have analyzed the process by which US lawmakers created path-breaking higher education programs that offered American women unprecedented support as they pursued college degrees. How effective were these programs in expanding women's access to higher education and, by extension, to the social and economic building blocks of full citizenship? Examining the effectiveness of federal financial aid policies for promoting women's social citizenship by way of increased educational attainment, this chapter examines whether this intent was effectively actualized.

Historically, the difficulty that many American women faced in pursuing higher education posed a significant barrier to their ability to achieve full social citizenship. To become fully incorporated into society, citizens must possess social rights, which include the right to income and the right to education.[3] As T. H. Marshall notes, the achievement of this type of social integration requires the democratization of "material enjoyment," and he highlights the importance of education for spreading "the components of a civilized and cultured life, formerly the monopoly of the few" throughout society.[4] He notes that, among a nation's youngest members, education represents a crucial mechanism for providing future adult citizens with the tools that they need to participate fully in society. Analogously, higher education facilitates full inclusion in society because it promotes socioeconomic well-being among those who gain it.[5] Historically, limited access to college degrees restricted women's access to the knowledge, skills, steady income, and economic independence that are associated with higher educational attainment. Considering the centrality of educational attainment to social citizenship, the difficulty that women faced in obtaining college degrees prior to the passage of landmark federal programs that used redistribution and government regulation in a way that promoted gender equality in higher educational attainment represented a significant barrier to women's achievement of full citizenship in the United States. The knowledge and skills that citizens derive from higher education foster high levels of social and economic stability and independence that, in turn, promote citizens' full incorporation into society.

Higher Education Policy and the Evolution of Women's Citizenship in the United States

Federal financial aid programs like work-study, Pell Grants, and federal student loans set a standard for government support whereby the US government assumed a measure of responsibility for the higher education of its citizens. Since their creation, the availability of federal financial aid has become a pivotal component in the calculus by which many families make decisions regarding their children's education. The availability of financial aid may determine not only where sons and daughters obtain postsecondary training but also whether they pursue higher education in the first place.[6]

Due to the substantial amount of aid provided and the number of students that it assisted, the creation of the GI Bill represents a watershed moment for higher education policy.[7] To be sure, the GI Bill extended government support to a select group of citizens—the overwhelmingly male population of World War II veterans who had been honorably discharged after serving in active duty for at least ninety days. The existence of compulsory military service prior to 1973 meant that the generous benefits of the GI Bill were granted to virtually an entire generation of American men. Indeed, a full 80 percent of men born in the 1920s were military veterans.[8] Through the student financial aid provisions of the GI Bill, the federal government expanded access to college for millions of men who might otherwise not have pursued higher education.

While the GI Bill paved the way to higher education for a considerable number of American men, an extremely small number of women utilized these benefits. Thus, women were largely excluded from early efforts by the federal government to support college students. Women would not experience these benefits en masse until fourteen years later, when lawmakers created federal student loans under the National Defense Education Act of 1958. The gender-egalitarian construction of this program, which provided student loans on the basis of need, effectively extended the federal commitment to supporting college

students while offering women their first broad-reaching opportunity to receive
government financial support for higher education. Subsequently enacted Pell
Grants shared this inclusive approach, thus furthering the trend of gender egalitarianism in government efforts to support college students.[9] Federal student
aid programs were developed with the goal of expanding access to higher education and, thus, promoting Americans' socioeconomic well-being. The question
remains as to whether these programs have actually succeeded in promoting
women's social citizenship by promoting greater educational attainment, higher
economic status, and increased social inclusion.

Scholars have long recognized the value of higher education to Americans'
social and economic well-being. Those who attain college degrees tend to earn
higher annual salaries, and they are more likely to be employed in jobs that
provide employee benefits such as pension plans, paid vacation and sick time,
parental leave, and options for flexible work arrangements. Citizens who attain
higher education are more likely to enjoy high social status, as the human capital gained in colleges and universities may render skills and experiences that
facilitate active civic and political engagement or even translate into advanta-
geous social and professional networks resulting in well-matched marriages,
friendships, and business associations.[10] They are also more likely to vote, to
contribute money to political campaigns, and to volunteer their time for political causes.[11] Considering the many benefits that emanate from the attainment
of a college degree, it seems understandable that Americans have come to view
higher education as a necessity—so much so that families frequently take on significant financial debt to fund postsecondary training for their children.[12]

While scholars recognize the value of higher education to Americans' socioeconomic well-being, we have yet to fully consider the effects that federal higher
education policies have had for gender parity in social citizenship.[13] To what
extent have women taken advantage of federal student aid programs, and have
they enjoyed access to these programs that compares to that of their male counterparts? How has the use of federal student aid programs affected women's socioeconomic status, and might these programs have contributed to the narrowing
of the gender gap in socioeconomic status that we have seen in recent decades?
While existing scholarship has provided valuable insights into the importance of
higher education for citizens' socioeconomic well-being, we have yet to empirically examine the relationship between federal higher education program usage
and gender parity in socioeconomic status. I hypothesize that, like the Social
Security program and Temporary Assistance to Needy Families (TANF)—
programs that are traditionally included under the conceptual umbrella of the
American "welfare state"—federal student aid programs represent a central
mechanism by which the state promotes greater socioeconomic status among

its citizens. Federal financial aid programs are distinct, however, in that they promote greater socioeconomic status not through income support, but by financing undergraduate education. Additionally, this analysis focuses on the gender
dynamics of federal student aid usage and the resulting effects for men's and
women's educational attainment.

The point of departure for this inquiry is the theory of policy feedback, which
contends that public policies have the capacity to alter citizens and the political environment. From this perspective, we consider the possibility that federal
student aid programs have helped citizens attain more education—a possibility that, as we will examine in chapter 7, may facilitate greater gender parity in
political participation. In this chapter, I examine the gender dynamics of federal
higher education program usage and consider the effects of program utilization
for men's and women's educational attainment, which policy feedback scholars
would describe as "resource effects" of policy utilization. The central hypothesis driving this analysis is that while the GI Bill exacerbated gender inequality
in socioeconomic status by expanding educational attainment for men but not
women, subsequently enacted financial aid programs that were broadly accessible to both genders have increased educational attainment for both men and
women and have, thus, promoted greater gender parity in socioeconomic status.
To test this hypothesis, I analyze the gender dynamics of GI Bill, federal student
loan, and Pell Grant usage and the effects of these programs for men's and wom-
en's educational attainment using data from three national surveys. A combination of descriptive statistics and multivariate analysis will permit me to examine
men's and women's higher education policy usage over time and the effects of
program usage for gender equality in educational attainment.

I find that, while the GI Bill significantly expanded men's access to college but
offered very little in the way of support for women interested in pursuing college degrees, federal student loans and Pell Grants have been widely accessible
to both women and men. Although the GI Bill appears to have fostered gender
disparity in educational attainment, I argue that the subsequently enacted financial aid programs promoted greater gender equality in socioeconomic status by
increasing the probability that women will attain advanced levels of education.
By making college more affordable, increasing the amount of time that students
can devote to academic work (as opposed to paid work), and promoting undergraduate degree completion, student financial aid programs constitute central
mechanisms by which US lawmakers have supported equal social citizenship for
women and men. It comes as little surprise that citizens place a great deal of
value in federal student aid programs; and, although they are more recent beneficiaries of direct government aid for education, I find that women assign particularly high value to these programs.

Data and Research Methods

Using data from three national surveys—the Social and Governmental Issues and Participation (SGIP) study (n = 1,400), the National Postsecondary Student Aid Study (NPSAS) (n = 137,800), and the Cooperative Institutional Research Program (CIRP) Freshmen Trends Archive (n ≈ 200,000)—this chapter uses empirical analysis to examine the gender dynamics of federal financial aid access and the impact that higher education policies have had on a central dependent variable: educational attainment for women and men. Each of these datasets offers unique insights into federal financial aid utilization and its effects. The CIRP Freshman survey provides data on the usage of federal student aid programs by men and women in their first year of college, while the NPSAS offers data on student aid usage for all enrolled college students. These datasets are especially useful for understanding trends in students' usage of federal financial aid over time. While CIRP and NPSAS data are limited to undergraduate students, the SGIP dataset provides data for a representative sample of Americans between the ages of eighteen and ninety-two. These data are especially valuable to this chapter's analysis because they not only permit us to consider higher education policy utilization for citizens born between the years of 1916 and 1990 but also enable us to use inferential statistical tools to empirically examine the relationship between financial aid policy usage and educational attainment.

The analysis that follows will proceed in two parts. The first stage explores descriptive statistics to understand general trends in the gender dynamics of federal student aid usage. I begin by using multivariate regression to investigate the determinants of financial aid usage. The dependent variable in these regression models—policy utilization—is measured using three dichotomous variables that correspond to whether or not (1 for an affirmative response, 0 for a negative response) respondents have used any federal student aid program, GI Bill benefits, federal student loans, or Pell Grants.[14] These models control for age, race, childhood socioeconomic status, and mother's educational attainment—independent variables that have been documented as strong predictors of social policy utilization.[15] Of particular interest to this analysis is the effect that gender has on program usage. To evaluate this effect, I include gender as the key independent variable in these models.

After considering who uses higher education programs and the factors shaping whether a student will or will not use federal student aid, I use a difference-in-differences analysis to examine the effect that eligibility for aid provided by the National Defense Education Act and the Higher Education Act has had on men's and women's college degree completion. I also consider the influence that the Title IX regulation has had on the gender dynamics of higher educational attainment. To measure respondents' highest level of completed education, I use an ordinal variable that is coded on a six-part scale: (1) less than high school, (2) high school diploma/GED, (3) technical school or some college, (4) two-year degree, (5) four-year degree, and (6) postbaccalaureate study/graduate or professional degree. To measure GI Bill, student loan, and Pell Grant utilization, the central independent variables of interest, I use the aforementioned dichotomous variables (coded as 1 for policy utilization, 0 for no policy utilization). I also include numerous variables representing additional indicators that scholars have shown to be significant determinants of educational attainment. Studies have shown that demographic and socioeconomic factors may shape educational attainment differently for women and men.[16] As such, I incorporate gender-separated models throughout this analysis, which permit me to examine the influence of these independent variables on educational attainment separately for women and men. To account for the influence of age on educational attainment, I include a variable measuring age in years (from eighteen to ninety-two). I expect older men and women to have significantly lower levels of educational attainment than their younger counterparts due to the dramatic increase in Americans' attainment of college degrees that we have seen in recent years. Because men enjoyed access to GI Bill benefits at higher rates than women, I suspect that older women will be significantly less likely than their male counterparts to attain high levels of education.

Scholars studying the relationship between race and educational attainment have found contradictory results when comparing white Americans with black Americans. Compared to whites of comparable status, one study found that blacks are somewhat more likely to attend college than their white counterparts.[17] A later study, on the other hand, revealed no significant differences in the educational attainment of blacks and whites who hail from similar socioeconomic backgrounds.[18] The relationship between race and educational attainment is similarly complex for Latinos. For this group of Americans, scholars have found that educational attainment tends to differ significantly according to ethnic groupings. Research has shown that Mexicans, for example, are significantly less likely than other Latinos to complete college degrees.[19] To control for the effects of race, I include two dichotomous variables that correspond to whether respondents identify as black (1 if black, 0 if white) or Hispanic (1 if Hispanic, 0 if white).

Other scholars have argued that socioeconomic background provides the strongest predictor of college attendance and graduation, as students from less privileged backgrounds are the most disadvantaged when it comes to higher educational access.[20] Research has shown that higher levels of parental income and wealth promote children's completion of bachelor's degrees.[21] To operationalize socioeconomic status, I include control variables for childhood socioeconomic status (five-point scale of family income compared to others at age sixteen, ranging from "far below average" to "far above average") and mother's educational attainment (nine-point scale ranging from "less than high school" to "PhD or professional degree").

Public policy scholars often find it difficult to isolate and control for endogenous personality characteristics that may bias observed relationships between independent variables and policy utilization. The CIRP Freshman survey data are particularly useful for addressing this challenge, as this data source includes measures that permit me to construct an index to control for ambitious personality characteristics that may condition whether individuals use federal student aid. This "go-getter" index consists of five parts: students' self-assessments of their (1) drive to achieve, (2) leadership ability, (3) competitiveness, (4) intellectual self-confidence, and (5) social self-confidence. For each variable, respondents rate themselves in relation to their peers (responses are on a five-point scale, ranging from "lowest 10%" to "highest 10%"). I suspect that having a "go-getter" personality will significantly increase the probability that men and women will use federal student aid but that controlling for this variable will not mitigate the influence of demographic and socioeconomic factors.

The Usage of Higher Education Policies

For the lawmakers who had championed federal financial aid programs, these policies represented an important tool for strengthening citizens' socioeconomic status by increasing their access to higher education. They believed that, by helping to make college more affordable, the government could expand educational opportunity in a way that permits more citizens to complete postsecondary degrees and to enjoy the social and economic benefits—such as increased income, financial stability, and greater social status—that they frequently yield. From that perspective, increasing access to higher education has been framed as a democratic imperative. Opening debate on the first federal student loan programs in 1957, Rep. Carl Elliott (D-AL) argued that "America's future success at home and abroad, in peace or war, depends on the education of her citizens. Democracy is based on that foundation. Whatever happens in America's classrooms during the next 50 years will eventually happen to America."[22] Eight years later, when lawmakers debated proposals for the Higher Education Act of 1965, US Education Commissioner Frances Keppell testified as to the necessity of federal support for increasing access to higher education.[23] Thus, the GI Bill, federal student loans, and Pell Grants were developed with the intention of substantially expanding access to higher education.

How effective have these programs been for achieving this end? This analysis considers the role that federal student aid programming has played in increasing

Americans' access to college and whether these programs have promoted gender equality in higher educational attainment since the 1950s. In examining this potential resource effect of federal student aid utilization, we must first consider the gender dynamics of historical trends in student aid usage. Have women and men taken advantage of federal education benefits at equitable rates, or has one gender tended to use financial aid at higher rates than the other? What determines higher education policy usage, and how valuable are these programs to beneficiaries? Given that the GI Bill disproportionately benefited men and the fact that women were infrequent beneficiaries of its generous education aid during the postwar era, I posit that federal student aid usage was an overwhelmingly male phenomenon prior to the advent of the National Defense Student Loan (NDSL) program in 1958. It seems plausible that the number of women receiving federal student aid increased substantially in the 1960s and continued to increase after 1965, with the creation of the need-based federal Pell Grant Program and the Guaranteed Student Loan (GSL) program. Unlike National Defense Student Loans, the GSL program guaranteed low-interest federal loans to students enrolled in accredited US higher educational institutions, irrespective of financial need.[24] Thus, I predict that this loan program also increased higher educational access for women and men, this time expanding opportunities for those who need financial support but who do not pass the means tests associated with the need-based programs. To assess the validity of these expectations, I begin by examining data indicating trends in overall financial aid usage and then consider data corresponding to each respective program.

Trends in Overall Federal Student Aid Usage

In assessing the relationship between financial aid utilization and higher educational attainment, understanding the reach of federal student aid is just as important as understanding its effects. The effectiveness with which the GI Bill, student loans, and Pell Grants have expanded educational opportunity is contingent upon how accessible these programs have been to Americans. Thus, the point of departure for this analysis is the question of whether women and men have historically enjoyed equitable access to federal student aid. I hypothesize that data will confirm scholars' finding that the GI Bill provided a significant source of educational support for American men—especially those in the most senior age cohorts.[25] I posit that student loans and Pell Grants, on the other hand, have been broadly accessible to both women and men because they have been constructed around the nongendered bases of need and college enrollment. Because these programs have been allocated without regard to military service or any such heavily gendered criterion, it stands to reason that women and men have been equally likely to take advantage of benefits in recent decades.

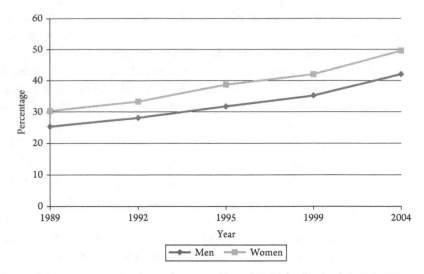

Figure 6.1 Percentage of undergraduates receiving federal financial aid, 1989–2004.
Note: For each of these years, the gender difference is statistically significant at α = 0.01. *Source*: US
Department of Education, National Postsecondary Student Aid Study (NPSAS).

Considering the gender dynamics of overall federal student aid program
usage in recent decades, Figure 6.1 shows the percentage of male and female
undergraduates receiving federal financial aid for select years.[26] Over the fifteen years presented, we see that the proportion of women and men who use
any type of federal student aid increased steadily, with women consistently
taking advantage of federal benefits at higher rates than men. Contrary to my
prediction that women and men will take advantage of federal student loans
and Pell Grants—the preponderance of federal aid offered in the years considered in this figure—at equal rates, we see that women have taken advantage of
benefits at higher rates than men in recent decades. From 1989 through 2004,
a statistically significant gender gap characterized federal student aid utilization; the proportion of undergraduate men reporting that they benefited from
student aid programs trailed that of women by an average of 6 percentage
points.[27]

Although women have used federal financial aid at higher rates than men in
recent decades, cohort analysis reveals that this was not always the case. Figure
6.2, which shows the percentage of Americans who have used federal student
aid by age cohort, offers an idea of the gender dynamics of financial aid utilization over time.[28] In accordance with my expectations, a broad and highly
significant gender gap in student aid utilization characterizes financial aid
usage among the most senior cohort of Americans, who were born between
1916 and 1934. This sharp difference in policy usage, I believe, reflects the
broad access to GI Bill benefits that men in this cohort of Americans enjoyed

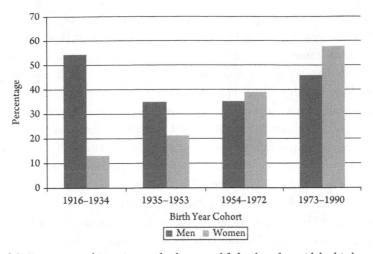

Figure 6.2 Percentage of Americans who have used federal student aid, by birth year cohort. *Notes:* These gender differences are statistically significant at α = 0.05 for the 1973–1990 cohort, at α = 0.01 for the 1935–1953 birth year cohort, and at α = 0.001 for the 1916–1934 birth year cohort. The gender gap for the 1954–1972 cohort is not statistically significant. *Source:* The Social and Governmental Issues and Participation (SGIP) study.

as they pursued higher education, in contrast to the extremely limited availability of federal aid for women in this group who pursued higher education. While 54.3 percent of all men born between 1916 and 1934 report having used federal student aid, only 13 percent of women born between these years report having done so. Men in the slightly younger cohort of Americans born between 1935 and 1953 are also significantly more likely to have used federal student aid than women in that age cohort. Approximately 34.8 percent of men in that group have used government benefits for higher education, compared to 21.2 percent of women. While men in the most senior cohorts of Americans are significantly more likely to have been the beneficiaries of federal student aid, this tendency does not hold for younger cohorts of Americans who were born between 1954 and 1990. For men and women born between 1954 and 1972, women are slightly more likely to use federal student aid benefits than men: 38.9 percent of women and 35.1 percent of men used student aid benefits. Among the youngest Americans who were born between 1973 and 1990, women are significantly more likely to report having used federal student aid than men: 57.7 percent of women born between 1973 and 1990 have used government financial support for higher education, compared to 45.8 percent of men in this age group.[29]

In accordance with my expectations, data suggest that federal student aid has provided a significant source of support for American undergraduates and that the dynamics of aid utilization vary according to age. Among men and women born between 1916 and 1953, who would most likely have begun college prior to 1972—the year that marked the creation of Pell Grants and the establishment of the Student Loan Marketing Association (Sallie Mae)—men are significantly more likely than women to have benefited from financial aid. For this group, only 17.3 percent of women report that they have received federal student aid benefits, while 35.8 percent of men report having done so. This contrasts sharply with the gender dynamics of financial aid receipt for the more junior cohorts of Americans who would likely have attended college after 1972. Data confirm that, since the mid-twentieth century, a significant portion of American women have joined men as the beneficiaries of federal student aid. As Figure 6.2 shows, women born after 1954—who fall between the ages of eighteen and fifty-four—use financial aid benefits at higher rates than their male counterparts: 43.7 percent of women have used federal student aid, compared to 38.4 percent of men. The absence of a significant difference in student aid utilization for men and women born between 1954 and 1972 signifies a period of gender parity in education policy usage; for the most junior cohort of Americans born between 1973 and 1990, we find that women are significantly more likely to benefit from federal aid than men.

Since the mid-1980s, the average amount of federal aid received by American undergraduates has increased steadily. This escalating amount likely reflects the ever-increasing cost of attending college in the United States. Although younger women are significantly more likely to use federal student aid than their male counterparts, men have received slightly greater amounts of student aid than women in recent years.[30] This difference may reflect the fact that women outnumber men as part-time students and as enrollees in two-year programs. Because the amount of aid awarded from means-tested programs reflects both student need and institutional costs, women's overrepresentation in these lower-cost programs may affect their average award amounts.[31]

Another possibility for the observation that men tend to receive higher amounts of financial aid than women is that men may still be more likely than women to receive veterans' benefits for higher education. Three percent of American undergraduates were veterans in the 2007–2008 academic year. Of those students, 73.1 percent were male, and 26.9 were female.[32] Although it is difficult to identify one particular cause for the observation that men tend to receive somewhat higher amounts of federal aid than women, women's greater presence in less costly postsecondary programs and the fact that men continue to make up the majority of GI Bill beneficiaries may contribute to this trend. In line with my expectations, overall higher education program utilization has increased in recent decades, as has the amount of federal aid awarded to students. Data from the US Department of Education's NPSAS and the Social and

Governmental Issues and Participation Study suggest that federal student aid has reached an increasing proportion of American undergraduates over time. Moreover, these data indicate that there has been a significant shift in the gender dynamics of policy utilization since the mid-twentieth century.

The Gender Dynamics of Federal Student Aid Usage

For the generation of Americans who defended the nation during World War II, the federal government offered a variety of benefits that promoted socioeconomic well-being. The prevalence of higher education policy usage among the men of this generation is striking. As we have seen, men born between 1916 and 1934 report having received federal student aid at dramatically higher rates than their female counterparts. Although the gender gap is not quite as impressive for the cohort of Americans born between 1935 and 1953, the trend holds: men are significantly more likely to have received federal support for funding higher education. Prior to the creation of federal student loans in 1958, the GI Bill was the only federal program that offered financial aid to college students. After its creation in 1944, more than 2 million citizens took advantage of GI Bill benefits, costing the federal government more than $5.5 billion.[33] Given the existence of conscription and the highly gendered nature of military service during the World War II era, it comes as no surprise that these veterans' benefits were awarded overwhelmingly to men. Of the 2.2 million World War II veterans who used the GI Bill to pursue college degrees, fewer than 65,000—a mere 3 percent—were women.[34] The significance of the GI Bill in promoting high levels of male enrollments in US colleges and universities in the postwar era is clear, as veterans made up approximately 70 percent of the male population in America's postsecondary institutions.[35]

Figure 6.3 reports GI Bill, student loan, and Pell Grant usage among men and women across age cohorts using data from the SGIP Study.[36] As we can see, the GI Bill provided financial support for generations of men pursuing college education, and its effects were particularly important for men born between 1916 and 1934.[37] For this group of men, 58.6 percent took advantage of the GI Bill. Although men in successive birth year cohorts have also benefited from GI Bill benefits, these proportions are considerably smaller: for men born between 1935 and 1953, 27.4 percent report receiving GI Bill benefits. Although the GI Bill has provided valuable support for generations of veterans pursuing higher education, it was particularly important to the most senior cohort of American men whose large numbers likely reflect the existence of military conscription during World War II and the Korean War. This program represents the original, albeit gender-biased, foundation of federal support for college students.

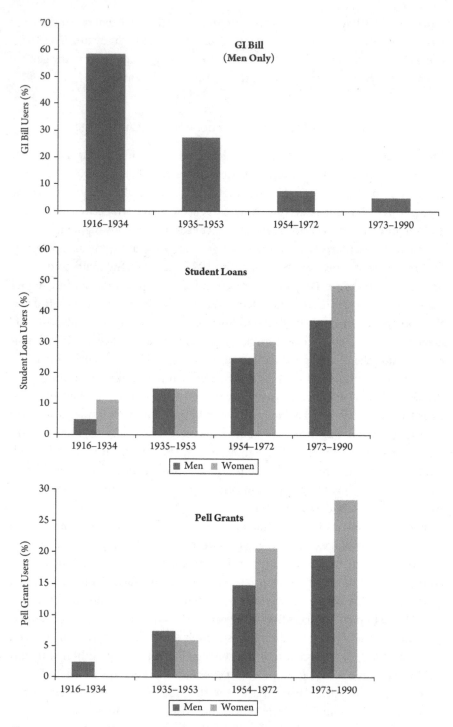

Figure 6.3 Federal financial aid utilization by birth year cohort. *Notes:* The gender differences in student loan and Pell Grant use for the 1973–1990 cohort are statistically significant at $\alpha = 0.05$. The remaining gender differences are not statistically significant. *Source:* The Social and Governmental Issues and Participation (SGIP) study.

If the creation of the GI Bill is distinctive because it initiated federal support for financing higher education while providing aid to a considerable number of men as they pursued college education, the creation of federal student loans is equally significant because it dramatically altered the gender dynamics of federal student aid utilization. Since the creation of federally subsidized student loans in 1958 and their expansion in subsequent years, student loans have become the dominant source of government support for both male and female college students. Thus, the creation of federal student loans marked the dawning of an altered, gender-egalitarian commitment to Americans pursuing postsecondary training. Data from the CIRP Freshman survey reveal that the percentage of men and women receiving NDSLs (popularly known as "Perkins Loans") during their first year of college has generally increased since the 1980s.[38] Between 1974 and 1998, on average, 12.7 percent of female college freshmen and 12.2 percent of male freshmen used NDSL benefits. Through most of the program's history, women received benefits at a slightly higher rate than men.

Like need-based loans, federal loans granted without regard to students' financial means have become increasingly available to men and women since the 1970s. Although women have tended to use need-based Perkins Loans at higher rates than men, men have been slightly more likely to use GSLs (popularly known as "Stafford Loans"), which are broadly targeted to students enrolled in accredited postsecondary institutions.[39] In 1974, 12.6 percent of male college freshmen reported that they received Guaranteed Student Loan benefits, compared to 11.4 percent of women. By 1989, 45 percent of women and 42.5 percent of men received Stafford Loans.[40] In less than twenty-five years, the proportion of men and women using non-need-based loans increased from approximately 10 percent to more than 40 percent, demonstrating an increased willingness of families across the income spectrum to borrow money to finance higher education.

Given the growth of student loan utilization in the years following the creation of the NDSL and GSL programs, it comes as little surprise that more recent data point to steady increases in the proportion of men and women benefiting from federal student loans. In a continuation of the aforementioned trends, more recent data from the National Postsecondary Student Aid Study indicate that the proportion of men and women using student loans has increased substantially in recent decades.[41] Among all undergraduates in 1989, 18 percent of women and 16.3 percent of men received federal student loans. By 2008, the percentage of female college students receiving federal student loans had increased to 37.6 percent, and the proportion of men using federal student loans reached 30.8 percent.

Cohort analysis of student loan utilization among all Americans corroborates this finding that student loan usage has increased considerably in recent decades.

Figure 6.3 reveals that student loan utilization increases as respondents' birth years ascend. In other words, the most junior cohorts of Americans use federal student loans at higher rates than their more senior counterparts. For men and women born in the 1916–1934 cohort, the 1954–1972 cohort, and the 1973–1990 cohort, a greater percentage of women report having used federal student loans than men.[42] Although these gender differences for the most senior cohorts of Americans do not reach statistical significance, women in the most junior cohort—those born between 1973 and 1990—are significantly more likely to use student loans than their male counterparts.[43] Overall, this evidence supports my expectation that federal student loans have been broadly accessible to both women and men. They also suggest that, in recent decades, this type of financial aid has become a particularly important source of support for women pursuing college degrees.

Pell Grants represent the other part of the newer, gender-egalitarian efforts of the federal government to expand access to postsecondary education. Data from the CIRP Freshman survey suggest that this program has worked in concert with student loans to promote greater access to higher education for American women and men. In the years following the creation of Pell Grants, the need-based program consistently provided financial aid for one-quarter to one-third of male and female college freshmen.[44] With the exception of 1974—when 24.7 percent of male freshmen and 23.6 percent of female freshmen received Pell Grants—women took advantage of Pell Grants at slightly higher rates than their male counterparts. By 1998, 32.6 percent of female college freshmen and 29.2 percent of male freshmen benefited from Pell Grants.[45] Overall, the percentage of men and women using Pell Grants remained steady in the years immediately following the program's creation. These data suggest that, per my expectations, federal Pell Grants have provided a significant source of financial support for students pursuing college degrees. Further, evidence supports the notion that—like federal student loans—the benefits of this program have been widely accessible to both male and female citizens.

Because of the means-tested nature of Pell Grant eligibility and the significant percentage of women and men who use benefits, evidence suggests that this program has successfully expanded access to higher education for citizens from less privileged socioeconomic backgrounds. Cohort analysis of SGIP survey data, as seen in Figure 6.3, reveals that Pell Grant utilization has been most prevalent among the youngest cohorts of American women and men. For Americans born after 1953, Pell Grants have provided a particularly important source of financial aid for women. Among those born between 1916 and 1953, relatively small proportions report having received Pell Grants. Consider the most senior cohort of Americans surveyed. For men and women born between 1916 and 1934, only 2.5 percent of men received Pell Grants, and no women benefited from the program. Among those born between 1935 and 1953, 7.3 percent of men report having used Pell Grants, compared to 5.9 percent of women.

A significant shift occurs for the cohorts born after 1953. For these groups, considerably greater percentages of respondents received Pell Grants, and women report using benefits at higher rates than their male counterparts. While 20.6 percent of women born between 1954 and 1972 indicate that they have received Pell Grants, 14.7 percent of men in this birth cohort indicate that they have benefited from the need-based grants. Similarly, for citizens born between 1973 and 1990, 28.4 percent of women report that they have used Pell Grants, compared to 19.6 percent of men.[46] These data suggest that citizens' usage of Pell Grants resembles that of student loans. In the decades after the program's creation, increasing proportions of men and women took advantage of benefits. Also, in recent years women have used program benefits at significantly higher rates than their male counterparts. Pell Grants have been integral to promoting equal educational opportunity for low-income men and women—especially those born after 1953.

Now that we have a sense of historical trends in GI Bill, student loan, and Pell Grant usage; the accessibility of each respective program; and the gender dynamics that characterize policy usage, we can consider the determinants of financial aid utilization.

Determinants of Federal Student Aid Usage

Thus far, we have seen that the gendered nature of GI Bill eligibility meant that this program, which provided the first federal financial aid for college students, was accessible primarily to men and was heavily used by those born between 1916 and 1934. The benefits of the federal student loan and Pell Grant programs that emerged after 1958 were allocated on the basis of gender-neutral criteria and, thus, were equally accessible to both women and men. The creation of student loans and Pell Grants heralded the birth of a new, gender-egalitarian support for higher education in which women enjoyed access to federal support for the pursuit of higher education along with men. Given what we have observed about the dynamics of men's and women's access to federal student aid, the question remains as to the determinants of higher education program usage. When financial aid is available, what determines whether someone will actually use it?

A primary objective of the GI Bill was to reward World War II veterans for their military service by offering generous financial support for those pursuing higher education. Thus, it seems plausible that gender and age—characteristics that we have identified as strong correlates of program utilization—would be significant predictors of GI Bill usage. Because so few women received benefits under this program in the postwar era, it would stand to reason that men are significantly more likely to use this program than women. Among men, I suspect that survey respondents who are older—and who are more likely to have served during military conflicts and to have been subject to the military draft—would be more likely to use these benefits than their younger counterparts.

While lawmakers created the GI Bill to reward military service, their original objective in providing student loans and their sustained purpose for providing Pell Grants was extending higher educational opportunity to capable but financially needy men and women. Thus, I predict that socioeconomic background will provide a strong determinant of student loan and Pell Grant utilization. For men and women from families with limited financial resources, I suspect that these federal programs offer benefits that are particularly attractive because they make higher education more affordable. Because student loans and Pell Grants represent the newest components of the federal government's student aid provisions, I suspect that age will also provide a significant predictor of policy utilization. While the benefits of the GI Bill were most accessible to older men, student loans and Pell Grants were targeted broadly to women and men. In recent years, federally subsidized student loans have come to replace grants as the government's preferred mechanism for aiding students. As a result, it seems plausible that younger Americans would be significantly more likely to take advantage of student loan benefits than older citizens.

In addition to socioeconomic background and age, I hypothesize that gender represents a significant determinant of student loan and Pell Grant utilization. Although these programs were made broadly available to both women and men, the possibility remains that families factor gender into the calculus that governs whether they allocate limited financial resources for the higher education of their sons and daughters. Echoing this chapter's introductory quote, Robert Hardesty, then-president of Southwest Texas State University and a former speechwriter for President Lyndon Jonson, recalled:

> If your parents were poor, you just didn't aspire to a higher education, unless you were lucky enough to receive one of the few private scholarships available. And if your parents were willing and able to scrimp and do without personal comforts to save enough money for a college education, it usually went to the son, not to the daughter.[47]

Policymakers, educational leaders, and economists alike have recognized that families historically incorporated gender into their decisions regarding economic investment in their children's education.[48] Many families have been dubious about spending limited funds to educate daughters who would presumably exit the labor force upon marriage. To avoid "wasting" money in this type of imprudent investment, some families reserved funds for sons who—in preparing for their roles as husbands and fathers—would use higher education to segue into stable and lucrative careers that would permit them to support their own families. If this is the case, federal student loans and Pell Grants may represent an important source of financial support for women—especially those from less advantaged socioeconomic backgrounds—who may be less likely to procure private resources to fund higher education.

For the logistic regression and ordinary least squares (OLS) regression results that I present throughout this chapter, I have used Clarify Software for STATA to estimate the substantive effects of statistically significant predictors on the outcome variable in corresponding models.[49] If, for example, gender provides a statistically significant variable in a model predicting GI Bill usage, Clarify makes it possible to gauge the magnitude of the effect that being male as opposed to female has on the probability of using the program. These probabilities are expressed as percentage-point increases or decreases. Each analysis includes only Americans who have obtained at least a high school diploma or a GED, as this level of education represents a fundamental requirement of federal student aid eligibility.

I use binary logistic regression analysis to consider the determinants of higher education policy usage among Americans who have earned at least a high school diploma or its equivalent.[50] In line with my expectations, the analysis indicates that gender and age provide statistically significant predictors of GI Bill utilization. Clarify results suggest that women are 10 percentage points less likely than men to use GI Bill benefits, and a man who was born in 1935 is 9 percentage points more likely to have used GI Bill benefits than a man who was born in 1972. These findings underscore the importance of the GI Bill for men and for more senior Americans, supporting previous evidence pointing to substantial GI Bill usage among men during the postwar era. The lack of statistical significance among the model's remaining coefficients suggests that race, childhood socioeconomic status, and mother's education offer little explanation for GI Bill use. Given that GI Bill benefits have been provided without means tests and on the basis of military service, the insignificance of demographic predictors is understandable.

When we consider the determinants of student loan usage among Americans, we find that survey data support my initial expectation that gender, age, and race would provide significant predictors of policy utilization. Gender represents a statistically significant predictor of student loan utilization, as women are more likely to use this program than men. When we consider the substantive effect of gender on student loan usage, we find that women are 8 percentage points more likely to use federal student loans than men. We also find that older Americans are significantly less likely than younger Americans to have received loans. Compared to someone who was born in 1972 (who would have been thirty-six years old in 2008), a citizen born in 1935 (who would have been seventy-three years old in 2008) is 27 percentage points less likely to have benefited from federal student loans. Like gender and age, race provides an additional factor that significantly shapes student loan utilization. Being African American corresponds to a 12-percentage-point increase in the probability of using student loans.[51] These results suggest that federal student loans have provided a particularly important source of aid for women and African Americans—groups that have borne much of the burden of US socioeconomic inequality—as they pursue college degrees. Additionally, these results confirm earlier evidence that student loans have been widely used among younger Americans, suggesting that the growing availability of student loans has been met with substantial usage among young citizens.

Consistent with my expectations and mirroring the findings for models predicting student loan usage, regression analysis indicates that gender, age, and race provide significant predictors of Pell Grant utilization. When we consider the effect of gender on Pell Grant utilization, survey data indicate that women are significantly more likely to receive this type of aid than men. Results suggest that women are 6 percentage points more likely than men to have benefited from Pell Grants. We also find that age has a considerable effect on whether Americans have taken advantage of Pell Grants. For example, a citizen who was born in 1935 is 15 percentage points less likely to have used Pell Grants than a citizen who was born in 1972. When we consider the significant effect of race on Pell Grant utilization, we find that being African American is associated with a 7-percentage-point increase in the probability that a citizen will use program benefits. In addition to gender, age, and race, this model also reveals that childhood socioeconomic status provides a significant predictor of Pell Grant usage. This contrasts with the statistically insignificant relationship between childhood socioeconomic status and student loan utilization. Moving from a childhood socioeconomic status that is "far below average" to one that is "far above average" yields a 9-percentage-point decrease in the probability of using Pell Grants. The significant effects of childhood socioeconomic status for Pell Grant utilization may reflect the means-tested nature of this program. Although Perkins Loans are need based, Stafford Loans are not; thus, socioeconomic background may not offer as robust a predictor of student loan usage as it does for Pell Grant receipt.

Moving beyond this focus on the determinants of usage for individual financial aid programs, examining the determinants of using any type of higher education benefits allows us to gain an overall sense of the factors that influence citizens' use of the policies. Results suggest that age, race, and childhood socioeconomic status emerge as central factors shaping financial aid utilization. Compared to those born in 1972, citizens born in 1935 are 21 percentage points less likely to have taken advantage of federal higher education programs.

Although race and childhood socioeconomic status have more modest substantive effects for the probability of using federal student aid, both of these variables influence the likelihood of using student aid programs. Compared to their white counterparts, black Americans are 12 percentage points more likely to use federal student aid. For socioeconomic background, we find that shifting childhood socioeconomic status from "far below average" to "far above average" corresponds to a 12-percentage-point decrease in the probability that a citizen will take advantage of federal student aid.

Overall, these results suggest that gender represents an important determinant of federal student aid usage and that its effect varies by student aid program. While women are significantly less likely than men to have taken advantage of GI Bill benefits, they are significantly more likely to use student loans and Pell Grants. Although older Americans are significantly more likely to use GI Bill benefits, federal student aid usage is significantly more prevalent among younger citizens, as they are more likely to use student loans and Pell Grants. We also see that African Americans and citizens from less privileged socioeconomic backgrounds are more likely to use federal student aid.

Binary regression analysis of the determinants of policy usage for women and men separately reveals similarly interesting findings.[52] When we consider only men, we find that age represents a significant determinant of GI Bill utilization: compared to a man who was born in 1972, a man born in 1935 is 35 percentage points more likely to have benefited from the GI Bill. We find that race, childhood socioeconomic status, and mother's education are not predictors of GI Bill utilization. This corroborates my prediction that the GI Bill's military service–based targeting rendered these demographic and socioeconomic characteristics less consequential than they would prove for citizens' use of subsequently enacted federal student aid programs. The gender-disaggregated findings generally echo the finding that demographic factors shape student loan utilization. For both men and women, those who are younger and those who are African American are significantly more likely to use student loans than older respondents and those who are white. When we compare more senior citizens to their younger counterparts, we find that men who were born in 1935 are 20 percentage points less likely to have used federal student loans than men who were born in 1972. For women, those born in 1935 are 33 percentage points less likely to have used federal student loans. Race is another demographic factor that shapes student loan utilization for women and men. For both genders, blacks are 12 percentage points more likely to use student loans than whites. Moving beyond demographic factors, we find that mother's educational attainment provides an additional significant predictor of student loan usage for men but not women. Data suggest that men whose mothers have more education are more likely to use student loans: increasing the educational attainment of a man's mother from a high school diploma to a four-year degree corresponds to an 8-percentage-point increase in the probability that he will use student loans.

What about the determinants of Pell Grant usage for men and women? As was the case for student loans, multivariate analysis suggests that older men and women are significantly less likely to take advantage of Pell Grants than those who are younger. Compared to those born in 1972, men born in 1935 are 8 percentage points less likely to be Pell Grant users. In an analogous comparison, we find that age has an even greater effect on whether women use Pell Grants. Compared to women born in 1972, those born in 1935 are 22 percentage points less likely to be Pell Grant beneficiaries. While race does not provide a significant determinant of whether men use Pell Grants, it appears to have significant effects for whether women use this program. We find that black women are 10 percentage points more likely to take advantage of Pell Grants than white women. While race influences program usage for women but not men, the reverse is true for socioeconomic background. Childhood socioeconomic status provides a significant predictor of men's Pell Grant usage: shifting a man's childhood socioeconomic status from "far below average" to "far above average" yields a 15-percentage-point decrease in the probability that he will have used Pell Grants.

Finally, we consider the variables shaping overall financial aid usage for women and men. Perhaps a reflection of the fact that men have consistently benefited from federal financial aid programs since their creation in the 1940s, age appears to have no significant effect on whether men use federal education benefits. For women, on the other hand, age represents a strong predictor of student aid utilization. Older women are significantly less likely to have benefited from federal financial education aid programs. Compared to a woman born in 1972, a woman born in 1935 is 37 percentage points less likely to have used any federal student aid. We also see that race significantly predicts financial aid policy usage for both women and men. Data suggest that blacks are significantly more likely to have taken advantage of federal student aid and that black men are 16 percentage points more likely than white men to use federal student aid, while black women are 11 percentage points more likely than white women to use these benefits. As these data indicate, demographic factors—particularly age and race—provide the strongest determinants of whether men and women use federal student aid.

Data from the 1998 CIRP Freshman survey corroborate these findings and suggest that demographic factors shape student aid utilization, even when we control for endogenous personality traits that could presumably shape whether individuals use federal student aid. Here, I use binary logistic regression analysis to predict higher education policy utilization among college freshmen.[53] The analysis suggests that women, African Americans, those whose parents have less income, those whose mothers have less education, and those who could be described as having ambitious, "go-getter" personalities are significantly more likely to use federal student aid. For both women and men, race (black) and having a "go-getter" personality are positively and significantly associated with higher education policy utilization. Parents' income and mother's education are significantly, but negatively, associated with using federal financial aid programs.

Overall, these findings suggest that, while American men are significantly more likely than women to have used GI Bill benefits, women are more likely to have used student loans and Pell Grants. Among men, GI Bill utilization is most prevalent among those who are older. In contrast, the benefits of federal student loans and Pell Grants have been significantly more available to younger citizens—both women and men. With the creation of the GI Bill in 1944, the federal government provided higher educational support for a generation of American men. Women, however, were excluded from this experience. By creating the federal student loan and Pell Grant programs, the US government provided financial support that would reach both women and men. These findings support my expectation that the creation of federal student loans and Pell Grants marked the emergence of a federal commitment to promoting greater educational attainment among women and men.

The Fortunate Ones?: How Student Aid Beneficiaries Think About Federal Education Program Usage

How do the beneficiaries of federal student aid view their usage of these programs? Central to this consideration of how program participants think about their use of education policies is whether they recognize student aid benefits as part of government social programming. According to Paul Pierson, traceability "involves two distinct tests: can visible outcomes be linked to government policy and can those policies be linked to someone who can be given credit or blame?"[54] For student financial aid policies, are women and men equally likely to trace these benefits to the federal government? I suspect that men—many of whom received generous GI Bill benefits from the state as a token of gratitude for military service—may be more likely than women to trace federal education policies to the government.

As shown in Table 6.1, we see that GI Bill beneficiaries appear to be acutely aware that program benefits were government social provisions. Sixty percent of GI Bill users trace program benefits to the federal government, while 57 percent of Pell Grant beneficiaries and 48 percent of student loan beneficiaries do so. Of the GI Bill, student loans, and Pell Grants, male beneficiaries are most likely to recognize the GI Bill as a government social program. Sixty-one percent of men who use the GI Bill confirm that they "have used a government social program,"

Table 6.1 **Recognition of Government Program Receipt Among Program Participants, by Gender**

	Percentage of Higher Education Program Recipients Saying: "*Yes, I Have Used a Government Social Program*"		
Program	*All Respondents*	*Men*	*Women*
GI Bill	60	61	50*
Student Loans	48	44	49
Pell Grants	57	53	60

Notes: These differences do not reach statistical significance. This may reflect the relatively small sample size included in this analysis.

*An extremely small number of women surveyed actually used GI Bill benefits. Of the 15 women who responded to the question of whether they have ever received GI Bill benefits, 8 indicated that they had.

Source: The Social and Governmental Issues and Participation (SGIP) study.

compared to 53 percent of men who used Pell Grants and 44 percent of men who used student loans.[55] Gender differences in traceability do not reach statistical significance.

The finding that the GI Bill represents the most traceable higher education program for men while the federal Pell Grant program represents the most traceable higher education program for women may indicate that these programs were widely recognized by their respective beneficiaries as having emanated from the federal government. Moreover, because receiving federal support in the form of monetary grants generally represents a positive experience, it would follow that those linking program provisions to the state would be likely to assign credit to the federal government for its generosity. For both men and women, federal student loan recipients are the least likely to recognize the federal government as the source of their benefits. This may be related to the process of applying for student loans. Given that students may apply for financial aid on their college campuses or in the comfort of their home, thanks to the Internet, applying for this type of government support typically does not involve a trip to a government building or direct interaction with a government employee. Moreover, when students fill out the FAFSA (Free Application for Federal Student Aid) form to apply for student aid, they may simply fail to realize that the aid for which they are applying comes from the US government.

What about the perceived value of federal student aid program usage? Do male and female program beneficiaries perceive benefits as helping to make education accessible and affordable? I expect that because student aid programs provide assistance that reduces the financial burden of obtaining a college degree, both women and men will perceive higher education programs as helping to make college accessible and affordable. Furthermore, I hypothesize that women will be especially likely to assign great value to financial aid usage because, at least historically, financing higher education through family support; full-time, part-time, or summer employment; or other private sources has been more difficult for women.[56]

When asked whether they agreed with the statement "I would not have considered higher education without benefits," 42.2 percent of women and 37.2 percent of men answered in the affirmative.[57] In regards to student loans, the principal mechanism by which the federal government supports students pursuing college degrees, women are again more likely to view federal financial aid as providing valuable assistance. When asked to characterize the extent to which student loans expanded educational opportunity, 47 percent of female college graduates responded that they expanded opportunity "a great deal," while 34.7 percent of male college graduates offered this same response.[58] Male and female student loan beneficiaries generally view these programs as having effectively expanded educational opportunity. Further, data suggest that women are particularly likely to view federal student loans as having significantly expanded their access to higher education.

Table 6.2, which further examines male and female college graduates' perceptions of how valuable federal student aid benefits were to their pursuit of higher education, provides additional evidence that student aid recipients—particularly women—assign considerable value to student aid benefits.[59] Among college graduates who report having used federal student aid, women are more likely than men to perceive these benefits as having enabled them to afford college: 41 percent of women and 38 percent of men strongly agree that, absent federal student aid, they would not have been able to afford higher education. Data also suggest that higher education policies help students attend high-quality institutions, minimize the total time needed to complete a college degree, and are viewed as facilitating access to valuable training. This evidence indicates that many male and female financial aid recipients recognize the value of government student aid for facilitating the successful completion of their degrees. In contrast to early experiences whereby women were largely excluded from GI Bill benefits, these findings suggest that women and men have come to share similar experiences with federal student aid programs.

Another way to gauge federal student aid beneficiaries' views of their program participation is to consider whether they have more positive attitudes toward the government than nonusers. Are financial aid recipients more likely than policy nonusers to agree that the federal government has provided opportunities for socioeconomic mobility and valuable assistance to those in need? It seems plausible that federal student aid users will have significantly more

Table 6.2 **The Value of Higher Education Policy Usage Among College Graduates, by Gender**

	Strongly Disagree	Disagree Somewhat	Neither	Agree Somewhat	Strongly Agree		
"I could not have afforded acquiring additional education without education benefits."							
Men	24%	21	0	18	38	=	101%
Women	14%	23	0	23	41	=	101%
"I would have attended a college of lesser cost, quality, or reputation without education benefits."							
Men	24%	16	1	30	28	=	99%
Women	23%	15	2	33	27	=	100%
"It would have taken me longer to acquire additional education without education benefits."							
Men	20%	17	1	27	35	=	100%
Women	19%	7	0	31	43	=	100%
"The education or training that I paid for with my student loan(s) was worth it."							
Men	8%	3	1	19	70	=	101%
Women	12%	3	1	11	74	=	101%

Notes: The total percentages may not equal 100 percent due to rounding. These differences do not reach statistical significance.

Source: The Social and Governmental Issues and Participation (SGIP) study.

positive attitudes toward the government than those who do not benefit from these programs because higher education program utilization offered a positive interaction with the government that facilitated long-term benefits—chiefly, the completion of a college degree.

Table 6.3 considers male and female college graduates' attitudes toward the government according to whether or not they received any type of federal student aid. For both male and female college graduates, higher education policy utilization is associated with more positive attitudes toward the government. Generally, college graduates who have received federal student aid are more likely to agree that the government has provided opportunities to improve living standards; however, the data suggest that men are significantly more likely to agree with this notion.[60] When we consider women and men separately, we again find that policy users are more likely than nonusers to agree that the government has provided opportunities to increase living standards.[61] Higher education program beneficiaries are also more likely to agree that government social programs have provided help during times of need.[62] Of course, student aid beneficiaries may also have experience with other government programs, and they may factor these experiences into their overall impressions of government support. While we cannot conclude that federal student aid is the sole driver of these attitudes,

Table 6.3 **Attitudes Toward Government Among College Graduates, by Gender and Higher Education Policy Usage and Nonusage**

		Disagree	*Neither*	*Agree*		
"Government has given me opportunities to improve my standard of living."						
Men	Nonusers	48	6	47	=	101%
	Users	32	1	68	=	101%
Women	Nonusers	43	7	50	=	100%
	Users	41	2	58	=	101%
"Government social programs have helped me in times of need."						
Men	Nonusers	59	11	30	=	100%
	Users	42	6	52	=	100%
Women	Nonusers	49	15	37	=	101%
	Users	36	10	55	=	101%

Notes: The sum of the percentages in some rows may not equal 100% due to rounding. The Disagree category includes the responses "strongly disagree" and "disagree somewhat," and the Agree category includes the responses "strongly agree" and "agree somewhat."

Source: The Social and Governmental Issues and Participation (SGIP) study.

data suggest that using higher education policies contributes to the tendency to view the state as providing valuable support.

Thus far, we have found that federal financial aid programs have provided valuable support for Americans pursuing higher education. The gender egalitarianism with which federal resources have been targeted, however, varies by program. The benefits of the GI Bill—the first federal program to offer direct financial aid to citizens pursuing college degrees—reached an overwhelmingly male population of veterans in the post–World War II era. Men born between 1916 and 1934 claimed benefits at considerably higher rates than their younger counterparts. While the GI Bill was a significant source of support for American men during the postwar era, we find that federal student loans and Pell Grants have been used by substantial portions of college students, both male and female. With the growth of student loan programs in recent decades, we have seen that these programs have come to represent a considerable source of support for younger citizens. In recent decades, student loans and Pell Grants have become the dominant source of federal support for college students.

When we consider the factors that compel citizens to use federal student aid—assuming the availability of said aid—we find that gender, age, and race provide strong predictors of GI Bill, student loan, and Pell Grant utilization. For the GI Bill, age and the gendered condition of military service prove the most powerful predictors of program utilization. Student loans and Pell Grants are widely used by both women and men, although women and younger Americans are significantly more likely to take advantage of these programs. While a significant proportion of American college students receive federal loans, fewer than half of beneficiaries recognize that these benefits come from the government; men and women are more likely to identify the GI Bill and Pell Grants as government social programs. For both genders, policy users largely view their use of federal student aid as a positive experience. Having considered the gender dynamics of federal student aid usage and beneficiaries' views regarding program receipt, we turn now to the effects of financial aid programs on higher educational attainment in the United States.

How Student Aid Usage Shapes Women's Educational Attainment

Thus far, we have seen that while the benefits of the GI Bill reached a broad but predominantly male segment of Americans during the postwar era, subsequently enacted federal student loans and Pell Grants have been widely used by both women and men. We have also seen that, since their creation, the student loan and Pell Grant programs have become the dominant mechanisms through which the federal government provides financial aid broadly to male and female students.

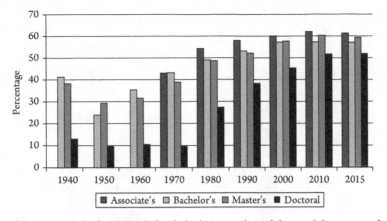

Figure 6.4 Percentage of associate's, bachelor's, master's, and doctoral degrees conferred to women, 1940–2015. *Note*: Data for the proportion of associate's degrees conferred to women are not available prior to 1970. *Source*: The National Center for Education Statistics (NCES).

In general, the gender dynamics of higher educational attainment have varied considerably over time, and the rates at which women have earned both undergraduate and graduate degrees has increased precipitously since the mid-twentieth century. Figure 6.4 shows the proportion of associate's, bachelor's, master's, and doctoral degrees conferred to women since 1940. It is interesting to note that in 1980, women earned the majority of associate's degrees, and by 1990, more than 50 percent of associate's, bachelor's, and master's degrees conferred in the United States. Although women trailed men in earning doctoral degrees into the early twenty-first century, by 2010 women earned a majority of PhDs as well.

I suspect that, especially among younger Americans, the emergence of a reversed gender dynamic whereby women earned a greater proportion of college and graduate degrees than men may reflect the impact of federal student aid programs that offered gender-egalitarian educational assistance. As a result, I expect that a causal relationship exists between federal student policy usage and higher educational attainment. I posit that the GI Bill provided significant resources to male beneficiaries that increased the probability that they would complete higher education during the postwar era. I also hypothesize that student loans and Pell Grants provided similar resources to women and men, thus increasing the likelihood of higher educational attainment for both genders.

Another mechanism by which federal student aid utilization can increase higher educational attainment is by increasing the time that low-income students can devote to academics. By precluding the necessity of working while attending college, I predict that federal student aid benefits significantly increase the time that students can devote to academics. Figure 6.5 displays the percentage of undergraduate men and women who, on average, devote fifteen or more hours per week to schoolwork outside of class. In line with my expectation, there

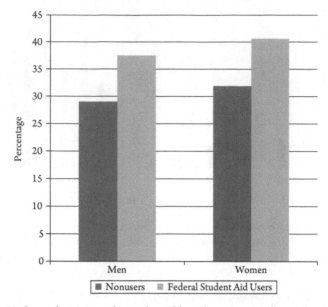

Figure 6.5 Undergraduates spending at least fifteen hours per week on schoolwork outside of class. *Note:* These differences between federal student aid users and nonusers are statistically significant at α = 0.001. *Source:* The 2008 National Postsecondary Student Aid Study (NPSAS).

appears to be a positive correlation between federal student aid usage and time devoted to academic work. Among male undergraduates, 37.5 percent of student aid beneficiaries spend at least fifteen hours each week doing academic work, compared to 29 percent of policy nonusers. Similarly, 40.6 percent of female undergraduates spend fifteen or more hours on schoolwork each week, while 31.9 percent of women who do not receive federal student aid do so.[63] The data suggest that undergraduates who benefit from federal student aid devote a significantly greater amount of time to academic work than those who do not. This represents an important mechanism by which federal student aid utilization increases the probability that students will successfully complete higher levels of education. This resource effect appears to be particularly beneficial to female student aid users, as they are significantly more likely to spend a substantial amount of time on academics.

Higher Education Policy Usage, Educational Ambition, and Educational Attainment

Descriptive statistics have suggested that federal student aid usage may be positively correlated with greater educational attainment because federal student aid makes college more affordable for men and women from less advantaged socioeconomic backgrounds and enables students to spend more time on schoolwork. Does using federal financial aid help program beneficiaries to obtain higher levels of education than they would have without government support? While it is the case that a financial aid recipient must be accepted into a college program to receive benefits, there is no guarantee that he or she will actually complete the degree and no guarantee that he or she will consider pursuing postgraduate education. Compared to those who have not used federal student aid, are the beneficiaries of government scholarships and loans more likely to obtain higher levels of educational attainment? The Social and Governmental Issues and Participation survey includes measures corresponding to a variety of demographic and background factors and measures of federal financial aid program usage that will allow us to examine the relative effects of these variables on women's and men's overall educational attainment. To investigate whether such a relationship exists, I empirically examine two relationships: (1) the relationship between federal student aid utilization and educational ambition and (2) the relationship between financial aid usage and actual educational attainment.

Educational ambition may provide a useful harbinger of educational attainment. I suspect that the usage of federal student aid programs may indirectly increase educational attainment by increasing the educational ambition of low-income students. Absent federal financial aid, undergraduates from less privileged socioeconomic backgrounds who face the burden of funding their own higher education may view the pursuit of advanced degrees as a prohibitively costly undertaking. Federal student aid beneficiaries, on the other hand, may be more likely to view advanced education as a feasible pursuit because federal support allows them to reserve limited financial resources for the task of financing advanced degrees, rather than undergraduate degrees. To test this possibility, I consider whether federal student aid utilization increases educational ambition among low-income students using data from the 2008 NPSAS. The central question driving this analysis is whether low-income undergraduates who benefit from federal student aid are more likely to plan on pursuing advanced education than those who do not.

Ordinal logistic regression analysis supports my hypothesis that student aid utilization promotes greater educational ambition for students coming from less privileged economic backgrounds.[64] Controlling for age, race, mother's education, and the possession of "go-getter" personalities, we find that federal student aid utilization provides a significant determinant of postgraduate educational plans among low-income college students.[65] For dependent undergraduates coming from low-income backgrounds—even when controlling for age, race, and ambitious, "go-getter" personality traits—federal higher education policy usage provides a statistically significant predictor of women's and men's intended higher educational attainment. The data suggest that women and men who use financial aid policies are more likely to express high levels of educational ambition than those who do not. Low-income male undergraduates who use federal student aid are 8 percentage points more likely to plan on earning a doctoral or professional degree than men who do not use these programs. Among their female counterparts, we find that women who receive student aid are 6 percentage points more likely to plan to earn a doctoral or professional degree than women who do not. These findings support my hypothesis that federal student aid utilization indirectly promotes higher educational attainment by promoting greater educational ambition among low-income students. In addition to revealing a significant relationship between federal student aid usage and educational ambition, these findings underscore the importance of higher education programs for making college more affordable for needy students.

What about the relationship between federal student aid utilization and the extent of educational attainment? The descriptive statistics presented in Figure 6.6 offer evidence that financial aid utilization is associated with higher levels of advanced degree completion for men and women. For men, 34.5 percent of college graduates who received federal student aid complete either a master's degree, a PhD, or a professional degree, compared to 31.8 percent of those who did not use financial aid. We find that female college graduates who use federal financial aid are significantly more likely to earn advanced degrees than those who do not benefit from these programs. For female college graduates, 37.6 percent of those who have used federal student aid programs have earned graduate degrees, compared to 26.1 percent of those who have not.[66]

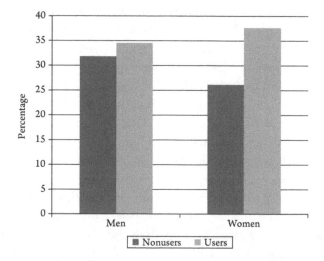

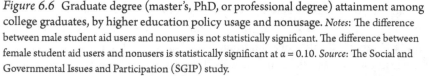

Figure 6.6 Graduate degree (master's, PhD, or professional degree) attainment among college graduates, by higher education policy usage and nonusage. *Notes:* The difference between male student aid users and nonusers is not statistically significant. The difference between female student aid users and nonusers is statistically significant at $\alpha = 0.10$. *Source:* The Social and Governmental Issues and Participation (SGIP) study.

Difference-in-differences analysis provides further support for the notion that federal higher education policies have promoted greater educational attainment among American women. In this portion of the analysis, I use quasi-experimental methods to consider whether eligibility for federal financial aid under the National Defense Education Act and the Higher Education Act, as well as protection under the Title IX regulation, has influenced women's and men's higher educational attainment.[67] I use three central estimating equations throughout the analysis, which correspond to the influence of the three aforementioned public policies. To examine the influence of the National Defense Education Act's (NDEA's) National Direct Student Loans, I use the equation

$$y_i = \alpha + \beta_1 \left(\text{Female} \times \text{post-1940}\right) + \beta_2 \text{Female} + \beta_3 \text{post-1940} + \varepsilon_i$$

where the dependent variable is the probability of graduating from college, and *post-1940* is a dichotomous measure of whether or not a respondent was a member of the birth year cohort that was born after 1940, who reached college age when federal financial aid had become available under the NDEA's student loan program in 1959. *Female* is a binary variable that corresponds to the respondent's gender (set to 0 for men, 1 for women).

I use a similar equation to estimate the influence that the Higher Education Act's (HEA's) Basic Educational Opportunity Grants—which became known as "Pell Grants"—have had on women's and men's college completion:

$$y_i = \alpha + \beta_1 \left(\text{Female} \times \text{post-1947}\right) + \beta_2 \text{Female} + \beta_3 \text{post-1947} + \varepsilon_i.$$

Here, *post-1947* is a dichotomous variable that measures whether or not a respondent is a member of the cohort born after 1947, who reached college age after 1966, during an era when the HEA's student aid benefits were available to college students.

Finally, I use a third equation to estimate the effect that protection under the Title IX regulation, which went into effect in 1976, had on the rate at which women and men complete college:

$$y_i = \alpha + \beta_1 \left(\text{Female} \times \text{post-1957}\right) + \beta_2 \text{Female} + \beta_3 \text{post-1957} + \varepsilon_i$$

where *post-1957* measures whether respondents are members of the cohort of Americans born after 1957, who reached college age after 1976, when the Title IX prohibition on sex discrimination in college admissions was in effect.

Table 6.4 shows the means for women and men on measures of college degree completion and on measures identified in the literature as relevant to higher educational attainment, such as race, childhood socioeconomic status, and parents' educational attainment. I examine the means for the cohorts of Americans

Table 6.4 **Difference in Means and Eligibility for National Defense Education Act Student Aid**

	College Freshmen Before 1959 (Born In/Pre-1940)		College Freshmen In/ After 1959 (Born Post-1940)		Difference-in-Difference
	Men	Women	Men	Women	
Age	75.172	75.365	42.395	42.824	0.235
	(0.649)	(0.562)	(0.552)	(0.512)	(1.978)
Childhood Socio-economic Status	2.548	2.742	2.689	2.701	−0.181
	(0.097)	(0.081)	(0.038)	(0.038)	(0.149)
Black	0.132	0.135	0.162	0.235	0.070
	(0.041)	(0.034)	(0.017)	(0.018)	(0.066)
Hispanic	0.048	0.072	0.132	0.128	−0.027
	(0.026)	(0.025)	(0.014)	(0.013)	(0.053)
Father Graduated College	0.036	0.091	0.301	0.259	−0.097
	(0.022)	(0.029)	(0.020)	(0.018)	(0.072)
Mother Graduated College	0.121	0.084	0.260	0.221	−0.001
	(0.039)	(0.028)	(0.019)	(0.017)	(0.070)
Some College	0.528	0.370	0.599	0.600	0.159
	(0.057)	(0.046)	(0.021)	(0.019)	(0.079)
College Grad	0.314	0.162	0.376	0.382	0.158
	(0.053)	(0.035)	(0.021)	(0.019)	(0.077)
N	77	111	553	643	1,378

Notes: Means are of Social and Governmental Issues and Participation random samples, weighted by sample weights. Standard errors are in parentheses.

whose birth years correspond to reaching college aid before and after the NDEA's financial aid benefits became available. We see that for the cohort of Americans born in or before 1940, 52.8 percent of men have completed some college, compared to 37 percent of women. For the younger cohort who were eligible for financial aid benefits under the NDEA, 59.9 percent of men and 60 percent of women had completed some college. For the cohort who reached college age before NDEA loans became available, 31.4 percent of men and 38.2 percent of women were college graduates. For the cohort who reached college age after the NDEA policy went into effect, 37.6 percent of men and 38.2 percent of women were college graduates. For women, the probability of graduating from college rose by a full 22 percentage points, compared to an increase of 6.2 percentage points for men.

I can use multivariate regression analysis to test the robustness of these differences. The results shown in Table 6.5 show the estimated effect of eligibility

Table 6.5 **Effect of Eligibility for National Defense Education Act Aid on the Probability of Being a College Graduate**

	(1) Difference-in-Differences	(2) Add Covariates
Female × Post-1940	0.158*	0.203*
	(0.077)	(0.082)
Female	−0.152*	−0.171*
	(0.072)	(0.077)
Post-1940	0.062	0.083
	(0.059)	(0.074)
Age		0.003*
		(0.001)
Childhood Socioeconomic Status		0.019
		(0.016)
Black		−0.099*
		(0.039)
Hispanic		−0.112
		(0.069)
Father Graduated College		0.185***
		(0.038)
Mother Graduated College		0.218***
		(0.039)
R^2	0.016	0.129
N	1,378	1,089

$^\dagger p \leq .1,$ * $p \leq .05,$ ** $p \leq .01,$ *** $p \leq .001.$

Note: Cells consist of unstandardized ordinary least squares regression coefficients; standard errors are in parentheses. Regressions are weighted by Social and Governmental Issues and Participation sample weights.

Source: Social and Governmental Issues and Participation study.

for aid provided by the National Defense Education Act alongside a comprehensive set of covariates that also shape the probability of completing college. The reduced model in column one suggests that eligibility for NDEA student aid corresponds to a 15.8-percentage-point increase in the probability that a woman will be a college graduate. The magnitude of the effect for women is greater than that for men—a 15.8-percentage-point increase, compared to a 6.2-percentage-point increase for men. This relationship holds when we add covariates: NDEA eligibility corresponds to a 20.3-percentage-point increase in the probability that women will earn a college degree, compared to an 8.3-percentage-point increase in the probability that men will do so.

The next set of results tests the estimated effect of eligibility for aid provided by the Higher Education Act on the likelihood that women and men would graduate from college. The means presented in Table 6.6 suggest that eligibility for HEA aid is associated with an increase in college completion for both women and men. For the cohort of respondents born in or before 1947, 51.2 percent of men and 42.8 percent of women had completed some college. For the cohort born after 1947 who were eligible for the aid provided by the Higher Education Act, 61 percent of men and 60.7 percent of women had completed some college. Similarly, for the cohort who reached college before the HEA's student aid went into effect, 33.8 percent of men had completed college, compared to 23.8 percent of women. For their counterparts who were eligible for HEA benefits when they reached college, 37.7 percent of men and 38.3 percent of women were college graduates—an increase of 3.9 percentage points for men and 14.5 percentage points for women.

Multivariate regression analysis confirms these results. The reduced model in column one of Table 6.7 suggests that eligibility for HEA student aid corresponds to a 10.6-percentage-point increase in the probability that women will graduate from college, compared to a 3.9-percentage-point increase for men. This finding holds when we add a comprehensive set of covariates. As column two shows, the estimated effect of eligibility for HEA student aid is 15.8 percentage points.

The final set of tables considers the effect that the Title IX regulation had on women's and men's educational attainment. Table 6.8 shows a difference-in-means analysis for the rates at which men and women who reached college age before and after Title IX went into effect completed college. We see that for the cohort born in or before 1957 who reached college age before the Title IX regulation went into effect, 57.9 percent of men and 45.5 percent of women completed some college. For the cohort born after 1957 who reached college age during an era in which Title IX regulated college admissions, 59.9 percent of men had completed some college, compared to 64.2 percent of women. The proportion of women completing some college increased by 18.7 percentage points, compared to an increase of 2 percentage points for men. When we turn to the rates at

Table 6.6 **Difference in Means and Eligibility for Basic Educational Opportunity Grant/Pell Grant Aid**

	College Freshmen Before 1966 (Born In/Pre-1947)		College Freshmen In/ After 1966 (Born Post-1947)		
	Men	*Women*	*Men*	*Women*	*Difference-in-Differences*
Age	69.854	71.290	40.151	40.429	−1.158
	(0.609)	(0.551)	(0.526)	(0.480)	(1.405)
Childhood Socio-economic Status	2.556	2.658	2.702	2.724	−0.080
	(0.078)	(0.063)	(0.040)	(0.040)	(0.120)
Black	0.126	0.166	0.167	0.237	0.030
	(0.029)	(0.029)	(0.018)	(0.019)	(0.054)
Hispanic	0.068	0.071	0.136	0.135	−0.003
	(0.021)	(0.019)	(0.016)	(0.014)	(0.043)
Father Graduated College	0.112	0.114	0.311	0.270	−0.043
	(0.027)	(0.025)	(0.022)	(0.020)	(0.059)
Mother Graduated College	0.163	0.107	0.265	0.229	0.020
	(0.032)	(0.024)	(0.021)	(0.018)	(0.056)
Some College	0.512	0.428	0.610	0.607	0.081
	(0.041)	(0.037)	(0.022)	(0.020)	(0.064)
College Grad	0.338	0.238	0.377	0.383	0.106
	(0.039)	(0.032)	(0.022)	(0.020)	(0.063)
N	131	158	414	509	1,360

Notes: Means are of Social and Governmental Issues and Participation random samples, weighted by sample weights. Standard errors are in parentheses.

which women and men graduate from college, we notice an interesting shift. For the pre–Title IX cohort of respondents who were born in or before 1957, 37 percent of men and 27.5 percent of women completed college. For the post–Title IX cohort who were born after 1957, 36.9 percent of men were college graduates, compared to 39.9 percent of women—an increase of 12.4 percentage points for women and a decline of 0.1 percentage points for men.

Table 6.7 **Effect of Eligibility for Higher Education Act Aid on the Probability of Being a College Graduate**

	(1) *Difference-in-Differences*	(2) *Add Covariates*
Female × Post-1947	0.106[+]	0.158*
	(0.063)	(0.068)
Female	−0.101[+]	−0.121*
	(0.055)	(0.060)
Post-1947	0.039	0.060
	(0.047)	(0.064)
Age		0.003*
		(0.001)
Childhood Socioeconomic		0.017
Status		(0.016)
Black		−0.096*
		(0.039)
Hispanic		−0.104
		(0.069)
Father Graduated College		0.186***
		(0.039)
Mother Graduated College		0.222***
		(0.039)
R^2	0.010	0.124
N	1,378	1,089

[+] $p \leq .1,$ * $p \leq .05,$ ** $p \leq .01,$ *** $p \leq .001.$

Note: Cells consist of unstandardized ordinary least squares regression coefficients; standard errors are in parentheses. Regressions are weighted by Social and Governmental Issues and Participation sample weights.

Source: Social and Governmental Issues and Participation study.

The regression analysis in Table 6.9 supports these findings. The reduced model suggests that the estimated effect of protection under Title IX on college completion is an increase of 12.6 percentage points for women and a decrease of 0.2 percentage points for men. When we add the list of covariates, we find that the effect is an estimated 16.5-percentage-point increase for women, compared to a 7.4-percentage-point decrease for men.

These results suggest that eligibility for the financial aid provided by the National Defense Education Act and the Higher Education Act and protection

Table 6.8 **Difference in Means and Protection Under Title IX Regulation**

	College Freshmen Before 1976 (Born In/Pre-1957)		College Freshmen In/ After 1976 (Born Post-1957)		
	Men	Women	Men	Women	Difference-in-Differences
Age	62.156 (0.556)	64.454 (0.568)	35.334 (0.487)	36.031 (0.442)	−1.601 (1.030)
Childhood Socio-economic Status	2.580 (0.054)	2.599 (0.049)	2.734 (0.048)	2.786 (0.047)	0.033 (0.100)
Black	0.139 (0.022)	0.197 (0.023)	0.172 (0.022)	0.236 (0.022)	0.006 (0.045)
Hispanic	0.069 (0.015)	0.085 (0.016)	0.158 (0.020)	0.145 (0.017)	−0.029 (0.036)
Father Graduated College	0.180 (0.024)	0.125 (0.020)	0.331 (0.027)	0.308 (0.023)	0.032 (0.049)
Mother Graduated College	0.180 (0.024)	0.121 (0.019)	0.287 (0.025)	0.254 (0.021)	0.026 (0.047)
Some College	0.579 (0.029)	0.455 (0.028)	0.599 (0.027)	0.642 (0.023)	0.167 (0.054)
College Grad	0.370 (0.029)	0.275 (0.025)	0.369 (0.026)	0.399 (0.023)	0.126 (0.052)
N	255	277	290	384	1,378

Notes: Means are of Social and Governmental Issues and Participation random samples, weighted by sample weights. Standard errors are in parentheses.

by Title IX's ban on sex discrimination in college admissions has contributed to an increase in women's college degree attainment. While results suggest that eligibility for the financial aid provided by the NDEA and HEA contributed to an increase in the probability that men would graduate from college, the Title IX regulation actually contributed to a slight decline in the rate at which men earn college degrees.[68]

Table 6.9 **Effect of Protection Under Title IX Regulation on Probability of Being a College Graduate**

	(1) *Difference-in-Differences*	(2) *Add Covariates*
Female × Post-1957	0.126*	0.165**
	(0.052)	(0.057)
Female	−0.095*	−0.096*
	(0.040)	(0.044)
Post-1957	−0.002	−0.074
	(0.038)	(0.059)
Age		0.000
		(0.002)
Childhood Socioeconomic Status		0.015
		(0.016)
Black		−0.097*
		(0.040)
Hispanic		−0.111
		(0.069)
Father Graduated College		0.182***
		(0.039)
Mother Graduated College		0.218***
		(0.039)
R^2	0.009	0.119
N	1,378	1,089

† $p \leq .1$, * $p \leq .05$, ** $p \leq .01$, *** $p \leq .001$.

Note: Cells consist of unstandardized ordinary least squares regression coefficients; standard errors are in parentheses. Regressions are weighted by Social and Governmental Issues and Participation sample weights.

Source: Social and Governmental Issues and Participation study.

Education Policy and Women's First-Class Citizenship

For more than seventy years, the US government has employed student financial aid as a mechanism for promoting the socioeconomic interests of its citizens. While the gendered criteria governing GI Bill eligibility have resulted in men's representing the principal recipients of this program's valuable benefits, the subsequently enacted federal student loan and Pell Grant programs—which extended benefits broadly to both women and men—have promoted gender parity in educational attainment in the United States. Moreover, by expanding access to higher education for American women, these programs have also promoted greater socioeconomic stability and independence for women. As such, these programs have promoted women's full incorporation into society and have, thus, enhanced women's status as full social citizens.

This chapter has considered the gender dynamics of federal student aid usage and the effects of policy utilization on women's social citizenship. At the outset, I hypothesized that the gender dynamics of federal student aid utilization vary across programs and that financial aid utilization promotes greater educational attainment. Empirical analysis of data from multiple surveys corroborates these predictions. Our examination of trends related to men's and women's financial aid utilization confirmed that men and women have enjoyed differential access to federal financial aid. The main source of this disparity is the fact that women were largely excluded from the benefits of the GI Bill during the postwar era. Federal student loans and Pell Grants, on the other hand, have been allocated on a more gender-egalitarian basis. This analysis has also found that federal student aid utilization significantly increases educational attainment for women and men. By making college affordable for low-income students and increasing the amount of time that students can devote to academic work, federal financial aid increases educational attainment among Americans.

The empirical analysis presented in this chapter has confirmed that, to fully appreciate the impact that federal financial aid programs have had on gender equality in the United States, we must consider the historical contexts from which they emerged. The GI Bill was the first federal policy that expanded access to higher education via the direct provision of financial aid. By providing millions of GIs with the opportunity to pursue higher education, the state essentially acted *in loco parentis* for an entire generation of American men, providing them with a new, relatively privileged brand of citizenship. In supporting veterans' pursuit of higher education, the federal government became a generous parent, and millions of GI Bill beneficiaries became its fortunate sons.

While the state assumed the responsibility of financing higher education for millions of American men, women were left to their own devices when it came to paying for higher education. Instead of receiving public aid to help pay for college, women continued to rely on private sources. Thus, the responsibility of paying for women's higher education was typically borne by families—assuming, of course, that it was undertaken at all. By reserving its generous financial support for men, the GI Bill exacerbated gender inequality in higher educational attainment and, in effect, socioeconomic status. American women would not experience the state's generosity in the form of higher education benefits until the creation of federal student loans and Pell Grants. Upon the emergence of these programs in the late 1950s and 1960s, both women and men could benefit from federal financial support as they pursued postsecondary education.

As this analysis has shown, the usage of Pell Grants and student loans significantly increases women's and men's educational attainment. This is a highly significant finding, considering that no previously enacted policy had this effect for women. The creation of Pell Grants and student loans marked the beginning of an era in which the state provided generous educational financial aid benefits to both its sons and its daughters. The results of this chapter suggest that federal financial aid policies have had important equalizing effects for the gender dynamics of American socioeconomic status. Not only have these policies significantly increased women's educational attainment, but also they have enhanced gender equality in social citizenship in the United States. By significantly increasing women's access to college degrees and the social and economic benefits that are associated with higher education, landmark higher education policies supported women's full incorporation into American society.

7

Federal Student Aid and the Gender Dynamics of Political Citizenship

As a result of economic, social, and political disparities predicated upon women's and men's supposedly different natures, abilities, and roles, women's political voice—at least through formal channels—was a muted whisper well into the twentieth century. Because women's second-class civil, social, and political status suppressed their engagement in the public sphere, the nation's political landscape was a predominantly male arena, characterized by gender inequality in political citizenship, which consists of the right to exercise political power or to influence the selection of others who will do so.[1] Although the passage of the Nineteenth Amendment in 1920 guaranteed women the right to vote and provided women with full civil citizenship, their status as second-class political citizens continued for decades following women's suffrage. Throughout these years, women's participation in political activities like voting, contacting elected officials, and contributing to political causes trailed that of men.[2] Although women had participated in protests, rallies, and various forms of grassroots activism to advocate causes like abolition, temperance, and women's suffrage, their social movement activity had historically occurred outside of the male-dominated institutions of American government.[3] Inequality in the rates at which men and women engaged in political activities at the mass level represented a chronic challenge to gender parity in terms of political citizenship.

The 1960s marked a turning point for gender-equal political citizenship, as higher education programs helped to expand access to knowledge and skills that promote political engagement. As chapter 6 demonstrated, student financial aid policies enacted during the mid-twentieth century helped women gain access to greater socioeconomic status. This chapter continues the investigation of the relationship between federal student aid programs and women's citizenship, this time considering how these programs have helped women to participate as full and equal members of the polity. With the dawning of the 1960s came important changes in the gender dynamics of US mass politics.[4] Over the subsequent fifty years, women's political participation increased substantially, and the gender gap in US political engagement narrowed considerably.[5] Although studies show that the gender dynamics of contemporary US politics can be characterized by residual inequalities—women are still, for example, less likely than men to express high levels of interest in politics, to feel efficacious, to serve as elected officials, and to contribute money to political candidates—women's participation in activities like voting and volunteering on political campaigns began to increase significantly in the 1960s and 1970s.[6]

The Gender Dynamics of Mass-Political Engagement in the United States

Given that the overall rates at which Americans engage in political activities like voting and attending political meetings have declined in recent decades, it is interesting to note that the decline has been more pronounced for men than for women. As Table 7.1 illustrates, 72 percent of men reported voting in the 1964 presidential election, compared to 67 percent of women.[7] Since 1980, however, American women have voted at higher rates than their male counterparts, and, in every subsequent presidential election, the percentage of eligible women voting has been higher than the proportion of eligible men.[8] In 2004, 60 percent of women and 56 percent of men turned out to vote.[9] From 1964 to 2004, the voter turnout of male citizens has declined by 16.2 percentage points, compared to 6.6 percentage points for women. Thus, the decline in men's voter turnout is almost 150 percent greater than the decline in women's turnout.

The amplification of women's political voice and the narrowing gender gap in political engagement have extended beyond voter turnout to include a number of political activities.[10] Although Americans now attend political meetings at lower rates than they did in the 1960s, the decline for men has been steeper than the decline for women—more than six times greater. Historical data also reveal increasing gender parity in the rates at which men and women contribute money to political campaigns. While men had long outpaced women as contributors to political campaigns, recent years have seen virtual parity in the rates at which men and women report doing so.[11] Moreover, as Table 7.1 shows, the rate of increase in women's participation by contributing money exceeded the rate of increase for men.

In addition to these shifts in the gender dynamics of electoral participation, political meeting attendance, and contributing money to political campaigns, scholars have suggested that, since the 1990s, women and men have been equally likely to contact congressional representatives and sign petitions.[12] It appears that political parties have taken note of women's increasing political engagement

Table 7.1 **Percentage Change in Participation in Various Political Activities by Gender**

	1964	*2004*	*% Change*
Voted in Presidential Election			
Men	71.9%	56.3%	−16.2
Women	67.0	60.1	−6.6
Attended Political Meetings			
Men	9.9	6.9	−3.0
Women	7.8	7.4	−0.4
Donated Money to Political Campaign			
Men	12.2	12.5	+0.3
Women	9.5	12.6	+3.1
Contacted by a Major Party			
Men	27.4	39.8	+12.4
Women	24.8	45.6	+20.8
	1984	*2004*	*% Change*
Discussed Politics with Family			
Men	69.5	80.2	+10.7
Women	65.4	79.4	+14.0

Sources: The Center for American Women and Politics (CAWP); the American National Election Study (ANES) Cumulative Data File, 1948–2004.

in recent decades. Since 1964, women have increasingly indicated that they were contacted by at least one of the two major political parties.[13] Between 1964 and 2004, the rate at which men were mobilized by major political parties increased by 12.4 percentage points, compared to an increase of a full 20.8 percentage points for women. Over the course of forty years, the rate of increase in women's mobilization by political parties increased 67 percent more than that of men.

To take a final example of the narrowing gender gap in US political engagement, consider the rates at which male and female Americans discuss politics with their families.[14] While discussing politics with family members has become an increasingly popular political activity for all Americans in recent decades, this increase has been greater for women than for men. Although women's and men's participation in this form of political engagement grew, the rate of women's participation outpaced men's by 30 percent. As these trends illustrate, the 1960s marked a turning point for the gender dynamics of mass politics in the United States. Substantial increases in women's political interest, efficacy, and participation promoted greater gender parity in political engagement and, thus, women's movement from second-class to first-class political citizens.

Higher Education Policy, Educational Attainment, and Increasing Gender Parity in US Political Engagement

Scholars have characterized historical differences in men's and women's political engagement as a function of gender inequality in the possession of resources that facilitate political activity. Among these resources, political behavior scholars highlight education as one that has a particularly strong association with political engagement.[15] Numerous studies have demonstrated a strong relationship between educational attainment and political engagement, yielding the conventional wisdom among political scientists that higher levels of educational attainment are associated with high levels of political involvement.[16] Philip Converse calls education "the universal solvent" of political engagement, due to its powerful relationship with a broad range of factors associated with high levels of political participation, such as factual knowledge, attention to politics, and voter turnout.[17] "The educated citizen," he writes, "is attentive, knowledgeable, and participatory, and the uneducated citizen is not."[18] According to this school of thought, the mechanisms by which education promotes political participation include increasing knowledge, cognitive abilities, and skills; piquing political interest; teaching skills that lend themselves to civic and political participation, such as public speaking and organizational skills; increasing socioeconomic status; providing access to social networks that promote participation; and creating a sense of civic duty.[19] Studies have also shown that citizens with higher levels of education are more likely to be mobilized by interest groups, candidates, and other activists.[20]

While scholars have emphasized the positive association between education and political participation, in considering the narrowing of the gender gap in US political engagement, we have yet to consider whether public policy has played a role in shaping this trend. Dramatic increases in women's attainment of college degrees emerged in the wake of lawmakers' creation of both federal financial aid policies that provided valuable student aid and Title IX, which prohibited sex discrimination in college admissions. As we saw in chapter 6, federal higher education programs expanded equal opportunity for men and women in the United States and promoted women's social citizenship by significantly increasing the probability that they will earn college degrees. This chapter examines whether federal support for college students has any influence on gender equality in terms of political citizenship. How, I ask, have the landmark higher education programs enacted since the late 1950s influenced the gender dynamics of political citizenship in the United States?

This chapter uses a difference-in-differences strategy to examine the feedback effects of federal student aid programs for promoting gender equality in political citizenship in the United States. I focus on mass politics—particularly the influence of student aid utilization on men's and women's political interest, political efficacy, and participation in political activities. Analyzing data from the Social and Governmental Issues and Participation (SGIP) study, I test education-policy models of political engagement. These models combine previous explanations for political attitudes and involvement, which emphasize individual-level demographic and socioeconomic characteristics, with an institutional-level explanation that underscores the feedback effects of public policies.

I suspect that federal student aid programs promote gender equality in US political engagement by promoting high levels of political interest, efficacy, and participation for American women. This effect could happen in two ways, which I will outline briefly here and describe in depth later in this chapter. On one hand, federal student aid programs could have significant resource effects that promote gender parity in political engagement. That is, higher education policies could provide resources that restructure the costs and benefits associated with political engagement. As Sidney Verba, Kay Lehman Schlozman, and Henry Brady have argued, possessing resources, such as higher levels of education, income, and political capital, makes citizens more likely to engage in politics.[21]

On the other hand, federal higher education policy usage could have significant interpretive effects that contribute to an increase in political involvement. In this way, higher education programs could convey messages to beneficiaries and provide experiences that shape their attitudes toward government and their inclination to participate in political activities. As such, I suspect that federal higher education policies have promoted gender egalitarianism in political engagement through a combination of resource and interpretive effects. By providing women with resources—particularly educational attainment—and experiences that signal their status as first-class citizens, I posit, higher education programs have contributed to gender equality in terms of political citizenship.

In what follows we will see that, although empirical analysis fails to support the notion that eligibility for federal student aid directly increases the probability that women will display high levels of political engagement, these policies appear to have significant indirect influence on political engagement. By contributing to high levels of educational attainment, which the analysis in chapter 6 revealed, federal higher education programs promote high levels of political engagement.

Although American men are more likely than women to express high levels of
political interest and to be efficacious, and although men are slightly more likely
than women to engage in political activities like contributing money to political
candidates, this analysis suggests that federal student aid programs have played
a role in the declining gender gap in political engagement that we have seen in
the last fifty years.

Studying the Relationship Between Higher Education Policy and the Gender Dynamics of Political Citizenship

The fact that the narrowing of the gender gap in political engagement has
occurred in tandem with significant increases in women's higher educational
attainment comes as little surprise to scholars who extol the benefits of educational attainment for strengthening political citizenship.[22] The claim that education yields political engagement, however, does not go uncontested. Richard
Brody cast doubt on the notion that education and political participation are
causally related when he pointed out that recent increases in Americans' educational attainment was accompanied by a decline in electoral participation,
rather than an increase, as the conventional wisdom would lead us to expect.[23]
As a result of Brody's thought-provoking observation, scholars have debated
the nature of the relationship between educational attainment and political
engagement.

Some scholars argue that the two are spuriously related, as observed relationships between educational attainment and political engagement are the result
of confounding factors, rather than education. Cindy Kam and Carl Palmer use
propensity score matching to examine the existence of a causal relationship
between educational attainment and participation, taking into account preadult
experiences and predispositions.[24] They argue that the relationship between education and political involvement is one of correlation rather than causation, as
education serves as a proxy for individual-level predispositions and experiences.
Adam Berinsky and Gabriel Lenz reinforce the call to observe greater caution in
assessing the relationship between education and political participation.[25] Using
the high rates of educational attainment resulting from attempts to dodge the
Vietnam War draft as a natural experiment, they find evidence that college education may not cause greater political participation. After demonstrating that
high rates of education driven by draft avoidance did not yield higher rates of
voter participation in the United States, Berinsky and Lenz suggest that "factors
such as family background or cognitive skills may lead individuals to both attend
college and participate in politics."[26]

While some scholars reject the conventional wisdom that educational attainment causes political participation, others are slow to discard the possibility that education and political involvement are causally linked. In a response to Brody's observation that increases in individual-level education have occurred in tandem with a decline in mass-level electoral participation, Rachel Sondheimer and Donald Green draw upon experimental evidence to argue that education has a strong influence on voter turnout.[27] Referring to their experimental and quasi-experimental studies as "an important turning point in a literature that has for decades found itself mired in uncertainty about whether to attach a causal interpretation to the correlation between education and political participation," they conclude that educational attainment has a "profound" effect on voter participation.[28]

In separate studies, Alexander Mayer and John Henderson and Sara Chatfield take issue with Kam and Palmer's assertion that "higher education is not cause, but proxy."[29] They critique Kam and Palmer's propensity score matching technique, asserting that their analysis was based on biased estimates. Repeating Kam and Palmer's analysis using an alternative research design to correct for bias, Mayer finds evidence that college education "has a positive and substantively important causal effect on political participation."[30] Henderson and Chatfield assert that the flaws in Kam and Palmer's analysis cast a shadow on their claim that education serves as a proxy for other factors. While not ruling out the possibility that pre-existing factors may play a role in the relationship between education and political involvement, Henderson and Chatfield argue that higher education may cause increased political participation "on top of" the pre-existing factors that Kam and Palmer emphasize.[31]

In light of this ongoing debate regarding the nature of the relationship between education and political participation, and considering the limitations inherent in using regression analysis of survey data to examine the relationship between policy utilization and political engagement—namely, the possibility that confounding variables, rather than public policies, shape significant associations—I take caution in interpreting the results of this analysis, stopping short of inferring causality in any observed relationships between higher education program utilization and involvement in political activities.

The Feedback Effects of Government Programs on Political Engagement

Moving beyond models of political engagement that emphasize the centrality of individuals' demographic characteristics and socioeconomic status to political attitudes and participation, scholars studying the feedback effects of federal policy utilization for political involvement take seriously the possibility that public policies can alter citizens and the political environment.[32] Scholars have defined policy feedback as the ways in which policies influence subsequent political conditions and, as a result, may alter the ways in which social groups see themselves, what they expect from the political process, and their capabilities.[33] This concept of policy feedback introduces an additional element into the classic model of democratic policymaking: not only do citizens influence policies, but also these policies shape citizens. Studies examining the feedback effects of public policies recognize the importance of government programs to American politics and, as a result, provide rich, increasingly comprehensive models of political engagement. Policy feedback scholars have emphasized two mechanisms by which policy feedback operates: resource effects and interpretive effects.

Resource Effects

The resource effects of public policy utilization are transmitted by way of incentives, such as monetary payments, goods, and services, that have implications for citizens' material well-being and life opportunities.[34] These effects typically reshape the costs and benefits of engaging in certain political activities. Andrea Campbell's analysis of the relationship between Social Security usage and political engagement provides a useful example of the resource effects of public policies.[35] Her analysis demonstrates that Social Security provides valuable benefits that make its most dependent beneficiaries more likely to pay attention to politics and to engage in political activity if they suspect that their benefits are in danger. While high-income Americans tend to participate in political activities at higher rates than those with less income, Campbell finds an inverse relationship between income and Social Security–related participation: as income increases, political involvement actually declines.[36] In this case, the receipt of Social Security support—a valuable resource for many lower-income senior citizens—elevates their interest in politics, making them more likely to become politically involved should those benefits appear to be imperiled. By providing senior citizens with valuable financial resources and by entitling them to targeted government provisions, the state effectively uses government resources in a way that promotes political participation among low-income citizens—a group that is often found at the margins of American politics. Suzanne Mettler's study of the GI Bill provides further evidence of the resource effects that federal policies may have on mass political engagement.[37] She finds that the use of higher education and vocational training benefits provided by the GI Bill is significantly associated with greater educational attainment among veterans. By providing funding to veterans pursuing college degrees, the GI Bill made college affordable for many citizens who would not have otherwise been able to afford higher education; for many beneficiaries, it decreased the amount of time it took to complete their degrees; and it affected the trajectory of many veterans' careers, "enhancing their employment prospects and standard of living."[38]

Chapter 6 revealed that eligibility for the student aid provided under the National Defense Education Act (NDEA) and the Higher Education Act (HEA), and the institutional access provided by the Title IX regulation have promoted higher levels of educational attainment among men and women. Finding that educational attainment represents a significant determinant of political engagement would indicate that the federal higher education programs enacted since the late 1950s have exerted significant resource effects on the gender dynamics of political engagement in the United States. In the difference-in-differences analysis that follows, I will test whether there are significant resource effects by including the key independent variable "educational attainment."

Interpretive Effects

In addition to the possibility that landmark higher education policies might influence political engagement through resource effects, they could also shape Americans' political behavior by way of interpretive (or cognitive) effects. Interpretive effects are the ways in which policies serve as sources of information and meaning that shape citizens' inclination to participate in public affairs.[39] In this way, scholars note, public policies can send messages to program participants that indicate their value as citizens, while also teaching the appropriate roles of citizens and the government.[40] Interpretive effects tend to be closely related to the features of policy design, the form that benefits take, and the scope of eligibility. Lawmakers can use government programs to alter citizens in important ways.[41] Suzanne Mettler's study of the effects of GI Bill usage for civic and political engagement revealed significant interpretive effects, as GI Bill usage influenced beneficiaries' perceptions of their worth as citizens, sending messages that indicated their status as first-class citizens. Mettler notes, for example, that the "fair and efficient" implementation of the GI Bill made veterans "feel treated as respected citizens" and as though "government was for and about people like them."[42] As a result of these interpretive effects, the GI Bill promoted high levels of civic and political participation among veterans.[43]

The feedback effects of public policy utilization, however, do not always promote political engagement. In his study of the relationship between the use of government assistance and political engagement, Joe Soss demonstrates that participation in the Aid to Families with Dependent Children (AFDC) program suppresses political engagement due to beneficiaries' negative encounters with the government agencies charged with administering benefits.[44] He asserts that welfare recipients came to view themselves as low-status clients and were less likely to assert themselves when faced with program-related grievances. "These beliefs," according to Soss, "are strong enough to make clients retreat from decision-making processes that have the most profound and immediate consequences for their family."[45] Program participants generalize their experiences to characterize the broader political system. Because welfare policy receipt yields a decreased sense of external efficacy among program beneficiaries, it has the effect of suppressing their participation in politics.[46]

This analysis tests whether the student aid provided by the NDEA and the HEA or the Title IX regulation exert significant interpretive effects that promote greater political engagement among women. To consider this possibility, I use difference-in-difference specifications that identify the estimated effect of aid eligibility on survey respondents' political engagement.

An Education-Policy Model of Political Engagement

The purpose of this empirical analysis is to further our understanding of how public policies influence mass political attitudes and behavior by examining the feedback effects of federal higher education program usage on the gender dynamics of US political engagement. Have the financial aid and expanded institutional access provided by the NDEA, the HEA, and Title IX helped to narrow the gender gap in political interest, efficacy, and participation? Driving this investigation is an education-policy model of political participation that incorporates higher education policy eligibility as a central determinant in the model of political involvement. In what follows, I test my hypothesis that eligibility for student financial aid and protection under Title IX have significantly increased the propensity that women will participate in political activities and have, thus, contributed to the narrowing of the gender gap in political engagement that we have seen since the 1960s.

The education-policy model of political engagement resembles previous policy-centered models of political participation that emphasize the feedback effects of public policies and the mechanisms by which they influence mass political behavior. This is not to say that federal education policies are the only factors that matter for gender parity in citizens' political attitudes and political involvement. This analysis acknowledges and draws upon existing scholarship that emphasizes the demographic and socioeconomic determinants of political attitudes and participation. In doing so, I combine the individual-level insights of the political participation literature with the institutionally centered focus of the emerging literature on policy feedback.

Because federal higher education programs were created with the central purpose of expanding higher educational access and increasing the probability that students would attain high levels of education, I am particularly interested in their effectiveness for promoting gender equality in political engagement by way of greater gender egalitarianism in educational attainment. Drawing from the notion that public policies can "provide resources and create incentives for mass publics," I hypothesize that by promoting the resource of greater educational attainment, education policies decrease the costs associated with participating in politics, thereby increasing beneficiaries' ability to engage in political activities.[47] In other words, I posit that higher education programs that have been enacted since the mid-twentieth century—which have contributed to significant increases in women's educational attainment—have increased gender parity in political interest, efficacy, and participation.

Moreover, I suspect that these programs have conveyed to women the message that they are full and equal members of the political community and have, thus, promoted increased political engagement via interpretive effects. In the course of this analysis, we may see that eligibility for federal financial aid and protection under the Title IX regulation exerts positive interpretive effects, signaling beneficiaries' privileged status as full and equal citizens. As a result of such cues, Americans who had access to the benefits of these programs when they reached college age may exhibit high levels of political engagement. The education-policy model of political engagement emphasizes the resource and interpretive effects of higher education programs and their importance for political participation.

Data and Research Methods

Using the difference-in-differences approach that I used in chapter 6, this chapter examines empirically the feedback effects of eligibility for the NDEA's and HEA's financial aid benefits and the equal institutional access provided by Title IX for gender equality in political citizenship in terms of political engagement.[48] I again use data from the nationally representative 2008 SGIP study. For each of the programs mentioned previously, I begin by conducting a difference-in-means analysis to examine the differences in political engagement among women and men who reached college age before and after the landmark federal education programs went into effect. Then, I consider the effect that program eligibility has had for the gender dynamics of political engagement.

First, I test whether eligibility for the financial aid provided by the National Defense Education Act's National Direct Student Loan Program or the Higher Education Act's Basic Educational Opportunity Grant (BEOG)/Pell Grant program or expanded institutional access generated by the Title IX regulation has had a positive influence on women's political engagement. For the financial aid provided by the NDEA, the corresponding education policy model of political engagement can be represented by the following equation:

$$ENG_i = \alpha + \beta_1 \left(Female \times post\text{-}1940\right) + \beta_2 Female + \beta_3 post\text{-}1940 + \varepsilon_i$$

where the dependent variable is one of three measures of political engagement—political interest, political efficacy, or political participation. *Female* is a measure of gender (0 for male, 1 for female), and *post-1940* is a binary variable of whether an individual is a member of the birth year cohort that was born after 1940 and, thus, reached college age at a point when the NDEA's federal student loans were available.

I use a similar model to examine the effect of eligibility for financial aid provided by the Higher Education Act using the equation

$$ENG_i = \alpha + \beta_1 \left(Female \times post\text{-}1947\right) + \beta_2 Female + \beta_3 post\text{-}1947 + \varepsilon_i$$

where post-1947 corresponds to whether a respondent is a member of the birth year cohort that was born after 1947, who reached college age in or after 1966, which marked the beginning of the federal government's administration of the BEOG/Pell Grants.

Finally, the education policy model that considers whether the Title IX regulation has significantly shaped political engagement can be expressed using the following equation:

$$ENG_i = \alpha + \beta_1 \left(Female \times post\text{-}1957\right) + \beta_2 Female + \beta_3 post\text{-}1957 + \varepsilon_i$$

where post-1957 is a binary variable indicating whether or not respondents were born after 1957 and, thus, reached college age under the administration of Title IX's prohibition on sex discrimination in college admissions, which went into effect in 1976. In what follows, I use a combination of descriptive statistics and difference-in-differences analysis to consider the relationship between federal student aid utilization and the gender dynamics of political interest, political efficacy, and political participation.

Dependent Variables: Measures of Political Engagement

Political Interest

What effect does eligibility for federal higher education programs have on the gender dynamics of political interest? This question is central to any analysis of political engagement, as citizens who are more interested in politics are more

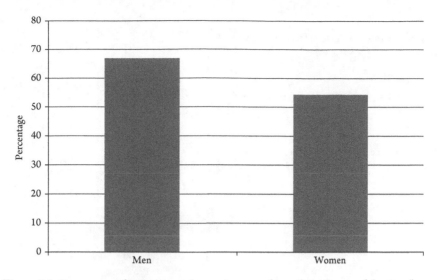

Figure 7.1 Percentage of Americans who are interested in politics "most of the time."
Note: Gender difference is statistically significant at α = 0.05. *Source*: The Social and Governmental
Issues and Participation (SGIP) study.

likely to engage in political activities.[49] SGIP survey data confirm scholars' asser-
tions that men are more likely than women to express high levels of political
interest. As Figure 7.1 shows, men are significantly more likely than women to
express high levels of political interest. When asked to describe the extent of
their interest in government and politics, 66.9 percent of male college graduates report that they are interested in politics "most of the time," compared to
54.3 percent of their female counterparts.

To test the education-policy model of political interest alongside dominant
explanations for citizens' attention to politics, I measure political interest using
a categorical variable that indicates the level of attention that respondents pay
toward politics. Responses range from 1 (interested in politics "hardly at all") to
4 (interested in politics "most of the time").[50]

Political Efficacy

Have federal higher education policies shaped the extent to which citizens feel that
the government responds to people like them or that they possess the knowledge
and skills necessary to influence government? Scholars examining the determinants of political efficacy and attitudes toward government have found significant
differences according to gender, and analysis of SGIP survey data corroborates
these findings.[51] The descriptive statistics presented in Figure 7.2 report the rates
at which male and female college graduates express high levels of political efficacy
using responses to two questions related to external efficacy and two questions

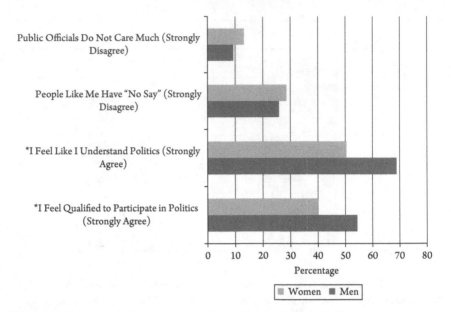

Figure 7.2 Percentage of respondents with high levels of political efficacy among college graduates, by gender. * Gender differences in high level of political efficacy are statistically significant at α = 0.05 for the responses "I feel like I understand politics" and "I feel qualified to participate in politics." *Source*: The Social and Governmental Issues and Participation (SGIP) study.

related to internal efficacy. Significant gender disparities characterize the possession of high levels of internal political efficacy among Americans.

While 68.8 percent of male college graduates strongly agree that they "have a pretty good understanding of the important political issues facing this country," 50.4 percent of women strongly agree with this statement. When asked whether they consider themselves well qualified to participate in politics, 54.3 percent of men strongly agree, compared to 40 percent of women. These high levels of internal political efficacy among male college graduates suggest that men are somewhat advantaged when it comes to political efficacy.

Do federal higher education policies have resource or interpretive effects that influence gender parity in Americans' political efficacy? To consider this question, I again draw on an education-policy model to examine the relationship between eligibility for federal student aid and Title IX protection and the gender dynamics of political efficacy. I operationalize political efficacy using a five-part index consisting of respondents' feeling that public officials care about citizens' preferences, agreement that people like them have a say in government, how well they feel they understand politics, how qualified they feel to participate in politics, and the extent to which they feel like "full and equal citizens."

Scholars have found that age represents an important determinant of political efficacy, as evidence indicates that Americans who are younger and those who are middle-aged tend to have higher levels of efficacy than elderly citizens.[52] To control for the effects of age, I include a control variable for age in years (from eighteen to ninety-two). Scholars examining the effects of race on political efficacy have found mixed results. While some have found lower levels of political efficacy among minority groups, others have found that minorities are no less likely than similar whites to express high levels of efficacy.[53] I control for the effects of race using dichotomous variables that represent self-identification as black (1 if black, 0 if white) and Hispanic (1 if Hispanic, 0 if white). For adults and children, those of lower socioeconomic status—particularly in terms of income—tend to express lower levels of efficacy.[54] Scholars have also noted the importance of education for political efficacy. Those with higher levels of education are more likely to feel politically efficacious and to express positive attitudes toward politics.[55] To account for the effects of socioeconomic status, I include controls for annual income (ten-point scale ranging from "less than $10,000" to "$150,000") and educational attainment (nine-point scale ranging from "less than high school" to "PhD or professional degree").

Political Participation

To what extent have federal higher education policies influenced citizens' involvement in activities geared toward directly altering the political system? I consider Americans' participation in mass political activities including voting, volunteering for political candidates, contributing to campaigns, contacting government officials, and participating in protests.[56] Data from the SGIP survey suggest that, among college graduates, the gender gap that has historically characterized political participation in the United States has narrowed significantly. In Figure 7.3 we see that, although men tend to engage in political activities at slightly higher rates than women, these gender differences are largely insignificant. The exception to this finding is men's significant advantage in contributing to political campaigns. While 52.2 percent of male college graduates have contributed money to political candidates, 43 percent of their female counterparts have done so.

To test an education-policy model of political participation, I use models that include a measure of the dependent variable political participation, which takes the form of an index of involvement in political activities consisting of four dichotomous indicators (which are coded as 1 for affirmative responses and 0 for negative responses): whether respondents ever (a) volunteered on a campaign, (b) contributed to a political candidate, (c) contacted a government official, and (d) participated in a protest or demonstration. This overall measure of political participation takes the form of an ordinal variable with scores ranging from 0 (representing the lowest level of political participation) to 1 (representing the highest level of political participation).

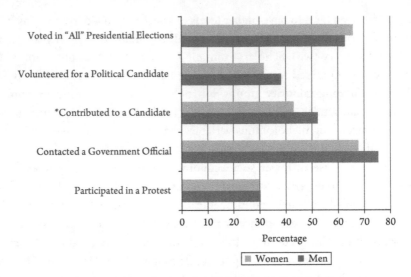

Figure 7.3 Percentage of respondents with high levels of political participation among college graduates, by gender. * Gender differences in high level of political participation are statistically significant at α = 0.05 for contributing to a political candidate. *Source*: The Social and Governmental Issues and Participation (SGIP) study.

Fostering Engagement?: Examining the Feedback Effects of Federal Higher Education Policies

Each year, federal higher education programs provide thousands of American women and men with financial aid that supports their educational pursuits. Does eligibility for federal education benefits promote gender parity in US political engagement? I posit that eligibility for student aid and protection by the Title IX regulation have promoted high levels of political interest, efficacy, and involvement among American women, which have counteracted historical gender disparities in Americans' political attitudes and participation. In the difference-in-differences analyses that follow, I examine the influence that federal higher education policies have had on gender equality in political engagement. I pay particular attention to the resource and interpretive effects of program utilization—as indicated by the coefficients corresponding to interaction variables that consider gender and birth year cohorts corresponding to eligibility for NDEA aid, eligibility for HEA aid, and protection by Title IX (post-1940, post-1947, and post-1957, respectively)—on educational attainment and predicted higher education policy utilization.

Table 7.2 shows a difference-in-means analysis that considers the effect of eligibility for National Defense Student Loans (NSDL) on political engagement. For political interest, efficacy, and participation, women and men in the cohort that had access to NDSL aid when they reached college age report lower levels

Table 7.2 **Difference in Means and Eligibility for National Defense Education Act Student Aid**

	Ineligible for Need-Based Financial Aid Born In/Pre-1940		Eligible for Need-Based Financial Aid Born Post-1940		
	Men	Women	Men	Women	Difference-in-Difference
Education	3.883	3.104	4.082	4.036	0.733
	(0.263)	(0.175)	(0.089)	(0.084)	(0.338)
Age	75.172	75.365	42.395	42.824	0.235
	(0.649)	(0.562)	(0.552)	(0.512)	(1.978)
Black	0.132	0.135	0.162	0.235	0.070
	(0.041)	(0.034)	(0.017)	(0.018)	(0.066)
Hispanic	0.048	0.072	0.132	0.128	-0.027
	(0.025)	(0.025)	(0.014)	(0.013)	(0.053)
Income	5.139	3.707	5.896	5.318	0.855
	(0.326)	(0.196)	(0.116)	(0.113)	(0.449)
Political Interest	3.573	3.187	3.331	3.122	0.177
	(0.095)	(0.095)	(0.037)	(0.039)	(0.150)
Political Efficacy	3.606	3.406	3.414	3.299	0.084
	(0.093)	(0.081)	(0.035)	(0.034)	(0.139)
Political Participation	0.403	0.308	0.356	0.296	0.035
	(0.034)	(0.029)	(0.013)	(0.012)	(0.049)
N	77	110	551	640	1,378

Notes: Means are of Social and Governmental Issues and Participation random samples, weighted by sample weights. Standard errors are in parentheses.

of political engagement than their more senior counterparts for whom these benefits were not available when they reached college. For political interest, for example, the mean response for men declines by 0.24, compared to a decline of 0.07 for women. Similarly, the magnitude of the decline in mean responses for political efficacy and political participation is smaller for women than men. This suggests that, although eligibility for student aid does not appear to promote high levels of political engagement for women or men, it may play an important role in the fact that declining political engagement among women is more modest than the decline among men.

These results hold when we incorporate a comprehensive set of covariates in the multivariate regression analysis in Table 7.3. Here we see that eligibility for

Table 7.3 Effect of Eligibility for National Defense Student Loans on the Probability of Engaging in Politics

	Political Interest		Political Efficacy		Political Participation	
	(1) Difference-in-Differences	(2) Add Covariates	(3) Difference-in-Differences	(4) Add Covariates	(5) Difference-in-Differences	(6) Add Covariates
Female × Post-1940	0.177	0.062	0.084	-0.027	0.035	-0.028
	(0.150)	(0.151)	(0.139)	(0.143)	(0.049)	(0.049)
Female	-0.386**	-0.259	-0.200	-0.181	-0.095*	-0.037
	(0.140)	(0.135)	(0.130)	(0.156)	(0.046)	(0.053)
Post-1940	-0.242*	0.230†	-0.191†	-0.167	-0.047	0.119**
	(0.116)	(0.135)	(0.108)	(0.128)	(0.038)	(0.043)
Female × Education		0.008		0.022		0.003
		(0.024)		(0.023)		(0.008)
Education		0.076***		0.092***		0.048***
		(0.018)		(0.017)		(0.006)
Age		0.014***		0.002		0.005***
		(0.002)		(0.002)		(0.001)

Black		–0.027	–0.085		–0.005
		(0.066)	(0.062)		(0.021)
Hispanic		–0.456***	0.083		–0.081*
		(0.122)	(0.113)		(0.039)
Income		0.014	0.035***		0.009**
		(0.011)	(0.010)		(0.004)
R²	0.018	0.107	0.008	0.121	0.012	0.203
N	1,378	1,134	1,364	1,125	1,372	1,131

† $p \leq .1$, * $p \leq .05$, ** $p \leq .01$, *** $p \leq .001$.

Note: Cells consist of unstandardized ordinary least squares regression coefficients; standard errors are in parentheses. Regressions are weighted by Social and Governmental Issues and Participation sample weights.

Source: Social and Governmental Issues and Participation study.

NDEA loans—as captured by the interaction term *Female × post-1940*—does not appear to promote high levels of political interest, efficacy, or participation. The models do, however, suggest that these programs exert significant resource effects as evinced by the positive influence of educational attainment on each measure of political engagement.

The means analysis in Table 7.4 further examines the influence of student aid eligibility on the gender dynamics of political engagement, this time focusing on eligibility for aid provided by the Higher Education Act's BEOG/Pell Grant Program. As was the case with NDEA loans, results

Table 7.4 **Social and Governmental Issues and Participation Summary Statistics**

	Ineligible for Need-Based Financial Aid Born In/Pre-1947		Eligible for Need-Based Financial Aid Born Post-1947		
	Men	Women	Men	Women	Difference-in-Difference
Education	3.909	3.413	4.097	4.042	0.441
	(0.196)	(0.147)	(0.097)	(0.089)	(0.275)
Age	69.854	71.290	40.151	40.429	−1.158
	(0.609)	(0.551)	(0.526)	(0.480)	(1.405)
Black	0.126	0.166	0.167	0.237	0.030
	(0.029)	(0.029)	(0.018)	(0.019)	(0.054)
Hispanic	0.068	0.071	0.136	0.135	−0.003
	(0.021)	(0.019)	(0.016)	(0.014)	(0.043)
Income	5.420	4.122	5.908	5.365	0.755
	(0.231)	(0.179)	(0.124)	(0.120)	(0.365)
Political Interest	3.546	3.309	3.311	3.074	0.000
	(0.068)	(0.068)	(0.040)	(0.042)	(0.121)
Political Efficacy	3.528	3.352	3.412	3.304	0.069
	(0.065)	(0.067)	(0.038)	(0.036)	(0.111)
Political Participation	0.408	0.332	0.350	0.287	0.013
	(0.025)	(0.023)	(0.014)	(0.012)	(0.040)
N	147	181	481	569	1,378

Notes: Means are of Social and Governmental Issues and Participation random samples, weighted by sample weights. Standard errors are in parentheses.

suggest that men and women who reached college age at a point when they could enjoy access to BEOG/Pell Grants report lower levels of political interest, political efficacy, and political participation than their more senior counterparts who were not eligible for these benefits when they reached college age.

The regression results presented in Table 7.5 corroborate this finding, suggesting that—like the student loans provided under the NDEA—eligibility for HEA financial aid did not yield a significant increase in the probability that women would express high levels of political interest and efficacy or that they would engage in political activities at high rates. The results do, however, suggest that education represents a strong determinant of political interest, political efficacy, and political participation, which suggests that while there may not be significant interpretive effects, BEOG/Pell Grants exert significant resource effects on political engagement by promoting high levels of educational attainment among beneficiaries, as we saw in chapter 6.

What about the Title IX regulation? The analysis of means that is presented in Table 7.6 suggests that, as we saw with the financial aid programs, protection under the Title IX regulation does not yield a substantial increase in political engagement. Rather, men and women in the cohort who reached college age at a time when higher educational institutions operated under the regulation's ban on sex discrimination in college admissions express lower levels of political interest, efficacy, and participation than their counterparts who reached college age before the Title IX regulation went into effect. This is confirmed by the regression models that appear in Table 7.7, which show that eligibility for Title IX has no significant interpretive effects that correspond to higher levels of political engagement. Yet, once again, results suggest that the influence of Title IX takes the form of resource effects: by promoting higher levels of educational attainment, the regulation indirectly promotes high levels of political engagement.

Contrary to my hypothesis that eligibility for NDEA benefits, eligibility for HEA benefits, and protection under Title IX would correspond to significant cognitive feedback effects on political engagement, these null findings reported in the difference-in-differences analyses suggest that this is not the case. Nevertheless, the results of this analysis suggest that high levels of educational attainment significantly increase the probability that respondents will engage in high levels of political involvement. Thus, federal student aid usage provides an important resource that mitigates gender inequality in political participation in the United States.

Table 7.5 **Effect of Eligibility for Higher Education Act Aid on the Probability of Engaging in Politics**

	Political Interest		Political Efficacy		Political Participation	
	(1) Difference-in-Differences	(2) Add Covariates	(3) Difference-in-Differences	(4) Add Covariates	(5) Difference-in-Differences	(6) Add Covariates
Female × Post-1947	0.000	-0.032	0.069	-0.015	0.013	-0.016
	(0.121)	(0.123)	(0.111)	(0.116)	(0.040)	(0.040)
Female	-0.237*	-0.191	-0.177†	-0.188	-0.076*	-0.049
	(0.107)	(0.143)	(0.099)	(0.134)	(0.035)	(0.046)
Post-1947	-0.235**	0.125	-0.116	-0.035	-0.058*	0.094*
	(0.090)	(0.117)	(0.083)	(0.110)	(0.030)	(0.038)
Female × Education		0.011		0.020		0.003
		(0.024)		(0.023)		(0.008)
Education		0.076***		0.092***		0.049***
		(0.018)		(0.017)		(0.006)
Age		0.012***		0.004†		0.005***
		(0.002)		(0.002)		(0.001)

	(1)	(2)	(3)	(4)	(5)	(6)
Black		-0.019		-0.091		-0.004
		(0.066)		(0.062)		(0.021)
Hispanic		-0.445***		0.076		-0.077†
		(0.122)		(0.113)		(0.039)
Income		0.016		0.033**		0.009**
		(0.011)		(0.010)		(0.004)
R^2	0.007	0.025	0.103	0.119	0.016	0.202
N	1,364	1,378	1,134	1,125	1,372	1,131

† $p \le .1$, * $p \le .05$, ** $p \le .01$, *** $p \le .001$.

Note: Cells consist of unstandardized ordinary least squares regression coefficients; standard errors are in parentheses. Regressions are weighted by Social and Governmental Issues and Participation sample weights.

Source: Social and Governmental Issues and Participation Study.

Table 7.6 Social and Governmental Issues and Participation Summary Statistics

	Ineligible for Need-Based Financial Aid Born In/Pre-1957		Eligible for Need-Based Financial Aid Born Post-1957		Difference-in-Difference
	Men	Women	Men	Women	
Education	4.089	3.516	4.042	4.158	0.689
	(0.134)	(0.116)	(0.109)	(0.100)	(0.230)
Age	62.156	64.454	35.334	36.031	-1.601
	(0.556)	(0.568)	(0.487)	(0.442)	(1.030)
Black	0.139	0.197	0.172	0.236	0.006
	(0.022)	(0.023)	(0.022)	(0.022)	(0.045)
Hispanic	0.069	0.085	0.158	0.145	-0.029
	(0.015)	(0.016)	(0.020)	(0.017)	(0.036)
Income	5.509	4.732	6.015	5.316	0.078
	(0.176)	(0.155)	(0.139)	(0.137)	(0.305)
Political Interest	3.494	3.289	3.267	3.018	-0.044
	(0.051)	(0.052)	(0.047)	(0.048)	(0.101)
Political Efficacy	3.498	3.350	3.393	3.291	0.046
	(0.047)	(0.050)	(0.045)	(0.041)	(0.093)
Political Participation	0.438	0.348	0.312	0.261	0.040
	(0.019)	(0.018)	(0.016)	(0.014)	(0.033)
N	286	313	342	437	1,378

Notes: Means are of Social and Governmental Issues and Participation random samples, weighted by sample weights. Standard errors are in parentheses.

Table 7.7 Effect of Protection Under Title IX Regulation on the Probability of Engaging in Politics

	Political Interest		Political Efficacy		Political Participation	
	(1) Difference-in-Differences	(2) Add Covariates	(3) Difference-in-Differences	(4) Add Covariates	(5) Difference-in-Differences	(6) Add Covariates
Female × Post-1957	−0.044 (0.101)	−0.110 (0.103)	0.046 (0.093)	−0.078 (0.097)	0.040 (0.033)	0.011 (0.033)
Female	−0.206** (0.078)	−0.162 (0.122)	−0.148* (0.072)	−0.159 (0.115)	−0.090*** (0.025)	−0.068† (0.039)
Post-1957	−0.227** (0.073)	0.221* (0.105)	−0.105 (0.067)	0.063 (0.098)	−0.124*** (0.025)	−0.087* (0.034)
Female × Education		0.011 (0.024)		0.021 (0.023)		0.004 (0.009)
Education		0.077*** (0.018)		0.093*** (0.017)		0.047*** (0.006)
Age		0.014*** (0.003)		0.005* (0.003)		0.002* (0.001)
Black		−0.015 (0.066)		−0.092 (0.062)		−0.004 (0.021)
Hispanic		−0.437*** (0.122)		0.078 (0.113)		−0.084* (0.039)

(continued)

Table 7.7 **Continued**

	Political Interest		Political Efficacy		Political Participation	
	(1) Difference-in-Differences	(2) Add Covariates	(3) Difference-in-Differences	(4) Add Covariates	(5) Difference-in-Differences	(6) Add Covariates
Income		0.016 (0.011)		0.031** (0.010)		0.012*** (0.004)
R^2	0.032	0.105	0.007	0.119	0.041	0.202
N	1,378	1,134	1,364	1,125	1,372	1,131

$^†p \le .1,$ * $p \le .05,$ ** $p \le .01,$ *** $p \le .001.$

Note: Cells consist of unstandardized ordinary least squares regression coefficients; standard errors are in parentheses. Regressions are weighted by Social and Governmental Issues and Participation sample weights.

Source: Social and Governmental Issues and Participation Study.

The Financial Aid Effect: Higher Education Policy Feedback and the Gender Dynamics of US Political Engagement

This analysis suggests that federal higher education programs have had important feedback effects for the gender dynamics of US political engagement. While existing models of political engagement have rightfully emphasized the importance of demographic and socioeconomic factors to political involvement, scholars are only beginning to attend to the significant feedback effects of public policy utilization on political engagement in the United States. Building on the work of policy feedback scholars who recognize that government programs are institutional factors that have the capacity to alter citizens and the political environment, this analysis has examined the feedback effects of eligibility for financial aid and expanded institutional access provided by federal higher education policies for gender equality in US political engagement. Throughout the analyses presented in this chapter, educational attainment proves to be positively associated with political engagement. As we saw in chapter 6, eligibility for federal student aid and protection under Title IX promote greater educational attainment for American women. Educational attainment, in turn, is a strong determinant of whether citizens will report high levels of political interest, efficacy, and participation.

By promoting higher educational attainment for women, federal financial aid programs have helped to narrow the gender gap in political engagement and have, thus, promoted greater gender parity in the United States. Evidence suggests that the higher-education-policy model of political participation provides a more comprehensive model of the determinants of political involvement than models that overlook the effects of public policies. While demographic and socioeconomic factors go a considerable way in explaining male and female political participation, these factors fail to account for the importance of public policies.

Higher education policies appear to have contributed to increasing gender equality in political engagement through important resource effects, but we do not find significant interpretive effects. A number of factors could explain why student aid does not appear to send messages that increase the probability that women will engage in politics. The fact that women were largely excluded from the benefits of the GI Bill may provide one explanation for this. The GI Bill had important interpretive effects that promoted high levels of political engagement among beneficiaries. Whereas GI Bill benefits were framed as rewards for service to the nation, subsequently enacted federal student aid programs—namely, federal student loans and Pell Grants—have allocated benefits on the basis of financial need or enrollment in accredited institutions of higher education. These programs have not been framed in a way that transmits clear, distinctive messages regarding beneficiaries' value as citizens in the way that the GI Bill did. Moreover, while GI Bill benefits were widely recognized as emanating from the federal government, many student loan and Pell Grant recipients may fail to recognize the federal government as the source of their benefits. As a result, beneficiaries may be less likely to think of their experiences with federal financial aid programs in a way that would influence their attitudes toward government or their inclination to participate in political activities.

Moreover, the absence of significant cognitive effects is not entirely surprising given that—for many respondents—a substantial amount of time had elapsed between the initial treatment (eligibility for student aid or eligibility for nondiscriminatory college admission under Title IX) and the occasion to report on political engagement in the SGIP survey. Nevertheless, the results of this analysis yield important implications for policymakers interested in promoting the welfare of American citizens by increasing gender parity in political engagement. This case provides a valuable example of how the provision of resources represents an important mechanism for increasing gender equality in political citizenship. The centrality of resource effects to the relationship between higher education policy utilization and political engagement mirrors Andrea Campbell's analysis of the federal Social Security program.[57] The difference between these policies, however, is that while Social Security provides valuable retirement benefits that prompt self-interested program recipients to guard their benefits via political participation, federal student aid programs promote political participation by providing resources that empower beneficiaries, rendering them better able to engage in political activities.

Lawmakers interested in promoting equal opportunity can implement social policies that provide citizens with resources that enhance their capacity to engage in politics. By providing valuable resources that significantly increase the probability that beneficiaries will attain higher levels of education, broad-reaching financial aid policies have contributed to significant increases in women's political interest, political efficacy, and involvement in political activities. These increases have contributed to a narrowing of the gender gap in American political engagement. In this way, federal higher education programs are instructive. Not only do they help to realize the promise of full and equal citizenship by promoting political engagement among a group that has traditionally been underrepresented in mass politics, but also they provide lessons as to how the state can successfully use social policy to promote gender equality in terms of political citizenship.

8

Citizenship by Degree

Promoting Equal Opportunity Through Higher Education

American women have come a long way in their journey toward full citizenship. Through much of the nation's history, women typically found it difficult to achieve economic independence and full incorporation into the public sphere. When it came to political engagement, they generally sat on the sidelines, relinquishing the power to determine the nation's course to men. Women's second-class citizenship belied the democratic ideals upon which the nation was founded, thereby representing a significant challenge to the authenticity of America's expressed political values. Since the 1960s, a combination of social, economic, and political strides have helped to usher women toward first-class citizenship. For example, the gender gap in political engagement has narrowed as women have become involved in political activities at increasing rates. Women now represent the majority of American voters, and they participate in a range of political activities, such as contacting elected officials and contributing money to political campaigns, at much higher rates than they did prior to the mid-twentieth century. The nation has also seen a significant increase in the number of women participating in politics at the elite level. Although women have yet to reach the highest elected offices in the national executive branch, women have run for and won local and statewide offices in increasing numbers over the past fifty years.

Conventional wisdom points to the emergence of feminism and the women's rights movement of the 1970s as the critical factor promoting enhanced opportunity for women in recent decades; yet, I have made the case that federal higher education policies—which were established prior to and apart from the feminist movement—represent a frequently overlooked factor that has played a central role in the advances that women have made. Using a combination of redistributive and regulatory policy, US lawmakers have helped to promote women toward the status of full and equal citizens. In a lethal one-two punch in a powerful assault on gender-unequal US higher education, lawmakers addressed resource disparities and institutional discrimination that had long suppressed the number of women graduating from the nation's colleges and universities.

Not only did financial aid programs created under the National Defense Education Act (NDEA) and the Higher Education Act (HEA) remove afford-ability as a formidable barrier to women's access to higher education, but also lawmakers invoked the state's regulatory power to ensure that institutions sub-jected women and men to the same admissions criteria. In doing so, they insti-tutionalized women's treatment as first-class citizens under US social policy and strengthened gender equality in social and political citizenship. In this way, landmark higher education policies have empowered women, a group that has historically occupied the margins of society, the economic landscape, and mass politics. By significantly expanding women's access to college degrees, these pro-grams helped pave the way for women to surpass men as the recipients of bach-elor's degrees, while also empowering women to become more economically independent, socially integrated, politically engaged members of the American citizenry.

The findings of this analysis also prompt a reconsideration of the traditional narrative of US welfare state development that has long cast southerners and nonliberals as inhibitors of progressive legislative efforts. To the contrary, by spearheading efforts to increase federal support for college students, a number of conservative and southern lawmakers supported some of the most conse-quential expansions of the American welfare state. Were it not for the handiwork of a small, but effective, group of policy entrepreneurs that included Southern Democrats and political moderates, these policy innovations might never have emerged from the political process. The successful passage of the NDEA, the HEA, and Title IX and their effectiveness for expanding access to higher edu-cation are largely the result of lawmakers' commitment to expanding access to higher education, their keen appreciation for the contemporaneous political context, their extensive knowledge of the political institutions within which they worked, and their strategic approaches to steering education policy proposals through the political process.

Higher education represents a critical building block of social, economic, and political inclusion, which in turn represent the pillars of first-class citizenship. By providing women—a group whose voices had historically sung *sotto voce* in mass politics—with greater access to higher education, national lawmakers used pub-lic policy to significantly increase the probability that women would participate as full and equal members of the polity. From the military service–based and, thus, overwhelmingly male targeting of the GI Bill in 1944 to the bold prohibi-tion of sex discrimination in college admissions established by Title IX in 1972, there can be no doubt that lawmakers have had extensive influence on gender egalitarianism in American colleges and universities. Public policymakers have used a combination of redistributive financial aid programs and institutional regulation to influence who gains the knowledge, skills, and socioeconomic benefits that emanate from higher education—benefits that, in turn, facilitate political interest, efficacy, and involvement. By wielding such considerable influence over who enjoys access to higher education, the federal government has helped to shape the gender dynamics of higher educational attainment in the United States and, thus, the gender dynamics of social and political citizenship.

Different Women: Intersectionality and Higher Education Policy

It remains to be seen whether federal higher education policies have had identical feedback effects for all American women. Given the intersectionality of gender, race, class, and age, it seems unlikely. Research has shown that the benefits provided by federal student aid programs have been particularly valuable to minority women, whose status as "double minorities" is accompanied by intensified social and economic challenges.[1] As such, it seems plausible that black women and Latinas, for example, would be particularly receptive to higher education policies and particularly sensitive to their feedback effects for civic engagement and political participation. Because of minority women's early integration into the labor force and their frequent omission from the gendered division of labor that emphasized the virtue of domesticity and "Republican Motherhood," these women may have been especially amenable to the benefits that completing a college degree could yield. I suspect that programs facilitating access to higher education provided highly valued benefits to minority women, such as increased income and pathways to more prestigious, better-paying occupations, as well as positive interactions with the federal government.

For women relegated to the margins of society, higher education programs may have also represented an effective antipoverty mechanism that increased the probability that beneficiaries and their families would achieve socioeconomic stability. Furthermore, for women who had long been relegated to domestic work, college degrees could yield substantial social mobility, providing access to professions like teaching, social work, and nursing, which were associated with heightened social prestige. Considering the findings of this analysis—especially the valuable resource effects that federal student aid policies have transmitted to all women—it seems likely that such resource effects would be particularly valuable to minority women. Future studies might consider the relationship between federal student aid utilization and women's political activism during the struggle for civil and women's rights. In addition to increasing access to higher education, federal higher education programs have facilitated women's involvement in mass politics.

194

It also remains to be seen whether government aid for students shaped the activism of female political elites working in political action committees and in formal governmental institutions, like the US Congress. Scholars have shown that lawmakers' personal identities shape policy outcomes and that the political views of women and men diverge on a number of pivotal issues. Congresswomen are more likely than their male counterparts to support bills related to women's issues.[2] As the number of women earning college degrees has increased, so too has the number of women running for and winning election to local, statewide, and national political office. Although at the time of this writing women have yet to reach the highest echelons of the nation's executive branch, women are serving in city councils, county commissions, the national and state-level legislatures, governors' mansions, and courthouses in increasing numbers. The women who attain these positions are overwhelmingly college graduates, and many of them have obtained advanced degrees. Considering the significant influence that federal higher education programs have had for gender equality in mass politics, it seems likely that these policies also shape elite politics.

Not Your Daddy's Education Program?: Higher Education Policies and American Men

Following the creation of federal policies expanding women's access to higher education, we have seen significant change in the status of American men in higher education. A puzzling trend that has occurred in tandem with recent increases in women's higher educational attainment is a decline in the rate at which men earn bachelor's degrees. The year 1981 marked the beginning of a significant gender gap, whereby women consistently outpaced men as the recipients of undergraduate degrees. By 2010, women earned 57 percent of bachelor's degrees, compared to just under 43 percent for men.[3] This substantial gender gap in college degree attainment is puzzling, especially when we consider that this dynamic was reversed in the 1960s.

Scholars seeking to explain this new gender gap in women's and men's higher educational attainment have offered a range of explanations, such as the possibility that deficiencies in noncognitive skills (such as the ability to follow directions, time management, and organizational skills) and low levels of motivation contribute to boys' and men's declining higher educational attainment. Research has shown that male students are less likely than their female peers to engage in precollege activities like academic camps and workshops that could increase the probability that they will persist in college and complete their degrees.[4] Another explanation could be that, while young men once viewed a college degree as a key that would unlock lucrative occupations, they have increasingly aspired to jobs that do not require an advanced education.[5]

Along these same lines, scholars have shown that young women are more likely to have completed college preparatory courses in most academic areas than young men.[6] Boys are more likely than girls to require special education accommodations and to be diagnosed with attention deficit/hyperactivity disorder.[7] Boys are also more likely to be suspended from school, to be held back, and to drop out altogether. Scholars have even pointed to what they term the "feminization of education" in the United States—the idea that American schools, and their increasingly female teaching staff, disadvantage and alienate boys by forcing students to adapt to customs and procedures that do not come easily to boys, who are naturally more rambunctious than girls.[8] Perhaps the most compelling explanation for this decline is rooted in broader, societal factors such as economic trends and the influence of social movements. Some have focused on the fact that there is a significant wage premium for women—in other words, the financial benefits of obtaining higher education are greater for women than for men.[9] Thus, the calculus by which Americans decide whether to invest in higher education may vary by gender.

Some have pointed to the possibility that by expanding women's access to higher education, the federal government has contributed to the significant decline in men's higher educational attainment and, further, their declining political engagement. Did the passage of Title IX, which overtly promoted women's inclusion in colleges and universities, precipitate the decline in men's higher educational attainment? To be clear, women and men have enjoyed equal access to federal grants and student loans under the programs created by the National Defense Education Act and the Higher Education Act. Moreover, Title IX has not promoted bias against men in higher education; it merely says that there will be no sex discrimination in admissions decisions. Both women and men are covered by that protection. As such, it would be difficult to make the case that Title IX is directly responsible for men's declining presence in higher education. Nonetheless, in making it illegal to discriminate against women in college admissions, the passage of Title IX marked the end of an era in which men were guaranteed a majority of seats at American higher educational institutions. Thus, after 1972, men and women would have to compete for each of those seats. While Title IX is not responsible for the declining presence of men in American colleges, the regulation has contributed to significant societal shifts that have challenged traditional gender norms in higher education.

Title IX has also challenged traditional family norms. As women have obtained higher education in greater numbers, and as they have moved into the public sphere at greater rates, women have come to enjoy greater economic independence than their foremothers. It could be the case that, as women have obtained higher levels of education and the socioeconomic benefits that come with it, the traditional family structure—which has long placed men in the role of "breadwinner"—has broken down. As a result, men may not feel as compelled to attend college for the purpose of getting high-paying jobs that will provide the primary source of income for their families. Another possibility is that, since the 1980s, high rates of incarceration have contributed to the decreasing rates at which men graduate from college and to their declining political participation. These potential explanations fall beyond the scope of this analysis; however, on the whole, women's large-scale movement into higher education appears to have significantly altered the gender dynamics that traditionally governed men's and women's family decisions. Understanding why men have fallen behind in college degree attainment represents an important puzzle for scholars of political science and public policy.

Unlocking Democratic Citizenship with Public Policy

The role that higher education policies have played in supporting women's movement toward first-class citizenship has important implications for how we think about public policy and its value as a mechanism for achieving national goals. The National Defense Education Act, the Higher Education Act, and Title IX represent a two-pronged policy approach that reshaped the gender dynamics of American colleges and universities. First, the NDEA and HEA redistributed federal resources in a way that removed cost as a barrier to higher education for women. Then, lawmakers used the Title IX regulation to eradicate the institutional barriers that limited women's access to colleges and universities. This two-pronged approach was necessary to effectively increase women's access to higher education. The funds provided by the NDEA and HEA would not reach maximum effectiveness until Title IX removed institutional barriers that suppressed women's admission to college. The redistributive policies alone were not enough to correct the problem of unequal access to higher education.

While the NDEA's and the HEA's redistributive federal student aid programs and the Title IX regulation took contrasting approaches to achieve the common end of increasing access to higher education, both approaches have been equally important to enhancing gender equality in higher education and political engagement. Although Title IX boldly promoted women's access to the nation's colleges and universities by banning sex discrimination in admissions policies, the NDEA and the HEA helped the nation to fathom the revolutionary idea of women's equal presence in postsecondary institutions. These early financial aid policies reshaped how Americans conceptualized higher education and conventional notions of which citizens are best suited for higher learning.

The development of these programs also highlights the centrality of political context to the extent to which lawmakers can address social problems. In the case of women's restricted access to college degrees, lawmakers working in 1958 could not remove all of the barriers that limited women's access to higher education at once. Objections to an extensive federal role in higher education limited the range of action they could take to promote broad inclusion in colleges and universities. Accordingly, the NDEA took a measured step in that direction by providing women and men, broadly, with financial support for college. Seven years later, in passing the HEA, policymakers extended this support. Again, they invoked redistributive policy, which best suited the political context of the 1960s.

In 1972, the policy context had shifted to one that privileged regulatory policy, and lawmakers effectively invoked federal regulation to compel higher educational institutions to provide women and men with equal access to college admission. In addition to highlighting the importance of political context to the viability and effectiveness of particular policy alternatives, this analysis has also demonstrated the power of this two-pronged, mixed-policy approach for ameliorating inequality that is rooted in both individual- and institutional-level challenges. In the case of combating gender inequality in higher education, it seems unlikely that the use of only redistributive policy or only regulatory policy would have proven as effective as the two-pronged approach. As a result of these policies, women gained more opportunities to venture into higher educational institutions and gender discrimination became increasingly apparent. Moreover, as women excelled in college—meeting and often exceeding the performance of their male counterparts—such discrimination became all the more intolerable.

Giving the Gift of Class: Higher Education Policy and the American Welfare State

The creation of broad-reaching federal support for individuals interested in pursuing higher education represents an important innovation in American social policy. Higher education policies have significantly expanded access to colleges and universities for millions of citizens. Without the financial assistance provided under the National Defense Education Act and the Higher Education Act and the egalitarian access to higher educational institutions that Title IX guaranteed, it is unlikely that women would currently represent the majority of American college students. These programs significantly expanded women's access to higher education and the social and economic benefits that emanate from it. Federal higher education programs enacted since the mid-twentieth century have important implications for how we conceptualize the American welfare state, for the future of higher education policy, and for the long-term effectiveness of higher education programs as a component of US social policy.

The purpose of the welfare state is to safeguard the social and economic well-being of the nation's citizens. As such, federal student aid programs represent an innovative approach to pursuing this end and cause us to expand our conceptualization of the welfare state. Unlike the nation's most prominent welfare state programs—such as Temporary Assistance to Needy Families (TANF), food stamps, and Medicaid—which are often demonized as the hallmarks of "big government" and criticized for providing handouts to the undeserving poor, financial aid programs have largely avoided such criticism by attaching federal resources to the generally respected pursuit of higher education. This is in large part due to the fact that education programs coincide with Americans' more positive attitudes toward measures that promote equal opportunity than those that support equal outcomes. The beneficiaries of government grants and loans must pair this support with their own efforts, which are crucial to completing a degree. A postsecondary degree, in turn, provides a credential that is associated with greater access to well-paying jobs and long-term socioeconomic stability. Although the government helps students access the path to higher education, it is incumbent on them to actually complete an academic program before they can reap the full benefits of the aid provided. Most Americans who receive federal benefits are expected to repay them, and all beneficiaries engage in academic work toward a college degree. Therefore, federal student aid policies institutionalized what I would term an "earned redistribution" of government funds, challenging the politically inflammatory representation of federal assistance as government handouts.

Considering the vitality of federal higher education programs to the socioeconomic and political well-being of American citizens, expanding these programs could represent an effective and politically viable way to increase economic opportunity in the United States and to thus strengthen the welfare state. Emphasizing the "earned" nature of redistributive student aid programs could provide an effective way to secure support for additional higher education programs that provide women and men with valuable resources. Moreover, federal efforts to promote equality using higher educational programming could provide lawmakers operating in the context of considerable polarization and legislative gridlock with a politically valuable tool for expanding the social welfare state. Using this type of framing that emphasizes the task-oriented nature of federal financial aid, student assistance programs would likely join popular and politically resilient programs like Social Security in casting beneficiaries as worthy recipients of the government's largesse. I have demonstrated that federal higher education policies have promoted increased higher educational attainment and political engagement among women, a group that has been historically marginalized in education and mass politics. As such, it is in the nation's democratic interest that we not only protect these programs but also strengthen them to provide politically underrepresented groups with access to higher education.

The success of these landmark policies for increasing access to higher education also has important implications for the methods by which lawmakers use public programming to support college students. As government support for higher education has expanded to reach more Americans—irrespective of income or financial need—and as lawmakers have come to rely most heavily on student loans, this form of support now dominates the student aid landscape. Federal grants, on the other hand, represent an ever-dwindling item on the menu of student assistance.[10] In a political context characterized by considerable hostility toward policies that resemble traditional welfare state programs like TANF and food stamps, federally subsidized student loans represent the most politically viable method of redistributing federal funds to assist college students.

Considering the value of higher education for promoting socioeconomic stability and political engagement among the nation's citizens, American lawmakers would do well to find ways to continue expanding higher educational access for citizens and to provide them with support as they pursue college degrees. As would be expected from the prevalence of student loans, American students now face an ever-increasing amount of debt, and women appear to be particularly affected by this trend. During the 2011–2012 academic year, 42.6 percent of women undergraduates used federal student loans, compared to 37.3 percent of men. In addition to borrowing money at higher rates than men, women also borrow slightly larger amounts. That same year, women borrowed an average of $6,570, compared to an average of $6,550 for men.[11] If women are disproportionately burdened by the weight of federal student loans, it could mean that they face additional related challenges like difficulty securing the financial resources necessary to pursue graduate or professional training, to purchase a home, or to start a family. As such, this type of burden would endanger the legacy of federal higher education programming for promoting full citizenship for American women.

To decrease the amount of debt that Americans take on when pursuing college degrees, policymakers might consider expanding the availability of federal grants and scaling back the nation's dependence on student loans. One way to do this would be to adjust the criteria that the government considers when determining students' dependency status and the amount of money that families are expected to allocate toward higher education. Under the current system, regardless of students' actual living situation, most single, childless undergraduate students under the age of twenty-four are considered financial dependents for the purposes of calculating financial aid rewards. Even if these students are not actually financially supported by their parents, they are required to provide their parents' financial information as they apply for federal financial aid. This system effectively limits the number of students who are eligible for federal grants. Allowing more students to apply for federal aid as independents would render many more students available for this type of aid.

All things considered, this analysis suggests that to fully understand the progress that American women have made in the last half century, we must take into account the landmark federal higher education programs that have contributed to the dramatic increase in women's higher educational attainment. The National Defense Education Act, the Higher Education Act, and Title IX have made significant contributions to women's movement toward equal status as citizens, particularly when it comes to incorporation into American social, economic, and political life. While the GI Bill promoted men's political participation in the postwar era, I have argued that subsequently enacted Pell Grants, student loans, and Title IX promoted greater gender parity in American politics by significantly increasing the likelihood that women would obtain higher levels of education. In passing these programs, US lawmakers played a central role in promoting women to first-class citizenship.

Appendix A

VARIABLES USED IN EMPIRICAL ANALYSES

Table A.6.1 **Variables Used in Analysis of Social and Governmental Issues and Participation Study Data**

Variable	Range	Coding
Educational Attainment	1–9	As an independent variable: Indicates highest level of education coded into nine categories: (1) less than high school; (2) high school diploma/GED; (3) technical or vocational school; (4) some college; (5) two-year degree; (6) four-year degree; (7) some graduate school; (8) master's; (9) PhD or professional degree
	1–6	As a dependent variable in ordinal logistic regression models: Indicates highest level of education coded into six categories: (1) less than high school; (2) high school diploma/GED; (3) technical school or some college; (4) two-year degree; (5) four-year degree; (6) postcollege study/graduate or professional degree
Employment Status	0, 1	Indicates whether respondent is employed (1) or not (0)
Employer-Provided Health Plan	0, 1	Indicates whether the respondent possesses an employer-provided health plan, coded as yes (1) or no (0)
Any Higher Education Policy Usage	0, 1	A combined variable measuring whether respondents took advantage of one or more of the following programs: Pell Grants, student loans, and the GI Bill
Pell Grant Usage	0, 1	Indicates whether respondent ever received Pell Grants (1) or not (0)
Student Loan Usage	0, 1	Indicates whether respondent ever received student loans (1) or not (0)
GI Bill Usage	0, 1	Indicates whether respondent ever received GI Bill benefits (1) or not (0)

(continued)

Table A.6.1 **Continued**

Variable	Range	Coding
Gender	0, 1	The respondent's gender, coded as 1 for female and 0 for male
Age	18–92	The respondent's age in years
Black	0, 1	The respondent's racial self-identification: those identifying as black or African American are coded as 1; those identifying as white are coded as 0; all others are coded as missing
Hispanic	0, 1	The respondent's racial self-identification: those identifying as Hispanic are coded as 1; those identifying as white are coded as 0; all others are coded as missing
Childhood Socioeconomic Status	1–5	Respondent's family income compared to others at age sixteen; ranges from 1 ("far below average") to 5 ("far above average")
Income	1–10	Respondent's annual total household income coded into ten categories from 1, which corresponds to less than $10,000 annually, to 10, which corresponds to $150,000 or more
Mother's Education	1–9	Indicates mother's highest level of education coded into nine categories: (1) less than high school; (2) high school diploma/GED; (3) technical school; (4) some college, no degree; (5) two-year degree; (6) four-year degree; (7) some postcollege education; no degree; (8) master's degree; (9) PhD or professional degree
Homeownership	0, 1	Whether the respondent is a homeowner (1) or not (0)
Political Information Index	4 parts	Index consisting of respondents' ability to identify the vice president, the branch that determines whether laws are constitutional, the percentage of congressional votes necessary to override a presidential veto, and the party controlling the House of Representatives
Political Efficacy Index	5 parts	Index consisting of feeling that public officials care about citizens' preferences, people like the respondent have a say in government, understanding politics, feeling qualified to participate, and feeling like "full and equal citizens"
Government Opportunity	1–5	Belief that the government has offered opportunities to increase standard of living: coded 1 (strongly disagree) through 5 (strongly agree)

Table A.6.1 **Continued**

Variable	Range	Coding
Full Citizenship	1–5	Feeling like a "full and equal citizen," organized into five categories from (1) disagree strongly to (5) agree strongly
Qualified to Participate	1–5	Feeling qualified to participate in politics, organized into five categories from (1) disagree strongly to (5) agree strongly
Owe Back to Country	1–5	Indicates respondents' agreement with the notion of owing back to the country, organized into five categories from (1) disagree strongly to (5) agree strongly
Political Interest	1–4	General interest in government and public affairs coded as 1 (hardly ever) through 4 (most of the time)

Table A.6.2 **Variables Used in Analysis of 2008 National Postsecondary Student Aid Study Data**

Variable	Range	Coding
Ultimate Education Planned	1–4	Indicates the highest level of education that the student intends to attain, coded into four categories: (1) associate's degree or professional certificate; (2) bachelor's degree; (3) master's degree/post–master's certificate; (4) PhD or professional degree
Age	12–76	Indicates the respondent's age on August 1, 2007
Race (Black)	0, 1	Indicates whether the respondent identifies as black (1) or white (0)
Mother's Education	1–6	Mother's highest level of educational attainment: (1) less than high school; (2) high school diploma/GED; (3) vocational training/some college; (4) associate's degree; (5) bachelor's degree; (6) master's/PhD/or first professional degree
Go-Getters	6 parts	A six-part index of student's participation in high school activities that correspond to confidence, ambition, and leadership characteristics: (1) participation in student government; (2) participation in departmental clubs; (3) membership in a high school fraternity or sorority; (4) participation in community service organizations; (5) membership in a special interest group; (6) received any type of leadership award (each individual activity is represented by a dichotomous variable)
Federal Student Aid Usage	0, 1	A combined variable measuring whether respondents took advantage of one or more of the following programs: Pell Grants, Stafford Loans, Perkins Loans, and veterans' benefits

Table A.6.3 **Variables Used in Analysis of Cooperative Institutional Research Program Freshman Survey Data**

Variable	Range	Coding
Gender	0, 1	The respondent's gender, coded as 1 for female and 0 for male
Age Group	1–6	Indicates the respondent's age bracket, coded into six groups: (1) sixteen years old or younger; (2) seventeen years old; (3) eighteen years old; (4) nineteen years old; (5) twenty years old; (6) age twenty-one or older
Black	0, 1	The respondent's racial self-identification: those identifying as black or African American are coded as 1; those identifying as white are coded as 0; all others are coded as missing
Parent's Income	1–14	Indicates parent's annual income, by brackets ranging from (1) "less than $6,000" to (14) "$200,000 or more"
Mother's Education	1–5	Indicates mother's highest level of educational attainment: (1) less than grammar school/some high school; (2) high school graduate; (3) nondegree postsecondary training/some college; (4) college degree/some graduate school; (5) graduate or professional degree
Go-Getters Index	5 parts	Index consisting of respondent's self-assessment of competitiveness, drive to achieve, leadership ability, intellectual self-confidence, and social self-confidence relative to peers
Any Higher Education Policy Usage	0, 1	Indicates whether respondent has used one or more of the following federal student aid policies: Pell Grants, Supplemental Educational Opportunity Grants (SEOGs), work-study, Stafford Loans (GSL), Perkins Loans (NDSL), or "other federal student aid"; affirmative responses are coded as 1, negative responses as (0)

Table A.7.1 **Variables Used in Analysis of Social and Governmental Issues and Participation Study Data**

Variable	Range	Coding
Female	0, 1	The respondent's gender, coded as 1 for female and 0 for male
Age	18–92	The respondent's age in years
Black	0, 1	The respondent's racial self-identification: those identifying as black or African American are coded as 1; those identifying as white are coded as 0; all others are coded as missing

Table A.7.1 **Continued**

Variable	Range	Coding
Hispanic	0, 1	The respondent's racial self-identification: those identifying as Hispanic are coded as 1; those identifying as white are coded as 0; all others are coded as missing
Childhood Socioeconomic Status	1–5	Respondent's family income compared to others at age sixteen; ranges from 1 ("far below average") to 5 ("far above average")
Income	1–10	Respondent's annual total household income coded into ten categories from 1, which corresponds to less than $10,000 annually, to 10, which corresponds to $150,000 or more
Mother's Education	1–9	Indicates mother's highest level of education coded into nine categories: (1) less than high school; (2) high school diploma/GED; (3) technical school; (4) some college, no degree; (5) two-year degree; (6) four-year degree; (7) some postcollege education, no degree; (8) master's degree; (9) PhD or professional degree
Educational Attainment	1–9	As an independent variable: indicates highest level of education coded into nine categories: (1) less than high school; (2) high school diploma/GED; (3) technical or vocational school; (4) some college; (5) two-year degree; (6) four-year degree; (7) some graduate school; (8) master's; (9) PhD or professional degree
Veteran	0, 1	Indicates whether the respondent has served in the armed forces (1) or not (0)
Any Higher Education Policy Usage	0, 1	A combined variable measuring whether respondents took advantage of one or more of the following programs: Pell Grants, student loans, and the GI Bill
Predicted Higher Education Policy Usage	0, 1	Propensity scores representing the probability that the respondent would adopt Pell Grant, student loan, or GI Bill benefits
Voting in Presidential Elections	1–5	Rate of voting in presidential elections: (1) "never voted"; (2) "rarely voted"; (3) "voted in some"; (4) "voted in most"; (5) "voted in all"
Campaigned	0, 1	Indicates whether respondent ever volunteered on a political campaign (1) or not (0)

(continued)

Table A.7.1 **Continued**

Variable	Range	Coding
Contributed	0, 1	Indicates whether respondent ever donated money to a political candidate or cause (1) or not (0)
Contacted	0, 1	Indicates whether respondent ever contacted a government official (1) or not (0)
Protested	0, 1	Indicates whether respondent ever participated in a protest or march (1) or not (0)
Political Participation Index	4 parts	Index consisting of whether respondents have ever volunteered on a political campaign, donated money to a political candidate or cause, contacted a government official, and participated in a protest or march
Political Efficacy Index	5 parts	Index consisting of feeling that public officials care about citizens' preferences, people like the respondent have a say in government, understanding politics, feeling qualified to participate, and feeling like "full and equal citizens"
Political Interest	1–4	Indicates the respondent's level of interest in politics: (1) "hardly at all"; (2) "only now and then"; (3) "some of the time"; (4) "most of the time"

Appendix B

SUPPLEMENTARY FIGURES AND TABLES

Table B.3.1 **Interest Groups Active in the Debate over Federal Aid to Education in 1957**

Supporters	# Members	Opponents	# Members
AFL-CIO	15,000,000	American Legion	2,800,000
National Congress of Parents and Teachers	10,130,000	Chamber of Commerce of the United States	1,700,000
The General Federation of Women's Clubs[a]	5,500,000	American Farm Bureau Federation	1,623,222
National Education Association	659,190	American Medical Association	150,000
United Mine Workers	600,000	National Association of Real Estate Boards	58,000
National Association for the Advancement of Colored People (NAACP)	300,000	National Association of Manufacturers	21,500
National Farmers' Union	274,119	National Economic Council	2,000
Brotherhood of Railroad Trainmen	210,708	Southern States Industrial Council	2,000
American Association of University Women	136,738	Investment Bankers Association of America	—[b]
American Veterans of World War II and Korea	125,000	National Conference of State Taxpayers Associations	—[c]

(continued)

Table B.3.1 **Continued**

Supporters	# Members	Opponents	# Members
National Council of Jewish Women	107,000	Defenders of the American Constitution	—[d]
International Association for Childhood Education	81,000		
American Federation of Teachers (AFL-CIO)	50,000		
Jewish War Veterans	45,000		
Americans for Democratic Action	39,000		
American Association of University Professors	37,000		
Order of Railway Conductors and Brakemen	35,000		
American Vocational Association	32,000		
American Veterans Committee	25,000		
American Home Economics Association	24,000		
American Library Association	20,000		
National Association of Social Workers	20,000		
National Child Labor Committee	13,000		
American Institute of Architects	10,700		
National Consumers League	10,000		

Table B.3.1 **Continued**

Supporters	# Members	Opponents	# Members
American Association of School Administrators	9,200		
Unitarian Fellowship for Social Justice	400		
American Parents Committee	400		
National Jewish Welfare Board	—[e]		
Council of Chief State School Officers	—[f]		
National School Boards Association	—[g]		
Railway Labor Executives' Association	—[h]		
Cooperative League of the USA	—[i]		

[a] The General Federation of Women's Clubs attended the first meeting of the Conference on Federal Aid to Education, but it did not formally testify in favor of or against federal school aid.

[b] 799 banks and investment houses.

[c] 37 states.

[d] Membership unavailable.

[e] 350 Jewish community centers and Young Men's and Young Women's Hebrew Associations.

[f] 53 state school officials.

[g] 43 state school boards.

[h] 22 chief executive officers of railway labor organizations.

[i] 20 cooperative organizations.

Source: "Who's For, Against U.S. School Aid?," *Congressional Quarterly Weekly Report*. Week ending April 19, 1957, 495–496.

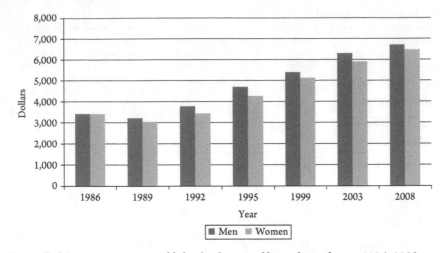

Figure B.6.1 Average amount of federal aid received by undergraduates, 1986–2008.
Note: Dollar amounts are given in current dollars, thus reflecting actual amounts prevailing during specified years. *Source*: US Department of Education, National Postsecondary Student Aid Study (NPSAS).

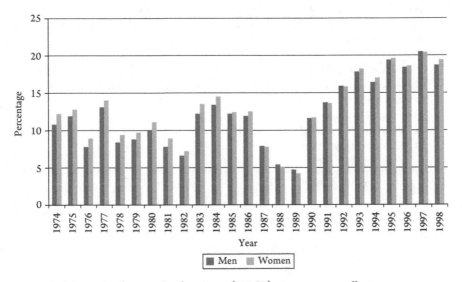

Figure B.6.2 National Direct Student Loan (NDSL) usage among college freshmen, 1974–1998. *Note:* These gender differences are statistically significant at $\alpha = 0.001$.
Source: Cooperative Institutional Research Program (CIRP) Freshman survey.

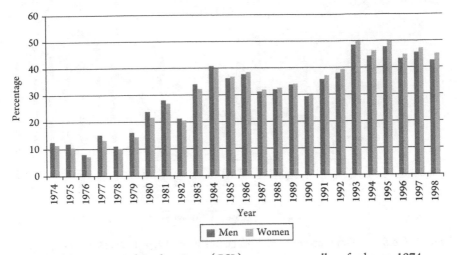

Figure B.6.3 Guaranteed Student Loan (GSL) usage among college freshmen, 1974–1998. *Note:* These gender differences are statistically significant at α = 0.001. *Source*: Cooperative Institutional Research Program (CIRP) Freshman survey.

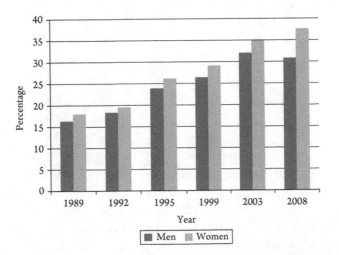

Figure B.6.4 Percentage of undergraduates receiving federal loans, 1989–2008. *Source*: US Department of Education, National Postsecondary Student Aid Study (NPSAS).

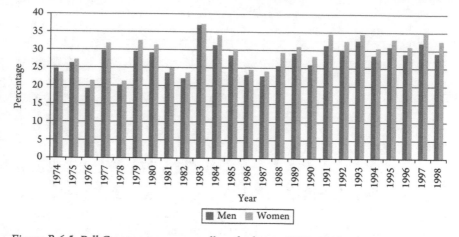

Figure B.6.5 Pell Grant usage among college freshmen, 1974–1998. *Note:* These gender differences are statistically significant at α = 0.001. *Source:* Cooperative Institutional Research Program (CIRP) Freshman survey.

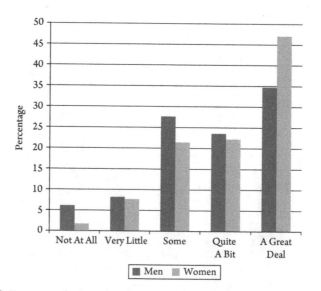

Figure B.6.6 Extent to which student loans expanded educational opportunity among college graduates, by gender. *Note:* These gender differences do not reach statistical significance. *Source:* The Social and Governmental Issues and Participation (SGIP) study.

Table B.6.1 **Determinants of Higher Education Policy Usage**

	GI Bill	Student Loans	Pell Grants	Any Higher Education Policy
Gender	−2.858***	.391**	.463**	.010
	(.424)	(.144)	(.173)	(.132)
Age	.057***	−.042***	−.037***	−.026***
	(.010)	(.005)	(.006)	(.004)
Black	−.241	.536**	.473*	.511**
	(.458)	(.186)	(.209)	(.178)
Hispanic	—	.143	−.574	.039
		(.371)	(.488)	(.356)
Childhood Socioeconomic Status	.035	−.082	−.184†	−.124†
	(.170)	(.081)	(.096)	(.075)
Mother's Education	−.101	.055	.008	.049
	(.086)	(.037)	(.044)	(.035)
−2 log likelihood	355.36	1,171.36	900.70	1,335.18
Goodness of Fit	103.60	110.80	62.53	60.85
Cox and Snell R^2	.102	.101	.058	.057
N	1,028	1,105	1,104	1,105

$^†p \le .1,$ $^*p \le .05,$ $^{**}p \le .01,$ $^{***}p \le .001.$

Notes: Cells consist of binary logistic regression coefficients in the numerator and standard errors in parentheses.

Analysis includes respondents who have earned at least a high school diploma or its equivalent.

Source: The Social and Governmental Issues and Participation (SGIP) study.

Table B.6.2 **Determinants of Higher Education Policy Usage, by Gender**

	GI Bill	Student Loans		Pell Grants		Any Higher Ed Policy	
	Men	Men	Women	Men	Women	Men	Women
Age	.070***	−.033***	−.049***	−.020*	−.050***	−.002	−.050***
	(.011)	(.008)	(.007)	(.009)	(.008)	(.006)	(.007)
Black	−.646	.558[†]	.539*	.331	.580*	.644*	.467[†]
	(.569)	(.295)	(.244)	(.353)	(.267)	(.277)	(.242)
Hispanic	—	−.300	.540	−1.182	−.205	−.514	.582
		(.564)	(.522)	(.931)	(.600)	(.529)	(.542)
Childhood Socio-economic Status	.058	−.140	−.034	−.329*	−.087	−.076	−.157
	(.188)	(.125)	(.107)	(.152)	(.123)	(.111)	(.105)
Mother's Education	−.098	.097[†]	.015	.047	−.014	.074	.024
	(.093)	(.052)	(.053)	(.065)	(.061)	(.047)	(.052)
−2 log likelihood	270.52	551.23	615.48	400.89	490.53	661.84	640.94
Goodness of Fit	56.47	37.72	73.83	13.38	52.93	9.82	83.32
Cox and Snell R^2	.123	.073	.128	.027	.093	.019	.143
N	421	493	612	492	612	493	612

[†] $p \leq .1$, * $p \leq .05$, ** $p \leq .01$, *** $p \leq .001$.

Notes: Cells consist of binary logistic regression coefficients in the numerator and standard errors in parentheses. Analysis includes respondents who have earned at least a high school diploma or its equivalent.

Source: The Social and Governmental Issues and Participation (SGIP) study.

Table B.6.3 **Determinants of Higher Education Policy Usage Among College Freshmen: Logistic Regression Results**

	All	*Men*	*Women*
Gender	.035***		
	(.006)		
Age Group	.000	−.007	.006
	(.006)	(.008)	(.008)
Black	.185***	.110***	.241***
	(.011)	(.016)	(.014)
Parent's Income	−.303***	−.294***	−.310***
	(.001)	(.002)	(.002)
Mother's Education	−.068***	−.090***	−.049***
	(.003)	(.004)	(.004)
"Go-Getters"	.080***	.132***	.031***
	(.005)	(.007)	(.007)
−2 log likelihood	693,684.63	316,839.18	376,623.08
Goodness of Fit	90,959.96	37,473.82	52,999.46
Cox and Snell R^2	.145	.134	.152
N	144,447	62,578	81,869

$^+ p \le .1,\, ^* p \le .05,\, ^{**} p \le .01,\, ^{***} p \le .001$.

Notes: Cells consist of binary logistic regression coefficients in the numerator and standard errors in parentheses.

Source: The 1998 Cooperative Institutional Research Program (CIRP) Freshman survey.

Table B.6.4 **Determinants of Ultimate Educational Plans Among Low-Income College Students, by Gender and Federal Student Aid Usage**

	Men	Women
Age	−.050	−.047
	(.039)	(.029)
Race (Black)	.069	.432***
	(.122)	(.094)
Mother's Education	.042	.063[†]
	(.042)	(.035)
"Go-Getters"	1.792***	.785***
	(.247)	(.183)
Federal Student Aid Usage	.670***	.426***
	(.141)	(.115)
−2 log likelihood	2,508.47	4,207.08
Pseudo R²	.033	.016
N	1030	1700

† p ≤ .1, * p ≤ .05, ** p ≤ .01, *** p ≤ .001.

Notes: Cells consist of ordinal logistic regression coefficients in the numerator and standard errors in parentheses. "Low-income" students are those whose annual family income is less than $30,000.

Source: The 2008 National Postsecondary Student Aid Study (NPSAS).

Table B.6.5 **Determinants of Educational Attainment Among Americans, by Gender and Higher Education Policy Adoption**

	Basic Model		GI Bill	Student Loans		Pell Grants	
	Men	Women	Men	Men	Women	Men	Women
Age	.015**	−.006	.021***	.026***	.009†	.019***	.000
	(.005)	(.005)	(.006)	(.006)	(.005)	(.006)	(.005)
Childhood Socioeconomic Status	.212*	.164†	.185†	.274**	.183*	.296**	.169†
	(.098)	(.087)	(.104)	(.100)	(.089)	(.100)	(.088)
Black	−.365	−.085	−.426	−.642*	−.269	−.449†	−.166
	(.250)	(.206)	(.261)	(.258)	(.210)	(.254)	(.208)
Hispanic	.473	−.434	.492	.628	−.589	.740†	−.361
	(.440)	(.453)	(.444)	(.446)	(.464)	(.447)	(.454)
Mother's Education	.233***	.394***	.270***	.224***	.419***	.226***	.403***
	(.043)	(.046)	(.046)	(.043)	(.047)	(.043)	(.047)
GI Bill Usage			.641*				
			(.280)				
Student Loan Usage				1.629***	1.479***		
				(.199)	(.187)		
Pell Grant Usage						1.383***	.780***
						(.238)	(.205)
−2 log likelihood	1,346.92	1,414.90	1,186.27	1,234.08	1,393.48	1,346.92	1,345.12
Goodness of Fit	1,539.50	1,751.43	1,436.97	1,633.86	1,881.91	1,623.08	1,856.58
Cox and Snell R^2	.095	.179	.127	.219	.272	.160	.202
N	498	541	428	498	541	497	541

† $p ≤ .1$, * $p ≤ .05$, ** $p ≤ .01$, *** $p ≤ .001$.

Notes: Cells consist of ordinal logistic regression coefficients in the numerator and standard errors in parentheses. Analysis includes respondents who have earned at least a high school diploma or its equivalent.

Source: The Social and Governmental Issues and Participation (SGIP) study.

Appendix C

ADDITIONAL EMPIRICAL STRATEGIES FOR POLICY FEEDBACK ANALYSIS

To check the robustness of the analyses presented in chapters 6 and 7, I use additional empirical strategies. Logistic regression analysis also reveals a striking relationship between federal student aid adoption and educational attainment for both women and men.[1] These results corroborate the findings from descriptive statistics that suggest a positive correlation between higher education program adoption and educational attainment. The results of inferential statistical analysis support my expectation that federal student aid adoption promotes greater educational attainment for male and female beneficiaries. GI Bill, student loan, and Pell Grant adoption appear to significantly increase the probability that citizens will attain high levels of education.

Two-stage least squares regression analysis offers an additional approach for investigating the influence that higher education programs have had on the gender dynamics of political engagement. To address one of the most formidable challenges to the study of policy feedback—the possibility that endogenous personality factors, rather than policy usage, shape users' attitudes and behaviors—I use two-stage regression modeling. This technique permits me to minimize the effects of selection bias that could distort observed outcomes of policy adoption for political interest, efficacy, and participation.[2] Throughout this analysis, I draw upon a combination of gender-aggregated and gender-disaggregated models that provide insight into the gender dynamics of political engagement in the United States and permit me to predict the effects that higher education policy adoption has for gender equality in mass-level politics.[3]

***

I draw upon statistical models that use the variable "predicted higher education policy usage" to operationalize the interpretive effects of student aid adoption. The statistical significance of these coefficients would suggest that program usage shapes political engagement through political learning, through the transmission of political messages, or by otherwise altering how beneficiaries conceptualize their roles as citizens.

Addressing Endogeneity Through Comprehensive Controls and Two-Stage Modeling

Policy feedback research is challenged by the possibility of endogeneity bias, which occurs when seemingly significant effects of policy usage merely represent correlation between policy adoption and the error term.[4] The possibility that pre-existing variables condition the outcomes that we observe for political attitudes and participation represents one of the most pressing challenges facing policy feedback analysis. There may be ways in which those who utilize federal student aid policies differ from those who do not. In such cases, the effects of higher education policy usage could simply mask the effects of ambitious, "go-getter" personalities that predispose individuals to not only take advantage of student aid but also engage in political activity. These differences—rather than the effects of program participation—may cause the outcomes that we observe. One way to combat the effects of endogeneity is by working to minimize omitted variable bias, controlling for explanatory variables that have been established in the literature as significant influences on political engagement—particularly gender, age, race, income, and educational attainment.

In addition to comprehensive controls, policy feedback scholars have identified two-stage regression analysis as a valuable method for controlling for this type of selection bias. This technique involves a multistep regression procedure that enables us to more confidently predict the influence that higher education policy usage has on political engagement. I again use the Clarify Software for Interpreting and Presenting Statistical Results to generate substantive estimates for the relative influence of significant variables.

Stage One

Using two-stage modeling enables me to control for characteristics that could potentially obscure the effects of higher education policy usage on political engagement.[5] This approach uses instrumental variables that reflect the propensity of adopting higher education policies, which allows me to minimize the effects of selection bias. In the first stage of the analysis, which appeared in chapter 6, I used binary logistic regression models to produce an instrumental variable that predicts higher education policy usage (see Table B.6.1).[6] This permits me to generate propensity scores for the entire sample of respondents that correspond to the likelihood that they will use federal student aid.

The dependent variable for these models is a binary measure of federal financial aid adoption (1 for an affirmative response, 0 for a negative response). The independent variables used to measure the effects of demographic factors are age (measured in years) and race (1 for black, 0 for white). To account for socioeconomic background, I include a self-assessment of childhood socioeconomic status relative to the respondent's peer group (five-category scale from "far below average" to "far above average") and a variable measuring mother's educational attainment (nine-point scale from "less than high school" to "PhD or professional degree"). Because the second stage of this analysis uses both gender-aggregate and gender-disaggregate models to examine the relationship between higher education policy adoption and political participation, I generate propensity scores that will make up the central independent variables. These scores correspond to each individual model: the aggregate model, which includes all respondents; the disaggregated model for men; and the disaggregated model for women.

Stage Two

The regression models presented here reflect the second stage of the two-stage modeling process. These stage two models predict political interest (Table C.7.1), political efficacy (Table C.7.2), and political participation (Table C.7.3) using an education policy model of political engagement. Because, as chapter 6 has shown, the use of federal student aid is positively associated with educational attainment, I use the independent variable "educational attainment" to operationalize the resource effects of higher education policy usage. Resource models of political engagement have indicated that citizens who have more education, more prestigious occupations, and greater income tend to participate in politics at higher levels than those who do not share these socioeconomic characteristics.[7]

Education is a particularly important factor in the calculus of political participation. In addition to providing information and skills that facilitate political learning and, thus, involvement in political activities, scholars have argued that education increases the normative impetus to engage in politics, as educational institutions may bestow upon students a heightened sense of civic duty.[8] The regression analysis in chapter 6 showed that men and women who use federal higher education programs are significantly more likely to attain high levels of education. In controlling for educational attainment in this analysis—using an eight-point scale (with values corresponding to levels of educational attainment ranging from "high school diploma/GED" to

Table C.7.1 **Determinants of Political Interest: Ordinal Logistic Regression Results (Stage Two)**

	Basic	Any Higher Education Policy	Basic		Any Higher Education Policy	
			Men	Women	Men	Women
Female	−.512***	−.576***				
	(.126)	(.131)				
Age	.031***	.038**	.032***	.031***	.033***	.034
	(.004)	(.014)	(.006)	(.005)	(.007)	(.025)
Black	.042	−.048	.112	.041	.385	.015
	(.162)	(.321)	(.251)	(.215)	(.534)	(.331)
Hispanic	−.780*	−.697*	−1.418	−.014	−1.490*	−.053
	(.316)	(.332)	(.449)	(.457)	(.585)	(.569)
Educational Attainment (Resource Effects)	.153***	.149***	.128**	.185***	.126*	.183***
	(.035)	(.036)	(.051)	(.049)	(.053)	(.050)
Income	.048$^+$	.045$^+$	.064*	.036	.051	.039
	(.026)	(.027)	(.040)	(.035)	(.042)	(.036)
Predicted Higher Education Policy Usage (Interpretive Effects)		1.026			−1.102	.214
		(2.095)			(2.774)	(2.302)
−2 log likelihood	2,044.33	1,975.35	921.05	1,117.58	868.02	1,102.41
Goodness of Fit	2,774.86	2,895.58	1,412.37	1,399.64	1,422.72	1,503.99
Cox and Snell R²	.097	.101	.098	.083	.096	.085
N	1,032	976	498	533	468	507

$^+$ p ≤ .1, * p ≤ .05, ** p ≤ .01, *** p ≤ .001.

Notes: Cells consist of ordinal logistic regression coefficients in the numerator and standard errors in parentheses. Analysis includes respondents who have earned at least a high school diploma or its equivalent.

Source: The Social and Governmental Issues and Participation (SGIP) study.

Table C.7.2 **Determinants of Political Efficacy: Ordinal Logistic Regression Results (Stage Two)**

	Basic	Any Higher Education Policy	Basic		Any Higher Education Policy	
			Men	Women	Men	Women
Female	−.226*	−.279*				
	(.110)	(.114)				
Age	.011**	−.001	.006	.015***	.008	−.001
	(.003)	(.012)	(.005)	(.005)	(.006)	(.022)
Black	−.077	.189	.106	−.226	.041	−.015
	(.146)	(.285)	(.219)	(.198)	(.456)	(.299)
Hispanic	−.156	−.210	.040	−.431	−.011	−.229
	(.297)	(.309)	(.421)	(.425)	(.531)	(.520)
Educational Attainment (Resource Effects)	.237***	.243***	.234***	.253***	.236***	.252***
	(.031)	(.031)	(.043)	(.044)	(.045)	(.045)
Income	.079***	.077***	.064†	.087**	.039	.100**
	(.023)	(.024)	(.034)	(.032)	(.036)	(.034)
Predicted Higher Education Policy Usage (Interpretive Effects)		−1.814			.627	−1.399
		(1.858)			(2.364)	(2.073)
−2 log likelihood	5,465.56	5,281.33	2,619.53	2,814.84	2,510.17	2,741.65
Goodness of Fit	17,612.25	18,388.46	7,749.20	9,321.72	8,014.43	9,790.64
Cox and Snell R²	.115	.118	.098	.127	.092	.133
N	1,023	970	493	530	464	505

†p ≤ .1, * p ≤ .05, ** p ≤ .01, *** p ≤ .001.

Notes: Cells consist of ordinal logistic regression coefficients in the numerator and standard errors in parentheses. Analysis includes respondents who have earned at least a high school diploma or its equivalent.

Source: The Social and Governmental Issues and Participation (SGIP) study.

Table C.7.3 **Determinants of Political Participation: Ordinal Logistic Regression Results (Stage Two)**

	Basic	Any Higher Education Policy	Basic		Any Higher Education Policy	
			Men	Women	Men	Women
Female	−.335** (.115)	−.363** (.119)				
Age	.029*** (.004)	.055*** (.012)	.024*** (.005)	.034*** (.005)	.035*** (.006)	.017 (.028)
Black	.016 (.153)	−.447 (.298)	−.041 (.230)	.098 (.208)	−1.137* (.479)	.248 (.313)
Hispanic	−.876** (.334)	−.891** (.346)	– 1.531*** (.476)	−.066 (.469)	−.634 (.580)	.120 (.567)
Educational Attainment (Resource Effects)	.322*** (.032)	.313*** (.033)	.294*** (.045)	.369*** (.047)	.267*** (.047)	.359*** (.048)
Income	.057* (.024)	.065** (.025)	.103** (.036)	.022 (.034)	.109** (.037)	.022 (.035)
Predicted Higher Education Policy Usage (Interpretive Effects)		4.279* (1.947)			7.661** (2.486)	−1.498 (2.179)
−2 log likelihood	2,804.21	2,724.63	3,171.03	1,421.24	1,306.90	1,400.92
Goodness of Fit	3,656.71	3,677.01	1,772.86	1,896.75	1,758.89	1,941.22
Cox and Snell R²	.182	.189	.197	.171	.218	.169
N	1,030	974	497	532	467	507

† p ≤ .1, * p ≤ .05, ** p ≤ .01, *** p ≤ .001.

Notes: Cells consist of ordinal logistic regression coefficients in the numerator and standard errors in parentheses. Analysis includes respondents who have earned at least a high school diploma or its equivalent.

Source: The Social and Governmental Issues and Participation (SGIP) study.

"graduate degree")—I control for the resource effects of higher education policy adoption.[9]

To capture the remaining influence of federal student aid usage—namely, the interpretive effects, which are derived from the experience of policy adoption, in and of itself—I use the instrumental variable "predicted higher education adoption" (with scores corresponding to probabilities ranging from 0 to 1), which I generated in stage one of the analysis.[10] This method is useful because it corrects for the possibility that, because higher education policy usage is not a randomly assigned "treatment," its observed effects for political participation may simply reflect characteristics that are endogenous to program participants, rather than the effects of policy usage. This technique enables us to consider how citizens' experiences with federal financial aid programs—and the messages that these programs transmit regarding their value as citizens—affect political engagement.

In addition to these key independent variables, the stage two regression models also include comprehensive control variables aimed at minimizing the problem of omitted variable bias. As such, I incorporate independent variables to control for competing explanations that scholars have offered for political engagement. First, I control for demographic factors that have been consistently shown to influence political attitudes and involvement. Research has demonstrated that age provides a significant determinant of political engagement and that older Americans tend to participate in political activities at higher rates than younger Americans.[11] I operationalize age using a variable that measures age in years (ranging from eighteen to ninety-two). Scholars have also shown race to be a significant determinant of political engagement. While Anglo-Whites and African Americans exhibit similar levels of political involvement, Latinos tend to have lower levels of participation.[12] I measure race using binary variables that signify whether respondents are black (1 if black, 0 if white) or Hispanic (1 if Hispanic, 0 if white). Finally, gender represents an additional demographic predictor of political engagement—one that is particularly important to this analysis. Scholars have noted the importance of gender as a determinant of political involvement, arguing that, for most political activities, women tend to be less politically engaged than men.[13] In this analysis, aggregate models of participation include female (0 if male, 1 if female) as a control variable, and disaggregated models divide the population according to this characteristic. Scholars have also shown that political participation is higher among those who have more income.[14] Models include a control variable for annual household income (ten-point scale ranging from "less than $10,000" to "$150,000 or more").

In the regression models examining the determinants of political interest, efficacy, and participation for women, the finding of significant, positive coefficients for educational attainment suggests that federal student aid adoption has resource effects that promote high levels of political engagement for women and men. These models fail to reveal significant interpretive effects when it comes to the effect of policy use on political interest, efficacy, and participation for women. However, the models in Table C.7.3 suggest that higher education policies have had significant interpretive effects for men's political engagement, which likely reflects the influence of the G.I. Bill.

NOTES

Chapter 1

1. Catherine R. Stimpson, ed., *Discrimination against Women: Congressional Hearings on Equal Rights in Education and Employment* (New York: R. R. Bowker Company, 1973), 131.
2. Hanna Rosin, "The End of Men," *Atlantic Monthly,* July 2010, http://www.theatlantic.com/magazine/archive/2010/07/the-end-of-men/8135/. I should note, at the outset, that gender—as opposed to sex—is the focus of this analysis, as the concept of gender includes the socially, culturally, and politically constructed categories in which I am interested. Gender, race, class, and other constructs intersect with one another in ways that preclude the possibility that gender works in the same way for all women and all men. Bearing this in mind, I recognize that gender is not an independent force.
3. US Department of Labor (Women's Bureau), "Civilian Labor Force by Sex, 1948-2015 Annual Averages"; see also Tamala M. Edwards, Tamerlin Drummond, Elizabeth Kaufman, Anne Moffett, Jacqueline Savaino, and Maggie Sieger, "Who Needs a Husband?," *Time Magazine,* July 2007, http://www.time.com/time/magazine/article/0,9171,997804-6,00.html.
4. A cobreadwinner is a wife who brings in at least 25 percent of the family's earned income but less than her partner's income. See Sarah Jane Glynn, "Breadwinning Mothers, Then and Now." Center for American Progress, 2014. https://www.dol.gov/wb/stats/Civilian_labor_force_sex_48_15_txt.htm. In 2011, 12 percent of American families with at least one child under the age of 18—more than eighty-three million families—were headed by a single mother. Single fathers represent a much smaller proportion of American single-parent families. In 2011, 2 percent of American family groups (1.7 million families) with children under the age of 18 were headed by single fathers. See US Census Bureau, "Profile America Facts for Features: Mother's Day: May 13, 2012," 2012, http://www.census.gov/newsroom/releases/archives/facts_for_features_special_editions/cb12-ff08.html.
5. Although the passage of the Nineteenth Amendment extended voting rights to white women, African American women would have to wait until the passage of the 1965 Voting Rights Act to exercise their right.
6. See, for example, Gail Collins, *When Everything Changed: The Amazing Journey of American Women from 1960 to the Present* (New York: Little, Brown and Company, 2009); Susan M. Hartman, *From Margin to Mainstream: American Women and Politics Since 1960* (Philadelphia: Temple University Press, 1989); Ruth Rosen, *The World Split Open: How the Modern Women's Movement Changed America* (New York: Penguin Books, 2000).
7. Throughout this analysis, I use the term "political engagement" to signify both political participation (e.g., voting, contributing money to a political campaign, or volunteering for a candidate) and attitudes toward government (e.g., political interest and political efficacy).

8. Scholars have begun to explore the relationship between federal support for higher education and citizens' socioeconomic status, life chances, and political participation. Prominent examples include Suzanne Mettler's *Soldiers to Citizens: The G.I. Bill and the Making of the Greatest Generation* (New York: Oxford University Press, 2005) and Suzanne Mettler and Eric Welch's "Civic Generation: Policy Feedback Effects of the G.I. Bill on Political Involvement over the Life Course," *British Journal of Political Science* 34, no. 3 (2004): 497–518.

9. Judith N. Shklar, *American Citizenship: The Quest for Inclusion* (Cambridge, MA: Harvard University Press, 1991), 2.

10. Ibid., 13–14.

11. Ibid., 16.

12. This suffrage did not, however, include black women who would generally have to wait until the passage of the Voting Rights Act of 1965 for guaranteed suffrage.

13. Theda Skocpol, *Protecting Soldiers and Mothers: The Political Origin of Social Policy in the United States* (Cambridge, MA: Harvard University Press, 1992).

14. Suzanne Mettler, *Dividing Citizens: Gender and Federalism in New Deal Public Policy* (Ithaca, NY: Cornell University Press, 1998).

15. T. H. Marshall, *Citizenship and Social Class and Other Essays* (New York: Cambridge University Press, 1950), 28.

16. Ibid., 28–29.

17. Ibid., 10–11.

18. Ibid., 11.

19. Ann Shola Orloff, "Gender and the Social Rights of Citizenship: The Comparative Analysis of Gender Relations and Welfare States," *American Sociological Review* 58, no. 3 (1993): 303–328.

20. Marshall, *Citizenship and Social Class and Other Essays*, 11.

21. Andrea Louise Campbell, *How Policies Make Citizens: Senior Political Activism and the American Welfare State* (Princeton, NJ: Princeton University Press, 2003), 28–32;> Sidney Verba and Norman H. Nie, *Participation in America: Political Democracy and Social Equality* (New York: Harper & Row, 1972), 2–3.

22. See, for example, Skocpol, *Protecting Soldiers and Mothers*; Margaret Weir, Ann Shola Orloff, and Theda Skocpol, "Understanding American Social Politics," in *The Politics of Social Policy in the United States*, ed. Margaret Weir, Ann Shola Orloff, and Theda Skocpol (Princeton, NJ: Princeton University Press, 1988), 16. For additional insights into how social movement politics have influenced the capacity of citizens to voice claims for equality, see, e.g., Phillip Ayoub, *When States Come Out: Europe's Sexual Minorities and the Politics of Visibility* (New York: Cambridge University Press, 2016), and Chris Zepeda-Millan, "Perceptions of Threat, Demographic Diversity, and the Framing of Illegality: Explaining (Non) Participation in New York's 2006 Immigrant Protests," *Political Research Quarterly* 67, no. 4 (2014): 880–888.

23. Claudia Goldin, "The Quiet Revolution That Transformed Women's Employment, Education, and Family," *American Economic Review* 96, no. 2 (2006): 1–21, 5.

24. Elizabeth Warren and Amelia Tyagi, *The Two-Income Trap* (New York: Basic Books, 2003).

25. Kristi Andersen, "Working Women and Political Participation, 1952-1972," *American Journal of Political Science* 19, no. 3 (1975): 439–453.

26. Nancy Burns, Kay Lehman Scholzman, and Sidney Verba, *The Private Roots of Public Action: Gender, Equality, and Political Participation* (Cambridge, MA: Harvard University Press, 2001), 214.

27. Ibid., 202.

28. Goldin, "The Quiet Revolution," 13; Claudia Goldin, Lawrence F. Katz, and Ilyana Kuziemko. "The Homecoming of American College Women: The Reversal of the College Gender Gap," *Journal of Economic Perspectives* 20, no. 4 (2006): 133–156, 152–153.

29. Claudia Goldin and Lawrence F. Katz, "The Power of the Pill: Oral Contraceptives and Women's Career and Marriage Decisions," *Journal of Political Economy* 110, no. 4 (2002): 730–770; Goldin, Katz, and Kuziemko. "The Homecoming of American College Women," 152–153.

30. Barbara Miller Solomon, *In the Company of Educated Women: A History of Women and Higher Education in America* (New Haven, CT: Yale University Press, 1985), 201–202.
31. Anderson, "Working Women and Political Participation," 441.
32. Jane J. Mansbridge, *Why We Lost the ERA* (Chicago: University of Chicago Press, 1986).
33. Although the scope of this analysis centers on women's political participation at the mass level, it is important to recognize that, in spite of resilient gender inequality in representation among elected officials, women's presence in US political institutions has grown since the mid-twentieth century. The percentage of women winning election to the US Congress increased steadily after Jeannette Rankin became the first woman to win election to the House in 1917. This steady increase gave way to a dramatic jump in 1993, the "Year of the Woman," which saw an unprecedented forty-seven women elected to the national legislature.
34. Verba and Nie, *Participation in America*; Sidney Verba, Kay Lehman Schlozman, and Henry E. Brady, *Voice and Equality: Civic Volunteerism in American Politics* (Cambridge, MA: Harvard University Press, 1995).
35. Verba and Nie, *Participation in America*; Verba, Schlozman, and Brady, *Voice and Equality*; Raymond E. Wolfinger and Steven J. Rosenstone, *Who Votes?* (New Haven, CT: Yale University Press, 1980).
36. Burns, Schlozman, and Verba, *The Private Roots of Public Action*, 142; Louis Menand, "Reimagining Liberal Education," in *Education and Democracy: Re-imagining Liberal Learning in America*, ed. Robert Orrill (New York: College Entrance Examination Board, 1997), 3; Wolfinger and Rosenstone, *Who Votes?*, 18.
37. Henry E. Brady, Kay Lehman Schlozman, and Sidney Verba, "Prospecting for Participants: Rational Expectations and the Recruitment of Political Activists," *American Political Science Review* 93, no. 1 (1999): 153–168, 162; Steven J. Rosenstone and John Mark Hansen, *Mobilization, Participation, and Democracy in America* (New York: Longman, 1993).
38. M. Margaret Conway, Gertrude A. Stuernagel, and David W. Ahern, *Women and Public Policy: A Revolution in Progress*, 3rd ed. (Washington, DC: CQ Press, 2005), 6.
39. Goldin, Katz, and Kuziemko. "The Homecoming of American College Women," 133–156.
40. National Center for Education Statistics (NCES) Homepage, US Department of Education, 2011, http://www.nces.ed.gov.
41. This figure is particularly noteworthy when we consider that in 1947, at the high point of gender inequality in higher education, there were 2.3 male students for each female student in American colleges and universities. See Goldin, Katz, and Kuziemko, "The Homecoming of American College Women."
42. Scott Jaschik, "Women Lead in Doctorates," *Inside Higher Ed*, 2010, http://www.insidehighered.com/news/2010/09/14/doctorates.
43. Mabel Newcomer, *A Century of Higher Education for American Women* (New York: Harper & Brothers Publishers, 1959), 152.
44. In the case of scholarships during the 1950s, Michael McPherson and Morton Schapiro note that "the policies schools adopted in awarding scholarships were largely uncoordinated and idiosyncratic, often reflecting the views of particular donors." See Michael McPherson and Morton Schapiro, *The Student Aid Game: Meeting Need and Rewarding Talent in American Higher Education* (Princeton, NJ: Princeton University Press, 1988), 6.
45. Data are reported in constant 2014–2015 dollars. The cost to attend a public college or university in 1963–1964 was $1,796, compared to $6,371 during the 2014–2015 academic year. For private colleges and universities, the cost of tuition and fees rose from $7,766 in 1963–1964 to $26,184 in 2014–1915. US Department of Education, National Center for Education Statistics, Table 330.10, "Average Undergraduate Tuition and Fees and Room and Board Rates Charged for Full-Time Students in Degree-Granting Postsecondary Institutions, by Level and Control of Institution: 1963-64 through 2014-15."
46. Suzanne Mettler, "Bringing the State Back In to Civic Engagement: Policy Feedback Effects of the G.I. Bill for World War II Veterans," *American Political Science Review* 96, no. 2 (2002): 351–365; Mettler, *Soldiers to Citizens*; Mettler and Welch, "Civic Generation," 497–518.
47. John Bound and Sarah Turner, "Going to War and Going to College: Did World War II and the G.I. Bill Increase Educational Attainment for Returning Veterans?," *Journal of Labor*

Economics 20, no. 4 (2002): 784–815; Mettler, *Soldiers to Citizens*; Keith Olson, "The G.I. Bill and Higher Education: Success and Surprise," *American Quarterly* 25, no. 5 (1973): 596–610; Keith Olson, *The G.I. Bill, the Veterans, and the Colleges* (Lexington, KY: University of Kentucky Press, 1974); Marcus Stanley, "College Education and the Midcentury G.I. Bills," *Quarterly Journal of Economics* 118, no. 2 (2003): 671–708.

48. Bound and Turner, "Going to War and Going to College," 809.

49. Olson, "The G.I. Bill and Higher Education," 597.

50. Mettler, *Soldiers to Citizens*.

51. Linda Gordon, *Pitied but Not Entitled: Single Mothers and the History of Welfare, 1890-1935* (New York: Free Press, 1994); Mettler, *Dividing Citizens*; Skocpol, *Protecting Soldiers and Mothers*.

52. Michael J. Bennett, *When Dreams Came True: The GI Bill and the Making of Modern America* (Washington, DC: Brassey's, 1996), 202.

53. Theda Skocpol, "Targeting Within Universalism: Politically Viable Policies to Combat Poverty in the United States," in *The Urban Underclass*, ed. Christopher Jencks and Paul E. Peterson (Washington, DC: Brookings Institution, 1991).

54. Andrea Louise Campbell, "Self-Interest, Social Security, and the Distinctive Participation Patterns of Senior Citizens," *American Political Science Review* 96, no. 3 (2002), 565–574; Theodore J. Lowi, "American Business, Public Policy, Case-Studies, and Political Theory," *World Politics* 16, no. 4 (1964): 677–715, 688–690; Jacob S. Hacker, "The Historical Logic of National Health Insurance: Structure and Sequence in the Development of British, Canadian, and U.S. Medical Policy," *Studies in American Political Development* 12 (1998): 57–130; Lorraine M. McDonnell, "Repositioning Politics in Education's Circle of Knowledge," *Educational Researcher* 38, no. 6 (2009): 417–427; Suzanne Mettler and Joe Soss, "The Consequences of Public Policy for Democratic Citizenship: Bridging Policy Studies and Mass Politics," *Perspectives on Politics* 2, no. 1 (2004): 55–73, 60; Paul Pierson, "When Effect Becomes Cause: Policy Feedback and Political Change," *World Politics* 45, no. 4 (1993): 595–628.

55. Campbell, "Self-Interest, Social Security, and the Distinctive Participation Patterns of Senior Citizens," 565–574; Campbell, *How Policies Make Citizens*, 28–32.

56. Verba, Schlozman, and Brady, *Voice and Equality*.

57. Pierson, "When Effect Becomes Cause"; Joe Soss, "Lessons of Welfare: Policy Design, Political Learning, and Political Action," *American Political Science Review* 93, no. 2 (1999): 363–380; Mettler and Soss, "The Consequences of Public Policy for Democratic Citizenship," 62; Mettler, *Soldiers to Citizens*; Ann Schneider and Helen Ingram, "Social Construction of Target Populations: Implications for Politics and Policy," *American Political Science Review* 87, no. 2 (1993): 34–347, 334.

58. Schneider and Ingram, "Social Construction of Target Populations," 334.

59. Mettler and Soss, "The Consequences of Public Policy for Democratic Citizenship," 56.

60. Soss, "Lessons of Welfare."

61. Staffan Kumlin and Bo Rothstein, "Making and Breaking Social Capital: The Impact of Welfare-State Institutions," *Comparative Political Studies* 38, no. 4 (2005): 339–365.

62. Mettler, *Soldiers to Citizens*.

Chapter 2

1. Elizabeth Sanders, "Mildred Rowe Sanders, a Life," Eulogy shared with author. December 16, 2011.

2. US Department of Commerce, Bureau of the Census, "Educational Attainment of the Population 25 Years Old and Over in the United States: 1940," April 23, 1942; "A Half-Century of Learning: Historical Census Statistics on Educational Attainment in the United States, 1940 to 2000: Detailed Tables," http://www.census.gov/hhes/socdemo/education/data/census/.

3. See, for example, Christopher J. Lucas, *American Higher Education: A History* (New York: Palgrave Macmillan, 2006), 109; Solomon, *In the Company of Educated Women*, 2.

4. Elizabeth M. Tidball, Daryl G. Smith, Charles S. Tidball, and Lisa E. Wolf-Wendel, *Taking Women Seriously: Lessons and Legacies for Educating the Majority* (Phoenix, AZ: Oryx Press, 1999), 10.

5. It comes as little surprise that throughout the nineteenth and twentieth centuries, women's higher educational attainment has been correlated with their labor force participation: women who have earned college degrees are more likely to enter the labor force than their less educated counterparts. Barbara Sicherman, "College and Careers: Historical Perspectives on the Lives and Work Patterns of Women College Graduates," in *Women and Higher Education in American History: Essays from the Mount Holyoke College Sesquicentennial Symposia*, ed. John Mack Faragher and Florence Howe (New York: W.W. Norton & Co., 1988), 135.

6. Lawrence E. Gladieux, Jacqualine E. King, and Melanie E. Corrigan, "The Federal Government and Higher Education," in *American Higher Education in the Twenty-First Century: Social, Political, and Economic Challenges*, ed. Philip G. Altbach, Robert O. Berdahl, and Patricia J. Gumport (Baltimore, MD: Johns Hopkins University Press, 2005), 163. As Logan Wilson notes, those who insist that the federal government has historically refrained from intervening in higher education tend to be uninformed about the government's "heavy commitment" to higher education or reluctant to admit that the nation's government and its college students are engaged in a "permanent and growing partnership." Logan Wilson, "The Federal Government and Higher Education," in *Education and Public Policy*, ed. Seymour E. Harris and Alan Levensohn (Berkeley, CA: McCutchan Publishing, 1965), 60. Historically, the political currency of localism has held more weight in regards to primary and secondary education as opposed to postsecondary education. See David Carleton, *Landmark Congressional Laws on Education* (Westport, CT: Greenwood Press, 2002), 5–6.

7. Roger L. Geiger, "The Ten Generations of American Higher Education," in *American Higher Education in the Twenty-First Century: Social, Political, and Economic Challenges*, ed. Philip G. Altbach, Robert O. Berdahl, and Patricia J. Gumport (Baltimore, MD: Johns Hopkins University Press, 2005), 39. Harvard's movement away from its strict Calvinist roots in the eighteenth century reflected the rise of tolerance and cosmopolitanism at the institution.

8. Geiger, "The Ten Generations of American Higher Education," 42–43.

9. Ibid., 41. Nevertheless, we should note that churches funded the majority of the nation's colleges and universities until the end of the Civil War. Newcomer, *A Century of Higher Education for American Women*, 6.

10. Geiger, "The Ten Generations of American Higher Education," 42; see also Lucas, *American Higher Education*, 109.

11. Lawrence E. Gladieux and Thomas Wolanin, *Congress and the Colleges: The National Politics of Higher Education* (Lexington, MA: Lexington Books, 1976), 4. Linda K. Kerber, "'Why Should Girls Be Learn'd and Wise?': Two Centuries of Higher Education for Women as Seen Through the Unfinished Work of Alice Mary Baldwin," in *Women and Higher Education in American History: Essays from the Mount Holyoke College Sesquicentennial Symposia*, ed. John Mack Faragher and Florence Howe (New York: W.W. Norton & Co., 1988), 21; John R. Thelin, *A History of American Higher Education*, 2nd ed. (Baltimore, MD: Johns Hopkins University Press, 2011), 55.

12. Although women were not among the exceedingly small portion of the population who received college education during the colonial period, citizens were a bit more lenient when it came to the gender gap in basic education, which is illustrated by improvements in women's literacy rates by the late seventeenth century. See, for example, Kerber, "'Why Should Girls Be Learn'd and Wise?'," 20.

13. Lucas, *American Higher Education*, 161; Leslie Miller-Bernal, "Coeducation: An Uneven Progression," in *Going Coed: Women's Experiences in Formerly Men's Colleges and Universities, 1950-2000* (Nashville, TN: Vanderbilt University Press, 2004), 4; Newcomer, *A Century of Higher Education for American Women*, 26–28; Tidball, Smith, Tidball, and Wolf-Wendel, *Taking Women Seriously*, 6.

14. Kerber, "'Why Should Girls Be Learn'd and Wise?'," 41.

15. Ibid.

16. Carleton, *Landmark Congressional Laws on Education*, 4–5; Gladieux, King, and Corrigan, "The Federal Government and Higher Education," 163; Gladieux and Wolanin, *Congress and the Colleges*, 3.
17. Thelin, *A History of American Higher Education*, 41.
18. Geiger, "The Ten Generations of American Higher Education," 43.
19. As John Thelin notes, the question of whether the University of Georgia or the University of North Carolina can claim to be the nation's first state university "is a matter of dispute" between the two schools. While the University of Georgia (UGA) received its state charter in 1785, the University of North Carolina (UNC) received its charter in 1789. Still, UNC began to admit students in 1795, while UGA enrolled its first students in 1801. Thelin, *A History of American Higher Education*, 45.
20. Thelin, *A History of American Higher Education*, 75.
21. Joel Spring, *The American School: From the Puritans to No Child Left Behind*, 7th ed. (New York: McGraw-Hill, 2008), 316.
22. Geiger, "The Ten Generations of American Higher Education," 50.
23. Lynn Peril, *College Girls: Bluestockings, Sex Kittens, and Coeds, Then and Now* (New York: W.W. Norton & Co., 2006), 49; Thelin, *A History of American Higher Education*, 42.
24. Geiger, "The Ten Generations of American Higher Education," 51.
25. Christopher P. Loss, *Between Citizens and the State: The Politics of American Higher Education in the 20th Century* (Princeton, NJ: Princeton University Press, 2012), 3; Thelin, *A History of American Higher Education*, 41–42.
26. Lucas, *American Higher Education*, 121–122.
27. Solomon, *In the Company of Educated Women*, 12. In correspondence to a friend, he described his motives for educating his daughters as such: "The chance that in marriage [Martha] will draw a blockhead I calculate at about fourteen to one," he said. "The education of her family will probably rest on her own ideas and directions without assistance." According to Jefferson, although his daughter's education may have eventually proven convenient—for example, in the case that she made an unfortunate match in marriage—it was not essential. National Women's History Museum (NWHM), "Women's Changing Roles as Citizens of a New Republic," 2007, https://www.nwhm.org/online-exhibits/education/1700s_2.htm.
28. Lucas, *American Higher Education: A History*, 161.
29. Linda D. Gordon, *Gender and Higher Education in the Progressive Era* (New Haven, CT: Yale University Press, 1990), 18; Miller-Bernal, "Coeducation: An Uneven Progression," 4.
30. Esbach, *The Higher Education of Women in England and America 1865-1920*, 83; Newcomer, *A Century of Higher Education for American Women*, 29; Peril, *College Girls*, 43. Supporters of higher education for women raised doubts regarding Clarke's findings, pointing out that the small sample of students upon which his analysis rests proves insufficient for making his grave conclusions. Esbach, *The Higher Education of Women in England and America 1865-1920*, 85.
31. Gordon, *Gender and Higher Education in the Progressive Era*, 16; Lucas, *American Higher Education*, 161. As historian John Faragher notes, historical data indicate there may have been some truth to these fears. Among women who graduated from college prior to World War I, for example, at least 25 percent of them never married. Moreover, the movement of women into higher education occurred in tandem with a decline in the nation's fertility. By 1900, the total fertility rate for American women had fallen to fewer than four children. John Faragher, "Introduction," in *Women and Higher Education in American History: Essays from the Mount Holyoke College Sesquicentennial Symposia*, ed. John Mack Faragher and Florence Howe (New York: W.W. Norton & Co., 1988), xi.
32. Lucas, *American Higher Education*, 161–162.
33. Newcomer, *A Century of Higher Education for American Women*, 49–50.
34. Linda Kerber, "The Republican Mother: Women and the Women and the Enlightenment— An American Perspective," *American Quarterly* 28, no. 2 (1976): 187–205; see also Linda Eisenmann, "Introduction," in *Historical Dictionary of Women's Education in the United States*, ed. Linda Eisenmann (Westport, CT: Greenwood Press, 1998), xii; Gordon, *Gender and Higher Education in the Progressive Era*, 14; Peril, *College Girls*, 19; Spring, *The American School*, 143. It is important to note that the concept of Republican Motherhood applied primarily to white women. The omission of women of color from Republican Motherhood reflected the

fact that effectively performing this duty was largely predicated on the ability to wield spiritual authority in the private sphere. Stereotypical depictions casting women of color as lacking self-control and possessing easily compromised morals and values invalidated their claim to moral authority in the home and precluded their assumption of this vital role. See, for example, Peril, *College Girls*, 99.

35. Esbach, *The Higher Education of Women in England and America 1865-1920*, 11.
36. Ibid., 44; Gordon, *Gender and Higher Education in the Progressive Era*, 21; Tidball, Smith, Tidball, and Wolf-Wendel, *Taking Women Seriously*, 11. At the turn of the century, it was not uncommon for male students to frown upon unabashed academic consciousness among their peers. Not only was enthusiastic study "frowned upon as excessive," common wisdom held that "it was 'poor form' to earn anything better than the 'gentleman's C' in one's courses." Lucas, *American Higher Education*, 208.
37. Gordon, *Gender and Higher Education in the Progressive Era*, 17.
38. Miller-Bernal, "Coeducation: An Uneven Progression," 4; Newcomer, *A Century of Higher Education for American Women*, 58; Rosalind Rosenberg, "The Limits of Access: The History of Coeducation in America," in *Women and Higher Education in American History: Essays from the Mount Holyoke College Sesquicentennial Symposia*, ed. John Mack Faragher and Florence Howe (New York: W.W. Norton & Co., 1988), 110; Spring, *The American School*, 143.
39. Lucas, *American Higher Education*, 121.
40. Spring, *The American School*, 143; Peril, *College Girls*, 35; Solomon, *In the Company of Educated Women*, 24. There is some debate as to whether the Georgia Female College was truly the nation's first women's college. Some historians argue that the curriculum at Georgia Female College—a school that was known to admit twelve-year-olds—was not rigorous enough to merit the distinction. Mary Sharp College, which was founded in 1853 in Winchester, Tennessee, and Elmira Female College, which was founded in 1855 in Elmira, New York, have each been recognized as the first college to admit women. See Peril, *College Girls*, 35–36, and Solomon, *In the Company of Educated Women*, 24.
41. Geiger, "The Ten Generations of American Higher Education," 51.
42. Rosenberg, "The Limits of Access," 109.
43. Gordon, *Gender and Higher Education in the Progressive Era*, 16; Lucas, *American Higher Education*, 160.
44. Gordon, *Gender and Higher Education in the Progressive Era*, 26.
45. Kerber, "'Why Should Girls Be Learn'd and Wise?'," 20. The most prominent of these women's colleges became popularly known as "the Seven Sisters": Barnard, Mount Holyoke, Radcliffe, Smith, Tulane, Vassar, and Wellesley. Thelin, *A History of American Higher Education*, 180–181.
46. Geiger, "The Ten Generations of American Higher Education," 50; Burns, Schlozman, and Verba, *The Private Roots of Public Action*, 142; Lucas, *American Higher Education*, 122; Miller-Bernal, "Coeducation: An Uneven Progression," 3; Tidball, Smith, Tidball, and Wolf-Wendel, *Taking Women Seriously*, 11. Oberlin also had the distinction of being the first college to integrate by admitting black students in 1833. Eisenmann, "Introduction," xv; Miller-Bernal, "Coeducation: An Uneven Progression," 3.
47. Lucas, *American Higher Education*, 162; Newcomer, *A Century of Higher Education for American Women*, 35; Thelin, *A History of American Higher Education*, 55. The emergence of coeducation did not mean the death of women's colleges. To the contrary, in the decades following Oberlin's admission of women, a number of women's institutions appeared in the South. Many southerners thought it best to send young women to local colleges where they could ensure the curriculum's moral and religious propriety, rather than to the "renegade" colleges of the North. Similar concerns among Catholic families drove the increase in Catholic women's institutions during the late nineteenth century. Thelin, *A History of American Higher Education*, 84.
48. Ruth Bordin, *Women at Michigan: The Dangerous Experiment, 1870s to the Present* (Ann Arbor, MI: University of Michigan Press, 2001), 3–4.
49. Eisenmann, "Introduction," xv; Kerber, "'Why Should Girls Be Learn'd and Wise?'," 41. The University of Iowa was the first public institution of higher education to adopt coeducation, when it admitted women as one-third of its student body in 1855. Peril, *College Girls*, 44.

50. Gordon, *Gender and Higher Education in the Progressive Era*, 212–224.
51. Newcomer, *A Century of Higher Education for American Women*, 153; Gordon, *Gender and Higher Education in the Progressive Era*, 24.
52. Newcomer, *A Century of Higher Education for American Women*, 153.
53. Geiger, "The Ten Generations of American Higher Education," 53. At Cornell University, founder Ezra Cornell expressed a commitment to founding a university where "any person" could find support to undertake "any study." However, Ezra Cornell's egalitarian sentiments seem to have been most closely tied to his commitment to ensuring poor students the same access to high-quality education as their well-heeled counterparts, because women were not included among the university's initial matriculants. During the university's early years, Ezra Cornell insisted that, while the schools' administrators sincerely wanted to include women, a lack of appropriate accommodations for female students precluded their admission. Women's rights activists Elizabeth Cady Stanton and Susan B. Anthony pressured him to uphold the promise of "any person, any study" when it came to women. Esbach, *The Higher Education of Women in England and America 1865-1920*, 105–106; Gordon, *Gender and Higher Education in the Progressive Era*, 23.
54. Peril, *College Girls*, 51; Tidball, Smith, Tidball, and Wolf-Wendel, *Taking Women Seriously*, 10. Although 41 percent of colleges were open to women in 1869, fewer than 1,400 women received degrees that year, compared to the 8,000 men who did. It is similarly important to note that, for some institutions, the term "coeducation" was used to signify the presence of exactly one female student. Newcomer, *A Century of Higher Education for American Women*, 37; Tidball, Smith, Tidball, and Wolf-Wendel, *Taking Women Seriously*, 10–12.
55. According to Barbara Solomon, black women's absence from higher education reflected the fact that their parents were poor and the simple fact that "most schools did not want them." Solomon, *In the Company of Educated Women*, 76.
56. Eisenmann, "Introduction," xiv.
57. Peril, *College Girls*, 40. The first black woman to receive a bachelor's degree in the United States was Mary Jane Patterson. The daughter of fugitive slaves earned a degree from Oberlin College in 1862. Esbach, *The Higher Education of Women in England and America 1865-1920*, 153; Peril, *College Girls*, 40.
58. Peril, *College Girls*, 69.
59. Peril, *College Girls*, 49.
60. Tidball, Smith, Tidball, and Wolf-Wendel, *Taking Women Seriously*, 11.
61. Esbach, *The Higher Education of Women in England and America 1865-1920*, 44; Gordon, *Gender and Higher Education in the Progressive Era*, 17. In fact, no classes were held on Mondays so that the women students could do the men's laundry. Their own laundry, however, had to be tended to during each woman's free time.
62. Lucas, *American Higher Education*, 162.
63. Rosenberg, "The Limits of Access," 114.
64. Lucas, *American Higher Education*, 213–214.
65. Esbach, *The Higher Education of Women in England and America 1865-1920*, 108; Rosenberg, "The Limits of Access," 111.
66. Esbach, *The Higher Education of Women in England and America 1865-1920*, 107; Newcomer, *A Century of Higher Education for American Women*, 27.
67. Rosenberg, "The Limits of Access," 113.
68. Thelin, *A History of American Higher Education*, 182.
69. Rosenberg, "The Limits of Access," 113.
70. Ibid., 109; see also Gordon, *Gender and Higher Education in the Progressive Era*, 14–15.
71. Spring, *The American School*, 143.
72. Geiger, "The Ten Generations of American Higher Education," 51; Thelin, *A History of American Higher Education*, 75.
73. President Buchanan's veto revolved around southern lawmakers' objection to the prospect of federal intervention into education. Thelin, *A History of American Higher Education*, 75.
74. Gladieux and Wolanin, *Congress and the Colleges*, 5; Gladieux, King, and Corrigan, "The Federal Government and Higher Education," 164; Thelin, *A History of American Higher Education*, 75.

75. Carleton, *Landmark Congressional Laws on Education*, 30; Esbach, *The Higher Education of Women in England and America 1865-1920*, 101; Solomon, *In the Company of Educated Women*, 44; Spring, *The American School*, 137–138. This emphasis on promoting practical education reflects Congressman Justin Morrill's 1848 assertion that American colleges would do best to "lop off a portion of the studies established centuries ago as the mark of European scholarship and replace the vacancy [with] those of a less antique and more practical value." Lucas, *American Higher Education*, 153–154.

76. Gordon, *Gender and Higher Education in the Progressive Era,* , 18; Peril, *College Girls*, 44.

77. Steven Brant and Jerome Karabel, *The Diverted American Dream: Community Colleges and the Promise of Educational Opportunity in America, 1900-1985* (Oxford University Press, 1989), 3; Carleton, *Landmark Congressional Laws on Education*, 34.

78. Carleton, *Landmark Congressional Laws on Education*, 27.

79. Geiger, "The Ten Generations of American Higher Education," 52.

80. Carleton, *Landmark Congressional Laws on Education*, 53; Esbach, *The Higher Education of Women in England and America 1865-1920*, 101; Lucas, *American Higher Education*, 155.

81. Spring, *The American School*, 316.

82. Lucas, *American Higher Education*, 213.

83. Thelin, *A History of American Higher Education*, 155; see also Peril, *College Girls*, 17.

84. Gordon, *Gender and Higher Education in the Progressive Era*, 6.

85. Thelin, *A History of American Higher Education*, 169.

86. Brant and Karabel, *The Diverted American Dream*, 4; Solomon, *In the Company of Educated Women*, 46.

87. Geiger, "The Ten Generations of American Higher Education," 55.

88. Miller-Bernal, "Coeducation: An Uneven Progression," 5. In the case of the University of Michigan, the school's reluctant administrators adopted coeducation as a more cost-effective alternative to building a separate school for women. Rosenberg, "The Limits of Access," 110.

89. Miller-Bernal, "Coeducation: An Uneven Progression," 5; Rosenberg, "The Limits of Access," 111.

90. Miller-Bernal, "Coeducation: An Uneven Progression," 5.

91. Thomas D. Snyder and Sally A. Dillow, *Digest of Education Statistics 2009* (Washington, DC: NCES, US Department of Education, 2010); "Historical National Population Estimates: July 1, 1900 to July 1, 1999," Population Estimates Program, 2000, http://www.census.gov/population/estimates/nation/popclockest.txt.

92. Carol S. Pearson, Donna L. Shavlik, and Judith G. Touchton, *Educating the Majority: Women Challenge Tradition in Higher Education* (New York: Macmillan Publishing Company, 1989), 16.

93. Pearson, Shavlik, and Touchton, *Educating the Majority*, 16; Solomon, *In the Company of Educated Women*, 64–65.

94. Esbach, *The Higher Education of Women in England and America 1865-1920*, 109; Thelin, *A History of American Higher Education*, 184. Prominent coordinate colleges included Harvard's "Harvard Annex" (later named Radcliffe), Brown's Pembroke College, Tufts's Jackson College, and Tulane's Sophie Newcomb College. Thelin, *A History of American Higher Education*, 180–184.

95. Esbach, *The Higher Education of Women in England and America 1865-1920*, 107; Gordon, *Gender and Higher Education in the Progressive Era*, 43; Lucas, *American Higher Education*, 214.

96. Peril, *College Girls*, 46.

97. Gordon, *Gender and Higher Education in the Progressive Era*, 43–44.

98. Ibid., 43; Rosenberg, "The Limits of Access," 116.

99. Solomon, *In the Company of Educated Women*, 71.

100. Newcomer, *A Century of Higher Education for American Women*, 151–152; Pearson, Shavlik, and Touchton, *Educating the Majority*, 16; Solomon, *In the Company of Educated Women*, 71–72.

101. In 1906, these women attended Newcomb College, Tulane's female coordinate institution. Solomon, *In the Company of Educated Women*, 72.

102. Ibid., 70.

103. Ibid., 71.
104. Ibid., 73.
105. Ibid.
106. Thelin, *A History of American Higher Education*, 199.
107. Geiger, "The Ten Generations of American Higher Education," 59–60.
108. In an attempt to strengthen vocational education during this period, federal lawmakers passed the Smith-Hughes Act of 1917, which provided federal support for vocational education at the high school level. Carleton, *Landmark Congressional Laws on Education*, 7.
109. Geiger, "The Ten Generations of American Higher Education," 58.
110. Lucas, *American Higher Education*, 232; Brant and Karabel, *The Diverted American Dream*, 5–6.
111. Snyder and Dillow, *Digest of Education Statistics 2009*.
112. Franklin D. Roosevelt, "Executive Order 7086 Establishing the National Youth Administration," June 26, 1935, online by Gerhard Peters and John T. Woolley, *The American Presidency Project*.
113. Florence Fleming Corley, "The National Youth Administration in Georgia: A New Deal for Young Blacks and Women," *Georgia Historical Quarterly* 77, no. 4 (1993): 728–756, 729.
114. Olen Cole Jr., "Black Youth in the National Youth Administration in California, 1935-1943," *Southern California Quarterly* 73, no. 4 (1991): 390.
115. Richard A. Reiman, *The New Deal & American Youth: Ideas & Ideals in a Depression Decade* (University of Georgia Press, 1992), 121.
116. Ibid., 1.
117. Ibid., 2.
118. Linda Eisenmann, *Higher Education for Women in Postwar America, 1945-1965* (Baltimore, MD: Johns Hopkins University Press, 2006), 3; Miller-Bernal, "Coeducation: An Uneven Progression," 8.
119. Peril, *College Girls*, 46; Tidball, Smith, Tidball, and Wolf-Wendel, *Taking Women Seriously*, 12. The former scenario was illustrated as early as the Civil War when the University of Wisconsin and a number of other male colleges admitted women to fill their classrooms. See Miller-Bernal, "Coeducation: An Uneven Progression," 4.
120. Philip G. Altbach, "Patterns in Higher Education Development," in *American Higher Education in the Twenty-First Century: Social, Political, and Economic Challenges*, ed. Philip G. Altbach, Robert O. Berdahl, and Patricia J. Gumport (Baltimore, MD: Johns Hopkins University Press, 2005), 20.
121. Eisenmann, *Higher Education for Women in Postwar America, 1945-1965*, 3–4; Pearson, Shavlik, and Touchton, *Educating the Majority*, 16–17.
122. Eisenmann, *Higher Education for Women in Postwar America, 1945-1965*, 49.
123. Goldin, Katz, and Kuziemko, "The Homecoming of American College Women."
124. Ibid., 135–136.
125. Mettler, *Soldiers to Citizens*, 7–11; see also Bound and Turner, "Going to War and Going to College," 787.
126. The creation of the GI Bill was a truly groundbreaking event. Before its creation in 1944, the federal government's activity in the area of higher education was confined to the donation of federal land for college building (the Morrill Land-Grant Acts) and federal assistance for vocational education (the 1917 Smith-Hughes Act). In 1944, however, lawmakers institutionalized direct student aid in the form of grants to help military veterans pursue postsecondary training.
127. Bound and Turner, "Going to War and Going to College," 789–790; Gladieux, King, and Corrigan, "The Federal Government and Higher Education," 174; Mettler, "Bringing the State Back In to Civic Engagement," 354; Miller-Bernal, "Coeducation: An Uneven Progression," 8–9. The exception to the criteria of honorable discharge and ninety days of service is early discharge due to disability sustained during duty.
128. Olson, "The G.I. Bill and Higher Education," 596.
129. Eisenmann, *Higher Education for Women in Postwar America, 1945-1965*, 54; Thelin, *A History of American Higher Education*, 267.

130. Bound and Turner, "Going to War and Going to College," 785; Conway, Stuernagel, and Ahern, *Women and Public Policy*, 22; Eisenmann, *Higher Education for Women in Postwar America, 1945-1965*, 28; Mettler, *Soldiers to Citizens*; Rosalind Rosenberg, *Divided Lives: American Women in the Twentieth Century* (New York: Hill and Wang, 2008), 166.

131. Geiger, "The Ten Generations of American Higher Education," 61.

132. Linda Eisenmann, "Educating the Female Citizen in a Post-war World: Competing Ideologies for American Women, 1945-1965," *Educational Review* 54, no. 2 (2002): 133–141, 133.

133. Mettler, *Soldiers to Citizens*, 144.

134. Bennett, *When Dreams Came True*, 202.

135. Eisenmann, *Higher Education for Women in Postwar America, 1945-1965*; Mettler, *Soldiers to Citizens*, 7–11.

136. Mettler, *Soldiers to Citizens*, 146.

137. Margot Canaday, "Building a Straight State: Sexuality and Social Citizenship Under the 194 G.I. Bill," *Journal of American History* 90, no. 3 (2003): 935–957, 956.

138. Mettler, *Soldiers to Citizens*, 146.

139. Edward Humes, *Over Here: How the G.I. Bill Transformed the American Dream* (Orlando, FL: Harcourt, 2006), 204.

140. Eisenmann, "Educating the Female Citizen," 133. Data from the US Department of Education illustrate these trends. After 1940, the rates at which men earned bachelor's degrees increased sharply, peaking around 1950 and then declining—perhaps as a result of male participation in the Korean War from 1950 through 1953. National Center for Education Statistics (NCES), 2011.

141. Unlike women, American men also enjoyed access to a broad range of scholarships that offered a valuable source of private funding for those pursuing college degrees. David Drennen, for example, attended Marietta College on a partial football and basketball scholarship. The youngest of six children born and raised in Marietta, Ohio, David excelled in both academics and sports. In high school, he was a member of the National Honor Society, but it was his talent in football, basketball, and track that proved especially helpful when he began college in 1951. The availability of sports scholarships helped David to fund his degree in physics. David C. Drennen, correspondence with author. January 18, 2012. Prior to the 1970s, only a small number of scholarships—especially sports scholarships—were available to women.

142. Eisenmann, *Higher Education for Women in Postwar America, 1945-1965*, 55.

Chapter 3

1. Angelica Cervantes, Marlena Creusere, Robin McMillion, Carla McQueen, Matt Short, Matt Steiner, and Jeff Webster, "Opening the Doors to Higher Education: Perspectives on the Higher Education Act 40 Years Later," 2005, https://www.tgslc.org/pdf/HEA_History.pdf.

2. Lee W. Anderson, *Congress and the Classroom: From the Cold War to "No Child Left Behind"* (University Park, PA: Pennsylvania State University Press, 2007), 1–7; Christopher T. Cross, *Political Education: National Policy Comes of Age* (New York: Teachers College Press, 2010), 2; Charlotte A. Twight, *Dependent on D.C.: The Rise of Federal Control over the Lives of Ordinary Americans* (New York: Palgrave, 2002), 134.

3. Eisenhower's previous efforts suggested that, while he disagreed with federal aid for students, he considered the task of improving school infrastructure to be worthy of federal intervention. During the early years of his presidency, he presented—albeit unsuccessfully—numerous proposals for school construction. See Anderson, *Congress and the Classroom*, 42; Barbara Barksdale Clowse, *Brainpower for the Cold War: The Sputnik Crisis and National Defense Education Act of 1958* (Westport, CT: Greenwood Press, 1981), 46. The strength of the administration's commitment to providing support for school infrastructure seems questionable, however, considering the failure of a unified Republican government to act on proposed legislation. Cross, *Political Education*, 7. Reluctance on the part of the Eisenhower administration and ambivalence among conservatives in Congress regarding the desirability of expanding the federal government's role in education likely inhibited action in this area.

4. Andersen, "Working Women and Political Participation, 1952-1972"; Verba and Nie, *Participation in America.*

5. See, for example, Mettler, *Dividing Citizens.*

6. Skocpol, *Protecting Soldiers and Mothers.*

7. Sally A. Davenport, "Smuggling-In Reform: Equal Opportunity and the Higher Education Act 1965-80" (PhD diss., Johns Hopkins University, 1982), 32; James L. Sundquist, *Politics and Policy: The Eisenhower, Kennedy, and Johnson Years* (Washington, DC: Brookings Institution, 1968), 176. A widely held misconception is that the NDEA provided money primarily for science and technology fields. While the program did provide money for the purchase of science equipment for grade schools, support for higher education was much more general. Although students who had demonstrated strong performance in science, mathematics, and foreign language were given "special consideration" during the review of applications for undergraduate loans, awards were ultimately provided irrespective of the area of postsecondary study that the recipient pursued. As Wayne Urban notes, popular conceptualizations of the NDEA as a science and mathematics program are "grossly oversimplified." Wayne J. Urban, *More Than Science and Sputnik: The National Defense Education Act of 1958* (Tuscaloosa, AL: University of Alabama Press 2010), 5.

8. John W. Kingdon, *Agendas, Alternatives, and Public Policies,* 2nd ed. (New York: Longman, 2003).

9. Carl Elliott Sr. and Michael D'Orso, *The Cost of Courage: The Journey of an American Congressman* (Tuscaloosa, AL: University of Alabama Press, 1992), 151.

10. Clowse, *Brainpower for the Cold War,* 43; Urban, *More Than Science and Sputnik,* 17.

11. Jennifer Cohron, "A Profile in Courage: Inaugural Award Capped Stellar Life, Career of Carl Elliott," *Daily Mountain Eagle,* December 22, 2013, C1–C3.

12. See, for example, John D. Skrentny, *The Minority Rights Revolution* (Cambridge, MA: Belknap Press of Harvard University Press, 2002), 67.

13. Anderson, *Congress and the Classroom,* 21–56; Carleton, *Landmark Congressional Laws on Education,* 113; Clowse, *Brainpower for the Cold War,* 49; Cross, *Political Education,* 12; Elliott and D'Orso, *The Cost of Courage,* 141; Virginia Van der Veer Hamilton, *Lister Hill: Statesman from the South* (Chapel Hill, NC: University of North Carolina Press, 1987), 224; C. Ronald Kimberling, "Federal Student Aid: A History and Critical Analysis," in *The Academy in Crisis: The Political Economy of Higher Education,* ed. John W. Sommer (New Brunswick, NJ: Transaction Publishers, 1995), 69–70; Sidney C. Sufrin, *Administering the National Defense Education Act* (Syracuse, NY: Syracuse University Press, 1963), 2; Twight, *Dependent on D.C.,* 143; Urban, *More Than Science and Sputnik,* 77. The Eisenhower administration— facing the pressure of public opinion favorable to federal education aid—reluctantly went along with these proposals. Neither the president nor conservative members of Congress believed that the *Sputnik* "crisis" was as grave a situation as others claimed it to be. Anderson, *Congress and the Classroom,* 44; Clowse, *Brainpower for the Cold War,* 136; Robert A. Divine, *The Sputnik Challenge* (New York: Oxford University Press, 1993), 165; Twight, *Dependent on D.C.,* 145. It has even been suggested that the magnitude of the threat posed by the Soviet Union's space innovations was intentionally amplified by lawmakers and members of the media who saw an opportunity to pass federal education legislation. Clowse, *Brainpower for the Cold War,* 136; Twight, *Dependent on D.C.,* 144.

14. I should note that, historically, "manpower" has been conceptualized as a gender-neutral concept that refers to the work of both men and women. During the Cold War, the term was used to describe the productive potential of the population in its entirety.

15. *Congressional Quarterly Weekly Report* (Washington, DC: Congressional Quarterly, 1956), 8.

16. William J. Reese, *America's Public Schools: From the Common School to "No Child Left Behind"* (Baltimore, MD: Johns Hopkins University Press 2005), 225.

17. See Appendix B, Table B.3.1.

18. Joel H. Spring, "In Service to the State: The Political Context of Higher Education in the United States," in *The Academy in Crisis: The Political Economy of Higher Education,* ed. John W. Sommer (New Brunswick, NJ: Transaction Publishers, 1995), 59; Spring, *The American School,* 403; J. J. Valenti, "The Recent Debate on Federal Aid to Education Legislation in the United States," *International Review of Education* 5, no. 2 (1959): 189–202, 192. The NEA was a strong supporter of general aid to education, but the organization had a difficult time

advocating for such aid in the face of weakened credibility stemming from many Americans' association of the NEA with progressive (also known as "life adjustment") education. Progressive education—which emphasized students' ability to cope with society and various life situations over a rigorous focus on traditional academic subjects—was viewed by many as a failing pedagogical framework and as the cause of the shortcomings in American education. Anderson, *Congress and the Classroom*, 41; Herbert M. Kliebard, *The Struggle for the American Curriculum, 1893-1958*, 2nd ed. (New York: Routledge, 1995), 226.

19. Anderson, *Congress and the Classroom*, 47; Kliebard, *The Struggle for the American Curriculum*, 228; Paul E. Marsh and Ross A. Gortner, *Federal Aid to Science Education: Two Programs* (Syracuse, NY: Syracuse University Press, 1963), 25–26; Spring, "In Service to the State," 59.

20. *Congressional Quarterly Weekly Report* (Washington, DC: Congressional Quarterly, 1957), 495–496; Valenti, "The Recent Debate on Federal Aid to Education Legislation in the United States," 193.

21. Anderson, *Congress and the Classroom*, 8.

22. Ibid., 51; see also Clowse, *Brainpower for the Cold War*, 42; Twight, *Dependent on D.C.*, 145–146. Interestingly, the issue of federal control had such political currency that it was even appropriated by proponents of federal student aid who favored extensive general aid, as opposed to aid narrowly allocated for particular academic areas. From their perspective, the federal government had no right to target federal support to students pursuing training in particular fields of study. Doing so, they argued, would involve an inappropriate level of federal control over American college students.

23. Charles E. Lindblom, "The Science of 'Muddling Through,'" *Public Administration Review* 19, no. 2 (1959): 79–88; Aaron Wildavsky, *The Politics of the Budgetary Process* (Boston, MA: Little, Brown, 1964).

24. Lindblom, "The Science of 'Muddling Through,'" 84.

25. Ibid.

26. See, for example, Edwin Amenta, Elisabeth S. Clemens, Jefren Olsen, Sunita Parikh, and Theda Skocpol, "The Political Origins of Unemployment Insurance in Five American States," *Studies in American Political Development* 2 (1987): 137–182; Hugh Heclo, *Modern Social Policies in Britain and Sweden: From Relief to Income Maintenance* (New Haven, CT: Yale University Press, 1974); Mettler, *Dividing Citizens*; Pierson, "When Effect Becomes Cause"; Paul Pierson, *Dismantling the Welfare State?: Reagan, Thatcher, and the Politics of Retrenchment* (New York: Cambridge University Press, 1994).

27. Pierson, "When Effect Becomes Cause," 609.

28. Public Law 85–864, "The National Defense Education Act"; see also Anderson, *Congress and the Classroom*, 50.

29. Kingdon, *Agendas, Alternatives, and Public Policies*; Frank R. Baumgartner and Bryan D. Jones, *Agendas and Instability in American Politics* (Chicago: University of Chicago Press, 1993).

30. Kingdon, *Agendas, Alternatives, and Public Policies*, 166.

31. *The Congressional Record*, Wednesday, April 19, 1989, 101st Congress, 1st session, House of Representatives, Vol. 135, No. 47.

32. Baumgartner and Jones, *Agendas and Instability in American Politics*, 54.

33. Ibid., 42.

34. Stewart McClure, Oral History Interview: "With Lister Hill on the Labor Committee" (Interview #3), January 11, 1983, Senate Historical Office Oral History Project, 117, http://www.senate.gov/history.

35. Clowse, *Brainpower for the Cold War*, 7–8.

36. Ibid., 13; Marsh and Gortner, *Federal Aid to Science Education*, 24.

37. Divine, *The Sputnik Challenge*, 159–165; Elliott and D'Orso, *The Cost of Courage*, 158; Twight, *Dependent on D.C.*, 145–146.

38. In the wake of the *Sputnik* launches, US leaders believed that Soviet schools were superior to American schools. Public opinion data, however, indicate that the general population was slower to arrive at this conclusion. In a survey conducted by the Opinion Research Corporation, 33 percent of Americans expressed the belief that schools in the Soviet Union did a better job of educating students in science and mathematics than their counterparts in the United States. Spring, *The American School*, 95.

39. Elliott and D'Orso, *The Cost of Courage*, 149–150; Judith A. Gouwens, *Education in Crisis: A Reference Handbook* (Santa Barbara, CA: ABC-CLIO, 2009), 6–7; Van der Veer Hamilton, *Lister Hill*, 224. In his memoir, Carl Elliott described the anxiety that gripped the United States in the wake of the first *Sputnik* launch as "sheer panic" and an "utter sense of crisis and doom." Elliott and D'Orso, *The Cost of Courage*, 149.

40. Clowse, *Brainpower for the Cold War*, 13; Arthur S. Flemming, "The Philosophy and Objectives of the National Defense Education Act," *Annals of the American Academy of Political and Social Science* 327 (1960): 132–138, 134; Marsh and Gortner, *Federal Aid to Science Education*, 24.

41. Clowse, *Brainpower for the Cold War*, 12.

42. Ibid., 8.

43. Ibid., 11; Reese, *America's Public Schools*, 230.

44. This was not the first time that education had been emphasized as a mechanism for meeting national goals. As Lee Anderson notes, "The Smith-Hughes Act did this in the context of World War I." Anderson, *Congress and the Classroom*, 42; see also Kliebard, *The Struggle for the American Curriculum*, 228. The Smith-Hughes Act provided federal funds to support programming for vocational education. As the first federal program to provide direct support for schools, the Smith-Hughes Act provides a compelling example of lawmakers' use of higher education policy for purposes of social engineering. After World War I, the number of young people enrolled in American schools had increased dramatically. Christopher Cross asserts that "by 1917 the percentage of 14- to 17-year-old children enrolled in schools had grown in less than 30 years from 7% to almost 30%." Cross, *Political Education*, 2. As such, the Smith-Hughes Act of 1917 was intended to support an education system faced with the task of providing a growing population of young people with skills necessary for productive citizenship and active participation in the nation's economy. The Serviceman's Readjustment Act ("The GI Bill") of 1944, which was passed after World War II, represents another prominent example of the federal government using education to achieve national goals. After World War II, lawmakers provided veterans with financial support for pursuing postsecondary education and vocational training. Central to the legislative intent of the GI Bill was the purpose of rewarding veterans for military service. Mettler, *Soldiers to Citizens*.

45. President Dwight D. Eisenhower, "Our Future Security," Radio and Television Address to the American People, November 13, 1957, http://www.presidency.ucsb.edu/ws/?pid=10950.

46. Ibid.; Spring, *The American School*, 402.

47. Clowse, *Brainpower for the Cold War*, 54; Van der Veer Hamilton, *Lister Hill*, 228.

48. "Champions of Education," *New York Times*, August 21, 1958.

49. Dr. Mary Allen Jolley, interview by author, tape recording, October 7, 2016.

50. Stewart McClure, Oral History Interview: "With Lister Hill on the Labor Committee" (Interview #3), January 11, 1983, Senate Historical Office Oral History Project, 77, http://www.senate.gov/history.

51. Jennifer Cohron, "Caught Between Elliott and Wallace," *Daily Mountain Eagle*, December 29, 2013, A1–A10.

52. Van der Veer Hamilton, *Lister Hill*, 224.

53. Elliott and D'Orso, *The Cost of Courage*, 43–58, 126–127.

54. *Congressional Quarterly Weekly Report* (Washington, DC: Congressional Quarterly, 1956), 677.

55. *Congressional Quarterly Weekly Report* (Washington, DC: Congressional Quarterly, 1958), 575.

56. Rather than interpreting women's subdued mid-twentieth-century activism as "the doldrums." See, for example, Leila J. Rupp and Verta Taylor, *Survival in the Doldrums: The American Women's Rights Movement, 1945 to the 1960s* (New York: Oxford University Press, 1987).

   A. Lanethea Mathews-Gardner offers a revisionist interpretation of this period that views the postwar activities of women's groups as "a critical period in which women remained politically active and feminist ideas germinated in a variety of institutions and organizations." In so doing, she recognizes the importance of the 1950s and early 1960s as a "critical period" wherein women's civic organizations "became political," adopting more centralized, professionalized, and modernized structures. A. Lanethea Mathews-Gardner, "The Political

Development of Female Civic Engagement in Postwar America," *Politics & Gender* 1, no. 4 (2005): 547–575, 549–551.

57. Mathews-Gardner, "The Political Development of Female Civic Engagement in Postwar America," 553.

58. "The Quarter's Polls," *Public Opinion Quarterly* 9, no. 2 (Summer 1945): 223–257.

59. Roper Commercial Survey, July 5, 1950–August 5, 1950. Survey by *Life* magazine, conducted by Roper Organization. Based on a national adult sample of 2,990 interviews. Dataset Archive Number: USRCOM1950-040.

60. Skocpol, *Protecting Soldiers and Mothers*.

61. Thomas Borstelmann, *The Cold War and the Color Line: American Race Relations in the Global Arena* (Cambridge, MA: Harvard University Press, 2001); Mary L. Dudziak, *Cold War Civil Rights: Race and the Image of American Democracy* (Princeton, NJ: Princeton University Press, 2000).

62. Skrentny, *The Minority Rights Revolution*, 67.

63. Gareth Davies, *See Government Grow: Education Politics from Johnson to Reagan* (Lawrence, KS: University Press of Kansas, 2007), 287.

64. Eisenmann, *Higher Education for Women in Postwar America, 1945-1965*, 14–15.

65. Ibid., 15.

66. Elliott and D'Orso, *The Cost of Courage*, 151.

67. Stewart McClure, Oral History Interview: "With Lister Hill on the Labor Committee" (Interview #3), January 11, 1983, Senate Historical Office Oral History Project, 77, http://www.senate.gov/history.

68. Stewart McClure, Oral History Interview: "The National Defense Education Act" (Interview #4), January 28, 1983, Senate Historical Office Oral History Project, 95, http://www.senate.gov/history.

69. Dr. Mary Allen Jolley, interview by author, tape recording, October 7, 2016.

70. R. Douglas Arnold, *The Logic of Congressional Action* (New Haven, CT: Yale University Press, 1990).

71. In a telling characterization, Sen. Lister Hill described the challenge of passing a federal education bill as simultaneously avoiding "the Scylla of race and the Charybdis of religion." Van der Veer Hamilton, *Lister Hill*, 225; see also Urban, *More Than Science and Sputnik*.

72. *Congressional Quarterly Weekly Report* (Washington, DC: Congressional Quarterly, 1958), 34. The student loan component of the Hill-Elliott proposal coincided with contemporary public opinion regarding the use of loans as a mechanism for increasing higher educational access. In response to a Gallup poll conducted in January of 1958, 77 percent of Americans agreed that the federal government should establish long-term loans for students who wished to attend college. Only 15 percent of respondents disagreed.

73. Stewart McClure, Oral History Interview: "The National Defense Education Act" (Interview #4), January 28, 1983, Senate Historical Office Oral History Project, 95, http://www.senate.gov/history.

74. Dr. Mary Allen Jolley, interview by author, tape recording, October 7, 2016.

75. Elliott and D'Orso, *The Cost of Courage*, 153–154.

76. Kingdon, *Agendas, Alternatives, and Public Policies*, 201.

77. Elliott and D'Orso, *The Cost of Courage*, 153 (emphasis theirs).

78. Cross, *Political Education*, 10; see also Stewart McClure, Oral History Interview: "With Lister Hill on the Labor Committee" (Interview #3), January 11, 1983, Senate Historical Office Oral History Project, 86, http://www.senate.gov/history.

79. Clowse, *Brainpower for the Cold War*, 121.

80. The central importance of the race issue to the eventual passage of broad-reaching federal student aid could be seen as an indicator that the racists in Congress were empowered in ways that sexists were not. It is true that one-party dominance in the South gave southern members of Congress a great deal of power when it came to thwarting efforts to pass federal student aid. Yet, it would be more accurate to say that the racists in Congress were mobilized in a way that the sexists—although these groups need not be mutually exclusive—were not because federal student aid was framed as a race issue, rather than a gender issue or one that was of particular interest to women.

81. Elliott and D'Orso, *The Cost of Courage,* 154.

82. See, for example, Kliebard, *The Struggle for the American Curriculum,* 229.

83. *Congressional Record,* 58th Congress, 2nd session, 682.

84. Anderson, *Congress and the Classroom,* 1–5, 55.

85. Clowse, *Brainpower for the Cold War,* 71.

86. Stewart McClure, Oral History Interview: "With Lister Hill on the Labor Committee" (Interview #3), January 11, 1983, Senate Historical Office Oral History Project, 95, http://www.senate.gov/history. Chairman Barden was not the only formidable opponent of federal education proposals. For the better part of the eight months that they were considered by Congress, the Hill-Elliott and Smith-Kearns bills would languish in the House Rules Committee. Chaired by another conservative Democrat, Howard W. Smith (D-VA), this committee had been a virtual graveyard for previous education proposals. As the chairman of the House Rules Committee in the late 1950s, Smith wielded considerable power and was described as "perhaps more powerful than any other single man in Congress at that time." Elliott and D'Orso, *The Cost of Courage,* 156. Commenting on the significance of clearing the Rules Committee for successfully passing higher education legislation, Carl Elliott recalled that "delivering the National Defense Education Act to the Rules Committee was like sending it into a black hole," and if Chairman Smith prevailed, "it would never have been heard of again." Elliott and D'Orso, *The Cost of Courage,* 157.

87. Within the House Education and Labor Committee, Chairman Barden's decision to reject the dominant practice of adhering to seniority when selecting subcommittee chairs in 1957 may have also enhanced the probability that an education bill would successfully emerge from the committee. In filling the last of five subcommittee chairs, Barden made the unconventional decision to skip over Rep. Adam Clayton Powell (D-NY) to appoint a fellow southerner, the more-junior Carl Elliott. While Elliott acknowledged that Chairman Barden's decision may have been based on racism, he maintained that "for me and the rest of the committee members eager to finally get an education bill in motion" the decision was fortunate because "any subcommittee headed by Adam Clayton Powell was dead in the water from the beginning." This view was rooted in the political controversy created by Powell's insistence that federal education programs be nondiscriminatory, which invoked the ire of Southern Democrats, who represented locales that would presumably use federal funds to support segregated school systems. Elliott and other members of the Education and Labor Committee believed that the representative from Alabama could produce higher education proposals that dealt with school segregation in a fashion that would be less inflammatory than any method that Powell was sure to adopt.

88. Elliott and D'Orso, *The Cost of Courage,* 142.

89. Ibid., 142–144. The very existence of these subcommittees represented a veritable coup for federal aid supporters. As Carl Elliott noted, "The subcommittee is typically the first step— through its research and hearings—toward launching a bill." Elliott and D'Orso, *The Cost of Courage,* 142. This triumph for the liberal coalition represents one of the earliest harbingers of the NDEA's imminent success.

90. Elliott and D'Orso, *The Cost of Courage,* 143.

91. Clowse, *Brainpower for the Cold War,* 52; Elliott and D'Orso, *The Cost of Courage,* 143–146. Among the previously enacted federal programs that Elliott and his staff studied were the Morrill Land-Grant Act of 1862, the Smith-Hughes Act of 1917, and the George-Barden Act of 1946. Clowse, *Brainpower for the Cold War,* 103.

92. Elliott and D'Orso, *The Cost of Courage,* 158.

93. Clowse, *Brainpower for the Cold War,* 127; Elliott and D'Orso, *The Cost of Courage,* 157–158.

94. Elliott and D'Orso, *The Cost of Courage,* 159.

95. The National Education Association (NEA) maintained a strong presence throughout the hearings on the NDEA, emphasizing their preference for general aid to schools. Elliott and D'Orso, *The Cost of Courage,* 154; Spring, *The American School,* 403. Greatly surpassing the $1 billion proposed by the Hill-Elliott measure, the NEA advocated for a program of federal student aid that would provide $4.5 billion to be allocated over a five-year period. This proposal included provisions for at least twenty thousand scholarships for high school graduates pursuing college education. *Congressional Quarterly Weekly Report* (Washington, DC: Congressional

Quarterly, 1957), 1340. Calling the demand "enraging," Carl Elliott noted that the NEA lobbied for general aid in an amount that was almost five times as much as the $1 billion requested in the Hill-Elliott proposal. He complained that "the NEA folks could never seem to understand that the only way to get some pie is a slice at a time." Elliott and D'Orso, *The Cost of Courage*, 154.

96. Stewart McClure, Oral History Interview: "The National Defense Education Act" (Interview #4), January 28, 1983, Senate Historical Office Oral History Project, 95, http://www.senate.gov/history.

97. Anderson, *Congress and the Classroom*, 21.

98. Ibid., 52–53. The issue of federal control over education proved so politically potent that it was appropriated by *supporters* of federal student aid, like Rep. George McGovern (D-SD), who objected to policy proposals that would limit the scope of federal student aid by targeting it to students pursuing education in fields deemed directly related to national security.

99. Clowse, *Brainpower for the Cold War*, 125–126; Cross, *Political Education*, 12; Elliott and D'Orso, *The Cost of Courage*, 168–169; Valenti, "The Recent Debate on Federal Aid to Education Legislation in the United States," 194.

100. Clowse, *Brainpower for the Cold War*, 43–45. This issue had thwarted the efforts of President Harry Truman and members of the Eighty-First Congress who had shown interest in enacting federal aid for education but had abandoned that objective when opposition to allocating federal aid to parochial schools appeared to mount a substantial political challenge.

101. Clowse, *Brainpower for the Cold War*, 43; Elliott and D'Orso, *The Cost of Courage*, 152.

102. See *Brown v. Board of Education of Topeka*, 347 U.S. 483 (1955). It is interesting to note that while Rep. Carl Elliott and Sen. Lister Hill emphasized the nondiscriminatory nature of the bill when working to secure the support—or to preclude the opposition—of Catholic churches, Adam Clayton Powell, and the National Association for the Advancement of Colored People (NAACP), both Hill and Elliott had signed the 1956 "Southern Manifesto" in which Southern Democrats—including Senators Strom Thurmond (D-SC), Walter George (D-GA), William Fulbright (D-AK), and Harry Byrd (D-VA)—criticized the Supreme Court's desegregation decision in *Brown v. Board of Education of Topeka*. Regardless of where Hill and Elliott stood on the issue of school desegregation, the fact that they strategically framed the NDEA so that it was vague enough to provide nondiscriminatory aid while failing to affect the racial order of southern educational institutions ultimately promoted greater inclusion of women in American higher education. Concern over whether proposed federal social policies could be leveraged to force desegregation in the South was not limited to the area of higher education. Lawmakers voiced similar concerns, for example, regarding health care policies during the mid-twentieth century. The 1965 passage of Medicare offers a prominent example of another federal program that harnessed receipt of government support to requirements of equal opportunity. See David Barton Smith's *The Power to Heal: Civil Rights, Medicare, and the Struggle to Transform America' Health Care System* (Nashville, TN: Vanderbilt University Press, 2016), and David Blumenthal and James Morone's *The Heart of Power: Health and Politics in the Oval Office* (Oakland, CA: University of California Press, 2010).

103. "Scholarship and Loan Program," Hearings Before the Subcommittee on Education and Labor, House of Representatives, 85th Congress, 1st Session, on Bills Relating to a Federal Scholarship Program, Hearings Held from August 12, 1957–April 3, 1958 (Washington, DC: US Government Printing Office, 1958), 14.

104. Ibid., 19.

105. Ibid., 14.

106. Ibid., 19.

107. Ibid., 2.

108. Ibid., 65–56.

109. Ibid., 523.

110. "Science and Education for National Defense," Hearings Before the Committee on Labor and Public Welfare, United States Senate, 85th Congress, Held from January 21–March 13, 1958 (Washington, DC: US Government Printing Office, 255).

111. "Scholarship and Loan Program Part 1," Hearings Before the Subcommittee on Special Education, Committee on Education and Labor, House of Representatives, 85th Congress, 1st Session, on Bills Relating to a Federal Scholarship Program, Hearings Held from August 12, 1957–November 4, 1957, 254–255.

112. See, for example, Eisenmann, *Higher Education for Women*, 15–16. The Soviet Union's purported commitment to equal rights for women had been an important component in Marxist ideology and had been highlighted in a 1963 constitution that proclaimed that women and men should enjoy equal rights "in all spheres of economic, state, cultural, social and political life." Skrentny, *The Minority Rights Revolution*, 75.

113. "Scholarship and Loan Program," 544.

114. "Science and Education for National Defense," Hearings Before the Committee on Labor and Public Welfare, United States Senate, 85th Congress, Held from January 21–March 13, 1958 (Washington, DC: US Government Printing Office, 1958), 1138.

115. The mid-twentieth century represents a transitional period for women's activism in the United States. As Jo Freeman notes, "By 1950, the 19th century organizations which had been the basis of the suffrage movement—the Women's Trade Union League, the General Federation of Women's Clubs, the Women's Christian Temperance Union, the National American Women's Suffrage Association—were all either dead or a pale shadow of their former selves." Jo Freeman, "The Origins of the Women's Rights Movement," in *Changing Women in a Changing Society*, ed. Joan Huber. (Chicago: University of Chicago Press, 1973), 40.

116. Elliott and D'Orso, *The Cost of Courage*, 158.

117. Stewart McClure, Oral History Interview: "With Lister Hill on the Labor Committee" (Interview #3), January 11, 1983, Senate Historical Office Oral History Project, 78, http://www.senate.gov/history.

118. Nancy MacLean, *American Women's Movement, 1945-2000: A Brief History with Documents* (Boston: Bedford/St. Martin's, 2009), 7. One exception to this trend is the fact that some women's groups continued to actively advocate for the Equal Rights Amendment (ERA) in the 1950s.

119. Clowse, *Brainpower for the Cold War*, 27.

120. The issue was also dropped by organizations not wanting to broach the topics of federal control and the ways in which a federal higher education program would affect states' rights. In 1952, for example, the General Federation of Women's Clubs jettisoned education from its policy agenda due to the controversy that the issue caused regarding civil rights issues. See Mathews-Gardner, "The Political Development of Female Civic Engagement," 560.

121. *Congressional Quarterly Weekly Report* (Washington, DC: Congressional Quarterly, 1958), 1001.

122. Lister Hill, Carl Elliott, and other proponents of federal student aid understood that by successfully clearing the formidable hurdle represented by the House Rules Committee with a 266–108 vote, the NDEA had achieved an important triumph. Elliott and D'Orso, *The Cost of Courage*, 168.

123. Dale Short, "Hitting the Ground Running," *Daily Mountain Eagle*, April 6, 2014. This recognition of Carl Elliott's considerable skill as a lawmaker is echoed by Mary Allen Jolley, who recalls that in an effort to build relationships with his colleagues, Elliott sought a position on the House Administration Committee. During the 1950s, this committee was charged with general organizational and housekeeping duties for the chamber. According to Jolley, "[Carl] had to give assignments for parking places, he had to go recount elections—he didn't have to sweep the floor, but it was just practically that. And, so that was the housekeeping stuff. But, you made good relationships when you could handle that and handle it well, because people cared about where they parked." Dr. Mary Allen Jolley, interview by author, tape recording, October 7, 2016.

124. *Congressional Quarterly Weekly Report* (Washington, DC: Congressional Quarterly, 1958), 16715; see also Clowse, *Brainpower for the Cold War*, 130; Valenti, "The Recent Debate on Federal Aid," 192. The Powell amendments emerged at the behest of civil rights advocates, particularly Clarence Mitchell of the National Association for the Advancement of Colored People (NAACP). Cross, *Political Education*, 9–10; Sundquist, *Politics and Policy*, 177. Arguing against the allocation of federal funds to school construction aid programs that

supported segregated schools, Powell complained that "Negro people have waited many, many years for this hour of democracy to come and they are willing to wait a few more years rather than see a bill passed that will . . . build a dual system of Jim Crow Education." Cross, *Political Education*, 10; Sundquist, *Politics and Policy*, 165–166.

125. *The Congressional Record—House*, 85th Congress, 2nd session, August 8, 1958, Vol. 104, p. 16694.

126. Clowse, *Brainpower for the Cold War*, 130; Divine, *The Sputnik Challenge*, 164.

127. Clowse, *Brainpower for the Cold War*, 19. This Cold War ideology shaped President Dwight Eisenhower's posture toward defense in the 1950s. As David L. Snead notes, he was primarily concerned with achieving three goals—"preserving a way of life, building a strong military, and overseeing a prosperous economy." David L. Snead, *The Gaither Committee, Eisenhower, and the Cold War* (Columbus: Ohio State University Press, 1998), 17. While the loyalty oath outraged many liberals, it helped to reconcile the bill with Cold War objectives.

128. Citing their dissatisfaction with the basic premise of the NDEA, Representatives Ralph W. Gwinn, Clare Hoffman, and Donald Nicholson in the House and Sen. Strom Thurmond in the Senate signed their respective committees' reports as members of the minority opposed to the measure. See Anderson, *Congress and the Classroom*, 49–50.

129. *Congressional Quarterly Weekly Report* (Washington, DC: Congressional Quarterly, 1958), 1059.

130. Clowse, *Brainpower for the Cold War*, 132.

131. Anderson, *Congress and the Classroom*, 27, 53; Clowse, *Brainpower for the Cold War*, 130; Elliott and D'Orso, *The Cost of Courage*, 168–170.

132. Clowse, *Brainpower for the Cold War*, 136–137.

133. Spring, "In Service to the State," 59.

134. *Congressional Record*, 85th Congress, 2nd session, 19612.

135. Elliott and D'Orso, *The Cost of Courage*, 170–171.

136. Anderson, *Congress and the Classroom*, 55.

137. Clowse, *Brainpower for the Cold War*, 138.

138. *Congressional Quarterly Weekly Report* (Washington, DC: Congressional Quarterly, September 4, 1958).

139. Dr. Hubertien H. Scott's remarks during the "Carl Elliott Commemoration Ceremony" at the University of Alabama when the congressman's Profiles in Courage award was presented to the university for safe keeping in September of 2015. From Dr. Mary Jolley's papers.

140. Letters from Dr. Mary Jolley's papers.

141. Homer D. Babbidge Jr. and Robert M. Rosenzweig, *The Federal Interest in Higher Education* (New York: McGraw-Hill, 1962), 51 (emphasis theirs); see also Alice M. Rivlin, *The Role of the Federal Government in Financing Higher Education* (Washington, DC: Brookings Institution, 1961), 119.

142. Stewart McClure, Oral History Interview: "The National Defense Education Act" (Interview #4), January 28, 1983, Senate Historical Office Oral History Project, 95, http://www.senate.gov/history.

143. Skrentny, *The Minority Rights Revolution*, 185; see also Kliebard, *The Struggle for the American Curriculum*, 229.

144. Van der Veer Hamilton, *Lister Hill*, 275; see, for example, Rivlin, *The Role of the Federal Government*, 78.

145. Rivlin, *The Role of the Federal Government*, 77.

146. Ibid., 78.

147. Ibid., 77.

148. Ibid.

Chapter 4

1. Reese, *America's Public Schools*, 226; see also Hugh Davis Graham, *The Uncertain Triumph: Federal Education Policy in the Kennedy and Johnson Years* (Chapel Hill, NC: University of North Carolina Press, 1984), 69; George A. Kizer, "Federal Aid to Education: 1945-1963," *History of Education Quarterly* 10, no. 1 (1970): 84–102, 93.

2. Graham, *The Uncertain Triumph*, 7–9; Kizer, "Federal Aid to Education: 1945-1963, 93. The platform set forth by the Democratic Party included a program for higher education aid that would provide grants to the states to address their most pressing educational needs, particularly classroom shortages and low teacher salaries. The education proposal included in the Republican Party's platform, on the other hand, focused on providing federal funds for elementary and high school classroom construction in needy districts. Kizer, "Federal Aid to Education: 1945-1963," 93.

3. Skocpol, "Targeting Within Universalism."

4. In 1972, Basic Educational Opportunity Grants were renamed Pell Grants in honor of Sen. Claiborne Pell (D-RI). Guaranteed Student Loans were renamed Stafford Loans in honor of Sen. Robert T. Stafford (R-VT) in 1988.

5. As a November 5, 1965, *Time* editorial noted just days before the passage of the Higher Education Act, the higher education programs included in Lyndon Johnson's "Great Society" initiative, the NDEA, and other federal programs that performed "good deeds" for individual Americans altered the nature of federal support for citizens, turning "Uncle Sam" into "Big Daddy." In other words, the author felt that the federal government had assumed the generous—albeit deviant—role of a "Sugar Daddy," offering "a wonderland of federal paternalism that stretches from cradle to grave."

6. *Congressional Quarterly Weekly Report* (Washington, DC: Congressional Quarterly, July 23, 1965), 1419.

7. Michael D. Parsons, *Power and Politics: Federal Higher Education Policymaking in the 1990s* (Albany, NY: State University of New York Press, 1997), 37.

8. Graham, *The Uncertain Triumph*, 12.

9. Ibid.

10. "American Women: Report of the President's Commission on the Status of Women" (Washington, DC: Government Printing Office, 1963), 10.

11. Ibid.

12. Graham, *The Uncertain Triumph*, 20.

13. Ibid., 44; Kizer, "Federal Aid to Education: 1945-1963," 93–94. The issue of religion represented one of the most formidable challenges to Kennedy's efforts in the area of education. As Kizer notes, "[a] significant number of Protestants and non-Catholics were concerned with the impact John Kennedy's religion might have on educational issues in spite of reassurances from the candidate during his campaign." Kizer, "Federal Aid to Education: 1945-1963," 93. Additionally, Kennedy also had to deal with criticism from members of the Catholic Church who objected to the "double taxation" of Catholics that would almost certainly occur in the event that the federal government succeeded in passing a comprehensive federal aid program. If Catholic schools are excluded from federal funding, parents who pay for their children to attend such schools must also contribute to the pool of federal tax dollars that supports public education. Kizer, "Federal Aid to Education: 1945-1963," 94. Ironically, as Edith Green noted in a June 1963 article in the *Journal of Higher Education*, arguments asserting the unconstitutionality of providing federal funds for private, church-related colleges failed to recognize that "Baptist, Catholic, Lutheran, Presbyterian, and other denominational colleges have been receiving research grants for years from the Department of Defense, the National Institutes of Health, the Atomic Energy Commission, and other federal agencies." Edith Green, "Support of Higher Education: Expense or Investment?," *Journal of Higher Education* 34, no. 6 (1963): 332.

14. Graham, *The Uncertain Triumph*, 45.

15. Upon signing the Higher Education Facilities Act of 1962, President Johnson emphasized the significance of the legislation, calling it the "the most significant education bill passed by the Congress in the history of the Republic" and adding that "[the 1963] session of Congress will go down in history as the Education Congress of 1963." Graham, *The Uncertain Triumph*, 52. This statement, which Hugh Davis Graham characterizes as "hyperbolic," offers a preview of the strong and favorable attitude toward active federal intervention in higher education that would characterize the Johnson administration's subsequent policy initiatives.

16. James C. Hearn, "The Paradox of Growth in Federal Aid for College Students, 1965-1990," in *The Finance of Higher Education: Theory, Research, Policy, and Practice*, ed. Michael B. Paulsen and John C. Smart (New York: Agathon Press, 2001), 273.

17. Parsons, *Power and Politics*, 35–37; Davenport, "Smuggling-In Reform"; Francis Keppel, "The Higher Education Acts Contrasted: Has Federal Policy Come of Age?," *Harvard Educational Review* 57, no. 1 (1987): 49–67, 50; Spring, "In Service to the State," 60. Joel Spring quotes Sen. Daniel Patrick Moynihan as remarking that "once again higher education policy was deployed by the national government to serve external political needs, in this case to press further to fill out a central theme of the Kennedy and Johnson administration[s]—that of equality . . .. Higher education was a means of obtaining goals elsewhere in the political system." Spring, "In Service to the State," 60.

18. *Congressional Quarterly Weekly Report* (Washington, DC: Congressional Quarterly, 1965), 61; see also José Chávez, "Presidential Influence on the Politics of Higher Education: The Higher Education Act of 1965" (PhD diss., University of Texas at Austin 1975), 52–56. Davenport, "Smuggling-In Reform," 43–46.

19. Chávez, "Presidential Influence on the Politics of Higher Education," 53. Taking note of the challenges that President Kennedy had encountered when trying to promote his education agenda, Johnson used secret task forces during the policy design phase of the Higher Education Act. Doing so enabled the administration to craft its proposal sans public scrutiny. Graham, *The Uncertain Triumph*; Parsons, *Power and Politics*, 36.

20. Chávez, "Presidential Influence on the Politics of Higher Education," 53; Graham, *The Uncertain Triumph*, 66; Paul Manna, *School's In: Federalism and the National Education Agenda* (Washington, DC: Georgetown University Press, 2006), 76–77. Included in the report submitted by the task force was Gardner's prescient recommendation that lawmakers establish a separate US Department of Education with the purpose of better coordinating the government's education programs. Graham, *The Uncertain Triumph*, 66. Although this suggestion did not gain traction during the Johnson administration, the Department of Education Organization Act of 1979 (PL 96–88) separated the Department of Health, Education, and Welfare (HEW) into the Department of Education and the Department of Health and Human Services.

21. Chávez, "Presidential Influence on the Politics of Higher Education,". Prior to that point in time, National Defense Student Loans (NDSLs), which were created as part of the NDEA, provided the bulk of federal student aid. Hearn, "The Paradox of Growth in Federal Aid for College Students, 1965-1990," 274.

22. Lyndon B. Johnson, "Remarks to the Delegates to the White House Conference on Education," Book II Pub. Papers July 21, 1965.

23. Davenport, "Smuggling-In Reform," 133.

24. Flemming, "The Philosophy and Objectives of The National Defense Education Act," 133; Gladieux and Wolanin, *Congress and the Colleges*, 15; Susan B. Hannah, "The Higher Education Act of 1992: Skills, Constraints, and the Politics of Higher Education," *Journal of Higher Education* 67, no. 5 (1996): 498–527, 503.

25. William D. Ford, "The Higher Education Act After 20 Years: Old Dreams and New Realities," Lyndon B. Johnson Distinguished Lecture, Southwest Texas State University, San Marcos, TX, November 7, 1985.

26. Parsons, *Power and Politics*, 35–36.

27. Parsons, *Power and Politics*, 37. Earlier that year, the same strategy had enabled the Johnson administration to move the Elementary and Secondary Education Act through Congress in only three months.

28. Graham, *The Uncertain Triumph*, 80; see also Chávez, "Presidential Influence on the Politics of Higher Education,"; Parsons, *Power and Politics*, 36.

29. Parsons, *Power and Politics*, 36.

30. Chávez, "Presidential Influence on the Politics of Higher Education," 57–58.

31. Ibid., 60–62.

32. Ibid., 63.

33. "Higher Education Act of 1965 (H.R. 3220)," Hearings before the Subcommittee on Education and Labor (Washington, DC: US Government Printing Office, 1965), 30.

34. Graham, *The Uncertain Triumph*, 81–82; Parsons, *Power and Politics*, 38.

35. *Congressional Quarterly Weekly Report* (Washington, DC: Congressional Quarterly, 1965), 76–76; Chávez, "Presidential Influence on the Politics of Higher Education," 52–53.

36. *Congressional Quarterly Weekly Report* (Washington, DC: Congressional Quarterly, 1965), 78.
37. Ibid., 63.
38. "Education Legislation-1963," Vol. 7, Hearings Before the Subcommittee on Education, Committee on Labor and Public Welfare, United States Senate, 4020.
39. *Congressional Record*, 88th Congress, 2nd session, 13573.
40. *Congressional Record*, 88th Congress, 2nd session, 10898.
41. Chávez, "Presidential Influence on the Politics of Higher Education," 70.
42. Ibid., 72.
43. "Higher Education Act of 1965 (H.R. 3220)," Hearings Before the Subcommittee on Education and Labor (Washington, DC: US Government Printing Office, 1965), 61–62.
44. Evidence provided to the subcommittee from a document entitled "Financial Aid to College Students, 1963-64" by Elizabeth W. Haven and Robert E. Smith further illustrates this gender-neutral approach to considering the Higher Education Act. The authors of this publication note that, while women were once widely regarded as less likely to assume the responsibility of a college loan, women and men were equally likely to obtain student loans to pay for college. In 1960, for instance, 49 percent of college freshmen who had received student loans were women. "Higher Education Act of 1965 (H.R. 3220)," Hearings Before the Subcommittee on Education and Labor (Washington, DC: US Government Printing Office, 1965), 455.
45. "Higher Education Act of 1965 (H.R. 3220)," Hearings Before the Subcommittee on Education and Labor (Washington, DC: US Government Printing Office, 1965), 659.
46. Ibid., 502.
47. "Higher Education Act of 1965 (S. 600)," Subcommittee Hearings (Washington, DC: US Government Printing Office, 1965), 301. Thelma Thomas Daley of the American Personnel and Guidance Association submitted a statement to the committee that offered high school students' thoughts regarding the proposed Higher Education Act of 1965. Reflecting on the program, a young woman named Joan remarked that "one of the major problems I face is money and so many scholarships are for such a little bit." Mike, the son of a steelworker, concurred: "I was exposed to the framework of Government loans in the 10th grade. It was like alleviating a hanging problem; it gave me a feeling that the money will be there and I'll have a chance." George, whose father was blind and who was supported by the welfare department in his county, echoed the financial concerns expressed by Joan and Mike: "on the road to college are many problems to be faced—the biggest of these is money. Money can affect grades and handicap functional participation. I want aid. I want my life to mean something." A final example of needy high school students' thoughts regarding the provisions of the Higher Education Act can be found in the comments of Lucy, a tenant farmer's daughter, who said, "I would love to be able to attend a good school. Maybe this bill is my salvation . . . . If I could obtain a loan, a grant, and a scholarship, maybe my dreams will come true." As this sample of quotes illustrates, the financial assistance provided by the HEA resonated with both male and female students. "Higher Education Act of 1965 (S. 600)," Subcommittee Hearings (Washington, DC: US Government Printing Office, 1965), 856–857.
48. *Congressional Record*, 88th Congress, 2nd session, 11182.
49. *Congressional Record*, 88th Congress, 2nd session, 18824.
50. The activities of national women's organizations faced numerous challenges in the 1960s, particularly significant declines in membership. As Kristin Goss and Theda Skocpol note, the mid-1960s marked the beginning of significant declines in membership for women's organizations. In the American Association of University Women, for example, the percentage of female college graduate members "dropped by 4 percent between 1945 and 1965, and then plunged by 80 percent" in the three decades after 1966. Kristin Goss and Theda Skocpol, "Changing Agendas: The Impact of Feminism on American Politics," in *Gender and Social Capital*, ed. Brenda O'Neil and Elisabeth Gidengil (New York: Routledge, 2006), 348. Rather than boasting broad memberships drawing upon women from all racial and socioeconomic backgrounds, women who engaged in feminist politics in the 1960s tended to be well-educated, middle-class women. Joyce Gelb and Marian Lief Palley, *Women and Public Policies: Reassessing Gender Politics* (Charlottesville, VA: University Press of Virginia, 1996), 38.

51. Goss and Skocpol, "Changing Agendas," 323.
52. Ibid., 324.
53. Ibid., 329.
54. "Higher Education Act of 1965 (H.R. 3220)," 701–705.
55. Ibid., 601–602.
56. Ibid., 598.
57. Dorothy McBride-Stetson, *Women's Rights in the USA: Policy Debates and Gender Roles*, 3rd ed. (New York: Routledge, 2004), 143.
58. "Higher Education Act of 1965," Hearings Before the Subcommittee on Education of the Committee on Labor and public Welfare, United States Senate, 89th Congress, 1st session on S. 600, Part I (Washington, DC: US Government Printing Office).
59. *Congressional Record*, 88th Congress, 2nd session, 4662.
60. "Higher Education Act of 1965 (H.R. 3220)," 649.
61. Ibid.
62. McBride-Stetson, *Women's Rights in the USA*, 144.
63. "Higher Education Act of 1965 (H.R. 3220)," 6627. Echoing this idea that the HEA could support women as they pursue skills that would promote valuable labor force participation, Walter J. Tribbey, president of the Draughton School of Business in Oklahoma City, Oklahoma, submitted a column authored by Dr. Benjamin Fine for the record. In it, Fine emphasizes the need for women in many fields, saying: "With the increasing complexity of American business and professional life, there is a growing demand for educated young women with stenographic skills who are versed in specialized fields such as legal medical, engineering or technical secretaries . . .. Because of the scramble by business executives, the young lady—and occasional young man—with a specialized training can count on an excellent salary and sound job security." "Higher Education Act of 1965 (H.R. 3220)," 535–536.
64. 111 Congressional Record—House, 89th Congress, 1st session, August 26, 1965, Made Special Order (H. Res. 527), 21944.
65. "Higher Education Act of 1965 (S. 600)," Subcommittee Hearings (Washington, DC: US Government Printing Office 1965), 1097–1098. Once it became clear that federal student loans were likely to be included in whatever higher education proposal emerged from Congress, representatives from the banking industry, including the American Bankers Association and the United States Aid Fund, made clear their support of government subsidies to banks offering student loans. They did, however, express opposition to government discretion over the interest rates attached to the loans and the terms of repayment.
66. "Higher Education Act of 1965 (S. 600)," Subcommittee Hearings (Washington, DC: US Government Printing Office, 1965), 1284.
67. Robert C. Albright, "Education Tax Credits Defeated," *Washington Post,* February 5, 1964, A1.
68. Graham, *The Uncertain Triumph*, 82.
69. Chávez, "Presidential Influence on the Politics of Higher Education," 117–118.
70. Ibid., 125–134.
71. *Congressional Quarterly Weekly Report* (Washington, DC: Congressional Quarterly, 1965), 1765, 2117.
72. Differences in the speed with which each chamber acted on the Higher Education Act suggests that the Senate provided less contentious ground for proposed higher education legislation than the House of Representatives. As John Walsh notes, the HEA emerged from the House Education and Labor Committee on July 14, 1965, but went without activity until August 26. In the Senate, on the other hand, the HEA emerged from committee on September 1 and passed the following day. John Walsh, "Congress: Higher Education Act Including Scholarship for Needy Passed in Final Days of Session," *Science, New Series* 150, no. 3696 (1965): 591–594, 592.
73. *Congressional Quarterly Weekly Report* (Washington, DC: Congressional Quarterly, 1965), 1827. Surprisingly, once the HEA came up for debate on the Senate floor, the bulk of debate pertained not to the aforementioned amendments, but to a disagreement as to the bill's effects for the level of control wielded by the federal educational bureaucracy over fraternal organizations. The primary source of contention was the appropriate reach of the US education commissioner's power. Specifically, lawmakers disagreed as to whether the commissioner could

deny federal higher education benefits to students attending institutions at which fraternities engaged in racial, religious, or creed-based discrimination. Chávez, "Presidential Influence on the Politics of Higher Education," 134–135. Once members inserted language clarifying that control over the practices of fraternities and sororities fell outside of the education commissioner's purview, the Senate passed its version of the Higher Education Act on September 2, by a vote of seventy-nine to three. The bill that emerged from the Senate differed from the House measure in two main respects: first, the Senate proposal included items geared toward improving elementary and secondary school teaching—particularly the establishment of a National Teacher Corps. Second, the Senate bill authorized $4.7 billion for fiscal years 1966–1970, while the House bill included only authorizations for fiscal year 1966. *Congressional Quarterly Weekly Report* (Washington, DC: Congressional Quarterly, 1965), 1827.

74. Walsh, "Congress: Higher Education Act Including Scholarship for Needy Passed in Final Days of Session," 592.
75. Chávez, "Presidential Influence on the Politics of Higher Education," 121 and 136–137.
76. Walsh, "Congress: Higher Education Act Including Scholarship for Needy Passed in Final Days of Session," 591.
77. In the House, 75 Republicans favored the HEA, while 41 opposed it; 238 Democrats voted for the bill, while 22 opposed it.
78. *Congressional Quarterly Weekly Report* (Washington, DC: Congressional Quarterly, 1965), 2117.
79. Lyndon B. Johnson, "Remarks at Southwest Texas State College Upon Signing the Higher Education Act of 1965," Book II Pub. Papers 1102, November 8, 1965.
80. *Congressional Quarterly Weekly Report* (Washington, DC: Congressional Quarterly, 1965), 2337.

Chapter 5

1. Quoted from a statement made during the 1970 congressional hearings on discrimination against women. See Stimpson, ed., *Discrimination Against Women*, 131.
2. Marvella Belle Hearn was the future Marvella Bayh—wife of Indiana senator and Title IX cosponsor Birch Bayh (D-IN). While sex discrimination dashed her hopes of attending the University of Virginia, Bayh's experience made a significant impression on her husband, who became a champion for women's equal access for higher education in the US Senate. Sen. Birch Bayh, interview by author, tape recording, March 1, 2011; see also Jeff Jacobs, "Champion of the Title IX Era," *Hartford Courant,* January 20, 2004, http://articles.courant.com/2004-01-20/sports/0401200283_1_civic-center-uconn-women-dodd.
3. Gender discrimination was not limited to students: those who were hired into college faculty positions earned less money than their male counterparts and were less likely to be promoted. See Stimpson, ed., *Discrimination Against Women*, 47.
4. Katherine Hanson, Vivian Guilfoy, and Sarita Pillai, *More Than Title IX: How Equity in Education Has Shaped the Nation* (Lanham, MD: Rowman and Littlefield Publishers, 2009), xvi.
5. Davis, *Moving the Mountain,* 212; Karen Blumenthal, *Let Me Play: The Story of Title IX, the Law that Changed the Future of Girls in America* (New York: Anthem Books for Young Readers, 2005).
6. "Title IX: A Sea Change in Gender Equity in Education," Archived Information, US Department of Education, https://www2.ed.gov/pubs/TitleIX/part3.html.
7. Scholars have devoted a great deal of attention to examining the effects that Title IX has had for gender equality in athletics. In their analysis of Title IX's effectiveness for promoting gender equality, for example, political scientist Eileen McDonagh and journalist Laura Pappano argue that, by constructing requirements for equal access to athletic opportunities around the assumption that women and girls should play on separate teams from men and boys, Title IX perpetuates the notion that women and men are not equal. Similarly, Elizabeth Sharrow examines the role that Title IX has played in shaping how policymakers think about "athletes" versus "female athletes," arguing that the policy has provided a mechanism for lawmakers to fuse biological sex into policy implementation. Beyond examining the relationship between Title IX and gender equity in athletics, legal scholars have recognized Title IX's significance

for promoting women's civil rights. See Eileen McDonagh and Laura Pappano, *Playing with the Boys* (New York: Oxford University Press, 2008); Elizabeth M. Sharrow, "'Female Athlete' Politic: Title IX and the Naturalization of Sex Difference in Public Policy," *Politics, Groups, and Identities* 5, no. 1 (2017): 46–66; see also Linda Jean Carpenter and R. Vivian Acosta, "Women in Intercollegiate Sport: A Longitudinal Study Thirty Three Year Update, 1977-1910"; Amanda Ross Edwards, "Why Sport? The Development of Sport as a Policy Issue in Title IX of the Education Amendments of 1972," *Journal of Policy History* 22, no. 3 (2010): 300–336.

8. NCWGE 2007, 5.
9. As Charles E. Lindblom notes, incremental policy change is characterized by modest adjustments to existing policies. This differs from what Frank R. Baumgartner and Bryan D. Jones describe as "short bursts of dramatic change" that significantly reform or otherwise alter public policy. See Lindblom, "The Science of 'Muddling Through,'" 79–88; Baumgartner and Jones, *Agendas and Instability in American Politics*.
10. For historical analysis and data related to women's political and socioeconomic standing, see Burns, Schlozman, and Verba, *The Private Roots of Public Action*; the Center for American Women and Politics (CAWP), 2014, http://www.cawp.rutgers.edu; *Congressional Quarterly Weekly Report* (Washington, DC: Congressional Quarterly, 1972), 597.
11. Scholars have focused largely on the effects of Title IX for promoting gender equality in athletics. As Anna Edwards notes, athletics became the focal point of Title IX when the executive branch, in implementing the legislation, charged the judicial branch with reviewing the policy in sports-related court cases. See, for example, McDonagh and Pappano's (2008) study on the regulation's effects for athletics. McDonagh and Pappano, *Playing with the Boys*.
12. Bernice Sandler, interview by author, tape recording, March 23, 2011.
13. Bernice Sandler, interview by author, tape recording, March 23, 2011.
14. The situation at Columbia University exemplified the disdain that many institutions held for this type of federal oversight. Administrators at Columbia flatly refused to submit a proposal for improving sex discrimination in hiring and employment on campus, and they also refused to provide the Office of Civil Rights with institutional data on women and minorities. As a result, the government withheld all federal grants from Columbia from November of 1971 until March of the following year. See *Congressional Quarterly* 1972, 599.
15. Bernice Sandler, interview by author, tape recording, March 23, 2011.
16. After achieving an exemplary record as a student in Oregon, Green hoped to pursue a career in law. However, because a legal career would have been incongruous with accepted gender norms of the day, Green's family and academic advisers urged her to pursue a more gender-appropriate profession: teaching. Although Green distinguished herself as a first-rate educator, she forever regretted relinquishing her dreams of becoming a lawyer. See Cynthia E. Harrison's Oral History interview with former congresswoman Edith S. Green, December 18, 1978.
17. Cynthia E. Harrison's Oral History interview with former congresswoman Edith S. Green, December 18, 1978.
18. Margaret Dunkle, interview by author, tape recording, January 5, 2012.
19. *Congressional Quarterly Weekly Report* (Washington, DC: Congressional Quarterly, 1972), 597.
20. Margaret Dunkle, interview by author, tape recording, January 5, 2012.
21. Ibid.
22. Hanson, Guilfoy, and Pillai, *More Than Title IX*, 8.
23. The Fourteenth Amendment of the US Constitution also failed to ensure that women received equal treatment by higher educational institutions. As Rep. Martha Griffiths noted in advocating for the Equal Rights Amendment (ERA), the Supreme Court had never recognized women as a class that is entitled to equal protection of the law as provided under the Fourteenth Amendment. See Susan L. Greendorfer, "Title IX Gender Equality, Backlash, and Ideology," *Women in Sport and Physical Activity Journal* 7 (1998): 69; *Congressional Quarterly Weekly Report* (Washington, DC: Congressional Quarterly 1972), 597.
24. *The Congressional Record*—Senate, 92nd Congress, 1st session, February 28, 1972, 5804.
25. Margaret Dunkle, interview by author, tape recording, January 5, 2012.

26. Ibid.
27. Blumenthal, *Let Me Play*, 47. The ERA had been introduced in Congress every year since 1923, repeatedly failing to garner enough support to amend the Constitution. See *Congressional Quarterly Weekly Report* (Washington, DC: Congressional Quarterly, 1972), 2590.
28. Representative Green's hearings on sex discrimination coincided with the House Education and Labor Committee's consideration of Section 805, her proposal to amend Title VI of the Civil Rights Act (HR 16098) to include a prohibition against sex discrimination in federally funded programs. See *Congressional Record* 1997, H4217.
29. Stimpson, ed., *Discrimination Against Women*, xiii.
30. Andrew Fishel and Janice Pottker, *National Politics and Sex Discrimination in Education* (Lexington, MA: D.C. Heath and Company, 1977), 96; Bernice Sandler, interview by author, tape recording, March 23, 2011.
31. Stimpson, ed., *Discrimination Against Women*, 23.
32. Ibid., 62.
33. Ibid., 165; also Bernice Sandler, interview by author, tape recording, March 23, 2011.
34. *Congressional Record* 1971, 30156.
35. Blumenthal, *Let Me Play*, 31.
36. Stimpson, ed., *Discrimination Against Women*, 12; see also US Department of Education, "Title IX: 25 Years of Progress," 3.
37. Bernice Sandler, interview by author, tape recording, March 23, 2011.
38. Title VI of the Civil Rights Act denied federal financial assistance to programs and activities that engaged in discrimination on the basis of race, nationality, or religion-based discrimination. See Skrentny, *The Minority Rights Revolution*, 231.
39. *Congressional Quarterly Weekly Report* (Washington, DC: Congressional Quarterly, 1970), 2055.
40. *Congressional Quarterly Weekly Report* (Washington, DC: Congressional Quarterly, 1970), 1700.
41. Joseph A. Califano, *Governing America: An Insider's Report from the White House and the Cabinet* (New York: Simon and Schuster, 1981), 263; *Congressional Record,* 1971, 30156.
42. *Congressional Quarterly Weekly Report* (Washington, DC: Congressional Quarterly, 1971), 483.
43. Ibid.
44. Ibid., 484.
45. Sen. Birch Bayh, interview by author, tape recording, March 1, 2011. An unsung hero, Representative Green's keen political acumen was crucial to the development and eventual implementation of Title IX and other landmark higher education policies that expanded women's access to higher education. As Marilyn Stapleton, Green's former chief of staff, noted, the congresswoman had a strong record of successfully championing legislation—a fact shaped, no doubt, by her intelligence and courage, her work ethic, and her excellent skills as a debater. As Stapleton noted, "When Mrs. Green got up to speak, a hush would go over the [House] floor" (interview with M. Stapleton, 2012). These skills proved indispensable in championing equal opportunity for American women. A great deal of Representative Green's effectiveness as a legislator was a function of her commitment to being well prepared. As her son, Richard Green, noted, "She had a reputation as being one of the members of Congress who did her homework. Something that most of them did not do." As a result, Green's office was often characterized as "a hardship office" (interview with R. Green, 2012). Describing her experience on Edith Green's congressional staff, Marilyn Stapleton recalls that legislative aides "would spend all-nighters compiling notebooks and, days ahead of time, answering questions that [Representative Green] thought might come up or challenges to what she was trying to accomplish" (interview with M. Stapleton, 2012).
46. Margaret Dunkle, interview by author, tape recording, January 5, 2012.
47. Hanson, Guilfoy, and Pillai, *More Than Title IX*, 8; Matthews and McCune, *Why Title IX?*; McDonagh and Pappano, *Playing with the Boys*, 101–102; Skrentny, *The Minority Rights Revolution*, 231.
48. Rosemary Salomone, "The Legality of Single-Sex Education in the United States: Sometimes 'Equal' Means 'Different,'" in *Gender in Policy and Practice: Perspectives on Single-Sex and*

Coeducational Schooling, ed. Amanda Datnow and Lea Hubbard (New York: RoutledgeFalmer, 2002); Imram Valentin, "Title IX: A Brief History," Report (Washington, DC: US Department of Education, 1997); Ana M. Martinez and Kristen A. Penn, eds., *Women in Higher Education: An Encyclopedia* (Santa Barbara, CA: AFL-CIO, 2002), 239–241; Andrew Fishel, "Organizational Positions on Title IX: Conflicting Perspectives on Sex Discrimination in Education," *Journal of Higher Education* 47 (1976): 102; Janet M. Martin, *The Presidency and Women: Promise, Performance, & Illusion* (College Station, TX: Texas A&M University Press, 2003).

49. Margaret Dunkle, interview by author, tape recording, January 5, 2012. See also Jean C. Robinson, Barbara Barnhouse Walters, and Julia Lamber, "Title IX in the 1970s: From Stealth Politics to Political Negotiation" (paper presented at the Annual Meeting of the Midwestern Political Science Association, Chicago, IL, April 5, 2008); Blumenthal, *Let Me Play*, 35; Hanson, Guilfoy, and Pillai, *More Than Title IX*, 8–9; Bernice Sandler, interview by author, tape recording, March 23, 2011; Skrentny, *The Minority Rights Revolution*, 247.

50. Margaret Dunkle, interview by author, tape recording, January 5, 2012.

51. Bernice Sandler, interview by author, tape recording, March 23, 2011.

52. Given the importance of Title IX for promoting gender equality in higher education, it comes as little surprise that fabled accounts of the program's development have emerged in the wake of its passage. However, claims of fierce advocacy for the program at its birth are merely tall tales. As Margaret Dunkle notes, "There was just a handful of people who were [working on behalf of Title IX]. It's kind of like people who say they were at Woodstock." In actuality, "nobody marched for Title IX," said Dunkle; "it just wasn't done because it was under the radar." Margaret Dunkle, interview by author, tape recording, January 5, 2012. See also Kristin Goss, *The Paradox of Gender Equality: How American Women's Groups Gained and Lost Their Public Voice* (Ann Arbor, MI: University of Michigan Press, 2013), 55–58.

53. Margaret Dunkle, interview by author, tape recording, January 5, 2012.

54. Robinson, Walters, and Lamber, "Title IX in the 1970s."

55. Ibid.

56. US House, Committee on Education and Labor, 1971, 367.

57. Ibid., H39252.

58. US House, 1971, 273–278.

59. *Congressional Record,* 1971, 39252.

60. US House, 1971, H38639, H39248.

61. US House 1971, 1078.

62. Hanson, Guilfoy, and Pillai, *More Than Title IX*, 9. Not surprisingly, these elite institutions counted a number of House representatives and senators among the ranks of their distinguished alumni. For example, John Erlenborn, an opponent of Title IX, attended the University of Notre Dame. Another opponent of Title IX's ban on sex discrimination in admissions was Peter Peyser (R-NY), who was an alumni of Colgate University, which did not admit women until 1972.

63. US House. *Higher Education Act of 1971,* 1st session, H.R. 7248; *Congressional Record,* 1971, H3249.

64. US House, 1971, H39248-39249.

65. *Congressional Record—Senate,* 92nd Congress, 1st session, November 4, 1971, 39248. Representative Green expressed exasperation regarding the irony of Hesburgh's support for Erlenborn's exemption: "How a person as Chairman of the Civil Rights Commission of the United States can make eloquent statements about having to end discrimination in this country and then say it is perfectly all right to continue the discrimination against over 50 percent of the people in the country I do not know." See *Congressional Record,* 1971, 39250.

66. *Congressional Record—House,* 92nd Congress, 1st session, November 4, 1971, 39249–39250.

67. Ibid., 39251–39252.

68. US House, 1971, H39261; Fishel and Pottker, *National Politics and Sex Discrimination in Education,* 101.

69. *Congressional Record,* 1971, 30155. Unlike Title IX's trajectory in the House, Bayh's amendment was not considered during Senate subcommittee deliberations. As senators considered

the proposed higher education reauthorization bill in the Education Subcommittee of the Labor and Public Welfare Committee, busing emerged as the most contentious education issue. Busing became a part of the debate over higher education when a desegregation assistance package was added to the higher education aid proposals under consideration, and controversy surrounding the proposal significantly slowed Senate action on the bill. See Fishel and Pottker, *National Politics and Sex Discrimination in Education*, 99–100; *Congressional Quarterly Weekly Report* (Washington, DC: Congressional Quarterly, 1972), 2617.

70. *Congressional Record,* 1971, 30156.

71. A few months earlier, the US House of Representatives passed the Equal Rights Amendment by a 354–23 roll-call vote, and then the Senate passed it by a vote of 84–8. See *Congressional Quarterly Weekly Report* (Washington, DC: Congressional Quarterly, 1971), 2590. If the statute had won support from three-quarters (or thirty-eight) of the states, it would have become the newest amendment to the US Constitution. Although it failed to secure passage as a constitutional amendment, the passage of the ERA by the House and Senate demonstrated lawmakers' recognition that Americans were generally opposed to overt gender discrimination, just as they had opposed overt racial discrimination in the 1960s.

72. *Congressional Quarterly Weekly Report* (Washington, DC: Congressional Quarterly, 1971), 597.

73. *Congressional Quarterly Weekly Report* (Washington, DC: Congressional Quarterly, 1972), 112. Considering the long-standing correlation between traditional views regarding acceptable gender roles and conservative ideology, this Republican president's support for gender equality may seem surprising. However, it is important to note that members of the Republican Party had been among the early supporters of the Equal Rights Amendment. Opposing the protective labor laws that were championed by New Deal Democrats, Republicans in the late 1930s and early 1940s supported legislation that would entitle women to the same treatment as men under the law. Women's reform groups and New Deal Democrats, on the other hand, opposed a constitutional amendment that would institutionalize equal treatment for women and men, fearing that such an amendment would weaken labor laws that provided women with needed support. Democrats did not begin to express support for the Equal Rights Amendment until 1944. See Mettler, *Dividing Citizens*, 207–208; see also Wendy Sarvasy, "Beyond the Difference Versus Equality Policy Debate: Postsuffrage Feminism, Citizenship, and the Quest for a Feminist Welfare State," *Signs: Journal of Women in Culture and Society* 17, no. 2 (1992): 329–362.

74. While hesitant to openly object to banning sex discrimination in college admissions, opponents could safely object to the redistribution of resources in areas that were more closely in line with traditional gender roles. Thus, they focused on how Title IX would affect sports programs and the student bodies at all-male military academies. While lawmakers might have focused on other areas that would be directly transformed by Title IX, such as sex discrimination in faculty hiring, gender discrimination in vocational education, and policies regarding pregnant and parenting students, these issues did not offer the same political accessibility or redistribution-based contention that athletics and all-male military academies did. Thus, Title IX's opponents portrayed the potential outcomes of Title IX as a zero-sum game in which these traditionally masculine arenas would be the losers. Although these issues failed to prevent the passage of Title IX, they set the tone for subsequent political battles long after the principals had left the ring.

75. The senators were particularly amused by this line of questioning, and at one point Dominick quipped, "If I may say so, I would have had much more fun playing college football if it had been integrated." Blumenthal, *Let Me Play*, 44.

76. Ibid. Commenting on the idea of admitting women to military academies, General William Westmorland provided further evidence of contemporary views regarding appropriate social roles for women and men, saying, "Maybe you could find one woman in ten thousand who could lead in combat, but she would be a freak and we're not running the military academy for freaks." See Rick Atkison, *The Long Gray Line: The American Journey of West Point's Class of 1966* (New York: Holt and Holt, 1999), 408; see also Meena Bose, "Leadership Challenges in National Security," in *Rethinking Madam President: Are We Ready for a Woman in the White House?*, ed. Lori Cox Han and Caroline Heldman (Boulder, CO: Lynne Rienner, 2007).

77. Skrentny, *The Minority Rights Revolution*, 247.
78. Sen. Birch Bayh, interview by author, tape recording, March 1, 2011.
79. Valerie M. Bonnette, interview by author, tape recording, January 6, 2012.
80. Bernice Sandler, interview by author, tape recording, March 23, 2011.
81. US House, 1971, H38639.
82. *The Congressional Record—Senate*, 92nd Congress, 1st session, February 28, 1972, 5804.
83. Snyder and Dillow, *Digest of Education Statistics*, 297.
84. Fishel and Pottker, *National Politics and Sex Discrimination in Education*. Although the exemption of undergraduate programs at private institutions limited the reach of Title IX, it is important to note that the majority of American undergraduate students attended public institutions.
85. In the House, both parties were fairly similarly divided regarding support for the omnibus education bill: 129 Democrats supported the legislation, while 104 voted against it; and 89 Republicans voted for the bill, compared to 76 who did not. Among Democrats, those representing districts in the North were more likely to support the bill than those from the South. Among northern Democrats, 109 members supported the Education Amendments, and 44 members opposed it. For Democratic members from southern districts, 20 voted for the education bill, while 60 voted against it. Opponents of the legislation generally took issue with its treatment of the busing issue. Conservative opponents wanted the bill to include more forceful antibusing measures, while liberal opponents felt that the bill's language was too conciliatory on the issue of busing. See *Congressional Quarterly Weekly Report* (Washington, DC: Congressional Quarterly, 1972), 1371; Califano, *Governing America*, 263; *Congressional Quarterly Weekly Report* (Washington, DC: Congressional Quarterly, 1972), 2805–2810.
86. McDonagh and Pappano, *Playing with the Boys*, 101.
87. Although Title IX would ultimately affect both public and private colleges and universities, its full reach was not immediately apparent in 1972. Initially, undergraduate admissions at private institutions were exempted from Title IX's ban on gender discrimination. Later, administrative regulations and court cases (e.g., *Grove City College v. Bell*) led to the inclusion of private colleges and universities under Title IX's prohibition on sex discrimination in admissions, as students in these institutions received federal financial aid.
88. "Access to Higher Education," The MARGARET Fund of NWLC, 2009, http://www.titleix.info/10-Key-Areas-of-Title-IX/Access-to-Higher-Education.aspx; Conway, Ahern, and Stuernagel, *Women and Public Policy*, 23–24; Hanson, Guilfoy, and Pillai, *More Than Title IX*; Martinez and Penn, eds. *Women in Higher Education*.
89. US Department of Education, "Title IX: 25 Years of Progress," Report, 1997, 3, http://www2.ed.gov/pubs/TitleIX/index.html.
90. *Congressional Record*, June 23, 1997, H4212.
91. Interview with V. Bonnette, 2012.
92. *Congressional Record*, 1997, H4217.
93. Baumgartner and Jones, *Agendas and Instability in American Politics*, 54.

Chapter 6

1. Excerpt from Cynthia E. Harrison's Oral History interview with former congresswoman Edith S. Green, December 18, 1978.
2. Williams is the author's grandmother, who has shared this story many times and was still kind enough to discuss her journey at length on May 20, 2015.
3. Marshall, *Citizenship and Social Class and Other Essays*, 25; Orloff, "Gender and the Social Rights of Citizenship," 305–307.
4. Marshall, *Citizenship and Social Class and Other Essays*, 47.
5. Scholars have also recognized that education yields benefits that extend beyond increased income and better labor market opportunities. It also yields nonpecuniary benefits like improved decision making, decreasing risky behaviors, and facilitating trust and civic engagement. See Philip Oreopoulous and Kjell G. Salvanes, "Priceless: The Nonpecuniary Benefits of Schooling," *Journal of Economic Perspectives* 25, no. 1 (2011): 159–184.

6. There is an extensive scholarship linking federal financial aid usage to college enrollment and completion. See, for example, Susan M. Dynarski, "Does Aid Matter? Measuring the Effect of Student Aid on College Attendance and Completion," *American Economic Review* 93, no. 1 (2003): 279–288; Deondra Rose, "Keys That Jingle and Fold: Federal Student Aid and the Expansion of Educational Opportunity for Black Women," *Journal of Women, Politics, and Policy* (2016): 1-22; Edward P. St. John, "The Impact of Student Financial Aid: A Review of Recent Research," *Journal of Student Financial Aid* 21, no. 1 (1991): 18–32; Edward P. St. John, R. Kirshstein, and J. Noell, "The Effects of Student Aid on Persistence: A Sequential Analysis of the High School and Beyond Senior Cohort," *Review of Higher Education* 14, no. 3 (1991): 383–406.

7. Bound and Turner, "Going to War and Going to College," 789–790; Mettler, "Bringing the State Back In to Civic Engagement."

8. Mettler, *Soldiers to Citizens*, 70.

9. In 1972, lawmakers amended the Higher Education Act of 1965 to include the Basic Educational Opportunity Grant (BEOG) program, which was renamed the "Pell Grant" program in 1980. The program that emerged in 1972 was derived largely from the need-based BEOG program that had originated in Title IV of the 1965 bill.

10. See, for example, David Brooks, *Bobos in Paradise: The New Upper Class and How They Got There* (New York: Simon & Schuster, 2001).

11. Verba, Schlozman, and Brady, *Voice and Equality*.

12. Warren and Tyagi, *The Two-Income Trap*.

13. See, for example, Burns, Schlozman, and Verba, *The Private Roots of Public Action*; Philip E. Converse, "Change in the American Electorate," in *The Human Meaning of Social Change*, ed. A. Campbell and P. Converse (New York: Russell Sage, 1972); Verba, Schlozman, and Brady, *Voice and Equality*.

14. For additional information regarding variable coding, see Appendix A, Table A.6.1.

15. Campbell, "Self-Interest, Social Security, and the Distinctive Participation Patterns of Senior Citizens," 565–574; Campbell, *How Policies Make Citizens*; Mettler, *Soldiers to Citizens*; Mettler and Welch, "Civic Generation," 497–518.

16. Karl L. Alexander and Bruce K. Eckland, "Sex Differences in the Educational Attainment Process," *American Sociological Review* 39, no. 5 (1974): 668–682; William H. Sewell and Vimal P. Shah, "Socioeconomic Status, Intelligence, and the Attainment of Higher Education," *Sociology of Education* 40, no. 1 (1967): 1–23. When considering the different factors that influence whether women and men earn college degrees, scholars have focused heavily on the influence of socioeconomic status and intellectual ability. For young women, socioeconomic status is a stronger determinant of college plans, attendance, and graduation than is intelligence. For men, intellectual ability provides a particularly strong determinant of college success. Alexander and Eckland, "Sex Differences in the Educational Attainment Process," 668–682; Sewell and Shah, "Socioeconomic Status, Intelligence, and the Attainment of Higher Education," 1–23. Scholars have also focused on the role that dominant gender ideologies play in educational attainment. In their analysis of the influence of egalitarian gender attitudes on the higher educational expectations of adolescent girls and boys, Davis and Pearce find that high school girls and boys who have more egalitarian attitudes regarding the work–family gender balance in families anticipate attaining higher levels of education. "Believing that women should have the same kinds of opportunities as men to have a career and that men should help equitably with household work and childcare inspires high school girls to expect to attain more education," they argue. For boys, they find that "having a more or less egalitarian work-family gender ideology is related to whether he will invest in higher education, but the effects are less pronounced." Shannon N. Davis and Lisa D. Pearce, "Adolescents' Work-Family Gender Ideologies and Educational Expectations," *Sociological Perspectives* 50, no. 2 (2007): 249–271.

17. Gail E. Thomas, Karl L. Alexander, and Bruce K. Eckland, "Access to Higher Education: The Importance of Race, Sex, Social Class, and Academic Credentials," *School Review* 87, no. 2 (1979): 133–156, 151.

18. Lee M. Wolfle, "Postsecondary Educational Attainment Among Whites and Blacks," *American Educational Research Journal* 22, no. 4 (1985): 501–525.

19. Lisettte M. Garcia and Alan E. Bayer, "Variations between Latino Groups in US Post-Secondary Educational Attainment," *Research in Higher Education* 46, no. 5 (2005): 511–533.

20. Thomas, Alexander, and Eckland, "Access to Higher Education," 151. Mary Beth Walpole notes that scholars have recognized students from low socioeconomic families as "educationally disadvantaged," but in focusing on educational inequality for students on the basis of race, ethnicity, gender, and sexual orientation, some have failed to recognize the importance of social family's socioeconomic status in shaping college completion. Mary Beth Walpole, "Socioeconomic Status and College: How SES Affects College Experiences and Outcomes," *Review of Higher Education* 27, no. 1 (2003), 45–46.

21. Dalton Conley, "Capital for College: Parental Assets and Postsecondary Schooling," *Sociology of Education* 74, no. 1 (2001): 59–72; Robert M. Hauser and Raymond Sin-Kwok Wong, "Sibling Resemblance and Intersibling Effects in Educational Attainment," *Sociology of Education* 62, no. 3 (1989): 149–171; Martha S. Hill and Greg J. Duncan, "Parental Family Income and the Socioeconomic Attainment of Children," *Social Science Research* 16, no. 1 (1987): 39–73. Parents also provide educational resources—such as access to reference books, dictionaries, and encyclopedias and a designated study space in the home—that are positively associated with higher educational attainment. Such resources appear to be particularly important to the ultimate postsecondary attainment of women. "The effect of women's resources," claims Jay Teachman, "may increase level of schooling attained by reducing the likelihood of choosing to enter roles (marriage, parenthood) that compete with additional education." Jay D. Teachman, "Family Background, Educational Resources, and Educational Attainment," *American Sociological Review* 52, no. 4 (1987): 548–557, 554.

22. "Scholarship and Loan Program," Hearings Before the Subcommittee on Education and Labor, House of Representatives, 84th Congress, 1st session, on Bills Relating to a Federal Scholarship Program, Hearings Held from August 12, 1957–April 3, 1958 (Washington, DC: US Government Printing Office, 1958), 1.

23. "Higher Education Act of 1965 (H.R. 3220)," Hearings Before the Subcommittee on Education and Labor (Washington, DC: US Government Printing Office, 1965), 301.

24. In 1988, the Guaranteed Student Loan program was renamed in honor of Sen. Robert Stafford (R-VT), becomingly popularly known as Stafford Loans.

25. See, for example, Bound and Turner, "Going to War and Going to College," 784–815; Mettler, *Soldiers to Citizens.*

26. Because data from the National Postsecondary Student Aid Study (NPSAS)—which the federal government, higher education associations, and researchers rely on as the primary source of federal financial aid data—are only available for years beginning in the mid-1980s, these data can only provide insight into the trends of federal student aid program usage by undergraduates and outcomes for educational attainment in recent decades. To examine trends over a longer term, I also consider data from the Cooperative Institutional Research Program (CIRP) Freshman surveys, which span from 1974 to 1998, and cohort analysis of Social and Governmental Issues and Participation (SGIP) data, which include a representative sample of Americans.

27. The significance of the difference between women's and men's responses was determined using a Chi-square test. Using an $\alpha = 0.01$ level of significance, we fail to reject the null hypothesis that there is no significant difference between proportions when p-values are greater than 0.01.

28. I construct age cohorts using the following categories: eighteen to thirty-five (born 1973–1990), thirty-six to fifty-four (born 1954–1972), fifty-five to seventy-three (born 1935–1953), and seventy-four to ninety-two (born 1916–1934). The mean age of college freshmen taking the Cooperative Institutional Research Program (CIRP) survey is eighteen years old. Considering this typical age of college entry, these age cohorts—ranging from the most senior to the most junior—correspond to students who would have begun their undergraduate education in four periods: 1934–1952, 1953–1971, 1972–1990, and 1991–2008.

29. These gender differences are statistically significant at a 99.9 percent confidence level for the seventy-four–to–ninety-two age cohort, a 99 percent confidence level for the fifty-five–to–seventy-three age cohort, and a 95 percent confidence level for the eighteen–to–thirty-five age cohort.

30. In 2008, for example, the average amount of federal aid received by undergraduate women—measured in current dollars that reflect actual amounts prevailing during specified years—was $6,472, compared to an average of $6,703 for men. See Appendix B, Figure B.6.1.

31. See, for example, Cecilia Elena Rouse, "What to Do After High School: The Two-Year Versus Four-Year College Enrollment Decision," in *Choices and Consequences: Contemporary Policy Issues in Education*, ed. Ronald G. Ehrenberg (Ithaca, NY: Cornell University Press, 1994).

32. Alexandra Walton Radford, Jolene Wu, and Thomas Weko, "Issue Tables: A Profile of Military Service Members and Veterans Enrolled in Postsecondary Education in 2001-08" (Washington, DC: US Department of Education, National Center for Education Statistics, 2009), 1, http://nces.ed.gov/pubs2009/2009182.pdf.

33. Olson, "The G.I. Bill and Higher Education," 596.

34. Bennett, *When Dreams Came True*, 202.

35. Men represented approximately 95.8 percent of World War II veterans. See *Census Atlas of the United States*, US Census Bureau, Population Division, http://www.census.gov/population/www/cen2000/censusatlas/. See also Bound and Turner, "Going to War and Going to College," 785; Conway, Steuernagel, and Ahern, *Women and Public Policy*, 22; Eisenmann, *Higher Education for Women in Postwar America, 1945-1965*, 28; Mettler, *Soldiers to Citizens*; Rosenberg, *Divided Lives*, 166.

36. Gauging women's GI Bill usage is difficult using data from the Social and Governmental Issues and Participation (SGIP) study because only fifteen women responded to the question of whether they have ever received GI Bill benefits. One-hundred-sixty men, in contrast, responded to this question. Thus, while the number of male respondents who responded to this question yields meaningful usage statistics, the number of women responding to this question is prohibitively small. Nonetheless, secondary data sources confirm women's vast underrepresentation among GI Bill beneficiaries. See, for example, Bennett, *When Dreams Came True*; Eisenmann, *Higher Education for Women in Postwar America, 1945-1965*; Mettler, *Soldiers to Citizens*.

37. It is important to note that, in addition to expanding access to college for a significant proportion of American men in the postwar era, approximately two-thirds of beneficiaries under the 1944 GI Bill used federal aid for vocational training. While 2.2 million World War II veterans used GI benefits to attend college, a full 5.6 million veterans used these benefits to attain vocational training. Mettler, *Soldiers to Citizens*, 42.

38. See Appendix B, Figure B.6.2.

39. See Appendix B, Figure B.6.3.

40. Although these gender differences may not seem substantial—in 2008, for example, 45 percent of women compared to 42.5 percent of men received Guaranteed Student Loans—these differences are statistically significant at the $\alpha = .001$ level.

41. See Appendix B, Figure B.6.4.

42. For the 1935–1953 birth year cohort, women and men used student loans at virtually equal rates: 14.8 percent of women and 14.7 percent of men used federal student loans.

43. Social and Governmental Issues and Participation Study, 2008.

44. See Appendix B, Figure B.6.5.

45. These differences are statistically significant at the $\alpha = .001$ level; however, this may reflect the large sample size of the CIRP Freshman survey.

46. The gender gap between women and men ages eighteen to thirty-five represents the only statistically significant differences in Pell Grant utilization across these four cohorts. This difference is significant at the $\alpha = .05$ level.

47. Robert L. Hardesty, "The Higher Education Act on Its 30th Birthday," LBJ Lecture, Southwest Texas State University, November 6, 1995.

48. See, for example, Gary Becker, *Human Capital: A Theoretical and Empirical Analysis, with Special Reference to Education*, 2nd ed. (University of Chicago Press, 1975); Jere R. Behrman, Robert A. Pollak, and Paul Taubman, "Do Parents Favor Boys?," *International Economic Review* 27, no. 1 (1986): 33–54.

49. See Gary King, Michael Tomz, and Jason Wittenberg, CLARIFY Software for Interpreting and Presenting Statistical Results, Version 2.1, http://gking.harvard.edu/clarify.

50. See results in Appendix B, Table B.6.1.

51. This echoes other research that has found that African Americans use financial aid programs at particularly high rates. See, for example, Rose, "Keys That Jingle and Fold," 1–22.
52. See results in Appendix B, Table B.6.2.
53. For information on variable coding, see Appendix A, Table A.6.3. See results in Appendix B, Table B.6.3.
54. Pierson, "When Effect Becomes Cause," 622.
55. It seems plausible that GI Bill traceability has fluctuated over time. For example, the program may have become less visible as the system of US military conscription was replaced with an all-volunteer military force in 1973.
56. See, for example, Becker, *Human Capital*; Cynthia E. Harrison, "Oral History: Edith Green," Oregon Historical Society; "Higher Education Act of 1965 (H.R. 3220)," Hearings Before the Subcommittee on Education and Labor (Washington, DC: US Government Printing Office, 1965). In 1958, US Undersecretary for the Department of Health, Education, and Welfare Dr. John A. Perkins alluded to these trends during debate over the first student loan programs. "If a family is perhaps pressed financially and they have sons and daughters," he stated, "they are apt to educate the sons before they will extend themselves to the daughters." He went on to describe women's difficulty securing alternative sources of support for higher education, explaining that "it is more difficult for young ladies to work themselves through college than it is for a young man to do so." "Scholarship and Loan Program," Hearings Before the Subcommittee on Education and Labor, House of Representatives, 85th Congress, 1st Session, on Bills Relating to a Federal Scholarship Program, Hearings Held from August 12, 1957–April 3, 1958 (Washington, DC: US Government Printing Office, 1958), 19. Throughout the course of testimony offered during this hearing, witnesses explained that the types of jobs offered to women students rarely offered enough remuneration to cover tuition and living expenses.
57. Social and Governmental Issues and Participation Study, 2008.
58. See Appendix B, Figure B.6.6.
59. The gender gaps presented in Table 6.2 do not reach statistical significance.
60. This gender gap is statistically significant at an $\alpha = .05$ level.
61. These between-gender and within-gender differences do not reach statistical significance.
62. The differences between women and men and the differences between female education policy users and nonusers do not reach statistical significance. The difference between male policy users and nonusers is statistically significant at an $\alpha = .05$ level.
63. These differences are statistically significant at the $\alpha = .001$ level. Significant gender differences also exist among federal student aid users and nonusers, respectively. Among both of these groups, women are significantly more likely to report spending at least fifteen hours per week on schoolwork outside of class (at the $\alpha = .001$ level).
64. See results in Appendix B, Table B.6.4.
65. The "go-getters" variable measures the extent to which respondents can be characterized as ambitious or enterprising using a six-part index. For more information on variable coding, please refer to Appendix A, Table A.6.2.
66. This difference is statistically significant at $\alpha = 0.10$.
67. This analysis uses a technique that is similar to the approach that Susan Dynarski used to investigate the effect of eligibility for Social Security survivors' benefits for college attendance and completion among students with deceased fathers. See Dynarski, "Does Aid Matter?," 279–288.
68. To test the robustness of these findings, I use a second technique—two-stage least squares regression analysis, which I summarize in Appendix C.

Chapter 7

1. Marshall, *Citizenship and Social Class and Other Essays*, 11.
2. American National Election Studies (ANES), "Guide to Public Opinion and Electoral Behavior," http://www.electionstudies.org/nesguide/gd-index.htm.
3. Conway, Steuernagel, and Ahern. *Women and Public Policy*, 9.

4. This analysis centers upon the gender dynamics of political engagement at the mass level; however, it is important to note that, since World War II, women have made great strides in elite politics as well. The percentage of women winning election to the US Congress increased steadily after Jeannette Rankin became the first woman to win election to the House in 1917. This steady increase gave way to a dramatic jump in 1993, the "Year of the Woman," which saw an unprecedented forty-seven women elected to the national legislature. In 2010, women held 16.8 percent of the seats in the US Congress.

5. Andersen, "Working Women and Political Participation, 1952-1972," 439–447; M. Margaret Conway, "Women and Political Participation," *PS: Political Science and Politics* 34, no. 2 (2001): 231–233.

6. Center for American Women in Politics (CAWP), "Women in Elective Office 2010," Factsheet, http://www.cawp.rutgers.edu; Burns, Schlozman, and Verba, *The Private Roots of Public Action*, 261; Conway, "Women and Political Participation," 231; Sidney Verba, Nancy Burns, and Kay Lehman Schlozman, "Knowing and Caring About Politics: Gender and Political Engagement," *Journal of Politics* 59, no. 4 (1997): 1051–1072; Andersen, "Working Women and Political Participation, 1952-1972," 441.

7. Center for American Women in Politics (CAWP), 2011, http://www.cawp.rutgers.edu.

8. It is important to note that this trend does not hold for the oldest cohort of American men and women. During the 2008 presidential election, for example, men who were seventy-five years of age and older voted at higher rates than their female counterparts.

9. Center for American Women in Politics (CAWP), 2011, http://www.cawp.rutgers.edu.

10. American National Election Studies (ANES), Cumulative Data File, 1948–2008.

11. Ibid.

12. These data from the American National Election Study and Margaret Conway's findings contradict those of Burns, Schlozman, and Verba, who contend that "for each kind of [political] activity except for attending protests, there is a gender difference, with women less active than men." Burns, Schlozman, and Verba, *The Private Roots of Public Action*, 64. These data and Conway's reference to scholarship produced in 1995 indicate that trends have changed since Burns, Schlozman, and Verba conducted their Citizen Participation Survey in 1990. Conway, "Women and Political Participation," 231–233.

13. American National Election Studies (ANES), Cumulative Data File, 1948–2008.

14. Ibid.

15. See, for example, Verba, Burns, and Schlozman, "Knowing and Caring About Politics," 1052; Kay Lehman Schlozman, Nancy Burns, and Sidney Verba, "Gender and the Pathways to Participation: The Role of Resources," *Journal of Politics* 56, no. 4 (1994): 963–990.

16. See, for example, Norman H. Nie, Jane Junn, and Kenneth Stehlik-Barry, *Education and Democratic Citizenship in America* (Chicago: University of Chicago Press, 1996); Rosenstone and Hansen, *Mobilization, Participation, and Democracy in America*; Verba, Schlozman, and Brady, *Voice and Equality*; Verba and Nie, *Participation in America*.

17. Converse, "Change in the American Electorate," 324–435.

18. Ibid., 324.

19. Burns, Schlozman, and Verba, *The Private Roots of Public Action*, 142; Verba, Schlozman, and Brady, *Voice and Equality*; Verba and Nie, *Participation in America*; Nie, Junn, and Stehlik-Barry, *Education and Democratic Citizenship in America*. David E. Campbell, "Civic Engagement and Education: An Empirical Test of the Sorting Model," *American Journal of Political Science* 53, no. 4 (2009): 771–786; Menand, "Re-Imagining Liberal Education," 3; Bruce A. Kimball, "Naming Pragmatic Liberal Education," in *Education and Democracy: Re-Imagining Liberal Learning in America*, ed. Robert Orrill (New York: College Entrance Examination Board, 1997); Wolfinger and Rosenstone, *Who Votes?*, 18.

20. Brady, Schlozman, and Verba, "Prospecting for Participants," 162; Rosenstone and Hansen, *Mobilization, Participation, and Democracy in America*.

21. Verba, Schlozman, and Brady, *Voice and Equality*.

22. See, for example, Conway, "Women and Political Participation," 231–233; Rosenstone and Hansen, *Mobilization, Participation, and Democracy in America*; Schlozman, Burns, and Verba, "Gender and the Pathways to Participation,"; Verba, Burns, and Schlozman, "Knowing and Caring About Politics," 1052; Verba, Schlozman, and Brady, *Voice and Equality*.

23. Richard A. Brody, "The Puzzle of Participation in America," in *The New American Political System*, ed. A. King (Washington, DC: American Enterprise Institute for Public Policy Research, 1975).
24. Cindy D. Kam and Carl L. Palmer, "Reconsidering the Effects of Education on Political Participation," *Journal of Politics* 70, no. 3 (2008): 612–631.
25. Adam J. Berinsky and Gabriel S. Lenz, "Education and Political Participation: Exploring the Causal Link," *Political Behavior* 33, no. 3 (2011): 357–373.
26. Ibid., 371.
27. Brody, "The Puzzle of Participation in America"; Rachel Milstein Sondheimer and Donald P. Green, "Using Experiments to Estimate the Effects of Education on Voter Turnout," *American Journal of Political Science* 54, no. 1 (2010): 174–189.
28. Sondheimer and Green, "Using Experiments to Estimate the Effects of Education on Voter Turnout," 185.
29. Alexander K. Mayer, "Does Education Increase Political Participation?," *Journal of Politics* 73, no. 3 (2011): 633–645; John Henderson and Sara Chatfield, "Who Matches? Propensity Scores and Bias in the Causal Effects of Education on Participation," *Journal of Politics* 73, no. 3 (2011): 646–658; Kam and Palmer, "Reconsidering the Effects of Education on Political Participation," 613.
30. Mayer, "Does Education Increase Political Participation?," 644.
31. Henderson and Chatfield, "Who Matches?," 648.
32. Lawrence Bobo and Franklin D. Gilliam Jr., "Race, Sociopolitical Participation, and Black Empowerment," *American Political Science Review* 84, no. 2 (1990): 377–393; Burns, Schlozman, and Verba, *The Private Roots of Public Action*; Eric Plutzer, "Becoming a Habitual Voter: Inertia, Resources, and Growth in Young Adulthood," *American Political Science Review* 96, no. 1 (2002): 41–56; Andersen, "Working Women and Political Participation, 1952-1972"; Jan E. Leighley and Jonathan Nagler, "Socioeconomic Bias in Turnout, 1964-1988: The Voters Remain the Same," *American Political Science Review* 86, no. 3 (1992): 725–736; Frederick Solt, "Economic Inequality and Democratic Political Engagement," *American Journal of Political Science* 52, no. 1 (2008): 48–60; Verba and Nie, *Participation in America*; Verba, Schlozman, and Brady, *Voice and Equality*; Wolfinger and Rosenstone, *Who Votes?*.
33. Mettler and Soss, "The Consequences of Public Policy for Democratic Citizenship," 60; Skocpol, *Protecting Soldiers and Mothers*, 58; see also Lowi, "American Business, Public Policy, Case-Studies, and Political Theory," 677–715; Pierson, *Dismantling the Welfare State?*.
34. Mettler and Soss, "The Consequences of Public Policy for Democratic Citizenship," 62; see also Mettler, *Soldiers to Citizens*, 12.
35. Campbell, "Self-Interest, Social Security, and the Distinctive Participation Patterns of Senior Citizens," 565–574.
36. Ibid., 569; see also Campbell, *How Policies Make Citizens*.
37. Mettler, *Soldiers to Citizens*.
38. Ibid., 88.
39. Mettler and Soss, "The Consequences of Public Policy for Democratic Citizenship," 60; see also Pierson, "When Effect Becomes Cause," 624.
40. Pierson, "When Effect Becomes Cause," 624; Joe Soss, "Lessons of Welfare," 363–380; Mettler and Soss, "The Consequences of Public Policy for Democratic Citizenship," 62; Mettler, *Soldiers to Citizens*; Schneider and Ingram, "Social Construction of Target Populations," 334.
41. Mettler and Soss, "The Consequences of Public Policy for Democratic Citizenship," 56.
42. Mettler, *Soldiers to Citizens*, 112.
43. This finding exemplifies Schneider and Ingram's argument that the social construction of groups targeted by public policies can have important effects for political outcomes.
44. Soss, "Lessons of Welfare," 363–380.
45. Ibid., 367.
46. Ibid.
47. Pierson, "When Effect Becomes Cause," 605.
48. See, for example, Campbell, *How Policies Make Citizens*; Mettler, "Bringing the State Back In to Civic Engagement," 351–365; Mettler, *Soldiers to Citizens*; Sarah K. Bruch, Myra Marx

Ferree, and Joe Soss, "From Policy to Polity: Democracy, Paternalism, and the Incorporation of Disadvantaged Citizens," *American Sociological Review* 75, no. 2 (2010): 205–226.

49. Verba, Burns, and Schlozman, "Knowing and Caring About Politics."

50. Please refer to Appendix A, Table A.7.1, for detailed information related to variable coding.

51. Linda Bennett and Stephen Earl Bennett, "Enduring Gender Differences in Political Interest," *American Politics Quarterly* 17, no. 1 (1989): 105–122; Burns, Schlozman, and Verba, *The Private Roots of Public Action*; Angus Campbell, Philip E. Converse, Warren E. Miller, and Donald E. Stokes, *The American Voter* (John Wiley & Sons, 1960); Verba, Burns, and Schlozman, "Knowing and Caring About Politics," 1051–1072.

52. Chung-Li Wu, "Psycho-Political Correlates of Political Efficacy: The Case of the 1994 New Orleans Mayoral Election," *Journal of Black Studies* 33, no. 6 (2003): 729–760.

53. William H. Form and Joan Huber, "Income, Race, and the Ideology of Political Efficacy," *Journal of Politics* 33, no. 3 (1971): 659–688; Marilyn H. Buehler, "Voter Turnout and Political Efficacy Among Mexican-Americans in Michigan," *Sociological Quarterly* 18, no. 4 (1977): 504–517; Wu, "Psycho-Political Correlates of Political Efficacy," 729–760.

54. Carole Pateman, *Participation and Democratic Theory* (Cambridge University Press, 1970); Wu, "Psycho-Political Correlates of Political Efficacy," 729–760.

55. Gabriel A. Almond and Sidney Verba, *The Civic Culture* (Little Brown & Co., 1965); Pateman, *Participation and Democratic Theory*, 48.

56. Although activities like debating political issues with a friend or family member may be geared toward changing political outcomes, they would not be the types of activities included in this analysis because they do not do so directly. As participation scholars have noted, we must be cautious when considering reported electoral participation, as Americans tend to over-report the rates at which they vote. Barbara A. Anderson and Brian D. Silver, "Measurement and Mis-measurement of the Validity of the Self-Reported Vote," *American Journal of Political Science* 30, no. 4 (1986): 771–785; Aage R. Clausen, "Response Validity: Vote Report," *Public Opinion Quarterly* 32, no. 4 (1968): 588–606; Jeffrey A. Karp, and David Brockington, "Social Desirability and Response Validity: A Comparative Analysis of Overreporting Voter Turnout in Five Countries," *Journal of Politics* 67, no. 3 (2005): 825–840; Brian D. Silver, Barbara A. Anderson, and Paul R. Abramson, "Who Overreports Voting," *American Political Science Review* 80, no. 2 (1986): 613–624. Thus, while I consider the gender dynamics of voting in presidential elections in my analysis of descriptive statistics, I omit this measure of political participation from the regression analysis.

57. Campbell, *How Policies Make Citizens*.

Chapter 8

1. Rose, "Keys that Jingle and Fold," 1-22.

2. Deborah L. Dodson, *The Impact of Women in Congress* (New York: Oxford University Press, 2006); Michele L. Swers, "Are Women More Likely to Vote for Women's Issue Bills Than Their Male Colleagues?," *Legislative Studies Quarterly* 23, no. 3 (1998): 435–448; Michele L. Swers, *The Difference Women Make: The Policy Impact of Women in Congress* (Chicago: The University of Chicago Press, 2002); Sue Thomas and Susan Welch, "The Impact of Gender on Activities and Priorities of State Legislators," *Western Political Quarterly* 44, no. 2 (1991): 445–456.

3. National Center for Education Statistics (NCES), Homepage, http://www.nces.ed.gov (US Department of Education, 2011).

4. Linda J. Sax, *The Gender Gap in College: Maximizing the Developmental Potential of Women and Men* (San Francisco, CA: Jossey-Bass, 2008). See also Fred Evers, John Livernois, and Maureen Mancuso, "Where Are the Boys? Gender Imbalance in Higher Education," *Higher Education Management and Policy* 18, no. 2 (2006): 1–13; Brian A. Jacob, "Where the Boys Aren't: Non-Cognitive Skills, Returns to School and the Gender Gap in Higher Education," *Economics of Education Review* 21, no. 6 (2002): 589–598; James O. O'Neil and Bryce Crapser, "Using the Psychology of Men and Gender Role Conflict Theory to Promote Comprehensive Service Delivery for College Men: A Call to Action," in *Masculinities in Higher Education: Theoretical and Practical Considerations*, ed. Jason A. Laker and Tracy Davis (New York: Routledge, 2011).

5. Serri Graslie, "The Modern American Man, Charted," NPR, accessed on July 30, 2014.
6. Elizabeth J. Allan, *Women's Status in Higher Education: Equity Matters* (San Francisco: Wiley Subscription Services, 2011).
7. O'Neil and Crapser, "Using the Psychology of Men and Gender Role Conflict Theory to Promote Comprehensive Service Delivery for College Men." Christina Hoff Sommers, *The War Against Boys: How Misguided Feminism Is Harming Our Young Men* (New York: Simon & Schuster, 2000).
8. Carole Leathwood and Barbara Read, *Gender and the Changing Face of Higher Education: A Feminized Future?* (New York: McGraw Hill, 2009). O'Neil and Crapser, "Using the Psychology of Men and Gender Role Conflict Theory to Promote Comprehensive Service Delivery for College Men."
9. Evers, Livernois, and Mancuso, "Where Are the Boys?," 1–13; Jacob, "Where the Boys Aren't," 589–598; Judith Kleinfeld, "The State of American Boyhood," *Gender Issues* 26, no. 2 (2009): 113–129.
10. See Suzanne Mettler, *Degrees of Inequality* (New York: Basic Books, 2014).
11. US Department of Education, National Center for Education Statistics, 2011-12 National Postsecondary Student Aid Study (NPSAS, January 2014), 12.

Appendix C

1. See results in Appendix B, Table B.6.5.
2. This two-stage approach to regression analysis has been used in other empirical examinations of policy feedback. See, for example, Mettler and Welch, "Civic Generation," 497–518.
3. Adopting the gender-disaggregated modeling approach that dominates political participation scholars' analyses of the gender dynamics of political involvement, I construct separate education policy models of participation for women and men. This approach takes into account "the heterogeneity within these two groups and, thus . . . differences among women and men." Burns, Schlozman, and Verba, *The Private Roots of Public Action*, 39. This technique does not, however, permit me to directly assess the differential effects of significant variables for women and men. To do this, I test gender-aggregated education-policy models of political interest, efficacy, and participation that incorporate gender as a control variable.
4. While scholars of policy feedback are acutely aware of the challenge posed by endogeneity bias and the imperative to effectively grapple with it (see, e.g., Mettler and Welch, "Civic Generation," 497–518), this challenge is by no means prohibitive. Many empirical investigations face the challenge of effectively dealing with this type of bias—indeed, scholars have gone so far as to argue that "there is not a single empirical paper that does not have endogeneity issues." Robert H. Chenhall and Frank Moers, "The Issue of Endogeneity within Theory-Based, Quantitative Management Accounting Research," *European Accounting Review* 16, no. 1 (2007): 173–195, 174. As such, policy feedback scholars must work to minimize the influence of endogeneity and selection bias in the analysis of data presently available and consider these challenges when constructing future survey instruments.
5. This two-stage approach to regression analysis has been used in other empirical examinations of policy feedback. See, for example, Mettler and Welch, "Civic Generation," 497–518, and Campbell, *How Policies Make Citizens*. Adopting the gender-disaggregate approach that dominates participation scholars' analyses of the gender dynamics of political involvement, I construct separate education policy models of participation for women and men. This approach takes into account "the heterogeneity within these two groups and, thus . . . differences among women and men." Burns, Schlozman, and Verba, *The Private Roots of Public Action*, 39. This technique does not, however, permit me to directly assess the differential effects of significant variables for women and men. To do this, I test gender-aggregate education-policy models of political participation that incorporate gender as a control variable. This allows me to use interaction variables to assess the magnitude and significance of differential effects.
6. See Table B.6.1.
7. Leighley and Nagler, "Socioeconomic Bias in Turnout, 1964-1988," 725–736; Solt, "Economic Inequality and Democratic Political Engagement," 48–60; Verba and Nie, *Participation in*

America; Verba, Schlozman, and Brady, *Voice and Equality*; Wolfinger and Rosenstone, *Who Votes?*.

8. Burns, Schlozman, and Verba, *The Private Roots of Public Action*, 142; Menand, "Re-Imagining Liberal Education,", 3; Kimball, "Naming Pragmatic Liberal Education"; Wolfinger and Rosenstone, *Who Votes?*.

9. This analysis excludes survey respondents who have not completed at least a high school diploma or its equivalent, as attaining this level of education is a prerequisite for eligibility for applying for admission to postsecondary education and, thus, for participation in higher education programs.

10. See Chapter 6, Tables 6.1 and 6.2.

11. Plutzer, "Becoming a Habitual Voter," 41–56; Verba, Schlozman, and Brady, *Voice and Equality*.

12. Verba, Schlozman, and Brady, *Voice and Equality*, 231.

13. Schlozman, Burns, and Verba, "Gender and the Pathways to Participation," 963–990; Verba, Burns, and Schlozman, "Knowing and Caring About Politics," 1051–1072; Susan Welch, "Women as Political Animals? A Test of Some Explanations for Male-Female Political Participation Differences," *American Journal of Political Science* 21, no. 4 (1977): 711–730.

14. Wolfinger and Rosenstone, *Who Votes?*.

BIBLIOGRAPHY

Abramson, Paul R. "Political Efficacy and Political Trust Among Black Schoolchildren: Two Explanations." *Journal of Politics* 34, no. 4 (1972): 1243–1275.

"Access to Higher Education." The MARGARET Fund of NWLC. 2009. http://www.titleix.info/ 10-Key-Areas-of-Title-IX/Access-to-Higher-Education.aspx.

Albright, Robert C. "Education Tax Credits Defeated." *Washington Post*, February 5, 1964, A1.

Alexander, Karl L., and Bruce K. Eckland. "Sex Differences in the Educational Attainment Process." *American Sociological Review* 39, no. 5 (1974): 668–682.

Almond, Gabriel A., and Sidney Verba. *The Civic Culture.* Boston: Little Brown & Co., 1965.

Altbach, Philip G. "Patterns in Higher Education Development." In *American Higher Education in the Twenty-First Century: Social, Political, and Economic Challenges*, edited by Philip G. Altbach, Robert O. Berdahl, and Patricia J. Gumport. Baltimore, MD: Johns Hopkins University Press, 2005, 15–37.

Amenta, Edwin, Elizabeth A. Clemens, Jefren Olsen, Sunita Karikh, and Theda Skocpol. "The Political Origins of Unemployment Insurance in Five American States." *Studies in American Political Development* 2 (1987): 137–182.

American National Election Studies (ANES). "Cumulative Data File, 1948-2008." http://www. electionstudies.org.

American National Election Studies (ANES). "Guide to Public Opinion and Electoral Behavior." http://www.electionstudies.org/nesguide/gd-index.htm.

"American Women: Report of the President's Commission on the Status of Women." Washington, DC: US Department of Labor, 1963.

Andersen, Kristi. "Working Women and Political Participation, 1952-1972." *American Journal of Political Science* 19, no. 3 (1975): 439–453.

Anderson, Barbara A., and Brian D. Silver. "Measurement and Mis-measurement of the Validity of the Self-Reported Vote." *American Journal of Political Science* 30, no. 4 (1986): 771–785.

Anderson, Lee W. *Congress and the Classroom: From the Cold War to "No Child Left Behind."* University Park: Pennsylvania State University Press, 2007.

Arnold, Douglas. *The Logic of Congressional Action.* New Haven, CT: Yale University Press, 1990.

Astin, Alexander W. "The Changing American College Student: Thirty-Year Trends, 1966-1996." *Review of Higher Education* 21, no. 2 (1998): 115–135.

Atkison, Rick. *The Long Gray Line: The American Journey of West Point's Class of 1966.* New York: Holt and Holt Co., 1999.

Ayoub, Phillip. *When States Come Out: Europe's Sexual Minorities and the Politics of Visibility.* New York: Cambridge University Press, 2016.

Babbidge Jr., Homer D., and Robert M. Rosenzweig. *The Federal Interest in Higher Education.* New York: McGraw-Hill, 1962.

Bassford, Kimberlee. *Patsy Mink: Ahead of the Majority*. Independent Documentary, 2008.

Baumgartner, Frank R., and Bryan D. Jones. *Agendas and Instability in American Politics*. Chicago: University of Chicago Press, 1993.

Becker, Gary. *Human Capital: A Theoretical and Empirical Analysis, with Special Reference to Education*. 2nd ed. Chicago: University of Chicago Press, 1975.

Bennett, Linda, and Stephen Earl Bennett. "Enduring Gender Differences in Political Interest." *American Politics Quarterly* 17, no. 1 (1989): 105–122.

Bennett, Michael J. *When Dreams Came True: The GI Bill and the Making of Modern America*. Washington, DC: Brassey's, 1996.

Berinsky, Adam J., and Gabriel S. Lenz. "Education and Political Participation: Exploring the Causal Link." *Political Behavior* 33, no. 3 (2011): 357–373.

Bernstein, Robert, Anita Chadha, and Robert Montjoy. "Overreporting Voting: Why It Happens and Why It Matters." *Public Opinion Quarterly* 65, no. 1 (2001): 22–44.

Blumenthal, David, and James Morone. *The Heart of Power: Health and Politics in the Oval Office*. Oakland: University of California Press, 2010.

Blumenthal, Karen. *Let Me Play: The Story of Title IX, the Law That Changed the Future of Girls in America*. New York: Anthem Books for Young Readers, 2005.

Bobo, Lawrence, and Franklin D. Gilliam Jr. "Race, Sociopolitical Participation, and Black Empowerment." *American Political Science Review* 84, no. 2 (1990): 377–393.

Bonnar, Deanne. "The Place of Caregiving Work in Contemporary Societies." In *Parental Leave and Child Care: Setting a Research and Policy Agenda*, edited by Janet Shibley Hyde and Marilyn J. Essex. Philadelphia: Temple University Press, 1991.

Borstelmann, Thomas. *The Cold War and the Color Line: American Race Relations in the Global Arena*. Cambridge, MA: Harvard University Press, 2001.

Bose, Meena. "Leadership Challenges in National Security." In *Rethinking Madam President: Are We Ready for a Woman in the White House?*, edited by Lori Cox Han and Caroline Heldman. Boulder, CO: Lynne Reinner, 2007.

Bound, John, and Sarah Turner. "Going to War and Going to College: Did World War II and the G.I. Bill Increase Educational Attainment for Returning Veterans?" *Journal of Labor Economics* 20, no. 4 (2002): 784–815.

Brady, Henry E., Kay Lehman Schlozman, and Sidney Verba. "Prospecting for Participants: Rational Expectations and the Recruitment of Political Activists." *American Political Science Review* 93, no. 1 (1999): 153–168.

Brant, Steven, and Jerome Karabel. *The Diverted Dream: Community Colleges and the Promise of Educational Opportunity in America, 1900-1985*. New York: Oxford University Press, 1989.

Brenner, Joanna, and Maria Ramas. "Rethinking Women's Oppression." *New Left Review* 144 (1984): 33–71.

Brody, Richard A. "The Puzzle of Participation in America." In *The New American Political System*, edited by A. King. Washington, DC: American Enterprise Institute for Public Policy Research, 1975, 287–324.

Brooks, David. *Bobos in Paradise: The New Upper Class and How They Got There*. New York: Simon & Schuster, 2001.

Brown v. Board of Education of Topeka. Supreme Court of the United States. May 31, 1955. *Legal Information Institute, Cornell University*. Web. March 18, 2011. http://www.law.cornell.edu.

Bruch, Sarah K., Myra Marx Ferree, and Joe Soss. "From Policy to Polity: Democracy, Paternalism, and the Incorporation of Disadvantaged Citizens." *American Sociological Review* 75, no. 2 (2010): 205–226.

Buehler, Marilyn H. "Voter Turnout and Political Efficacy Among Mexican-Americans in Michigan." *Sociological Quarterly* 18, no. 4 (1977): 504–517.

Burns, Nancy, Kay Lehman Schlozman, and Sidney Verba. *The Private Roots of Public Action: Gender, Equality, and Political Participation*. Cambridge, MA: Harvard University Press, 2001.

Burrelli, Joan. "Thirty-Two Years of Women in S&E Faculty Positions." Report. National Science Foundation, 2008. http://www.nsf.gov/statistics/infbrief/nsf08308/nsf08308.pdf.

Califano, Joseph A. *Governing America: An Insider's Report from the White House and the Cabinet.* New York: Simon and Schuster, 1981.

Campbell, Andrea Louise. "Self-Interest, Social Security, and the Distinctive Participation Patterns of Senior Citizens." *American Political Science Review* 96, no. 3 (2002): 565–574.

Campbell, Andrea Louise. *How Policies Make Citizens: Senior Political Activism and the American Welfare State.* Princeton, NJ: Princeton University Press, 2003.

Campbell, Angus, Philip E. Converse, Warren E. Miller, and Donald E. Stokes. *The American Voter.* New York: John Wiley & Sons, 1960.

Campbell, David E. "Civic Engagement and Education: An Empirical Test of the Sorting Model." *American Journal of Political Science* 53, no. 4 (2009): 771–786.

Canaday, Margot. "Building a Straight State: Sexuality and Social Citizenship Under the 1944 G.I. Bill." *Journal of American History* 90, no. 3 (2003): 935–957.

Carleton, David. *Landmark Congressional Laws on Education.* Westport, CT: Greenwood Press, 2002.

Castaneda, Cindy, Stephen G. Katsinas, and David E. Hardy. "Meeting the Challenge of Gender Equity in Community College Athletics." *New Directions for Community Colleges* 142 (2008): 93–105.

Census Atlas of the United States. U.S. Census Bureau, Population Division. http://www.census. gov/population/www/cen2000/censusatlas/.

Center for American Women in Politics (CAWP). "Fast Facts." 2009. http://www.cawp.rugters. edu.

Center for American Women in Politics (CAWP). 2010. "Women in Elective Office 2010." Fact Sheet. http://www.cawp.rutgers.edu.

Center for American Women in Politics (CAWP). 2011. http://www.cawp.rugters.edu.

Cervantes, Angelica, Marlena Creusere, Robin McMillion, Carla McQueen, Matt Short, Matt Steiner, and Jeff Webster. "Opening the Doors to Higher Education: Perspectives on the Higher Education Act 40 Years Later." 2005. https://www.tgslc.org/pdf/HEA_History. pdf.

Chávez, José. "Presidential Influence on the Politics of Higher Education: The Higher Education Act of 1965." PhD diss., University of Texas at Austin, 1975.

Chenhall, Robert H., and Frank Moers. "The Issue of Endogeneity within Theory- Based, Quantitative Management Accounting Research." *European Accounting Review* 16, no. 1 (2007): 173–195.

Clausen, Aage R. "Response Validity: Vote Report." *Public Opinion Quarterly* 32, no. 4 (1968): 588–606.

Clowse, Barbara Barksdale. Brainpower for the Cold War: The Sputnik Crisis and National Defense Education Act of 1958. Westport, CT: Greenwood Press, 1981.

Congressional Quarterly Weekly Report. Washington, DC: Congressional Quarterly, 1956.

Congressional Quarterly Weekly Report. Washington, DC: Congressional Quarterly, 1957.

Congressional Quarterly Weekly Report. Washington, DC: Congressional Quarterly, 1958.

Congressional Quarterly Weekly Report. Washington, DC: Congressional Quarterly, 1965.

Congressional Quarterly Weekly Report. Washington, DC: Congressional Quarterly, 1970.

Congressional Quarterly Weekly Report. Washington, DC: Congressional Quarterly, 1971.

Congressional Quarterly Weekly Report. Washington, DC: Congressional Quarterly, 1972.

Congressional Record, 85th Congress, 2nd session. August 8, 1958, 16694.

Congressional Record, 85th Congress, 2nd session. August 23, 1958, 19612.

Congressional Record 92nd Congress, 1st session. August 5, 1971, 30155.

Conley, Dalton. "Capital for College: Parental Assets and Postsecondary Schooling." *Sociology of Education* 74, no. 1 (2001): 59–72.

Converse, Philip E. "Change in the American Electorate." In *The Human Meaning of Social Change*, ed. A. Campbell and P. Converse. New York: Russell Sage, 1972, 263–338.

Conway, M. Margaret. "Women and Political Participation." *PS: Political Science and Politics* 34, no. 2 (2001): 231–233.

Conway, M. Margaret, Gertrude A. Stuernagel, and David W. Ahern. *Women and Public Policy: A Revolution in Progress.* 3rd ed. Washington, DC: CQ Press, 2005.

The Cooperative Institutional Research Program (CIRP). "Trends File." The Higher Education Research Institute (HERI) at UCLA, 2010. http://www.heri.ucla.edu.

Crittenden, Ann. *The Price of Motherhood: Why the Most Important Job in the World Is Still the Least Valued.* New York: Henry Holt, 2001.

Cross, Christopher T. *Political Education: National Policy Comes of Age.* New York: Teachers College Press, 2010.

Cushman, Clare, ed. *Supreme Court Decisions and Women's Rights: Milestones to Equality.* Washington, DC: Congressional Quarterly, 2001.

Davenport, Sally A. "Smuggling-In Reform: Equal Opportunity and the Higher Education Act 1965-80." PhD diss., Johns Hopkins University, 1982.

Davidson, Sue. *A Heart in Politics: Jeannette Rankin and Patsy T. Mink.* Seattle, WA: Seal Press, 1994.

Davis, Flora. *Moving the Mountain: The Women's Movement in America Since 1960.* New York: Simon & Schuster, 1991.

Davis, Shannon N., and Lisa D. Pearce. "Adolescents' Work-Family Gender Ideologies and Educational Expectations." *Sociological Perspectives* 50, no. 2 (2007): 249–271.

Dearden, Lorraine, Javier Ferri, and Costas Meghir. "The Effect of School Quality on Educational Attainment and Wages." *Review of Economics and Statistics* 84, no. 1 (2002): 1–20.

Divine, Robert A. *The Sputnik Challenge.* New York: Oxford University Press, 1993.

Dodson, Debra L. *The Impact of Women in Congress.* New York: Oxford University Press, 2006.

Dudziak, Mary L. *Cold War Civil Rights: Race and the Image of American Democracy.* Princeton, NJ: Princeton University Press, 2000.

Dynarski, Susan. "Does Aid Matter? Measuring the Effect of Student Aid on College Attendance and Completion." *American Economic Review* 93, no. 1 (2003): 279–288.

Eckelberry, R. H. "The Approval of Institutions Under the 'G.I. Bill.'" *Journal of Higher Education* 16, no. 3 (1945): 121–126.

"Education: Dead Calm for Federal Aid." *Time Magazine,* August 11, 1958. http://www.time.com/time/magazine/article/0,9171,825449,00.html.

Edwards, Amanda Ross. "Why Sport?: The Development of Sport as a Policy Issue in Title IX of the Education Amendments of 1972." Paper presented at the Annual Meeting of the Midwest Political Science Association, Chicago, IL, April 15, 2004. http://www.allacademic.com/meta/p83807_index.html.

Edwards, Tamala M., Tamerlin Drummond, Elizabeth Kaufman, Anne Moffett, Jacqueline Savaino, and Maggie Sieger. "Who Needs a Husband?" *Time Magazine.* 2007. http://www.time.com/time/magazine/article/0,9171,997804-6,00.html.

Eisenmann, Linda. "Introduction." In *Historical Dictionary of Women's Education in the United States,* edited by Linda Eisenmann. Westport, CT: Greenwood Press, 1998, xi–xx.

Eisenmann, Linda. "Educating the Female Citizen in a Post-War World: Competing Ideologies for American Women, 1945-1965." *Educational Review* 54, no. 2 (2002): 133–141.

Eisenmann, Linda. *Higher Education for Women in Postwar America, 1945-1965.* Baltimore, MD: Johns Hopkins University Press, 2006.

Elliott Sr., Carl, and Michael D'Orso. *The Cost of Courage: The Journey of an American Congressman.* Tuscaloosa: University of Alabama Press, 1992.

Erickson, Nancy S. "A Supreme Court First: Equal Protection Applied to Women." In *Historic U.S. Court Cases: An Encyclopedia,* 2nd ed., edited by John W. Johnson. New York: Routledge, 2001, 765–769.

Esbach, Elizabeth Seymour. *The Higher Education of Women in England and America 1865-1920.* New York: Garland Publishing, 1993.

Esping-Andersen, Gøsta. *Three Worlds of Welfare Capitalism.* Princeton, NJ: Princeton University Press, 1990.

"Essay: What Big Daddy, Alias Uncle Sam, Will Do for YOU." *Time Magazine.* November 5, 1965. http://www.time.com/time/magazine/article/0,9171,901770,00.html.

Faragher, John. "Introduction." In *Women and Higher Education in American History: Essays from the Mount Holyoke College Sesquicentennial Symposia*, edited by John Mack Faragher and Florence Howe. New York: W.W. Norton & Co., 1988, ix–xviii.

Fishel, Andrew. "Organizational Positions on Title IX: Conflicting Perspectives on Sex Discrimination in Education." *Journal of Higher Education* 47, no. 1 (1976): 93–105.

Fishel, Andrew, and Janice Pottker. *National Politics and Sex Discrimination in Education.* Lexington, MA: D.C. Heath and Company, 1977.

Flemming, Arthur S. "The Philosophy and Objectives of the National Defense Education Act." *Annals of the American Academy of Political and Social Science* 327 (1960): 132–138.

Ford, William. "The Higher Education Act After 20 Years: Old Dreams and New Realities." Lyndon B. Johnson Distinguished Lecture, Southwest Texas State University, San Marcos, TX, November 7, 1985.

Form, William H., and Joan Huber. "Income, Race, and the Ideology of Political Efficacy." *Journal of Politics* 33, no. 3 (1971): 659–688.

Freeman, Jo. "The Origins of the Women's Liberation Movement." In *Changing Women in a Changing Society,* edited by Joan Huber. Chicago: University of Chicago Press, 1973, 30–49.

Fullerton, Andrew S., Jefrey C. Dixon, and Casey Borch. "Bringing Registration into Models of Vote Overreporting." *Public Opinion Quarterly* 71, no. 4 (2007): 649–660.

Garcia, Lisette M., and Alan E. Bayer. "Variations between Latino Groups in US Post-Secondary Educational Attainment." *Research in Higher Education* 46, no. 5 (2005): 511–533.

Geiger, Roger L. "The Ten Generations of American Higher Education." In *American Higher Education in the Twenty-First Century: Social, Political, and Economic Challenges*, edited by Philip G. Altbach, Robert O. Berdahl, and Patricia J. Gumport. Baltimore, MD: Johns Hopkins University Press, 2005, 3–34.

Gelb, Joyce, and Marian Lief Palley. *Women and Public Policies: Reassessing Gender Politics.* Charlottesville, VA: University Press of Virginia, 1996.

"The Gender Wage Gap: 2008." Fact Sheet. 2009. Institute for Women's Policy Research. https://iwpr.org/publications/the-gender-wage-gap-2009-updated-september-2010/.

Gladieux, Lawrence E., and Arthur M. Hauptman. *The College Aid Quandary: Access, Quality, and the Federal Role.* Washington, DC: Brookings Institution, 1995.

Gladieux, Lawrence E., Jacqualine E. King, and Melanie E. Corrigan. "The Federal Government and Higher Education." In *American Higher Education in the Twenty-First Century: Social, Political, and Economic Challenges*, edited by Philip G. Altbach, Robert O. Berdahl, and Patricia J. Gumport. Baltimore, MD: Johns Hopkins University Press, 2005, 212–237.

Gladieux, Lawrence E., and Thomas R. Wolanin. *Congress and the Colleges: The National Politics of Higher Education.* Lexington, MA: Lexington Books, 1976.

Glynn, Sarah Jane. "Breadwinning Mothers, Then and Now." Center for American Progress. 2014. https://www.dol.gov/wb/stats/Civilian_labor_force_sex_48_15_txt.htm.

Goldin, Claudia. "The Quiet Revolution That Transformed Women's Employment, Education, and Family," *American Economic Review* 96, no. 2 (2006): 1–20.

Goldin, Claudia, and Lawrence F. Katz. "The Power of the Pill: Oral Contraceptives and Women's Career and Marriage Decisions." *Journal of Political Economy* 110, no. 4 (2002): 730–770.

Goldin, Claudia, and Lawrence F. Katz. *The Race between Education and Technology.* Cambridge, MA: Belknap Press/Harvard University Press, 2008.

Goldin, Claudia, Lawrence F. Katz, and Ilyana Kuziemko. "The Homecoming of American College Women: The Reversal of the College Gender Gap." *Journal of Economic Perspectives* 20, no. 4 (2006): 133–156.

Goldstein, Leslie Friedman. *The Constitutional Rights of Women: Cases in Law and Social Change.* Madison: University of Wisconsin Press, 1988.

Gordon, Linda D. *Gender and Higher Education in the Progressive Era.* New Haven, CT: Yale University Press, 1990.

Gordon, Linda. *Pitied but Not Entitled: Single Mothers and the History of Welfare, 1980-1935.* New York: Free Press, 1994.

Goss, Kristin A, and Theda Skocpol. "Changing Agendas: The Impact of Feminism on American Politics." In *Gender and Social Capital,* edited by Brenda O'Neil and Elisabeth Gidengil. New York: Routledge, 2006, 323–356.

Graham, Hugh Davis. *The Uncertain Triumph: Federal Education Policy in the Kennedy and Johnson Years.* Chapel Hill: University of North Carolina Press, 1984.

Green, Edith. "Support of Higher Education: Expense or Investment?" *Journal of Higher Education* 34, no. 6 (1963): 330–333.

Greendorfer, Susan L. "Title IX Gender Equity, Backlash and Ideology." *Women in Sport & Physical Activity Journal* 7, no. 1 (1998): 69.

Gutman, Amy. *Democratic Education.* Princeton, NJ: Princeton University Press, 1987.

Hacker, Jacob S. "The Historical Logic of National Health Insurance: Structure and Sequence in the Development of British, Canadian, and U.S. Medical Policy." *Studies in American Political Development* 12 (1998): 57–130.

Hamilton, Virginia Van der Veer. *Lister Hill: Statesman from the South.* Chapel Hill: University of North Carolina Press, 1987.

Hannah, Susan B. "The Higher Education Act of 1992: Skills, Constraints, and the Politics of Higher Education." *Journal of Higher Education* 67, no. 5 (1996): 498–527.

Hanson, Katherine, Vivian Guilfoy, and Sarita Pillai. *More Than Title IX: How Equity in Education Has Shaped the Nation.* Lanham, MD: Rowman and Littlefield Publishers, 2009.

Hardesty, Robert L. "The Higher Education Act on Its 30th Birthday." LBJ Lecture, Southwest Texas State University, 1995.

Harrison, Cynthia E. "Oral History: Edith Green." Oregon Historical Society, 1978.

Hearn, James C. "The Paradox of Growth in Federal Aid for College Students, 1965-1990." In *The Finance of Higher Education: Theory, Research, Policy, and Practice,* edited by Michael B. Paulsen and John C. Smart. New York: Agathon Press, 2001, 267–320.

Heclo, Hugh. *Modern Social Policies in Britain and Sweden: From Relief to Income Maintenance.* New Haven, CT: Yale University Press, 1974.

Henderson, John, and Sara Chatfield. "Who Matches? Propensity Scores and Bias in the Causal Effects of Education on Participation." *Journal of Politics* 73, no. 3 (2011): 646–658.

Hess, Frederick M. "Introduction." In *Footing the Tuition Bill: The New Student Loan Sector,* edited by Frederick M. Hess. Washington, DC: AEI Press, 2007, 1–18.

"Higher Education Act of 1965 (H.R. 3220)." Hearings Before the Subcommittee on Education and Labor. House of Representatives, 89th Congress, 1st Session. On H.R. 3220, and Similar Bills to Strengthen the Educational Resources of Our Colleges and Universities and to Provide Financial Assistance for Students in Post-Secondary and Higher Education. Washington, DC: US Government Printing Office, 1965.

Hill, Martha S., and Greg J. Duncan. "Parental Family Income and the Socioeconomic Attainment of Children." *Social Science Research* 16, no. 1 (1987): 39–73.

Humes, Edward. *Over Here: How the G.I. Bill Transformed the American Dream.* Orlando, FL: Harcourt, 2006.

Jaschik, Scott. "Women Lead in Doctorates." *Inside Higher Ed.* Website. 2010. http://www.inside-highered.com/news/2010/09/14/doctorates.

Johnson, Lyndon B. "Remarks to the Delegates to the White House Conference on Education." Book II Pub. Papers, July 21, 1965.

Johnson, Lyndon B. "Remarks at Southwest Texas State College upon Signing the Higher Education Act of 1965." Book II Pub. Papers 1102, November 8, 1965.

Kam, Cindy D., and Carl L. Palmer. "Reconsidering the Effects of Education on Political Participation." *Journal of Politics* 70, no. 3 (2008): 612–631.

Karp, Jeffrey A., and David Brockington. "Social Desirability and Response Validity: A Comparative Analysis of Overreporting Voter Turnout in Five Countries." *Journal of Politics* 67, no. 3 (2005): 825–840.

Keeter, Scott, Molly Andolina, and Krista Jenkins. *The Civic and Political Health of the Nation: A Generational Portrait.* 2002. http://www.civicyouth.org/research/products/Civic_Political_Health.pdf.

Keppel, Francis. "The Higher Education Acts Contrasted: Has Federal Policy Come of Age?" *Harvard Educational Review* 57, no. 1 (1987): 49–67.

Kerber, Linda. "The Republican Mother: Women and the Enlightenment-An American Perspective." *American Quarterly* 28, no. 2 (1976): 187–205.

Kerber, Linda K. "'Why Should Girls Be Learn'd and Wise?': Two Centuries of Higher Education for Women as Seen Through the Unfinished Work of Alice Mary Baldwin." In *Women and Higher Education in American History: Essays from the Mount Holyoke College Sesquicentennial Symposia,* edited by John Mack Faragher and Florence Howe. New York: W.W. Norton & Co., 1988, 18–42.

Kimball, Bruce A. "Naming Pragmatic Liberal Education." In *Education and Democracy: Reimagining Liberal Learning in America,* edited by Robert Orrill. New York: College Entrance Examination Board, 1997, 45–67.

Kimberling, C. Ronald. "Federal Student Aid: A History and Critical Analysis." In *The Academy in Crisis: The Political Economy of Higher Education,* edited by John W. Sommer. New Brunswick, NJ: Transaction Publishers, 1995, 69–93.

King, Gary, Michael Tomz, and Jason Wittenberg. CLARIFY: Software for Interpreting and Presenting Statistical Results. Version 2.1. 2003. http://gking.harvard.edu/clarify.

Kingdon, John W. *Agendas, Alternatives, and Public Policies.* 2nd ed. New York: Longman, 2003.

Kizer, George A. "Federal Aid to Education: 1945-1963." *History of Education Quarterly* 10, no. 1 (1970): 84–102.

Kliebard, Herbert M. *The Struggle for the American Curriculum, 1893-1958.* 2nd ed. New York: Routledge, 1995.

Krein, Sheila Fitzgerald. "Growing Up in a Single Parent Family: The Effect of Education and Earnings on Young Men." *Family Relations* 35, no. 1 (1986): 161–168.

Kumlin, Staffan, and Bo Rothstein. "Making and Breaking Social Capital: The Impact of Welfare-State Institutions." *Comparative Political Studies* 38, no. 4 (2005): 339–365.

Leighley, Jan E., and Jonathan Nagler. "Socioeconomic Bias in Turnout, 1964-1988: The Voters Remain the Same." *American Political Science Review* 86, no. 3 (1992): 725–736.

Li, Judith Ann. "Estimating the Effect of Federal Financial Aid on Higher Education: A Study of Pell Grants." PhD diss., Harvard University, 1999.

Lindblom, Charles E. "The Science of 'Muddling Through.'" *Public Administration Review* 19, no. 2 (1959): 79–88.

Lindgren, J. Ralph, and Nadine Taub. *The Law of Sex Discrimination.* St. Paul, MN: West Publishing Company, 1988.

List, Jill H., and Lee M. Wolfle. "The Effect of Father's Presence on Postsecondary Educational Attainment Among Whites and Blacks." *Research in Higher Education* 41, no. 5 (2000): 623–633.

Loss, Christopher P. *Between Citizens and the State: The Politics of American Higher Education in the 20th Century.* Princeton, NJ: Princeton University Press, 2012.

Lowi, Theodore J. "American Business, Public Policy, Case-Studies, and Political Theory." *World Politics* 16, no. 4 (1964): 677–715.

Lucas, Christopher J. *American Higher Education: A History.* New York: Palgrave Macmillan, 2006.

MacLean, Nancy. *American Women's Movement, 1945-2000: A Brief History with Documents.* Boston: Bedford/St. Martin's, 2009.

Mansbridge, Jane J. *Why We Lost the ERA.* Chicago: University of Chicago Press, 1986.

Manski, Charles F., and David A. Wise. *College in America.* Cambridge, MA: Harvard University Press, 1983.

Marsh, Paul E., and Ross A. Gortner. *Federal Aid to Science Education: Two Programs.* Syracuse, NY: Syracuse University Press, 1963.

Marshall, T. H. *Citizenship and Social Class and Other Essays.* Cambridge: Cambridge University Press, 1950.

Martin, Dallas. "Let the Past be Prologue: The Higher Education Act's 40-Year-History Is Important to Its Future." *University Business,* 2006: 25–26. http://www.universitybusiness.com.

Martin, Janet M. *The Presidency and Women: Promise, Performance, & Illusion.* College Station: Texas A&M University Press, 2003.

Martinez, Ana M., and Kristen A. Penn, eds. *Women in Higher Education: An Encyclopedia.* Santa Barbara, CA: ABC-CLIO, 2002.

Mathews-Gardner, A. Lanethea. "The Political Development of Female Civic Engagement in Postwar America." *Politics & Gender* 1, no. 4 (2005): 547–575.

Matthews, Martha, and Shirley McCune. *Why Title IX?* Washington, DC: Resource Center on Sex Roles in Education National Foundation for the Improvement of Education. US Department of Health, Education, and Welfare, Office of Education, 1997.

Mayer, Alexander K. "Does Education Increase Political Participation?" *Journal of Politics* 73, no. 3 (2011): 633–645.

McBride-Stetson, Dorothy. *Women's Rights in the USA: Policy Debates and Gender Roles.* 3rd ed. New York: Routledge, 2004.

McDonagh, Eileen, and Laura Pappano. *Playing with the Boys: Why Separate Is Not Equal in Sports.* New York: Oxford University Press, 2008.

McDonnell, Lorraine M. "A Political Science Perspective on Education Policy Analysis." In *Handbook on Education Policy Research,* edited by Gary Sykes, Barbara Schneider, and David N. Plank. New York: American Educational Research Association/Routledge, 2009, 57–70.

McDonnell, Lorraine M. "Repositioning Politics in Education's Circle of Knowledge." *Educational Researcher* 38, no. 6 (2009): 417–427.

McPherson, Michael S., and Morton Owen Schapiro. *Keeping College Affordable: Government and Educational Opportunity.* Washington, DC: Brookings Institution, 1991.

McPherson, Michael S., and Morton Owen Schapiro. *The Student Aid Game: Meeting Need and Rewarding Talent in American Higher Education.* Princeton, NJ: Princeton University Press, 1998.

Menand, Louis. "Re-Imagining Liberal Education." In *Education and Democracy: Re-Imagining Liberal Learning in America,* edited by Robert Orrill. New York: College Entrance Examination Board, 1997, 1–17.

Mettler, Suzanne. *Dividing Citizens: Gender and Federalism in New Deal Public Policy.* Ithaca, NY: Cornell University Press, 1998.

Mettler, Suzanne. "Bringing the State Back In to Civic Engagement: Policy Feedback Effects of the G.I. Bill for World War II Veterans." *American Political Science Review* 96, no. 2 (2002): 351–365.

Mettler, Suzanne. *Soldiers to Citizens: The G.I. Bill and the Making of the Greatest Generation.* New York: Oxford University Press, 2005.

Mettler, Suzanne. "The Transformed Welfare State and the Redistribution of Political Voice." In *The Transformation of American Politics,* edited by Paul Pierson and Theda Skocpol. Princeton, NJ: Princeton University Press, 2007, 191–222.

Mettler, Suzanne, and Eric Welch. "Civic Generation: Policy Feedback Effect of the G.I. Bill on Political Involvement over the Life Course." *British Journal of Political Science* 34 (2004): 497–518.

Mettler, Suzanne, and Joe Soss. "The Consequences of Public Policy for Democratic Citizenship: Bridging Policy Studies and Mass Politics." *Perspectives on Politics* 2, no. 1 (2004): 55–73.

Miller-Bernal, Leslie. "Coeducation: An Uneven Progression." In *Going Coed: Women's Experiences in Formerly Men's Colleges and Universities, 1950-2000.* Nashville: Vanderbilt University Press, 2004, 3–21.

Mink, Gwendolyn. *The Wages of Motherhood: Inequality in the Welfare State, 1917-1942.* Ithaca, NY: Cornell University Press, 1995.

Morse, John F. "Federal Aid to Students in Higher Education." In *Education and Public Policy,* edited by Seymour E. Harris and Alan Levensohn. Berkeley, CA: McCutchan Publishing, 1965.

Nam, Charles B. "Impact of the 'GI Bills' on the Educational Level of the Male Population." *Social Forces* 43, no. 1 (1964): 26–32.

Nam, Charles B. "Family Patterns of Educational Attainment." *Sociology of Education* 38, no. 5 (1965): 393–403.

National Center for Education Statistics (NCES). Homepage. US Department of Education, 2011. http://www.nces.ed.gov.

National Postsecondary Student Aid Study (NPSAS). Restricted-Access Data. US Department of Education: National Center for Education Statistics, 2008.

National Center for Education Statistics (NCES)/Institute for Education Statistics (IES). US Department of Education. https://nces.ed.gov.

National Women's History Museum (NWHM). "Women's Changing Roles as Citizens of a New Republic." 2007. https://www.nwhm.org/online-exhibits/education/1700s_2.htm.

Newcomer, Mabel. *A Century of Higher Education for American Women.* New York: Harper & Brothers Publishers, 1959.

Nie, Norman H., Jane Junn, and Kenneth Stehlik-Barry. *Education and Democratic Citizenship in America.* Chicago: University of Chicago Press, 1996.

Olson, Keith. "The G.I. Bill and Higher Education: Success and Surprise." *American Quarterly* 25, no. 5 (1973): 596–610.

Olson, Keith. *The G.I. Bill, the Veterans, and the Colleges.* Lexington: University of Kentucky Press, 1974.

Oreopoulous, Philip, and Kjell G. Salvanes. "Priceless: The Nonpecuniary Benefits of Schooling." *Journal of Economic Perspectives* 25, no. 1 (2011): 159–184.

Orloff, Ann Shola. "Gender and the Social Rights of Citizenship: The Comparative Analysis of Gender Relations and Welfare States." *American Sociological Review* 58, no. 3 (1993): 303–328.

Parsons, Michael D. *Power and Politics: Federal Higher Education Policymaking in the 1990s.* Albany: State University of New York Press, 1997.

Pateman, Carole. *Participation and Democratic Theory.* New York: Cambridge University Press, 1970.

Pearson, Carol S., Donna L. Shavlik, and Judith G. Touchton. *Educating the Majority: Women Challenge Tradition in Higher Education.* New York: Macmillan Publishing Company, 1989.

Peril, Lynn. *College Girls: Bluestockings, Sex Kittens, and Coeds, Then and Now.* New York: W.W. Norton & Co., 2006

Pierson, Paul. "When Effect Becomes Cause: Policy Feedback and Political Change." *World Politics* 45, no. 4 (1993): 595–628.

Pierson, Paul. *Dismantling the Welfare State?: Reagan, Thatcher, and the Politics of Retrenchment.* New York: Cambridge University Press, 1994.

Pierson, Paul. "The Study of Policy Development." *Journal of Policy History* 17, no. 1 (2005): 34–51.

Plutzer, Eric. "Becoming a Habitual Voter: Inertia, Resources, and Growth in Young Adulthood." *American Political Science Review* 96, no. 1 (2002): 41–56.

Price, Derek V. *Borrowing Inequality: Race, Class, and Student Loans.* Boulder, CO: Lynne Rienner Publishers, 2004.

Public Law 85–864. "The National Defense Education Act."

Quadagno, Jill. *The Color of Welfare: How Racism Undermined the War on Poverty.* New York: Oxford University Press, 1994.

Radford, Alexandria Walton, Jolene Wu, and Thomas Weko. "Issue Tables: A Profile of Military Service Members and Veterans Enrolled in Postsecondary Education n 2001-08." US Department of Education, National Center for Education Statistics, 2009. http://nces.ed.gov/pubs2009/2009182.pdf.

Reese, William J. *America's Public Schools: From the Common School to "No Child Left Behind."* Baltimore, MD: Johns Hopkins University Press, 2005.

Riley, Richard W. "The Role of the Federal Government in Education— Supporting a National Desire for Support for State and Local Education." *St. Louis University Public Law Review* 1997: 29–54.

Rivlin, Alice M. *The Role of the Federal Government in Financing Higher Education.* Washington, DC: Brookings Institution, 1961.

Robinson, Jean C., Pamela Barnhouse Walters, and Julia Lamber. "Title IX in the 1970s: From Stealth Politics to Political Negotiation." Paper presented at the Annual Meeting of the Midwest Political Science Association, Chicago, IL, April 5, 2008.

Rose, Deondra. "Keys That Jingle and Fold: Federal Student Aid and the Expansion of Educational Opportunity for Black Women." *Journal of Women, Politics, and Policy* (2016): 1–22.

Rosenberg, Rosalind. "The Limits of Access: The History of Coeducation in America." In *Women and Higher Education in American History: Essays from the Mount Holyoke College Sesquicentennial Symposia*, edited by John Mack Faragher and Florence Howe. New York: W.W. Norton & Co., 1988, 107–129.

Rosenberg, Rosalind. *Divided Lives: American Women in the Twentieth Century.* New York: Hill and Wang, 2008.

Rosenstone, Steven J., and John Mark Hansen. *Mobilization, Participation, and Democracy in America.* New York: Longman, 1993.

Rosin, Hanna. "The End of Men." *Atlantic Monthly*, July 2010. http://www.theatlantic.com/magazine/archive/2010/07/the-end-of-men/8135/.

Rupp, Leila J., and Verta Taylor. *Survival in the Doldrums: The American Women's Rights Movement, 1945 to the 1960s.* New York: Oxford University Press, 1987.

Russell, Anne. "Patsy Takemoto Mink: Political Woman." PhD diss., University of Hawaii, 1977.

Ryan, John F. "The Relationship Between Institutional Expenditures and Degree Attainment at Baccalaureate Colleges." *Research in Higher Education* 45, no. 2 (2004): 97–114.

Salomone, Rosemary. "The Legality of Single-Sex Education in the United States: Sometimes 'Equal' Means 'Different.'" In *Gender in Policy and Practice: Perspectives on Single-Sex and Coeducational Schooling*, edited by Amanda Datnow and Lea Hubbard. New York: RoutledgeFalmer, 2002, 47–73.

Sanders, M. Elizabeth. "Mildred Rowe Sanders, a Life." Eulogy shared with author. December 16, 2011.

Sapiro, Virginia. "The Gender Basis of American Social Policy." In *Women, the State, and Welfare: Historical and Theoretical Essays*, edited by Linda Gordon. Madison: University of Wisconsin Press, 1990, 36–54.

Sarvasy, Wendy. "Beyond the Difference Versus Equality Policy Debate: Postsuffrage Feminism, Citizenship, and the Quest for a Feminist Welfare State." *Signs* 17, no. 2 (1992): 329–362.

Schlozman, Kay Lehman, Nancy Burns, and Sidney Verba. "Gender and the Pathways to Participation: The Role of Resources." *Journal of Politics* 56, no. 4 (1994): 963–990.

Schneider, Anne, and Helen Ingram. "Social Construction of Target Populations: Implications for Politics and Policy." *American Political Science Review* 87, no. 2 (1993): 334–347.

"Scholarship and Loan Program," Hearings Before the Subcommittee on Education and Labor. House of Representatives, Eighty85th Congress, 1st Session. On Bills Relating to a Federal Scholarship Program. Hearings Held from August 12, 1957–April 3, 1958. Washington, DC: US Government Printing Office.

"Science and Education for National Defense." Hearings Before the Committee on Labor and Public Welfare, United States Senate, 85th Congress. Held from January 21–March 13, 1958. Washington, DC: US Government Printing Office.

Sharrow, Elizabeth M. "Female Athlete Politic: Title IX and the Naturalization of Sex Difference in Public Policy." *Politics, Groups, and Identities* 5, no. 1 (2017): 46–66.

Shklar, Judith N. *American Citizenship: The Quest for Inclusion.* Cambridge, MA: Harvard University Press, 1991.

Sicherman, Barbara. "College and Careers: Historical Perspectives on the Lives and Work Patterns of Women College Graduates." In *Women and Higher Education in American History: Essays from the Mount Holyoke College Sesquicentennial Symposia*, edited by John Mack Faragher and Florence Howe. New York: W.W. Norton & Co., 1988, 130–164.

Silver, Brian D., Barbara A. Anderson, and Paul R. Abramson. "Who Overreports Voting." *American Political Science Review* 80, no. 2 (1986): 613–624.

Skocpol, Theda. "Targeting Within Universalism: Politically Viable Policies to Combat Poverty in the United States." In *The Urban Underclass*, edited by Christopher Jencks and Paul E. Peterson. Washington, DC: Brookings Institution, 1991, 411–436.

Skocpol, Theda. *Protecting Soldiers and Mothers: The Political Origin of Social Policy in the United States*. Cambridge, MA: Harvard University Press, 1992.

Skrentny, John D. *The Minority Rights Revolution*. Cambridge, MA: Belknap Press, 2002.

Smith, David Barton. *The Power to Heal: Civil Rights, Medicare, and the Struggle to Transform America's Health Care System*. Nashville, TN: Vanderbilt University Press, 2016.

Snead, David L. *The Gaither Committee, Eisenhower, and the Cold War*. Columbus: Ohio State University Press, 1998.

Snyder, T. D., and S. A. Dillow. *Digest of Education Statistics 2009* (NCES 2010-013). Washington, DC: National Center for Education Statistics, Institute of Education Statistics, US Department of Education, 2010.

Social and Governmental Issues and Participation (SGIP) Study. 2008.

Solomon, Barbara Miller. *In the Company of Educated Women: A History of Women and Higher Education in America*. New Haven, CT: Yale University Press, 1985.

Solt, Frederick. "Economic Inequality and Democratic Political Engagement." *American Journal of Political Science* 52, no. 1 (2008): 48–60.

Sondheimer, Rachel Milstein, and Donald P. Green. "Using Experiments to Estimate the Effects of Education on Voter Turnout." *American Journal of Political Science* 54, no. 1 (2010): 174–189.

Soss, Joe. "Lessons of Welfare: Policy Design, Political Learning, and Political Action." *American Political Science Review* 93, no. 2 (1999): 363–380.

Spring, Joel H. "In Service to the State: The Political Context of Higher Education in the United States." In *The Academy in Crisis: The Political Economy of Higher Education*, edited by John W. Sommer. New Brunswick, NJ: Transaction Publishers, 1995, 45–66.

Spring, Joel. *The American School: From the Puritans to No Child Left Behind*. 7th ed. New York: McGraw-Hill, 2008.

Stanley, Marcus. "College Education and the Midcentury G.I. Bills." *Quarterly Journal of Economics* 118, no. 2 (2003): 671–708.

Stimpson, Catharine R., ed. *Discrimination Against Women: Congressional Hearings on Equal Rights in Education and Employment*. New York: R.R. Bowker Company, 1973.

St. John, Edward P. "The Impact of Student Financial Aid: A Review of Recent Research." *Journal of Student Financial Aid* 21, no. 1 (1991): 18–32.

St. John, Edward P., R. Kirshstein, and J. Noell. "The Effects of Student Aid on Persistence: A Sequential Analysis of the High School and Beyond Senior Cohort." *Review of Higher Education* 14 (1991): 383.

Stromquist, Nelly P. "Sex-Equity Legislation in Education: The State as Promoter of Women's Rights." *Review of Educational Research* 63, no. 4 (1993): 379–407.

Sufrin, Sidney C. *Administering the National Defense Education Act*. Syracuse, NY: Syracuse University Press, 1963.

Sundquist, James L. *Politics and Policy: The Eisenhower, Kennedy, and Johnson Years*. Washington, DC: Brookings Institution, 1968.

Swers, Michele L. "Are Women More Likely to Vote for Women's Issue Bills Than Their Male Colleagues?" *Legislative Studies Quarterly* 23, no. 3 (1998): 435–448.

Swers, Michele L. *The Difference Women Make: The Policy Impact of Women in Congress*. Chicago: University of Chicago Press, 2002.

Teachman, Jay D. "Family Background, Educational Resources, and Educational Attainment." *American Sociological Review* 52, no. 4 (1987): 548–557.

Thelin, John R. *A History of American Higher Education*. 2nd ed. Baltimore, MD: Johns Hopkins University Press, 2011.

Thomas, Gail E., Karl L. Alexander, and Bruce K. Eckland. "Access to Higher Education: The Importance of Race, Sex, Social Class, and Academic Credentials." *School Review* 87, no. 2 (1979): 133–156.

Thomas, Sue, and Susan Welch. "The Impact of Gender on Activities and Priorities of State Legislators." *Western Political Quarterly* 44, no. 2 (1991): 445–456.

Tidball, M. Elizabeth, Daryl G. Smith, Charles S. Tidball, and Lisa E. Wolf-Wendel. *Taking Women Seriously: Lessons and Legacies for Educating the Majority*. Phoenix: Oryx Press, 1999.

"Title IX at 30: Report Card on Gender Equity." Report. National Coalition for Women and Girls in Education, 2002.

Traugott, Michael W., and John P. Katosh. "Response Validity in Surveys of Voting Behavior." *Public Opinion Quarterly* 43, no. 3 (1979): 359–377.

Trumbull, John. *The Progress of Dulness*. New Haven, CT: Printed by Thomas and Samuel Green, 1773.

Turrittin, Anton H., Paul Anisef, and Neil J. MacKinnon. "Gender Differences in Educational Achievement: A Study of Social Inequality." *Canadian Journal of Sociology* 8 (1983): 395–420.

Twight, Charlotte A. *Dependent on D.C.: The Rise of Federal Control over the Lives of Ordinary Americans*. New York: Palgrave, 2002.

Urban, Wayne J. *More Than Science and Sputnik: The National Defense Education Act of 1958*. Tuscaloosa: University of Alabama Press, 2010.

US Census Bureau. "Historical National Population Estimates: July 1, 1900 to July 1, 1999." Population Estimates Program. 2000. http://www.census.gov/population/estimates/nation/popclockest.txt.

US Census Bureau. "Table 226. School Enrollment by Sex and Level." Statistical Abstract of the United States. 2002. http://www.census.gov/compendia/statab/2012/tables/12s0226.pdf.

US Census Bureau. "American Community Survey." 2009. http://www.census.gov/acs/www/.

US Census Bureau. "Current Population Survey." 2009. http://www.census.gov/cps.

US Census Bureau. "CPS Historical Tables: Educational Attainment." 2011. http://www.census.gov/hhes/socdemo/education/data/cps/historical/index.html.

US Census Bureau. "Educational Attainment in the United States: 2011." 2011. http://www.census.gov/hhes/socdemo/education/data/cps/2011/tables.html.

US Census Bureau. "Profile America Facts for Features: Mother's Day: May 13, 2012." 2012. http://www.census.gov/newsroom/releases/archives/facts_for_features_special_editions/cb12-ff08.html.

US Department of Education. "Title IX: 25 Years of Progress." Report. 1997. http://www.ed.gov/pubs/TitleIX/.

US House, Committee on Education and Labor. *Hearings Before the Special Subcommittee on Education*. Washington, DC: US Government Printing Office, 1971.

US House. *Higher Education Act of 1971*. Hearings. 92nd Congress, 1st Session, H.R. 7248. *Congressional Record* 118 (November 1, 1971): H38639.

US House. *Higher Education Act of 1971*. Hearings. 92nd Congress, 1st Session, H.R. 7248. *Congressional Record* 118 (November 4, 1971): H3249-39252.

US Public Law 92–318. 92nd Congress, 2nd Session (June 23, 1972).

Valenti, J. J. "The Recent Debate on Federal Aid to Education Legislation in the United States." *International Review of Education* 5, no. 2 (1959): 189–202.

Valentin, Iram. "Title IX: A Brief History." Report. Washington, DC: US Department of Education, 1997.

Verba, Sidney, Kay Lehman Schlozman, and Henry E. Brady. *Voice and Equality: Civic Volunteerism in American Politics*. Cambridge, MA: Harvard University Press, 1995.

Verba, Sidney, Nancy Burns, and Kay Lehman Schlozman. "Knowing and Caring About Politics: Gender and Political Engagement." *Journal of Politics* 59, no. 4 (1997): 1051–1072.

Verba, Sidney, and Norman H. Nie. *Participation in America: Political Democracy and Social Equality*. New York: Harper & Row, 1972.

Von Lohmann, Fred. "Single-Sex Courses, Title IX, and Equal Protection: The Case for Self-Defense for Women." *Stanford Law Review* 48, no. 1 (1995): 177–216.

Walpole, Mary Beth. "Socioeconomic Status and College: How SES Affects College Experiences and Outcomes." *Review of Higher Education* 27, no. 1 (2003): 45–73.

Walsh, John. "Congress: Higher Education Act Including Scholarship for Needy Passed in Final Days of Session." *Science, New Series* 150, no. 3696 (1965): 591–594.

Warren, Elizabeth, and Amelia Tyagi. *The Two-Income Trap*. New York: Basic Books, 2003.

Weir, Margaret, Ann Shola Orloff, and Theda Skocpol. "Understanding American Social Politics." In *The Politics of Social Policy in the United States*, edited by Margaret Weir, Ann Shola Orloff, and Theda Skocpol. Princeton, NJ: Princeton University Press, 1988, 3–36.

Welch, Susan. "Women as Political Animals? A Test of Some Explanations for Male-Female Political Participation Differences." *American Journal of Political Science* 21, no. 4 (1977): 711–730.

Wildavsky, Aaron. *The Politics of the Budgetary Process*. Boston, MA: Little, Brown, 1964.

Williams, Joan. *Unbending Gender: Why Family and Work Conflict and What to Do About It*. New York: Oxford University Press, 2000.

Wilson, Logan. "The Federal Government and Higher Education" In *Education and Public Policy*, edited by Seymour E. Harris and Alan Levensohn. Berkeley, CA: McCutchan Publishing, 1965.

Wolfinger, Raymond E., and Steven J. Rosenstone. *Who Votes?* New Haven, CT: Yale University Press, 1980.

Wolfle, Lee M. "Postsecondary Educational Attainment Among Whites and Blacks." *American Educational Research Journal* 22, no. 4 (1985): 501–525.

Wu, Chung-Li. "Psycho-Political Correlates of Political Efficacy: The Case of the 1994 New Orleans Mayoral Election." *Journal of Black Studies* 33, no. 6 (2003): 729–760.

Zepeda-Millan, Chris. "Perceptions of Threat, Demographic Diversity, and the Framing of Illegality: Explaining (Non)Participation in New York's 2006 Immigrant Protests." *Political Research Quarterly* 67, no. 4 (2014): 880–888.

INDEX

Page numbers followed by *f* or *t* indicate figures or tables, respectively. Numbers followed by n indicate notes.

College of William and Mary, 25
colleges and universities. *See* higher education; *specific institutions*
college students. *See* students
Collegiate School, 25
collegiate sports. *See* athletics
Collins, Gail, 227n6
colonial era, 25–26, 231n12
Columbia University, 34, 36, 251n14
community colleges, 107–108
Cone, Keith G., 94
Conference on Federal Aid to Education, 50, 209*t*
Constitutional Convention, 26
Converse, Philip E., 166, 256n13
Conway, Margaret, 260n12, 260n22
Cooperative Institutional Research Program (CIRP) Freshman Trends Archive, 6, 126, 135, 257n26, 257n28, 258n45; data, 128, 204*t*
Cooperative League of the USA, 209*t*
Cornell, Ezra, 30, 234n53
Cornell University, 34, 234n53
cosmopolitanism, 231n7
costs: for housing, 13; tuition and fees, 17, 229n45
Council of Chief State School Officers, 209*t*
coverture, 8
crisis politics, 43–77
Cross, Christopher, 240n44
cultural characterizations, 20

Daley, Thelma Thomas, 248n47
Dartmouth University, 100
data, 126–128, 173–174, 204*t*
Davenport, Sally, 84–85
Davies, Gareth, 58
Davis, Shannon N., 256n16
debt, 199–200
Defenders of the American Constitution, 208*t*
Delta Kappa Gamma, 70
democratic citizenship, 196–197
Democratic Party, 72–73, 246n2, 254n73. *See also specific politicians*
democratic policymaking, 169–170
demographics, 13, 142–143
dental degrees, 117
Department of Education Organization Act of 1979 (PL 96-88), 247n20
Department of Health and Human Services (HHS), 247n20
Depression, 36–38, 44–45
Derthick, Lawrence G., 53, 65–66, 68, 73–74
desegregation, 243n102, 254n69
developing institutions, 96
difference-in-differences approach, 7

discrimination: racial, 49, 105, 241n80; sex. *See* sex or gender-based discrimination
doctoral degrees, 149, 149*f*
domesticity, 13, 193
Dominick, Peter, 114, 254n75
Donovan, Hedley W., 84
double minorities, 193
double standards, 31–32
Drennan, David, 237n141
Dunkle, Margaret, 104–105, 109, 253n52
Durant, Henry, 29
Dynarski, Susan M., 256n6, 259n67

Eagle, Jay, 43
earned redistributions, 198–199
Eastland, James O., 96
education: of American women, 14–16; costs of undergraduate education, 13, 17, 229n45; determinants of ultimate plans among low-income college students, 216*t*; and educational attainment, 217*t*; federal aid for. *See* federal student aid; federal control over, 239n22, 243n98; feminization of, 195; gender gap in, 89–90, 90*t*; and higher education policy usage, 213*t*–215*t*; opportunity for, 212*f*; parent resources, 257n21; and political efficacy, 221, 223*t*; and political interest, 221, 222*t*; and political participation, 182–183, 182*t*, 183, 186*t*, 221–225, 224*t*; postsecondary. *See* higher education; practical, 235n75; progressive, 239n18; Republican Education, 25; sex discrimination in, 106; and ultimate educational plans among low-income college students, 216*t*; variables used in empirical analyses, 201*t*–203*t*, 203*t*–206*t*; vocational, 236n108, 258n37
educational ambition, 150–159, 155*t*, 157*t*, 158*t*
educational attainment: age and, 158, 160*t*, 217*t*; among college graduates, 152, 152*f*; federal student aid and, 148–159, 154*t*– 155*t*, 158*t*, 256n6; gender gap in, 15–16, 36–37, 39, 107, 117, 194, 256n16; higher education policy and, 152, 152*f*; political efficacy and, 177; political engagement and, 166–168, 170; race and, 127, 217*t*; socioeconomic status and, 127, 158, 160*t*, 217*t*, 256n16, 257n20; student loans and, 217*t*; Title IX protection and, 156, 158, 158*t*, 160*t*; voter participation and, 169; of women, 1–2, 6, 15, 15*f*, 23–24, 36–38, 89–90, 90*t*, 107, 148–152, 149*f*, 152*f*, 158–159, 159*t*, 160*t*, 166–168, 231n5, 231n12, 232n27, 232n31, 234n54, 256n16
Educational Development Act of 1958, 62